A STURDY RACE OF MEN

149 BRIGADE

To Jamie and Riley, my grandsons,

in the hope that they will never have to go to war.

A STURDY
RACE OF MEN

149 BRIGADE

A HISTORY OF THE NORTHUMBERLAND FUSILIERS TERRITORIAL BATTALIONS IN THE GREAT WAR

ALAN ISAAC GRINT

Pen & Sword
MILITARY

First published in Great Britain in 2018 by
Pen & Sword Military
an imprint of
Pen & Sword Books Ltd
Yorkshire – Philadelphia

Copyright © Alan Isaac Grint 2018
ISBN 978 1 52674 178 3

Printed and bound in the UK by TJ International Ltd, Padstow, Cornwall.

Pen & Sword Books Limited incorporates the imprints of Atlas, Archaeology,
Aviation, Discovery, Family History, Fiction, History, Maritime, Military,
Military Classics, Politics, Select, Transport, True Crime, Air World, Frontline
Publishing, Leo Cooper, Remember When, Seaforth Publishing,
The Praetorian Press, Wharncliffe Local History, Wharncliffe Transport,
True Crime and White Owl.

For a complete list of Pen & Sword titles please contact
PEN & SWORD BOOKS LIMITED
47 Church Street, Barnsley, South Yorkshire, S70 2AS, England
E-mail: enquiries@pen-and-sword.co.uk
Website: www.pen-and-sword.co.uk
PEN AND SWORD BOOKS
1950 Lawrence Rd, Havertown, PA 19083, USA
E-mail: Uspen-and-sword@casematepublishers.com
Website: www.penandswordbooks.com

CONTENTS

Our Roll of Honour

O lads, dear lads, who were loyal and true,
The worst of the fight was borne by you;
So the word shall go to cottage and hall,
Our battles are won by the men that fall.

When peace dawns over the countryside,
Our thanks shall be to the lads that died,
O quiet hearts, can you hear us tell
How peace was won by the men that fell?

These are the final verses of 'Our roll of Honour', a poem that
in the monthly publication, the St George's Gazette, would precede the
obituaries of officers who died in battle.

FOREWORD

In Eldon Square, in the centre of Newcastle upon Tyne, lies the war memorial erected by public subscription in 1923 to commemorate those who lost their lives in the Great War.

Across Northumberland, in our market towns, lie similar memorials erected by a grieving public who had seen their communities decimated by a war which had led to the deaths of thousands of their young men.

Despite the passage of time, memories of the war have never faded. Those memories linger within families, in our neighbourhoods, in our schools and in the public buildings erected in the 1920s to commemorate those who died by looking to the future.

Many books have been written about the Great War. They cover all perspectives and all theatres of war. Some are official histories, and some are the result of later research. Others are personal accounts written either at the time or recalled much later. All these sources have added to our knowledge of what happened in the Great War and the sacrifices it demanded.

Over the years, research has become easier for historians. Archives have opened up and the availability of information via the internet has greatly improved our understanding of the events of 1914-1918.

This book by Alan Grint on the 149 Brigade brings together historical fact and personal memory. It is not about a single battle or a single person. It is instead the story of what happened to a brigade from its formation in May 1915 after the disastrous losses at the Second Battle of Ypres the previous month to its disbandment four years later.

Alan Grint's endeavour has been a lifetime in the creation. His book reminds us of the young men of Northumberland who fought in that Brigade. It is about their devotion to their country's cause, their comradeship and their heroism. It reflects a huge amount of research and is a very significant contribution to our knowledge of what happened to so many innocent young men as they confronted the grim realities of war. It is painstakingly researched and is an exceptional narrative of the four years of the Brigade's existence. It is written with a skill and a passion for recording what happened and keeping that memory alive for future generations.

The Great War touched the lives of almost every household in the country. From the patriotic call to arms in 1914 through the horrors of the mud in Flanders and the Somme, this is indeed the story of 'a sturdy race of men'.

John Shipley, House of Lords

ACKNOWLEDGEMENTS

My book has been many years in the writing, and it is only through the tireless help and support of my wife, Julia, that it has seen the light of day. She has worked alongside me all the way.

In the gathering together of arcane bits of information I am indebted to a large number of knowledgeable individuals who have responded to my online searches, in particular to Graham Stewart, David Blanchard and others from the invaluable Great War Forum. My thanks also to Ian Johnson and Keith Riley, for their help and encouragement.

It is the personal accounts of the officers and men of the Territorial Battalions, those who spent a great part of their young lives fighting during the Great War, that bring my story to life. I have been most grateful to the institutions that have had the foresight to preserve these, especially the Imperial War Museum Archives and Oral Library: George Harbottle, Elmer Wilfred Cotton, Jack Dorgan, Joe Pickard, Percy Williams and Albert Edward Bagley – all are long gone but their memoirs remain an inspiration.

I am indebted to the helpful staff at a number of local institutions around Northumberland: the Central Library in Newcastle upon Tyne, the Northumberland Archives at Woodhorn and The Fusiliers Museum of Northumberland at Alnwick.

I would like to thank Alan Fidler and Steve Young of the Tynemouth World War 1 Project and Michael Hardy, Malcolm Anderson and Iain Mulch of Ryton and District War Memorials Project for allowing me to use a number of pictures of soldiers that appear on their web sites.

The maps and illustrations were diligently drawn by the talented and ever-patient Chloe Rodham, in many cases from rudimentary sketches I sent her. My thanks to Jon Wilkinson and Sarah Cook at Pen and Sword for their creativity and diligence. Thanks, too, to Lord Shipley of Gosforth, himself an ardent local historian, who was kind enough to write the foreword. I have made great efforts to trace the owners of the copyright of the extracts and images I have used. To those who gave their permission, my thanks, and to those with whom I was unable to make contact, I hope that they will understand the use of their images, for which I apologise.

INTRODUCTION

This book was written in memory of all ranks who gallantly served in the four Northumberland Fusilier Battalions of Territorial Force during the Great War.

Quo Fata Vocant
Whither the Fates Call

The genesis of 149 Brigade as one of the three brigades of the 50th (Northumbrian) Division took place in the middle of May 1915 when it superseded the Northumbrian Brigade. Just over three weeks previously, the four Territorial Force battalions of the Northumberland Fusiliers which made up the Northumbrian Brigade had left their garrisons on the north-east coast; they landed in France on 21 April and travelled north to the horrors of the Ypres Salient in Belgium. Without any introductory war experience, without any time for schooling at the front, the four battalions were propelled into the *Second Battle of Ypres,* to counterattack on two successive days an enemy greatly superior in numbers, machine guns and artillery and who were supremely confident following their use of gas. What followed was a massacre using instruments of industrial war: artillery, machine guns and poisoned gas. The Territorials' lionhearted advance against St Julien gave the British line – which was reeling and almost shattered – crucial time to re-organise and consolidate. A Staff Officer of the Regular Army regarded the attack by the Northumbrian Brigade as one of the finest feats of arms he had ever witnessed[1]. Following their harrowing rite of passage, after a brief respite the brigade was ordered back into the salient over the next four weeks, holding trenches between

Weiltje and Hooge. While at Hooge some elements of the Brigade supported an attack during the *Second Battle of Bellewaarde.* As the British position in the salient became more secure the brigade was dispatched to what was regarded as quieter sections of the front: Wulverghem and Armentières. The trenches at Armentières provided an extremely comfortable billet never experienced again during their subsequent three years at war. This was followed by seven weeks' training at Strazeele. Then, from late December 1915 – during miserable winter months – the 149 Brigade held the perilous trenches on the flank of Hill 60, a feat accomplished by sheer dogged endurance. Finally, in April, the brigade left the salient for what was reputably a quiet sector: the trenches facing the Wytschaete Ridge and covering Kemmel Hill. After a week, the renowned tranquillity of this area was shattered and fierce trench warfare began to rage, day and night. The trenches were constantly blighted by relentless enemy artillery and heavy trench mortars.

After four weeks of rest and training in the Meteren area, the 149 Brigade returned to the trenches on the Wytschaete Ridge, where they suffered enemy hostility even fiercer than that of their previous tour of duty in this sector. From the second half of July until the middle of August the brigade served in trenches in the quieter locations of St Eloi and Wulverghem. After this, the Fusiliers moved to the Somme, first to a training area near Henencourt where they prepared intensely for a major assault on 15 September 1916. This was the *Battle of Flers-Courcelette,* during which the brigade took severe casualties when a neighbouring division failed to capture High Wood. However, following the victory of 15 September, elements of the brigade were in action on a number of occasions as the Allies slowly pushed forward at great cost, wallowing in mud in the forward battle area, sometimes manning the line, sometimes providing work parties at others providing stretcher bearers as the enemy slowly retreated eastwards.

On 14 November, the brigade was involved in an ill-fated attack on Hook Sap and Gird Line, part of the outlying defences of the Butte de Warlencourt. This attack may be described as a forlorn hope – a diversion to draw enemy fire from a more promising advance on Beaucourt. Nonetheless, the 149 Brigade managed to take its objectives, although many of the assaulting troops were wiped out. Many a brave man perished that day. By now there were few men from Northumberland still within the ranks of the brigade and fewer still who had cheerfully volunteered in the heady days of April 1915. Those that survived went back into divisional rest at Brestle where they spent Christmas Day out of the line.

New Year's Day 1917: the brigade returned to the trenches south east of the Butte de Warlencourt. After a few weeks, the division was taken out of the line for a short rest at Dernancourt and then moved south to a French sector near Estrées, followed by another period out of the line in training as 'corps de Chasse' for the next big push: the *Arras Offensive*. After early successes, the front soon reverted to trench to trench fighting, similar to the attrition on the Somme. Significantly, elements of the 149 assaulted and recaptured – with few casualties – the important observation post of Wancourt Tower. Following this they spent the summer months holding various positions along the Arras sector, including an extended period in the Vis-Chérisy front where the trenches were sound and reliefs could generally be carried out in daylight.

By October the brigade had moved back to the Ypres Salient, where on 26 October they became embroiled in the *Third Battle of Ypres*. Three of the brigade's battalions attacked along a front south east of Houthulst Forest. Wading across a swamp in unrelenting rain against a strongly manned line of pill boxes, the brigade suffered, for no gain, over a thousand men killed or injured. To lick their wounds the men were given a well-deserved rest out of the line, although by 11 December they were back amongst the desolation, manning the trenches covering Passchendaele and providing working parties in the forward area which was shelled continuously.

At the end of January 1918, the brigade was reduced, as were many others, from four to three battalions: the 1/7 Battalion was transferred as a Pioneer Battalion to the 42nd (East Lancashire) Division. The slimmed-down brigade remaining within the 50th Division spent the next few months fighting for its very existence. Although the brigade was not involved in stemming the first thrust of the German Offensive across the Somme in March, it fought gallantly for the next ten days to repel the German onslaught. Their losses rose steadily until they were transferred to Flanders, where they were joined by a raft of replacements, many of whom were mere boys, who would fight with great tenacity during the next German Offensive in early April 1918. Withdrawn and reorganised, the brigade was sent southwards to a 'quiet' sector under French authority, little knowing that this sector had actually been selected for another of the Germany's offensives. In this cauldron, the brigade was practically annihilated and the three proud Territorial Force battalions were reduced to cadre strength, never to take the field again. Any survivors were scattered throughout the British Army.

In the meantime, the 1/7 Battalion, allocated the tasks of digging trenches, maintaining roads and providing working parties, saw direct action once again when, on 25 March during the German offensive on the Somme, they moved forward to hold a gap in the line near Achiet-le-Grand. After 5 April, as the pressure on this part of the front eased, the battalion resumed its duties as a Pioneer Battalion. Working in the back area they received their fair share of casualties from artillery fire.

From the middle of August, as the Allied advance to victory began, the battalion moved eastwards rapidly, mending roads and bridges as the front moved inexorably towards Germany. On 11 November, Armistice Day, the battalion was quartered at Hautmont, where they rested until the middle of December, when over three days they marched to Charleroi. Here demobilisation began until the battalion was reduced to cadre strength in March 1919. The remnants sailed to the United Kingdom in April 1919, nearly four years after they had sailed to France.

CHAPTER ONE

THE BEGINNING
THE ROUTE TO THE WESTERN FRONT

If I should die, think only this of me:
That there's some corner of a foreign field
That is for ever England. There shall be
In that rich earth a richer dust concealed.

From *'The Soldier'* by Rupert Brooke, written December 1914

From the Tyne to the Tweed, from the North Sea to the Cheviots, this is Northumberland, the home of the Fifth Regiment of the Line, the Northumberland Fusiliers. In the early 1900s this border county was as diverse as it was extensive: the coast and rivers, the fertile plains and the Cheviots were hinterland to the once industrial powerhouse of the south east of the county with its thriving coal mines, magnificent shipyards and Lord Armstrong's heavy engineering factories. Men from all over the British Isles were drawn there by the magnet of employment and opportunity: the streets were hardly paved with gold, but there was work.

The Northumberland Fusiliers was raised in 1674 as the Fifth Regiment of Foot, but by 1782 it had been given the regional designation – Northumberland. In 1836 it received the further distinction of being a fusilier unit, adopting the title Fifth (Northumberland Fusiliers) Regiment of Foot. Under the Childers reforms of 1881 when regimental numbering was abolished, the regiment was designated the county regiment of Northumberland including the towns of Newcastle upon Tyne and Berwick upon Tweed.

As far back as the 18th Century the county was home to a number of volunteer militia forces. A letter dated 12 May 1859 from General Sir John Peel, Secretary of State at the War Office, to the Lord Lieutenant of Northumberland, authorised him to raise a number of rifle corps under the powers granted to him under the Yeoman and Volunteers Consolidation Act of 1804. In Northumberland this led to the formation of three volunteer battalions. Further changes came after 1881 when militia units and volunteer rifle battalions were incorporated into the Northumberland Fusiliers. In 1883 the First Northumberland Rifle Volunteer Corps was renamed as the First Volunteer Battalion, the Second Northumberland Rifle Volunteer Corps was renamed as the Second Volunteer Battalion, and the First Newcastle upon Tyne Rifle Volunteer Corps was renamed the Third Volunteer Battalion. It was men from these volunteer battalions which would form the nucleus of the Territorial Force in 1908.

A squad of recruits at High Wood Rifle Range in 1893
"A" Company 1 Volunteer Battalion Northumberland Fusiliers
Back row: Tom Craigie, T. Appleby, James White, Unknown, W. Davison, T. Kearney
Second Row: Sgt Major H. Perry, Anthony Emerson, Jasper Stevenson, T. Robson
Front Row: J. G. Halliburton, W. Smith, J. Dodd, T. W. Halliburton.
Author's Collection

Drilling with rifles and firing at local ranges were the basic activities of the volunteers. Indeed, the skeleton of one such range can still be seen in the aptly named Target Wood, near Acomb. The National Rifle Association organised annual shooting competitions in which representatives from the Volunteer Rifle Corps throughout the country competed for the Queen's Medal.

The volunteer battalions held annual training camps, as would the post-1908 battalions of the Territorial Force. In 1893 this jamboree took place at Ripon Racecourse: over four hundred bell tents housed well over two thousand men from the Tyne and Tees Brigade. Private John Gibson of Hexham composed a song about the camp:

> *And there we meet upon the field*
> *Our comrades in the grey:*
> *From Allendale and Bellingham*
> *And marksmen true are they.*
> *From Corbridge and from Haltwhistle,*
> *Morpeth and Alnwick,*
> *From Belford and Berwick*
> *We find good men and true.*

Castleton Camp 1904
Author's Collection

The Third Volunteer Battalion at Conway Camp, 1906
Author's Collection

When the Boer War broke out in 1899, the regular army was weak in numbers. At the time it didn't seem much of a problem: expectations were that the war against a Boer army of untrained farmers would be brought to a rapid and successful conclusion. This was not to be the case. Initially, the War Office turned down offers from volunteers, but following the disasters of early December 1899, when the regular army suffered humiliating defeats, the official attitude changed.

On 2 January 1900, a Special Army Order authorised the raising of volunteer service companies by county regiments. Each service company was expected to register 116 men aged between 25 and 35, preferably unmarried, who were first class shots, physically fit, of good character and passed as efficient for the last two years. There was one problem: The Volunteer Act stated that volunteers were for *local* defence and were not allowed to serve abroad. This was circumvented by allowing the men to enlist in the *regular* army for one year; each volunteer battalion of a county regiment could now raise a company which, on arrival in South Africa, would be attached to its affiliated regiment under the orders of its commanding officer.

The three Northumberland volunteer battalions all rose to this challenge. The First Volunteer Battalion raised a special service company of two officers and eighty men: twenty-four were from Hexham, ten from Morpeth, eight each from Belford and Alnwick, nine from Bellingham, three from Allendale and six from Berwick. Prudhoe supplied one officer and five men, Corbridge one officer and four men, and Haltwhistle three men, including Sergeant Instructor Walton. One of the first to volunteer was Corporal G. Middlemiss, the postmaster in Glanton, North Northumberland. He had spent much of his life as a Volunteer, doing service with the Newcastle Engineers, Percy Artillery,

Lieutenant
William Ernest Stephenson
Courtesy of Lynn Yates

Northumberland Hussars and 'D' Company of the 1st Volunteer Battalion. Technically he was too old to fight overseas, but he regarded this service as his swansong and his persuasive powers earned him a ticket for the one year's service in South Africa. The Second Volunteer Battalion raised a Special Service Company in February 1900, whilst the Third Volunteer Battalion reported a month earlier that it had also raised a Special Service Company. Each served one year abroad. Another to volunteer was Lieutenant William Stephenson, 'F' Company (Newburn) 2nd Volunteer Battalion.

The campaign was not always an easy ride for these doughty volunteers: a number of them were killed, so that their particular corner of a foreign field lies under the glaring sun of South Africa. After the Boer War, until its reincarnation as the Territorial Force in 1908, life for its members continued as it had done before: annual camps, drilling and musketry. In 1907 the Robinson Cup for Drill Attendance and Musketry was won by Sergeant M. Dixon of 'I' Company 1st V.B.N.F.

Uniform of 1st Volunteer Battalion Northumberland Fusiliers, c. 1903
Courtesy of Graham Stewart

Transcript of the memorial plaque found in Hexham Abbey, to men from Hexham who served with the First Volunteer Battalion in the Boer War:

SOUTH AFRICAN WAR 1898-1902
THIS TABLET HAS BEEN ERECTED TO COMMEMORATE
THE PATRIOTISM OF THE FOLLOWING MEMBERS OF
THE HEXHAM Co OF THE 1st VOL. Bn NORTHUMBERLAND
FUSILIERS WHO VOLUNTEERED AND SERVED IN
THE BOER WAR 1898-1902, SOME OF WHOM LOST
THEIR LIVES IN THEIR COUNTRY'S CAUSE

Lieutenant G.F. Fisher

Corporal J.T. Porteus	Corporal E. Eddy
Pte R. S. Bantham	Pte J. McBride
J. Beswick	M. Matthews
W. Burn	J. E. Murray
R. Bulman	J. D. Ritson
J. Cathrae	J. Robinson
T. Cooke	J .W. Riley
T. Copper	Jos. Smith
J. Chester	J. W. Smith
W. A .Charlton	A .W. Snowball
J. Claude	J. Stonehouse
W. Davidson	J. W. Swinburne
W. A. French	(died of wounds in S Africa)
T. Harrison	W. Taylor
J. T. Hogarth	J. Tait
D. Houston	H. Towns
J. H. Hutchinson	J. Wilkinson
F. I'Anson	G. Wilkinson
(drowned in S Africa)	J. R. Ward
T. McGill	C.Wright
A. McIntosh	H. Welsh
H. Cooke	Bugler J. W. Robson

AND ALSO OF THE FOLLOWING TOWNSMEN, WHO
VOLUNTEERED AND DIED DURING THE SAID WAR

Trooper A. Smith, died of fever in S Africa
Trooper G. Nesham, died of fever in S. Africa
Trooper W. R. Pearson, died on return

A number of men who served in South Africa – either with the regular army or with the volunteer battalions – later joined the Territorial Force, some at its inception in 1908, others at the onset of hostilities in 1914. Andrew Cowan and his brother served with the Northumberland Yeomanry in South Africa. Andrew was taken prisoner by the Boers and later related to the press that his captors searched him for money but they found none as he had hidden it in his boot. In September 1914 he enlisted into the 1/7 Battalion Northumberland Fusiliers with the service number 7/1966. Rising to Sergeant, he was later posted to the 1/4 East Yorkshire Regiment (31288) and was killed in action on 29 March 1918. Another volunteer, William Hartley, had also seen action in South Africa with the Volunteer Battalion and joined the Territorial Force in Hexham soon after the Great War began. Like Andrew Cowan, his previous experience earned him early promotion. 4/1873 Corporal William Hartley was killed on 26 April 1915 and is buried at Seaforth Cemetery, Cheddar Villa near Ypres.

The Third Volunteer Battalion at Ripon Camp, 1907
Author's Collection

The Boer War exposed many faults in the structure and command of the British Army; these became the focus for structural changes within the United Kingdom's military, made urgent by the German Kaiser's headlong pursuit to challenge the supremacy of the British Empire on land and at sea. In 1903 the Navy was building ever larger ships, the Dreadnoughts, and both the Royal

Naval Volunteer Reserve and the Royal Marine Volunteers were formed. On the continent enormous armies were being conscripted; war was in the air. Until 1900 the volunteer battalions had never been part of the British Army, and, although individuals had acquitted themselves well in South Africa, as a body these volunteers would be no match against a well-trained invasionary force equipped with modern weaponry. Recognising this, Secretary of State Lord Haldane felt it wise to demand more in the way of training for volunteers. After much deliberation the Territorial Forces Act was passed by Parliament on 2 August 1907 and came into effect on 1 April 1908:

THE TERRITORIAL AND RESERVE FORCES ACT, 1907

(7 Edward VII, Cap. 9)

This act was designed to facilitate the reorganisation of His Majesty's military forces and for that purpose to authorise the establishment of County Associations and the raising and maintenance of a Territorial Force, and for amending the Acts relating to the Reserve Forces (2 August 1907). These County Associations were formed almost immediately. In Northumberland the work of the County Association began in January 1908. Its members were:

President: The Lord Lieutenant, Henry, 7th Duke of Northumberland.

Chairman: appointed by the Army Council: Lord Allendale .

Vice-Chairman: also appointed by the Army Council: Sir Francis Blake.

Military Members: fourteen, appointed by the Army Council as representatives of the Territorial Force of the late Yeomanry and Volunteer Forces of the County.

Representatives: one member each from the **County Council of Northumberland**, the **City Council of Newcastle upon Tyne**, the **Borough Council of Tynemouth** and the **University of Durham**.

Nine co-opted members representing **Coal Owners**, **Engineers**, **Ship Builders**, **Agriculture**, **Coal Miners**, **Boiler Makers**, **Shipwrights** and the **Amalgamated Union of Labour**.

Thus, Richard Haldane's prescience prompted the creation of the fledgling Territorial Force in Northumberland, of which the volunteer rifle battalions formed the core. The First Battalion was split into two, creating the 1/4 and 1/7 Battalions. The 1/4 was to recruit along the Tyne Valley with its headquarters in Hexham, whilst the 1/7 Battalion was to recruit in the area stretching from Berwick upon Tweed to Ashington, Morpeth and Bedlington in the south east of the county, with its headquarters in Alnwick. The Second Battalion became the 1/5, recruiting among the shipyard and industrial workers along the River Tyne and Gosforth, with its headquarters in Walker. The Third Battalion was designated the 1/6 Battalion; its headquarters remained in St George's Drill Hall off St Mary's Place with a remit to recruit within the city boundaries of Newcastle upon Tyne. At the same time as the formation of the infantry units, the Territorial Force also encompassed volunteers from the cavalry, medical and engineering units.

Rules for the numbering of soldiers were not published in the *Territorial Regulations 1908* and did not appear until the 1912 edition. However, it is evident that in Northumberland, the men who wanted to transfer from the three old pre-1908 Volunteer Battalions to the new battalions of the Territorial Force were numbered from '1'. It was not until May 1915 that the prefix numbers 4/, 5/, 6/ and 7/ were introduced to differentiate men from the four Territorial Battalions making up 149 Brigade. For clarity, I have used these prefixes anachronistically from the start of this book.

Some of the earliest recruits to the fledgling battalions from the Volunteer Battalions were: 4/1 Colour Sergeant Andrew George Richardson and 4/26 Private Ernest Copper who embodied [*sic*, this was a term used for the Territorial Forces] on 8 April 1908; 5/25 Sergeant John Thomas Peebles, who embodied on 7 April 1908; 6/10 Sergeant William Prudhoe Atkinson and 6/92 Sergeant James Atkins who embodied on 1 April 1908, and 7/57 Sergeant James Riddell who embodied on 3 April 1908.

In early 1917 a further change in the numbering of the Territorial Force was ordered under Army Council Instructions issued in late 1916. Units were given new, six figure numbers in blocks. The Northumberland Fusiliers were issued with the following blocks of numbers:

1/4th Battalion: 200001 – 240000

1/5th Battalion: 240001 – 265000

1/6th Battalion: 265001 – 290000

1/7th Battalion: 290001 – 315000

In 1908, within the Northumberland County Association, a number of committees were established to administer finance, clothing, equipment, recruiting, buildings, horses and transport, each comprising disparate groups of military and civilian members. These committees were supported by a full-time secretariat. There was one secretary, Captain A. L. Napier, initially situated at the Moot Hall in Newcastle; a chief clerk, an ex-Orderly Room Sergeant of the regular army; a finance, clothing and equipment clerk; an ex Quartermaster Sergeant from the regular army; a typist and two office boys. They had their work cut out.

All the financial affairs of the volunteer units had to be sorted. Existing drill halls and other Volunteer property was to be taken in charge: resolving the ownership was to prove extremely complicated, and led to the appointment of a surveyor, Major M. H. Graham, a former Volunteer officer. Legal problems were handled by a firm of solicitors, Wilkinson and Marshall. While these issues were being unravelled, between 1908 and 1911 new drill halls were built in Amble, Ashington, Haltwhistle, Hexham, Prudhoe and Whitley Bay. A crowning accomplishment was the construction of a large, central rifle range at Ponteland, opened by 1913 and completed by 1914.

At the onset of hostilities, all companies had their own homes:

1/4 Battalion, Northumberland Fusiliers

Headquarters and 'A' & 'G' Companies: The Armoury, Battle Hill, Hexham.
'B' Company: The Armoury, Bellingham.
'C' Company: John Martin Street, Haydon Bridge.
'D' and 'H' Companies: The Armoury, 6 Vane Terrace, Prudhoe.
'E' Company: The Drill Hall, Corbridge.
'F' Company: The Armoury, Town Hall Crescent, Haltwhistle.

1/5 Battalion, Northumberland Fusiliers

Headquarters and 'A', 'B' and 'C' Companies: The Drill Hall, Walker.
'D' Company: The Drill Hall, Newburn.
'E' and 'F' Companies: St George's Drill Hall, Wallsend.
'G' and 'H' Companies: The Drill Hall, Gosforth.

1/6 Battalion, Northumberland Fusiliers

Headquarters and 'A', 'B', 'C', 'D', 'E', 'F', 'G' and 'H' Companies: St George's Drill Hall, Newcastle upon Tyne.

1/7 Battalion, Northumberland Fusiliers

Headquarters and 'D' Company: 14 Fenkle Street, Alnwick.
'A' Company: Copper Chare, Morpeth.
'B' Company: The Drill Hall, Ashington.
'C' Company: The Armoury, High St, Belford.
'E' Company: The Drill Hall, Amble.
'F' Company: Rothbury.
'G' and 'H' Companies: Ravensdowne, Berwick upon Tweed.

Elsewhere, problems developed within the permanent staff of the new Territorial Unit. The 1/6 (City) Battalion reported that a concert held in the Drill Hall on 1 April 1908 had been attended by about 700 men in uniform. At the interval, all of those who wanted to transfer to the new force were invited to enlist that night. Only 225 men took the opportunity. Many of the older members of the volunteer battalion had decided to end their association with the military, although a number of these were not slow in coming forward in August 1914, when they saw the need.

To make matters worse, in May 1908 it was announced that Sergeant Instructors were to lose five shillings from their weekly wage due to a new payment rate for the Territorial Force. However, the news from the 1/4 Battalion was optimistic, reporting that by 25 April 1908, 14 officers and 290 men had joined. New companies were soon to form at Haltwhistle and Throckley which would boost numbers. Indeed, a month later they had 375 officers and men.

The County Associations were also responsible for the provision of clothing for their new recruits. In Northumberland, the infantry was provided with scarlet tunics bearing the gosling green facings of the Northumberland Fusiliers, worn with navy trousers and a peaked cap as parade dress. White metal buttons and insignia were used for these, as opposed to the gilded metal of the regular army. Also issued to each recruit was a 1902 pattern khaki service uniform for general wear on which gilded badges and buttons were worn.

Presentation of Colours to 1/4 Battalion
Newburn, 1922
Author's Collection

At the 1909 annual camp of the Northumberland Infantry Brigade at Magdalene Fields, Berwick, not all of the uniform changes had been implemented – the massed men wore a motley assortment of uniforms and civilian clothing. It was, however, from this camp that Colour Parties from the 1/5, 1/6 and 1/7 Battalions travelled to Windsor Castle, where on Saturday 19 June 1909, His Majesty King Edward VII presented Colours to 108 Territorial Force Infantry Battalions. Why the 1/4 did not go to London is not understood; they didn't receive their Colours until 1922 – on the football pitch at Newburn!

Recruiting for the new force became a serious objective. The (eventually) smart new uniforms, together with the opportunity to attend paid annual camps in an age when salaried holidays were unknown, were both good incentives. Jack

Dorgan of Ashington, a scout master, joined up largely because he enjoyed the training weekends away, as well as the fortnight when all four battalions of the Northumberland Territorial Force gathered *en masse*. Jack became a soldier of the 1/7 Battalion, and he gave an oral account – transcribed here – of his experiences during the two-week brigade camp:

> *We went to the seaside, a treat in itself, where we were housed in bell tents: ten to twelve men to a tent with their groundsheets and two blankets, sleeping on a straw filled palisade. Every morning the first hour was spent with PT instructors, followed by a shave and putting on of your uniform. After which, breakfast: bacon, egg and a fried drip. At 8.30am there was a parade of the brigade's four battalions followed with either a route march in the morning or afternoon. Lunch was always stew. We practised bayonet fighting every day with our bayonets attached to the Lee Enfield rifle.*[1]

Somewhat ironically, Dorgan later recalled that during his service he never used his bayonet in anger.

Men of the 1/4 Battalion Northumberland Fusiliers at Magdalene Field, Berwick, 1909
Courtesy Graham Stewart

Workers from industrial Northumberland, miners accustomed to claustrophobic underground conditions and poorly paid agricultural labourers – they were all entitled, as Territorials, to two weeks at the coast or in lush green countryside, with good food and evening entertainment. Successive yearly camps were held:

1908 was in Ripon, Yorkshire; 1909 was at Berwick upon Tweed; 1910 was in Richmond, Yorkshire (1/4 and 1/6 Battalions), Fourstones, Hexham (1/5 Battalion) and Moorlaws, Alnwick (1/7 Battalion); 1911 was at Bellister Camp, Haltwhistle; 1912 was at Scarborough, Yorkshire; 1913 was at Bridlington, Yorkshire; 1914 was at Greystoke, Cumberland.

Men of the 1/5 Battalion at Bellister Camp, 1911
Courtesy of Graham Stewart

It appears that at Berwick the men of the newly formed Territorial Force were on their best behaviour, as recorded in the Berwickshire Advertiser of 2 July 1909:

> *The recorder said he would pass from that to another matter, which was to him a source of great satisfaction and must be to the inhabitants of the town, and that was the fact that during the last month, as they all knew, there had been a large body of troops of the Territorial Force, he believed about 3,400 men, in camp in the Borough. These men of course passed their hours of pleasure and recreation in the town, and it was to him a particular source of satisfaction to be informed on the best official authority that the conduct of the men when in town was most excellent and most exemplary. Further that the most friendly feelings had at all times existed between the men in the force and the inhabitants of the town. He thought that was a source of gratification to all.*[2]

An officer of the 1/4 wrote about the camp at Scarborough:

After the absence of nine years the battalion is again encamped on the breezy heights of Scarborough Racecourse. We arrived here by special train on 16 June, in dull and threatening weather, but fortunately got settled down in camp without getting wet. Colonel J. F. Riddell made his annual inspection of the battalion on Tuesday 18 June. Unfortunately, rain had fallen heavily during the whole of the night and much difficulty was experienced in folding great coats and cleaning up uniforms saturated with rain. Our strength in camp is 18 officers and 625 men, by far the largest figure we have had since the inauguration of the Territorial Scheme. So far, our training has been conducted under fairly favourable conditions, the manoeuvring ground is, however, small and much intersected by 'Out of Bounds' patches, and the weather has only been moderately favourable, the days being showery and the nights cold and wet.[3]

Similarly, there were battalion notes for the 1/6 Battalion, Scarborough, dated 24 June 1912, also commenting on the strength of the battalion at the camp:

The total strength in camp is 634 non-commissioned men and twenty-two officers. This week the greater part of the battalion will go to Strensall for musketry.[4]

Men of 1/6 Northumberland Fusiliers in dress uniform at Scarborough Camp, 1912
Courtesy of Graham Stewart

Both of these battalions were of a reasonable size but were still considerably below the desired strength of just over a thousand men of all ranks.

Dorgan describes some of the training whilst at the camp at Scarborough:

Some tactical training was followed involving mock battles and so on. I was special on these. As a scout master I was in charge of the battalion scouts. Me and my battalion scouts were always used as the enemy, and would go out one hour beforehand lying in extended order across each side of the road awaiting the battalion on which we would open fire with dummy cartridges. As soon as the rifle fire was heard the advancing column would extend into the fields: No 1 Company to the left; No 2 Company to the right; No 3 to the left and so on. Each line of four would push one man through the hedge. As soon as they had got through the hedge they would extend right across the field, doubling up but always advancing forward. As soon as that happened the scouts would retreat to the next field and open fire again. The battalion was under fire as they went forward. After three or four fields me and my scouts would disappear leaving the battalion in extended order.[5]

Men of the 1/4 Battalion at their annual camp
Courtesy Graham Stewart

Section IX of the Territorial and Reserve Forces Act[6] deals with enlistment, service and discharge. In part 1(b) it states:

… shall be enlisted to serve for such a period as may be prescribed, not exceeding four years reckoned from the date of attestation.

Part 1(c) states:

… may be re-engaged within twelve months before the end of his current term of service for such a period as be prescribed not exceeding four years from the end of that term and on re-engagement shall make the prescribed declaration before a justice of the peace or an officer, and so from time to time.

Therefore, a man could leave the Territorial Force even in wartime when he had served four years – or at least that was the case until compulsory service came into force in early 1916.

These men were discharged under King's Regulations Paragraph 392(xxi), Time Expired:

7/643 Private John Brotherton from Morpeth embodied on 1 February 1909 and was discharged, Time Expired, on 15 February 1916 after serving seven years in the Territorial Force. He served on the Western Front from 21 April 1915 until 27 January 1916.

4/783 Private Richard Blackburn from North Walbottle embodied on 23 January 1911 and was discharged, Time Expired, on 22 January 1916 after serving five years with the Territorial Force. He fought on the Western Front from 20 April 1915 to 22 January 1916.

6/750 Private James Anderson from Byker attested on 2 January 1909, re-engaged on 21 January 1913 and 21 January 1914, and was Time Expired on 4 February 1916, after serving seven years with the Territorial Force. He served on the Western Front from 20 April 1915 to 4 February 1916.

The second Military Service Act of May 1916 put an end to this right:

The passing of the second Military Service Act in May 1916 removed the right of time expired Territorials to return to civilian life. Instead they found themselves automatically returned to the colours. Even so, some men serving in France preferred to allow themselves to be conscripted and join a strange unit, rather than remain with their chums, so they could spend time back in Britain.[7]

One such man was 6/1246 Lance-Corporal Samuel Carr who had joined the Territorial Force on 25 April 1910 and became Time Expired on 13 January 1917. Instead of remaining with his comrades, he opted to join the Royal Navy in November 1917 and served on HMS *Offa*, an M Class destroyer, as an Engine Room Artificer 4th Class.

An important aspect of the Act[8] defined the area of service of men in the Territorial Force. Section XIII of the Act stated:

Part 1:

Any part of the Territorial Force shall be liable to serve in any part of the United Kingdom, but no part of the Territorial Force shall be carried or ordered to go out of the United Kingdom.

Part 2:

Provided that it shall be lawful for His Majesty, if he thinks fit, to accept the offer of any part or men of the Territorial Force signified through their commanding officer to subject themselves to the liability –

(a) *To serve in any place outside the United Kingdom: or*

(b) *To be called out for actual military service for the purposes of defence at such places in the United Kingdom as may be specified in their agreement whether the Territorial Force is embodied or not; and upon any such offer being accepted, they shall be liable, whenever required during the period to which the offer extends, to serve or be called out accordingly.*

Part 3:

A person shall not be compelled to make such an offer, or be subjected to such liability as aforesaid, except by his own consent, and a commanding officer shall not certify any voluntary offer previously to his having explained to every person making the offer that the offer is purely voluntary on his part.

In a nutshell, the Territorial Force's role was to defend the United Kingdom. Its soldiers could be asked to serve overseas but in order to do so they were required to sign the Imperial Service Obligation. No man could be forced to do this. However, on the instigation of compulsory conscription in 1916 a man was required to serve overseas even if he had not signed the Imperial Service Obligation. Below is a transcription of the Imperial Service Obligation (Document E.624) from September 1914 when its take-up significantly increased:

> I (No.) (Rank) (Name) of the (Unit) do hereby agree, to subject to the conditions stated overleaf, to accept liability, in the event of national emergency, to serve in any place outside the United Kingdom, in accordance with provisions of the Territorial and Reserve Forces Act, 1907

CONDITIONS OF SERVICE.

1. On undertaking the liability to serve abroad in time of national emergency, an officer or man of the Territorial Force will be required to sign an agreement, on Army Form E. 624, in the presence of the Officer Commanding the Territorial unit to which he belongs, and, unless notification to the contrary is given to the Commanding Officer, the liability will continue as long as the officer's or man's engagement in the Territorial Force lasts.

2. The engagement on Army Form E. 624, of an officer or man of the Territorial Force to accept liability for service outside the United Kingdom in time of national emergency, will be to serve with his own unit, or with a part of his own unit, only. He cannot under this agreement, be drafted as an individual to any other unit.

3. Except as regards liability for foreign service, the conditions of the officer's or man's service in the Territorial Force will not be affected by this agreement.

4. A badge will be awarded to each individual accepting such liability for service outside the United Kingdom. This badge may be worn, when in uniform, on the right breast of the officer or man so long as the liability continues.

Conditions of Service of those signing E 624 for service overseas

If a soldier volunteered by signing E 624 for service overseas, he was entitled to wear above his right breast a badge inscribed Imperial Service, surmounted by a crown. If more than ninety per cent of a battalion volunteered for service abroad then the words 'Imperial Service' were placed below the unit's title in the Army List. It appears that, before the war, very few men volunteered to serve abroad, and by September 1913 only thirteen per cent of men had done so.

7/2125 Private George Crawford of Berwick wearing the Imperial Sevice Badge

On Tuesday 4 August 1914, when Britain and its Empire declared war on Germany, the Foreign Office issued the following official statement:

> *Owing to the summary rejection by the German Government of the request made by His Majesty's Government for assurances that the neutrality of Belgium will be respected, his Majesty's Ambassador in Berlin has received his passports and his Majesty's Government declared to the German Government that a state of war exists between Great Britain and Germany as from 11pm on 4 August 1914.*[9]

All across the United Kingdom people awoke on Wednesday 5 August to find that the country was at war with Germany. Days later, Great Britain and its Empire declared war on the Austro-Hungarian Empire, allies of Germany.

George Harbottle, who worked as a clerk for the ship-owning firm of Cairns Noble and Company, described how he enlisted in the City of Newcastle Battalion of the Territorial Force, the 1/6 Northumberland Fusiliers:

War was very much in all our minds, therefore, when I went over to South Northumberland Cricket ground in Gosforth on the Monday Bank Holiday afternoon [3 August 1914] where we were supposed to be playing a team from another club. Their team failed to turn up for some unexplained reason, no doubt connected with the war, for which the Territorial Force had already received its calling up papers.[10]

Instructions to 4/1003 Pte Robert Surtees Knots Renwick
to report for duty, dated 4 August 1914
Author's Collection

The four battalions of the Territorial Force in Northumberland had to be recalled from their annual camp at Greystoke in Cumberland. Harbottle recalls:

Several of us sat there in the sunshine and discussed what our personal action should be if, as seemed certain, war would be declared the next day. One of our number (Herbert Waugh) [6/1515 Waugh would eventually take a commission] was already a serving territorial with a Lance-Corporal's stripe in 'A' Company of the 1/6th Battalion Northumberland Fusiliers. This company was largely recruited from Quaysiders, other Commercial Houses and Banks. He had that morning received his calling up papers instructing him to report the following morning in uniform at the depot, St George's Hall, Newcastle. His view was that we should try and enlist in that Company which he knew was below full strength. Henry Laurence Benson, [Second Lieutenant 'A' Company 1/6 Battalion Northumberland Fusiliers, who died on 11 April 1916, mentioned in despatches] and I both decided to do just that and felt that as we both had been given considerable training in our respective schools' OTCs we would be regarded as acceptable recruits.[11]

Thus it was that on the following morning George went first to his workplace at the Commercial Exchange, where he worked as a junior chartering clerk. His intention was to sign up (embody) later that morning. Russel Cairns, one of the company's directors and a major in the Territorial Field Artillery, appeared in the office – in uniform – on his way to report for duty. He called all the staff together and informed them that if they wanted to join the army their jobs would be kept open and their pay would continue. Army pay at the time and throughout the war was one shilling (1s, or 12d [old pence]) per day for a private, and not a great deal more for NCOs. At the time, a loaf of bread cost 3d, tea was 2s per pound weight and sugar was 2p per pound weight.

On the Tuesday morning I went up to the Drill Hall but was told that they had no authority yet to accept new recruits but to come back in the evening. This I did with a number of others (including Laurie Benson). We were accepted, given our uniforms, had a medical inspection of a somewhat rudimentary character, and told to report at 9am the following day in uniform, when we would be fully equipped and sent to join the company which had already assembled in Tilley's huge dance hall in New Market Square.[12]

All over Northumberland at the onset of war, men flocked to Drill Halls to enlist following Lord Kitchener's call for volunteers. Some were old soldiers, willing to fight again for their country. Others, like George Harbottle, had already gained experience with their schools' OTCs. Another of these men was George Pears Walton who initially enlisted as a private with the 19 Battalion Northumberland Fusiliers, but since he'd spent three years with the Officer Training Corps at Sedbergh School, he was quickly gazetted Second Lieutenant and served with the 1/4 Northumberland Fusiliers.

Alnwick Alndale Juniors 1913-1914
Back Row: Alex Davidson (1/7, killed); T. Thompson (1/7); Robert Pattison (1/7, killed);,
Walter Clark, (1/7, killed); Ernest Cook (1/7, killed); Charles W. Murray (RAMC)
Front Row: Matt Hetherington (1/7); Walter Lockey (1/7); William Matthewson, (RFC);
Ted Hedley (1/7, killed); J. Johnson (1/7, wounded).
Referees: Frank Moir (ASC) and Victor Brewis (1/7)

Apart from those with previous experience there were many untrained and unprepared men who nonetheless saw it as their patriotic duty to sign up:

My premier reason for enlisting was before all else a spirit of patriotism and a kind of fighting instinct which I believe comes to all the British race at times, but it was the opportunity to be with my late office colleagues from Wigham Richardson Company, Walker Shipyard, that caused me to act. It was on 14 September 1914 that I passed the superficial medical and found myself in a recruit's squad, drilling at the Walker band field – we were taught squad and rifle fire at a miniature range at the last-mentioned place for a period of eight weeks. The hours were sharp and we went to our respective homes each evening.[13]

Courtesy of the Heritage Centre, Bellingham

1/4 Battalion leaving Hexham; they marched along Priestpopple (opposite)
Author's Own Collection
and down Loosing Hill to the railway station (above)
Courtesy of Graham Stewart

All four battalions saw massive enlistment in the opening weeks of the war. The 1/5 Battalion reported that between eighty and ninety men were required to bring the battalion up to establishment level. Recruitment began at 0900hrs on 10 August and by 1600hrs the same day they were up to full strength, with the men fully clothed and equipped and posted to their companies.

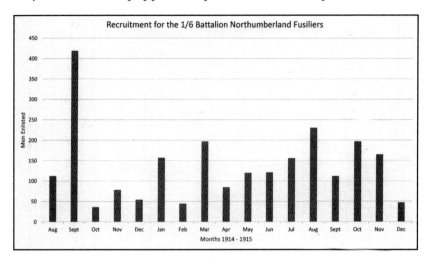

Initially, throughout August, the four battalions were billeted at a number of Co-operative Halls and schools throughout the county:

> As the schools were on holiday there were plenty of these available for temporary use as billets in addition to Co-operative Halls and Miner's Halls. Our next move was to West Moor Co-op Hall and then to Newsham Road School on the outskirts of Blyth, where it was our job to do guard duty at the harbour every night at various points. Undoubtedly the lighthouse at the end of the pier was both the most interesting and comfortable. That at the import dock was the least desirable on account of the multitude of rats milling about after dark.[14]

In September, the four battalions were brought together as a brigade in Gosforth Park; their billets were lines of tents in a large field just east of the track leading from the Race Course to the North Farm. Their time was filled on the parade ground, with rifle drill, musketry instruction and route marching. Officers and NCOs used the time to get to know their men and to develop the battalion's *esprit de corps*. In order to correspond with the structure of the regular army, the Territorial Force battalions were reduced from eight companies to four, each company having four platoons. The 1/7 Battalion was re-organized as follows:

'A' (Morpeth) Company and 'H' (Berwick) Company became Number 1 Company, commanded by Captain H. R. Smail.

'B' (Ashington) Company and 'D' (Alnwick) Company became Number 2 Company, commanded by Captain E. W. Milburn and Captain T. O. Wood second in command.

'C' (Belford) Company and 'F' (Rothbury) Company became Number 3 Company, commanded by Captain the Honourable J. A. Joicey and Captain the Honourable G. W. Liddell second in command.

'E' (Amble) Company and 'G' (Berwick) Company became Number 4 Company, commanded by Captain N. I. Wright and Captain V. Merrivale second in command.

The battalion was the basic tactical unit of the infantry of the British Army in the Great War. At full establishment it consisted of 1,007 men, of whom 30 were officers, and comprised a Battalion Headquarters (HQ) and four companies. The battalion was usually commanded by an officer with the rank of Lieutenant Colonel, with a Major as second in command. Battalion HQ also included three other officers: a Captain or Lieutenant filled the role of Adjutant (in charge of battalion administration); a Captain or Lieutenant was the Quartermaster (responsible for stores and transport); and an officer of the Royal Army Medical Corps was attached as Medical Officer.

The Battalion HQ also included the Regimental Sergeant Major (RSM, the most senior non-commissioned officer) plus a number of specialist roles filled by sergeants: Quartermaster, Drummer, Cook, Pioneer, Shoemaker, Transport, Signaller, Armourer (usually attached from the Army Ordnance Corps) and Orderly Room Clerk. A corporal and four privates of the Royal Army Medical Corps were attached to Battalion HQ for water and sanitary duties; a corporal and fifteen privates were employed as signallers; ten privates were employed as pioneers (on construction, repair and general engineering duties); eleven privates acted as drivers for the horse-drawn transport; sixteen were stretcher-bearers (these often being the musicians of the battalion band); six privates acted as officers' batmen (personal servants) and two as orderlies for the Medical Officer.

The companies were usually numbered A-D and at full establishment numbered 227 bodies. Each was commanded by a major or captain, with a captain as second in command. Each company had a small headquarters' contingent consisting of a company sergeant major (CSM), a company quartermaster sergeant (CQMS), two privates acting as batmen and three as drivers. The body of the company was divided into four platoons, each of which was commanded by a subaltern (a lieutenant or second lieutenant). In total, the four platoons consisted of eight sergeants, ten corporals, four drummers, four batmen and one hundred and eighty-eight privates. Each platoon was subdivided into four sections, each of twelve men under an NCO. For the new officers this was a great deal to learn and understand.

Further reorganisation followed with the introduction of the Imperial Service Obligation, as recounted by George Harbottle:

When we signed up it was on the usual terms of the Territorial Force which were for home defence only. It was then that we were requested to volunteer for foreign service which practically all did immediately, although a few, for various reasons, did not do so and eventually were transferred to the Second Line Battalion which was already building up.[15]

Private George Dando
with his trainer Private F. Watson
Author's Collection

Amongst the hurly burly of the territorials preparing for war and the horrors of the battles on the Western Front, people at home tried their best to get on with their lives. Sport was popular: football, rugby and boxing all continued to feature. In early 1915 at his billet in Ouseburn Schools, Private George Dando, trained by Private F. Watson, prepared to box as 'Young Dando' at the National Sporting Club. Private Dando, weighing in at a diminutive seven stones, fought a least two further fights at St James' Hall in Newcastle. In April, he defeated Young Swift of Plymouth over fifteen rounds and in November 1915, he beat the larger George Kilts in a bruising catch-weight contest, again over fifteen rounds.

By the end of October 1914, the camp in Gosforth Park had become a quagmire, leading to the removal of the Infantry Battalions to coastal defence duties: the 1/4 Battalion went to Princess Louise Road Schools in Blyth; the 1/5 Battalion went to Morpeth Road schools in Blyth; the 1/6 Battalion relocated to Seaton Sluice and the 1/7 Battalion to Cambois.

The 1/7 Battalion at Cambois

The 1/6 Battalion were ordered to Seaton Delaval and so be able to do sentry duty on the sand dunes at Seaton Sluice every night from dusk to dawn. Companies did this duty one night in four with the next day off to clean up, sleep and above all to remove the sand that had blown into all the working parts of our rifles.[16]

At this time, the four battalions were equipped with the long Lee-Metford rifle, unlike the regular army who were equipped with the shorter Lee-Enfield. The machine-gun sections were equipped with old fashioned Maxim guns. During this time at the coast, individuals who had not been passed fit for active service, as well as those pre-war men who had enlisted only for home defence duties and had not volunteered for active service abroad, were drawn together and marched away to form the nucleus of the second line battalions. The 2/4 and 2/5 Battalion were formed at Blyth on 23 and 22 November respectively, whilst the 2/6 Battalion was formed in Newcastle on 28 December 1914. The 2/7 Battalion had been formed much earlier, on 26 September 1914.

Reserve Battalion 2/4 Northumberland Fusiliers, No. 10 Platoon
Author's Collection

In January 1914 all the second line battalions were placed under the orders of 188 Brigade 63rd (2nd Northumbrian) Division. However, in June 1916 this division was broken up and transferred to 217 Brigade Division, 72nd Division. Only the 2/7 NF saw action overseas, when on 20 January 1917 they sailed to Egypt for duty as a Garrison Battalion.

Third line battalions were formed in June 1915 and became reserve battalions for their respective first line battalions serving overseas. In January 1917, the 21 Provisional Battalion became the 35 Battalion (Territorial Force) Northumberland Fusiliers. This battalion had been formed in 1915 from home service personnel from the Territorial Force Battalion of the Northumberland Fusiliers, and was based at Herne Bay in Kent. Similarly, on 1 January 1917, the 22 Provisional Battalion became the 36 (Territorial Force) Northumberland Fusiliers. These Provisional Battalions had been formed in 1915 from Home Service men of the four Territorial Force Battalions of the Northumberland

Fusiliers. The 36 Battalion embarked for France in May 1918 as a Garrison Guard Battalion and was attached to 178 Brigade (2nd North Midland) Division.

Men of the 2/7 Battalion Northumberland Fusiliers, Egypt
Courtesy of Paul Moss

Payday for men of the 21 Provisional Battalion, Northumberland Fusiliers
based at Herne Bay, Kent
Author's Collection

Officers of 4 Reserve Battalion, Northumberland Fusiliers, Scotton Camp, Catterick
St George's Day 1917
Author's Collection

The adjutant of the 1/4 Battalion wrote from Blyth on 22 December 1914 to the St George's Gazette thanking Mrs Fischer of Hexham and the ladies of the county for providing the battalion with three and half hundredweights of Christmas puddings for the men on coastal duties.[17]

The adjutant of the newly renamed 1/4 Northumberland Fusiliers wrote in February 1915 from billets in Blyth. He pointed out that the Foreign Service Battalion was now known as the 1/4 and the home service battalion as the 2/4 Battalion. He goes on to say, 'We are fully complete as regards personnel and are gradually completing as regards stores and equipment'.[18]

Even before the Territorial Forces disembarked on the Western Front there were sad losses to the ranks of the men who had enlisted. Some deaths were accidental, others came about because of the stress of the training being undertaken by these volunteers.

7/1227 Private William Cameron died on 14 October 1914, aged 22:

Fell on live rail. Accidental death was the verdict returned at an inquest held by Mr Coroner Appleby at Newcastle Infirmary on William Cameron (22), a private in 'C' Company of the 1/7th Battalion Northumberland Fusiliers stationed at Gosforth Park. Lance Corporal William Hall of the 1/7th Northumberland Fusiliers identified the deceased. He was a native of

Belford, and had lived at Alnwick for some time. On October 14, deceased's company left Gosforth Park for Earsdon. They crossed the railway at Benton Square Station, and word was passed along for the men to beware of the live rail. It happened that Cameron had reason to recross the railway. Witness soon after was informed that Cameron had fallen upon the live rail. On approaching Cameron, he found he was dead. Private Hughes, who was a member of the advance guard on October 14, stated that when on Shiremoor Bridge he saw Cameron crossing the railway. He got safely over one set of rails, when he stumbled and fell upon a live rail. Lance-Sergeant W Wright of the Royal Army Medical Corps, stated that Cameron was burnt on both knees, across the face, and on the thumb. He was dead when witnesses reached him.[19]

7/2555 Private John Crosby Stephenson died on 25 December 1914, aged 35:

The remains of Private Thomas Crosby of 7th Battalion Northumberland Fusiliers were interred with full military honours at Alnwick Cemetery on Tuesday afternoon. The coffin was placed on a lorry and covered with a union jack, the deceased's bayonet and cap being laid on top. Leaving Clayport where Private Crosby was billeted the cortege was headed by a firing party of twelve men and Sergeant Bootle. Six under bearers, comrades of the dead soldier, marched by the side of the lorry and behind followed the relatives, succeeded by the Company numbering 100, to which the deceased belonged. Second Lieutenant Frazer was in command. At the cemetery the burial service was conducted by Reverend W. D. Trotter. Three volleys were fired over the grave and the 'last post' sounded by the buglers.[20]

7/1817 Pte Alfred George Poole died on 20 April 1915, aged 28:

Tragedy at Cambois

One of the soldiers quartered at Cambois made a tragic discovery last night. In the reservoir he found the body of Private Alfred Poole of the 7th Northumberland Fusiliers. The body was conveyed to the mortuary at Blyth by PC Carr. Poole, who worked as a miner at Ashington prior to the war, was reported missing on April 20, the same day as his battalion left for France.[21]

Sergeants of 1/4 Battalion Northumberland Fusiliers at Hexham
Author's Collection

All through the year, men from the Territorial Force battalions were out on the streets trying to encourage new recruits. They were competing against representatives from new battalions that were forming after Kitchener's Appeal for volunteers. These were the 'Pals Battalions'. This extract from the St George's Gazette records the efforts of the 2/7 Battalion to secure future recruits:

On April 6, Easter Tuesday 1915, 150 territorials of the 2/7 Northumberland Fusiliers started on a five days' recruiting march through north Northumberland under the command of Captain R. H. Hodgkin, Second Lieutenants W. A. G. Darlington and A. Kent. On the first day they started out from Alnwick and marched to Wooler, via Whittingham and Glanton, accompanied by press photographers. At Wooler they received a 'royal reception' arranged by the ladies of the Red Cross and the clergy. Next day a meandering march of over 26 miles was undertaken ending in Cornhill, where the officers stayed with Captain and Mrs Collingwood. Next day they headed for Berwick by the way of Norham which was termed a 'comparative stroll'. Pipers of the Royal Scots were on hand as the soldiers entered into the town where they found a splendid tea provided by the Mayor. The next day, was on to Bamburgh, calling in at Belford where again we were well fed. On Saturday the troops swung into Alnwick where a very competent critic was heard to say, 'Marching like regulars'. The band also came in for great praise as being at the head of the procession but still found the energy to play the troops through inhabited parts on the road. The author sums up, 'We have the satisfaction of knowing that our efforts were not in vain as the recruiting numbers have improved considerably'.[22]

Men from Hexham, 1915
Author's Collection

Men of 1/7 Northumberland Fusiliers digging trenches along the North East coast
Author's Collection

Through the winter the four battalions manned the coastal defences along the south Northumberland coast until orders were received in April 1915 that all of the first line battalions were off to France to fight the enemy. For many, this was what they had been waiting for:

> *It was the chief topic of conversation: should we get there in time to be any good – should we get there at all? We very much resented what seemed to be the popular estimate of us, viz, that we were a sort of mobilised gentleman's club, quasi-military in character, officially recognised but not likely to be used in any serious military purpose. And then suddenly, one afternoon, the magic order came. Battalion to make immediate preparedness to entrain the next morning. And our destination? – No official information given on this point. Any unofficial information? Yes – France.*[23]

Not everyone felt as enthusiastic:

> *I was leaving a wife, home and friends and all I held dear to me behind and departing for an unknown destination with all the apprehension of death, wounds and hardship ahead. Packed together 8 per carriage and including full equipment, with blackened railway windows and hard seats we journeyed south …*[24]

Thus, the four battalions of the Territorial Force from Northumberland – at this time known as the Northumbrian Brigade – were destined for France, still carrying their outdated weapons.

CHAPTER TWO

SECOND YPRES-THE BATTLE OF ST JULIEN

We are the Dead. Short days ago
We lived, felt dawn, saw sunset glow,
Loved and were loved, and now we lie
In Flanders Fields.

From '*In Flanders Fields*' by Lieutenant Colonel John McCrae, MD

Early in April 1915, rumours were rife about the imminent departure overseas of the four battalions of the Northumbrian Brigade. Sure enough, on 18 April the transport section and machine gun sections of all four battalions left their billets along the Northumberland coast for Southampton from where they sailed in the darkness for Le Havre on the SS *Archimedes*.

Two days later, on Tuesday 20 April 1915, all four of the Territorial Battalions of the Northumberland Fusiliers: 1/4, 1/5, 1/6 and 1/7, prepared for embarkation for France. At this time, these four battalions were known as the 'Northumbrian Brigade'. The 1/7 left their base at Cambois where they had been on coastal duties near Blyth Harbour; after an inspection at their billets in the Council School, the battalion marched with the bands of the Reserve Battalion (2/7) through the crowded streets of Blyth to the railway station. The 1/6, stationed at Seaton Sluice, marched the few miles along the coast to Blyth Station. Each battalion occupied two trains as they sped southwards. The

War Diary of the 1/5 records that the strength of the Battalion was 27 officers and 915 other ranks. The trains stopped at York, Doncaster, and Lincoln, thence to Liverpool Street, arriving at about 1700hrs. George Harbottle of the 1/6 had been promoted to Lance Sergeant (three stripes but only a corporal's pay) and together with Corporal Gray and ten other ranks had the job of train guard, which meant policing the train when it stopped to be sure that no one got off and was left behind. From there they progressed to Folkestone, where each battalion boarded a vessel to cross the channel to Boulogne.

> *Needless to say, we were given no information about where we were going but knew that it was bound to be France because, for Egypt, there would have been some special equipment. The train skirted around London to the south coast where in the dead of night we were herded on board ship and after a comparatively smooth crossing arrived in Boulogne in the early hours of Wednesday, 21 April.*[1]

The 1/7 boarded the steamer *Invicta* at about 2300hrs, whilst the 1/5 boarded the SS *Victoria* and the 1/6 crossed in SS *Onward*, both of which had earlier weighed anchor and steamed into the darkness.

S S *Onward*
Author's Collection

38

The boats were jam-packed, each carrying over 1000 soldiers. Many of the families of those who traversed the channel that night knew nothing of where their men had gone – not until they began to receive notices of their death or that they had been wounded in battle. It was a perfect night for the journey:

> *A night of black velvet darkness and silence. Not a light of any kind, not a sound save the throbbing of the engines and the beat of the screws, not a whisper among the closely packed ranks of men on board the channel steamer which conveyed us across. The sea was brilliantly phosphorescent ... and every wave top was a gleam of sparkling light ... Ahead there gleamed a glistening phosphorous surge in the inky black sea and a long luminous lane – like the Milky Way – stretched before us. This was the wake of a destroyer ahead, mapping out as it were a luminous road for us to travel along. And so the 1/7 came to France, Unseen, but present, the Navy led and safeguarded us to our destination.*[2]

The four battalions disembarked throughout the night of 20-21 April. Once ashore, the men formed up and marched to St Martin's encampment, a tented enclave, where they rested for a number of hours until they marched on to Pont des Bricques, and waited until it was time to board a train that night at 2300hrs. They travelled in covered cattle trucks, thirty men to each truck. After a six-hour journey the Fusiliers were off-loaded at Cassel and marched to Winezeele where they were billeted, before moving eastwards towards Ypres and the front line. At this time, the six Allied divisions within the Ypres salient were facing seven divisions and two independent brigades of Duke Albrecht's Fourth Army.

By April 1915, Germany was manufacturing chlorine, in great quantities and at low cost, for use in the German dye industry. But chlorine had also been recognized as a killing agent; a vesicant, it causes death by stimulating the over-production of fluid in the lungs, leading to drowning. Carl Duisberg, head of IG Farben and Fritz Haber, head of the Kaiser Wilhelm Institute, were toiling furiously to find a method of discharging chlorine in large quantities into enemy trenches. Initial experiments with gas-filled shells had failed, although in the future – with a different method of filling – gas shells would be widely used by both sides. The solution proposed was to release the chlorine directly from pressurised cylinders using a favourable wind to carry the noxious cloud. By 22 April 1915, and contrary to the provisions of The Hague Conventions of 1899 and 1906, the Germans had put in place 600 cylinders, containing 160 tons of chlorine, opposite Langemarck. There had been various intimations that the Germans were contemplating the use of gas, including intelligence gleaned from a German prisoner revealing information about the enemy's plans, but it appears that little attention had been paid to the various reports.

The whole nature of the war changed on the afternoon of 22 April 1915, when soon after 1600hrs the German artillery shortened their range and began an intense bombardment of the French front-line trenches north of Ypres. These were held by the 87th Territorial and the 45th Algerian French Army Divisions, the latter division composed of white Zouave regiments from Algeria, African Light Infantry (white punishment battalions) and native Algerian riflemen. On their right were the 2 and 3 Brigades of the 1st Canadian Division, which was the first of the imperial divisions to arrive on the Western Front, in February 1915. The rest of the Ypres salient was held by three British regular divisions: the 5th, 27th and 28th. Into this maelstrom the Territorial Force battalions of the Northumberland Fusiliers were fast approaching. The afternoon of 22 April was sunny with a light east-west breeze. At 1700hrs two greyish green clouds were observed, one on either side of Langemarck, drifting close to the ground from the German front line towards the French trenches. Eventually these clouds spread laterally until they united into one long rolling bank of choking fog. This was immediately followed by an intense bombardment throughout the salient. Within minutes, thousands of Zouaves and Algerian riflemen were seen stumbling in panic as they made for the rear, clutching their throats, coughing, their faces turning an ashen purple. In their reeking, yellowed uniforms, they staggered blindly away across fields, through hedges and over ditches.

Plainly something terrible was happening. What was it? Officers, and Staff Officers too, stood gazing at the scene, awestruck and dumbfounded; for in the northerly breeze there came a pungent nauseating smell that tickled the throat and made our eyes smart. The horses and men were still pouring down the road, two or three men on a horse, I saw, while over the fields streamed mobs of infantry, the dusky warriors of French Africa; away went their rifles, equipment, even their tunics that they might run the faster. One man came stumbling through our lines. An officer of ours held him up with levelled revolver, "What's the matter, you bloody lot of cowards?" says he. The Zouave was frothing at the mouth, his eyes started from their sockets, and he fell writhing at the officer's feet.[3]

Within an hour, although a few stoical men remained at their posts, the front line had been abandoned; a gap of 8000 yards had been created in the Ypres defences. Some of the gas drifted onto the Canadian positions but they held their line. Canadian reinforcements filtered to the left into the gas-contaminated area and carried out a series of counterattacks which stemmed the advance of the German infantry. In many places along this gap the German infantrymen, naturally wary of this new form of warfare, dug in rather than pressing forward.

At Kitcheners' Wood (not named after Lord Kitchener but from the French 'Bois des Cuisiniers'), the 10 Battalion of the 2 Canadian Brigade was ordered to counterattack into the breach forged by the gas attack. They formed up after 2300hrs, with the 16 Battalion (Canadian Scottish) of the 3 Brigade arriving to support the advance. Both battalions charged with over 800 men, in waves of two companies each, at 2346hrs. Without reconnaissance, the battalions encountered hedges and ditches on the way to their objective, but, having been engaged in small-arms fire from the wood, they began an impromptu bayonet charge. The assault cleared the former oak plantation of Germans – but with a 75 per cent Canadian casualty rate.

The 1/7 left Winezeele the following day, which was 23 April – an auspicious date, since Saint George was the patron saint of the Northumberland Fusiliers. They marched through Poperinghe to Vlamertinghe Woods arriving at 1900hrs, where '3' and '4' Companies took up positions in reserve trenches whilst '1' and '2' Companies remained in support. To the east, artillery fire from both sides rumbled on and on, flaring uneasily in the night sky. From the afternoon of 20 April, a 42-centimetre howitzer had begun dropping 2000lb shells into Ypres with devastating results.

In the early hours of 24 April, Duke Albrecht ordered a second gas strike followed by an assault on the Canadian apex, in an attempt to cut off the Ypres salient. The attack was intended to overrun the Canadian trenches, capture the village of St Julien and strike into the heart of the salient as far as the Zonnebeke Ridge. At the same time, another attack would continue operations west of the Yser Canal. By this stage, some of the Canadians had been issued with makeshift respirators: these were cotton bandoliers to be wetted and tied over the mouth and nose if a gas cloud were detected. They were predictably ineffective: even when wearing them men would collapse to the floor of their trenches with weeping, blinded eyes and burning throats. German infantry would stride in behind the gas cloud wearing better protection. By 1400hrs on 25 April, Kitcheners' Wood was again in German hands. St Julien was still held by the Allies, although later that day it was captured as they retired to conform to a defensive line.

After taking over a line of trenches, the men of the 1/4 moved back into the wood where they had spent the night, building themselves shelters with branches, waterproof sheets and blankets.

> *They gave the men protection from the sun, which became very hot as the day wore on, and also concealed them from enemy aeroplanes of which we had quite a lot over us all day.*[4]

Bunbury was taken aback at how rapidly he and his men, newly arrived from home, were to be employed at the front:

> *We fully expected that we should be left in the reserve trenches for some days, as up till now all the troops that have come out have been put into billets some way in the rear of the front line, while first the officers, and then the NCOs and men are sent up to the trenches in small parties or by platoons to familiarise them with the conditions, previous to the battalion going up as a unit. We had scarcely finished tea, however, when we got orders to pack up and fall in ready to march off at once.*[5]

On the evening of 24 April all four battalions that made up the Northumbrian Brigade met up at the crossroads in Brandhoek and marched through Vlamertinghe. As they strode through the small town, the men could clearly see that it bore all the dismal trademarks of enemy fire:

By the time we arrived at the outskirts of Ypres the traffic of ammunition and ambulance wagons had ceased and we were alone on the road. The only noise we heard was the echo of our own steps and the occasional roar of a gun or a bursting shell. Suddenly we came across a corpse lying across the pavement and the gutter – it was the body of a peasant – his bundle was lying some yards away having been precipitated forward when he fell. Just over the canal bridge a timber wagon and two shattered horses came into view and we walked through the blood of these noble animals as we passed them on the road. We were now in the town proper – everywhere nothing but ruins could be seen – not a house but was either shattered by shells or gutted with fire. Many walls leaned at dangerous angles into the streets and in the dim light of night each ruin seemed to me to represent the work of some grinning demon who was lurking in hiding behind these ghostly houses. On our way, we passed more dead horses, which in many cases were in a state of decomposition and emitted a fearful odour of rottenness.[6]

Cloth Hall, Ypres, on fire.
Author's Collection

As the column reached Ypres at 2300hrs it began to rain, which soon developed into a downpour that continued all night; everyone was thoroughly soaked, chilled and uncomfortable.

> *Although the Germans had only commenced shelling the place a few days ago, the town was rapidly becoming a mass of ruins, and there were huge shell holes in the middle of the roads and streets, and a number of corpses lay about, while the whole town appeared absolutely deserted.*[7]

Passing through ravaged Ypres, all four battalions suffered incessant shell fire which fell with the rain on the once quaint and historic town. The 1/5 had its first taste of what was to be their existence for the next four years and took its first casualty to a random German shell:

> *My back and pack were struck by a shower of debris and flying dirt while quite a number of men fell and bled for their country. Jack Duncan was in front of me and received a severe wound from this, our first shell. He was carried onto the pavement and left for the attention of the doctor.*[8]

5/2523 Private John ('Jack') William Duncan was later discharged, on 28 September 1916, under KR Para 392(xvi) wounds, (Silver War Badge 170659).

Rumours abounded that there were enemy spies concealed in the ruins of Ypres whose job was to signal whenever British troops were passing through. Sure enough, as soon as the Northumbrian Brigade entered the town the shelling began. Their chosen route passed through the centre of Ypres near the ruins of the Cathedral and the Cloth Hall, once a landmark of great beauty. This point seemed to be the focus of the enemy's attention and every kind of shell including Jack Johnsons, incendiaries, high explosives, and shrapnel fell around them. (Jack Johnson was an Afro-American boxer who held the world heavyweight title until 5 April 1915; his name was used as slang for a heavy German shell that gave off a lot of smoke.) The brigade made good progress by keeping close to the edges of streets and squares, and by doubling past places where the houses had been blown apart. At this point the 1/4 had suffered no casualties. As they were about to leave the main square they were halted in their tracks as a result of brigades in front losing their way.

Here we were treated to a truly gorgeous spectacle, as the shells came hurtling over our heads and more often than not exploded right in one or other of these fine buildings, not more than 30 yards from where we stood, The incendiary shells in particular produced a wonderfully fine effect, as they seemed to set fire to the whole interior of these buildings, which appeared to burn furiously with a very bright flare, at the same time giving off dense clouds of smoke, which poured out of the roofless ruins; the grandeur of the sight of these splendid old buildings being consumed with flames, while the shells constantly burst against their walls or passed through their windows bereft of glass, enhanced by the darkness of the night, baffles description, and the only thing I could think of to liken it to was the burning of Rome.[9]

During the twenty minutes or so of waiting, the 1/4 did not take any casualties, but as they moved off a high explosive shell burst over the tail of the 1/7 who were in front of them:

We arrived at the outskirts of Ypres and marched through the square, the market place of Ypres. Shells were dropping on the cobbled stones and some of the lighter shells and the shrapnel were spreading right across the square and the Cloth Hall and the Cathedral were on fire. We had our first casualty in going through the square, Tommy Rachael, who was a postman in Ashington. He was marching behind me and he shouted out, he said 'I'm wounded'. Nobody would believe him and then somebody said, 'There is blood coming down his legs,' and another fellow said, 'Help him, help him somebody. He's not going to drop out. We are the Northumberland Fusiliers!' That was the spirit we had. As we reached the outskirts we didn't know where we were going, neither officers nor men. After having an hour or two's sleep just outside of Ypres we marched on in the early hours [of 24/25 April] under heavy shell fire.[10]

Lieutenant Armstrong of the 1/7 also recorded the events in Ypres:

At last, as it was night, we approached the ruins of Ypres, and the roar of the guns was tremendous. We marched past the famous Cloth Hall (even then badly knocked about), and began to move at the double so as to escape being shelled. It was too late, however, and we were brought to a halt in the grand square of Ypres, opposite the Cathedral. Shells were bursting all around us and the Brigadier seemed uncertain whether he should proceed. The first casualties occurred in number one platoon, a shell bursting at the head of the Battalion and wounding several men ... I had a close shave for a start, a shell bursting close to my platoon and wounding Private Henderson, who was next to me, in the foot.[11]

Once the Fusiliers had passed through the burning city the German artillery bombardment closed, confirming that the enemy had known where they were. On reaching Potijze the men, by now exhausted and unnerved, lay in the open trying to get some rest, the horrors of the last few hours reverberating through their minds. They clustered in small groups so as to minimise the risk of heavy losses from the enemy's shells, and as the downpour continued all night they were soon lying in water.

1/4 Battalion

At about 1630hrs on 25 April the 1/4 and 1/7 were sent forward to support 10 Brigade (4th British) Division in a counterattack against Kitcheners' Wood and St Julien, where they experienced their first real action. On receiving their orders, the 1/4 moved two companies forward, but they managed to advance further than intended. In great danger, they were forced to take shelter during daylight hours and to return to Wieltje in the dark.

Soon I became conscious of bullets whizzing by both ears and I quickly guessed I was being sniped at from within our own lines, so seeing a small mound of earth just ahead of me I doubled up to it, and no sooner had I done so than several bullets plumped into it from in front, which amply confirmed my suspicions. The mound I had sheltered behind was in a gap in a hedge, and at the other side of the field about 150 yards away and exactly in front of me was a ruined cottage from which I thought it was more than likely I was being sniped. My mound only gave me cover if I lay absolutely flat with my face practically on the ground, and as the bullets continued whistling close past and above me, and I had no weapon to attempt to reply with (only having a walking cane and my revolver with about ten cartridges), I had an awful five minutes, as I felt it was certain death if I attempted to go forward, and my only alternative was to remain there and funk it. I did not, however, take long to make up my mind, and said what I fully expected would be my last prayer, and mentally bade farewell to all my dear ones. I then first tried to draw my opponent's fire by raising my cap, but he was too old a hand to be deceived by this. I then also had a good look round, and saw what I thought was a ditch about 20 or 30 yards to my right, running down the hedge, on the side which was concealed from the cottage, and I determined to make a dash for this. Accordingly, hoping once again to draw his fire (which I really believe I did this time, as I heard several bullets whistle past), I made a feint at rising to the left of my cover, just showing myself for a brief instant on that side, and then immediately rising, and dashing off as fast as I could run to the right, and having safely reached the ditch, I threw myself into it, and crawled down the hedge till I got level with the cottage, where I reckoned I was at last safe from the attentions of the sniper. As I made my way along this ditch, which was half full of water, I came across the bodies of four men (including two Canadians and one Northumberland Fusilier) within a few yards of each other, who had probably been shot by the same sniper, while walking down behind the hedge believing themselves screened from view, and therefore safe; and this made me glad that I had chosen the greater security of the ditch. Having reached this point, I succeeded in summoning two men to me, and explained to them what I suspected, and told them to try and bag the sniper. This, by dint of careful stalking, they succeeded in doing, and going into the building to examine their handiwork afterwards, they found it was a German in British uniform. Looking back on this I have not the slightest hesitation in saying that this was my most unpleasant experience, as it was the only occasion on which I was conscious of being threatened with funk, and I regard it as almost miraculous that I escaped untouched, and most sincerely thank God.[12]

During this foray, the 1/4 lost one man: 4/2021 Private William Spence from Prudhoe. Three officers were injured: Captain D. H. Weir, RAMC (who sustained a shattered arm), Lieutenant C. M. Joicey, (shot through the leg) and Second Lieutenant W. Robinson (shot through the foot). Of the other ranks, thirty-three men were wounded. A further twenty men were reported missing, but many of these were lying low, reporting for duty the next day.

1/7 Battalion

The 1/7 crossed the canal near the Menin Gate and marched past the École de Jeunes Filles to a potato field at St Jean, a village north east of Ypres. Here Lieutenant Colonel G. S. Jackson informed his company commanders that at 1630hrs they were expected to lead an attack on the village of Fortuin, about three miles north east of Ypres.

> *You should have seen our faces. We had not the faintest notion before this that we were going to attack. We were tired out, very hungry indeed, and pretty jumpy besides. We had no idea where we were, who was on our right and left, we had never seen the country in daylight. All we were possessed of in the way of information was a very inferior small scale map.*[13]

While they were waiting for the order to advance, the men of the battalion lay down in a potato field in lines of platoons, spread out as far as possible, with an interval of two paces between each man. The attack was supported by a battery of six eighteen pounders that started to shell the terrain in front of the Northumbrians. The Germans responded by shelling the troops:

> *It was rather a trial waiting for the next one plopping on top of you. For the first hour I was in mortal funk, and then I got more or less used to it and brave enough to light a cigarette. Finally, I fell asleep to be wakened every now and then by a shower of mud and potatoes. I do not know how many people we lost in this field.*[14]

Finally, at 1630hrs the order was received for the 1/7 to advance. The battalion formed up with 'A' and 'B' Companies in the front line and 'C' and 'D' Companies in support. They advanced in lines of platoons, to a point 1000 yards from the enemy just behind a trench held by the Canadians, and took up positions. They were under heavy rifle fire. Even though they noticed troops retiring on their right flank, the battalion pushed on for a further 500 yards in the face of heavy machine-gun and rifle fire. Here the first line took shelter in a small ditch where, on their left, machine-gun fire was zipping from a cottage. They immediately directed heavy fire at the building, and a section on the left was sent off to work around it.

We finally came to rest about 500 yards from the Boches, and started to scratch holes with our entrenching tools, to get out of the rifle fire. Shortly afterwards a German plane came over close down, and he must have spotted us, because the Boche guns started shelling.[15]

After waiting three hours for promised artillery assistance, at 0900hrs the 1/7 realised that there were no troops on their left and right flanks and that their support troops had retired. Consequently, they fell back to a position on the right of the Canadians and remained till dark when they returned to Wieltje and bivouacked for the night.

Writing home from the front, a private in the 1/7 stated that it was on Sunday afternoon [25 April 1915] while digging trenches that a 'Jack Johnson' laid part of 'C' (Belford) Company out, killing the brothers Tom [Thomas Henry] and Will [Wilfred Hereward] Wake of Bamburgh and wounding Philip Wood.[16] See Chapter 13, 'Aftermath'.

At 1930hrs the Northumbrian Brigade was placed under the orders of the 1st Canadian Division to form their reserve. The morning of Monday 26 April 1915 saw all the battalions bivouacked at various sites around Wieltje. At 1015hrs, Brigadier General J. F. Riddell (Northumbrian Brigade) received an order from the commander of 10 Infantry Brigade to verify a report (sent in from the 28th Division) that the enemy had broken through the front line near Fortuin; if this were found to be true, the 1/5 were required to counterattack with whatever force he deemed necessary. Immediately, Lieutenant Colonel A. H. Coles, the commander of the 1/5, sent out an officer's patrol; soon afterwards the rest of his battalion followed on to Fortuin with orders to mount a counteraction if needed.

The War Diary[17] records that the battalion arrived at the point of the rumoured German breakthrough at 1140hrs and could find no evidence to suggest that it had happened. A message to this effect was sent to Brigade HQ, and in reply the Fusiliers were ordered to retire or – if that was deemed too dangerous – to dig in. By this time the battalion was being bombarded by shells and had already taken some casualties, so they replied that they would entrench and retire under the cover of darkness. The casualties were: two officers killed:

Captain Fountain Okey Colbourne Nash, 'D' Company, and Lieutenant Lindsay Bainbridge (attached to the Royal Engineers Signals Company – see Chapter 13, 'Aftermath') and one Fusilier killed: 5/1522 Private James Arnold, a Belfast man, a miner who lived in Walker on Tyne. A further sixty-eight Fusiliers were wounded, and one officer and thirty-one men were reported as missing. As bad as this sounds, as a result the 1/5 would take no part in the even more disastrous operation carried out by the other three battalions of the brigade on this fateful day.

Major Fountain Okey Colbourne Nash

1/5 Northumberland Fusiliers

Fountain was in born London in 1878, the son of Joseph and Laura Nash of Hampstead. He was educated at St Paul's School, London, and the University of London. He graduated in 1897 with a degree in civil engineering. Whilst in the employment of Rochdale Town Council he was granted associate membership of the Institute of Civil Engineers. In 1905 Fountain married Ella Heap Nash of Blackpool. Fountain secured his post as an officer of the Territorial Force in April 1911. He was killed on 26 April 1915, aged 37, and is buried in Birr Cross Road Cemetery. His headstone is inscribed:

HE GIVETH

MY BELOVED SLEEP

Later in the day, at 1330hrs, Brigadier General Riddell received further orders from the 1st Canadian Division that the Northumbrian Brigade was to attack St Julien, together with the Lahore Division and a further battalion from the 4th Division. The attack was scheduled for 1405hrs, with the supporting artillery opening fire at 1320hrs. Worryingly, none of the officers from the brigade had been given the chance to reconnoitre the ground around Wieltje and St Julien, one and three-quarter miles away: they had been given no intelligence on the position of either the enemy's or the Allied trenches. Worse still, they had no idea that the General Headquarters line was strongly wired and that there were only a few places through which troops could pass; there was no liaison between the artillery and the attacking forces. The other battalions employed in the assault had already moved forward, but the men of the Northumbrian Brigade had only thirty-five minutes to prepare; by 1350hrs they were on the move. In the scramble to obey orders, many of the men were not even supplied with extra ammunition.

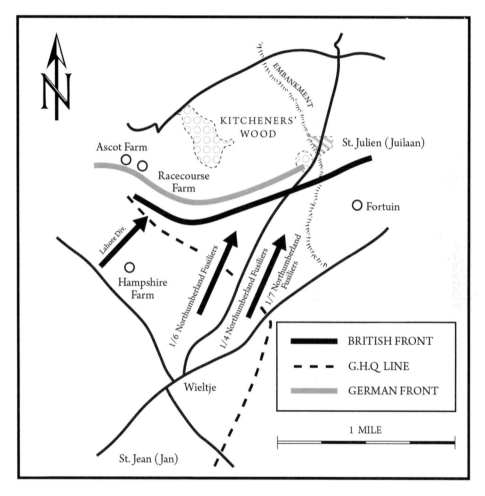

Attack of the Northumberland Brigade: 26 April 1915

The 1/4 (commanded by Lieutenant Colonel A. J. Foster) were ordered to attack on the right with their left flank on the Wieltje-St Julien road; the

1/6 (commanded by Lieutenant Colonel G. R. B. Spain) were on the left with their right flank on the Wieltje-St Julien road; the 1/7 (commanded by Lieutenant Colonel G. Scott Jackson) were to support the 1/4 Battalion. Thus, the Northumbrian Infantry Brigade (as an entity) was the first brigade of the Territorial Force to go into battle during the Great War.

> *As a mere NCO in our 'A' Company I knew nothing of this. All we knew was we had to 'fall in' with full equipment, i.e. full marching order with pack on our back, containing great coat and all our spare possessions. Add to this ammunitions pouches, rifle, haversack and entrenching tool, plus two extra bandoliers of ammunition just served out to us, it was obvious that we were well weighed down.*[18]

The troops moved off in full marching order. At about 1405hrs the leading battalion was suddenly brought up short by an impenetrable barrier of heavy duty barbed wire about ten yards deep – the GHQ line. This barricade was totally unexpected. Beyond it was the Allied front line (at 600 to 700 yards) and the enemy front line at 1200 yards. Their advance stalled as the heavily-equipped men tried to identify a way to negotiate the wire, and to make things worse, the narrow gaps they eventually found (or cut) caused them to bunch up as they struggled through, offering an easy target for concentrated enemy fire.

> *Where the huge casualties arose, it was not by the enemy attack on us, or our attack on the enemy but the fact that there was a great long line of reserve line barbed wire about 10 yards wide and about 4 feet high. There was a single gap. Garton, a brave officer – he had wire cutters and he stood there cutting another gap – of course he was killed. My section was through the gap straight away and most of the 1st and 2nd platoons was through the gap straight away – they hadn't got the range on us. Then when the rest of the battalion was trying to get through that gap they got murdered by machine gun and artillery fire.*[19]

The other two battalions suffered similarly from having had no proper reconnaissance. They were going in blind:

> *We were then in extended order in true drill-book fashion and advanced*

in short sharp rushes under whistle command. Our packs were a terrible encumbrance and so out came jack knives and we just cut the straps of each other's packs and left them behind. Those who did survive, lived for the next few months sans greatcoat and any spare clothing.[20]

The following is taken from the War Diary of the 1/6 Battalion, Northumberland Fusiliers:

The 1/6 Battalion within minutes of receiving their orders deployed into artillery formation with 'A' and 'B' Companies in the Front line and 'C' and 'D' Companies in the second line at fifty yards interval and two hundred yards distance. Directly we left the cover of the village [Weiltje] the enemy literally poured shrapnel into our ranks, inflicting heavy casualties. The first rush took us over a shallow hollow of meadow littered with dead and wounded, for the enemy's fire was intense. Up the rise we began to meet machine gun bullets, rifle fire and high explosive shells from all directions, which thinned our ranks considerably.[21]

The 1/6, on the left of the attack, suffered the largest number of casualties with six officers and fifty-eight other ranks killed. The officers included brothers Captains George Edward and Howard Tomlin Hunter and Lieutenants Arthur Richmond Garton (see Chapter 13, *Aftermath),* Edmund Mortimer and William Black Noble, and Second Lieutenant Edward Noel Mather. Many more would die of their wounds in the days that followed.

Mine was rather a flying visit to France and Belgium. We landed on 22 April and I was knocked at St Julien (Ypres) on 26 April. Between those dates we had a good deal of heavy marching and discomfort, which of course was only to be expected. I got a dose of shrapnel – one in the eyebrow, and the other in the top of my head … Lieutenant Garton died gallantly, just before me in the advance. He had quite coolly cut the wire entanglements, and I had just followed him through when he was killed by a bullet – a great loss to the company. Lieutenant Noel Mather was killed later on within a few feet of me, while we were firing from behind a hedge. There was great slaughter in that place and I think about 100 men were either killed or wounded there. Just before I was hit there were only half-a-dozen of us capable of firing. The

> *Germans had the range to a foot and dropped Jack Johnsons methodically all along the hedge. A sniper nearly got me there too. His bullet went through my clothing and shirt, but didn't touch me. It got the next man! On the whole, we had rather an exciting time from first to last.*[22]

Lord Kitchener had, in the past, been scornful about the abilities of the Territorials. However, in the House of Lords in 1915 he paid this tribute following the *Battle of St Julien*:

> *I want to tell you that the pushing up of the Northumbrian Division was one of the most glorious episodes of the war. They went up in broad daylight in skirmishing order in face of the most awful shell-fire. It seemed impossible that any of them would reach the trenches. Their exploits will bear comparison with Balaclava, and I hope the day will come when a more able pen than mine will tell the world of the deeds performed by our incomparable infantry in front of Ypres. I am thankful for the privilege of having the pleasure of congratulating them on their heroism, and offer them my undying admiration.*[23]

The actions of the Northumbrian Brigade bore witness to the pre-war training and stamina of men who were subjected to the nerve-racking experiences of a great battle only six days after leaving England. They advanced steadily into the face of violent machine gun and rifle fire. Most of this came from the heavily defended German position known as Kitcheners' Wood, on their left front, and was responsible for many of the casualties suffered by the 1/6.

The British front line was manned by two regular battalions: the 2nd Battalion Argyll and Sutherland Highlanders and the 1st Battalion Hampshire Regiment. Many of the Territorial survivors, including Lance Sergeant George Harbottle, tumbled into these trenches to gain some respite:

> *I remember asking the three standard questions required in the drill book – Are you short of ammunition? – Whereabouts are the enemy's lines? – What is the range? The answer I got from a Hampshire Corporal, 'We've boxes and boxes of ammo,' kicking one by his foot and then, 'Sit down and get your breath and don't worry about the Bosches, they were quiet enough until you lads made a stir!' I asked him if they were not joining in the attack to which he replied, 'Us! Good God no, we're not crazy.'*[24]

Soon enough, the order came for the remnants of the 1/6 to advance. George Harbottle reckoned there were about fifty of them, led by two officers: Lieutenants Fawcus and Dawson. They needed to negotiate the front line barbed wire – a problem, albeit nowhere near as intractable as that posed by the GHQ line. Without any artillery support and as machine gun bullets filled the air, isolated parties of the 1/6 managed to reach a position approximately 250 yards beyond the Allied front-line and to occupy some small trenches which were believed to have been occupied by the Germans.

Orders were also received by the 1/4 and 1/7 at about 1400hrs, just as the men had finished eating:

We had just finished our lunch, and shortly after 2pm we were rushed out of our trenches at a moment's notice and ordered to attack in a north easterly direction. These were the only orders we received, and on setting out we had no idea where our own front line trenches in this part of the front were situated, or what was the objective of our attack, though we afterwards discovered that we were attacking the German lines around the village of St Julien. [25]

At the 1/4 Battalion's bivouac, officers and men were lying in a field pitted with shell holes of various sizes, which provided some small safety against German shells, when Lieutenant Colonel Foster called together his company commanders. Within only two minutes they were back, announcing that the battalion was to attack the village of St Julien forthwith. At the 1/7 Battalion:

At about 2.15pm Colonel G. S. Jackson hurriedly called out the company commanders, and in two minutes they came rushing back with the news that we were to attack the village of St Julien immediately. We were to attack as yesterday, with two platoons of our company (Nos 3 and 4) in front and the other two (Nos 1 and 2) in support, moving out in artillery formation. We were not quite ready when the Brigadier [Riddell] accompanied by the Brigade-Major [Moore] and Staff Captain Hill came up, shouting for us to hurry as we were already behind time. We were on the move at 2.30pm. St Julien lay some three or four miles in a north east direction from Wieltje and our present lines. We had not the vaguest idea as to where our own front line was or indeed if there was one at all, or where the Germans were.[26]

Lance Corporal Jack Dorgan of the 1/7 painted a vivid picture of the carnage during the advance:

We suffered many casualties on the road up; many, many casualties. I remember a shell dropping when we were lying behind a hedge, and two men had both their legs taken off: both of these were Ashington lads. One lived a few minutes, and the other lived about half an hour. One was called Jackie Oliver and the other was Bob Young. Bob Young was the first to go. When he was hit he said, 'Will you take my wife's photograph out of my pocket?' He was sensible to the last and jokingly, as I thought, he kept saying to me, he says, 'Put my legs straight.' Well, he'd no legs to put straight, and I just made a movement, touched the lower part of his body. What could I do? He died with his wife's photograph in his hand.

Jackie Oliver had a brother in our Battalion and I shouted to our fellows who had to leave me with these two wounded men, 'Tell Weedy Oliver his brother's wounded.' He never recovered consciousness but eventually, sometime later, Weedy Oliver came back and was with his brother when he died. No doctors available. No first aid available. I don't know where they were, because our Battalion was still advancing towards the front line. I just had to leave them. I don't know where they were buried. I never saw them or heard of them again. I had to go as fast as I could to catch up with our Battalion.

We went on and on, and as we went up the Canadians and the Highlanders were retreating from the front line because they had been under gas. There was no gas masks, nothing for gas casualties, and all they had on was their bandage out of their first aid kit which every soldier carried in a pocket in his tunic, and they had these bandages on their eyes and there they were staggering back. Gas never affected me and there was fellows dropping behind all the time – I must have been one of the lucky ones. We came to the reserve trenches, but we didn't recognise them as trenches, nobody in them, they were all retired. So, we just jumped over, but we never reached the front line. The gas was too dense and then we had to retire. We never reached St Julien. I think we only got far as St Jean but, wherever it was, we had to retire from there. We didn't come out of the line for four days.[27]

The 1/7 moved up into the firing line to reinforce the 1/4, the men advancing at the double in extended order. They pushed forward by rushes, but could find no good firing position. The battalion suffered deplorable losses before they reached the shelter of a trench in front, also occupied by the Seaforth Highlanders.

> *There seemed to be thousands of German guns trained on us, while none of ours was speaking at all. A wide panoramic stretch of country was in view, with what was apparently the village of St Julien in the middle distance, and the vast Houthulst Forest farther behind. We had to go downhill into a slight valley, and then the ground began to rise again. Our casualties from the start were very severe but presently we came under terrible machine-gun fire and worse still we had to cross the barbed wire entanglements protecting one of our own rearward lines of trenches. As this was not cut and was accurately ranged upon by the Boches, our casualties were ghastly.[28]*

Lieutenant Cowan continued:

> *Presently we thought we saw the German trenches with their garrison – ready, it seemed, to surrender, as they appeared to be holding up their hands. By this time, of course we had deployed as yesterday but our lines were very thin now. We made ready to charge, but after all it transpired that this was our own front line held by the 2nd Seaforth Highlanders of the 4th Division and they were cheering us on. They expressed surprise at the way we had faced the music.[29]*

St Julien was also the subject of a letter quoted in one of the Berwick newspapers:

> *Private W. Kinghorn, Seaforth Highlanders, a Berwick man, who was wounded some time ago and is now back in the firing line, writes to his aunt, Mrs W Landless, 29 Palace Street, Berwick on 25 May: We have been in the great Battle of Ypres for a month, and we have had about enough for a little while. They are always using gas here again, but gained nothing by it. There is a very heavy artillery battle going on just now … I saw an awful lot of Berwick chaps the other night, and had a good chaff with them and I think that Berwick ought to be proud of them [1/7 NF]. I saw them the day they went into action for the first time. I watched them the whole time,*

and they were splendid, but of course, they all say they wish they were back in Berwick again.[30]

The remnants of the 1/7 found themselves beyond the front line trenches, situated just in front of St Julien; it was impossible to advance, as the air was thick with bullets. Although the sheltering men were convinced that they would be shelled, in the event this didn't happen, because the enemy had found far more interesting targets behind them: stretcher bearers were trying to take the wounded back and the Germans were doing their utmost, with all too much success, to blow them to bits.

We found that the only way to advance was for a few men under an officer or an NCO, to make a short rush forward and then to lie flat and regain their breath. It was a case of every man using his own intelligence with courage. We made a good deal of progress and took up a strong line with a hedge in front of it, which afforded some shelter. In front of this position was a large open field and at the other end of it, a few hundred yards distant, lay the village of St Julien and the Germans. To cross this field without adequate artillery support was impossible and yet we were ordered to advance. Our present position by the farm, however, was being shelled to such an extent that as far as our own safety went, it did not much matter where we were. We finished the last of these, and I was going to lie down, when I received a staggering blow on the back, and fell forward. I suffered an agonising pain, and soon felt another blow on the back, also extremely violent. I began to feel difficulty in breathing and wondered if I would ever leave this spot.[31]

At 1545hrs, as the attack was stalling, Brigadier General Riddell and his Brigade Major left the relative safety of the support trench in order to make contact with their battalion commanders. They moved stealthily towards Vanheule Farm but, when they were about 150 yards south of the buildings, Riddell was felled by a bullet through the head. Command of the Northumbrian Brigade devolved to Lieutenant Colonel Foster of the 1/4, whose first order was for the battalion to dig in. As the attack had stalled, the lives of the remaining soldiers hung by a thread. They dug in where they could and waited for the coat of darkness to cover them.

Brigadier General James Foster Riddell
149 Brigade

James was the only son of the late John Riddell and his first wife Jane. He was educated at Wellington School and Sandhurst. In April 1912, he married Margaret Christobel Scott of Surrey and in later years lived at Lesbury House, Lesbury, Northumberland. After Sandhurst he was gazetted to the Northumberland Fusiliers and served twenty years with the 2nd Battalion, initially in India. He returned to England in 1885.

During the Hazara Campaign of 1888, against the Kala Dhaka tribes of what nowadays is known as Pakistan he was mentioned in despatches for valour during the storming of the Chula Crag. He served with the Fusiliers during the Boer War and was then sent home to raise a 3rd Battalion at York, returning to his beloved 2nd Battalion. 1n 1904 he was appointed commander of the 3rd Battalion in South Africa until it was disbanded, finishing his tour of duty on the continent with the 2nd Battalion. In 1911 he was appointed Brigadier of the Northumberland Infantry Brigade (made up of four Territorial Force battalions of the Northumberland Fusiliers), and on the onset of war was gazetted Brigadier General. Throughout the winter of 1914/1915 this Territorial Brigade guarded the coastline and industrial centres of South Northumberland from the vicinity of Blyth.

In April 1915 James and his brigade embarked for France. Within days, his men were attacking over open country swept by fire from all levels in an attempt to capture St Julien. At about 3pm Riddell decided to move forward into the firing line, despite the advice of his staff, who urged him to remain in his Headquarters rather than risk facing the murderous fire. However, he was a brave man, who wanted to be alongside his men. He was shot by a sniper as he advanced across the battlefield. The bullet entered his head and he died instantaneously, aged 52. After the war his body was exhumed and buried in Tyne Cot Cemetery. His headstone is inscribed:

KILLED LEADING HIS MEN

BUT FIVE DAYS LANDED

SOLDIER AND GREAT GENTLEMAN

That day – one of tragedy for so many men – saw countless acts of heroism. Part time soldiers, who'd travelled to France expecting a role providing garrisons along the communication lines, had instead been propelled to the front within days of landing. They were tested, but they proved to be utterly dauntless amid the carnage.

An artist's impression of Privates Burrell and Martin crossing the fire-swept battlefield carrying ammuntion, for which they won Distinguished Conduct Medals.
Author's Collection

Privates 7/1180 George Burrell and 7/2188 Charles Martin from Morpeth were both awarded the Distinguished Conduct Medal. Their citations read:

Distinguished Conduct Medal

For conspicuous gallantry during the attack on St Jean on 26 April 1915, in carrying up a box of ammunition to the firing line, assisted by Private Martin [Private Burrell] across open ground and under heavy fire from the enemy. They advanced entirely unsupported and were cheered by their comrades for their bravery.

7/1180
Private
George
Burrell

7/2188
Private
Charles
Martin

At 2000hrs the battalions were ordered to retire. As dusk fell, Lieutenant Bunbury was given the distressing job of organising the bringing in of the wounded and the dead. The SDGW records that over fifty men from the 1/4 were killed during the attack, with well over 300 wounded. Many of these men would die in the days that followed. Although no officers were killed, a large number were injured, including Captains Chipper, Hunting and Plummer, Lieutenants Carrick and Speke and Second Lieutenant R. Allen. Those who were killed included 4/1592 Lance Corporal William Ernest Woodman from Hexham, who was subsequently mentioned in despatches; 4/1855 Private Arthur John Herdman of Humshaugh, and 4/1719 Private William Scott from Haydon Bridge. Others mentioned in despatches were Second Lieutenant D.T. Turner, 4/32 Sergeant John William Smith, 4/1640 Private A. Brown and 4/1517 Lance Corporal George Chadderton, who was also awarded the Distinguished Conduct Medal.

His citation states:

> *For conspicuous gallantry on 26 April 1915, during the advance, in volunteering to carry a message across the open and under heavy fire, from St Julien to Wieltje. He then returned with the answer and again volunteered for and performed the same duty, showing great courage throughout.*

Sammy, the regimental dog, went through the day with the 1/4 and although he was blown several feet into the air when a shell landed, he appeared none the worse for the experience!

The 1/7 reported the following casualties for the period 25 April to 2 May: Officers: 2 killed, including Second Lieutenant Alan Williamson Kent who died from his wounds on 27 April, and 12 wounded; Other Ranks: 19 killed, 217 wounded and 161 missing. For details see Appendix A.

> *It was exactly a week after we'd landed in France – just one week to the day – and the next afternoon when we were assembled as a Battalion after all that hectic week in Flanders, we found ourselves with four hundred and odd men out of nearly twelve hundred men who had landed in France. It was terrible, terrible. Most of my pals were gone, either killed or wounded, and I don't remember whether it was the Adjutant or Colonel who sent for me and he says, 'You are now a Corporal'. By then practically all the officers and NCOs were wiped out. And it was just one week since we'd come off the boat. All gone!* [32]

NORTHUMBERLAND TERRITORIALS
WHO FELL AT ST JULIEN

6/1546
Pte Albert Epstein

4/1872
Pte John Grierson

4/785
Sgt Victor Elton Scott

4/2190
Pte John Shepherd

4/2279
Pte George Pearson

4/1404
Pte William Soulsby

4/2275
Pte William Fox

6/1803
Pte Francis W Moore

7/1665
Pte Fred Irving

7/2295
Pte Frederick Lyons

4/1756
Pte John Edward Adams

4/1327
Pte Joseph Cunningham

4/836
Pte Obediah Armstrong

7/1301
Pte John E Harrison

6/20019
Cpl James Binning

7/1949
LCpl James Goodfellow

NORTHUMBERLAND TERRITORIALS
WHO FELL AT ST JULIEN

4/1348
Pte James Fenwick

4/1756
Pte Alfred Blacklock

6/3213
Pte Alexander Burgess

7/2786
Pte Albert Ernest Nichol

6/2877
Pte Benjamin Baston

5/2458
Pte David Keith Tulloch

4/616
Pte Matthew Hudson

4/1592
Cpl Ernest Woodman

6/2378
Pte Ernest Beattie

6/2853
Pte Thomas Job Raynor

6/1000
Pte Thomas Wardle

4/1981
Pte John Thompson

6/2748
LCpl F J Strazenburg

6/1509
Pte Gilbert Grayson

7/1443
Cpl William McLeod

4/539
Cpl John Robson

Sammy

There are many stories of animals in the Great War. One of the most interesting tales concerns Sammy, a terrier who was the mascot of the 1/4 Northumberland Fusiliers. Sammy was adopted by the soldiers at their Drill Hall in Hexham. When the 1/4 marched off on 20 April 1915 for service in France, Sammy climbed onto the train with them and duly arrived in France as part of the new detachment. Six days later these Fusiliers were involved in the attack on St Julien and, as were many of his human comrades in arms, he was wounded and gassed. Happily he survived and stayed with the Fusiliers for over a year sharing the hardships of living in the trenches. However, in the autumn of 1916 he was accidentally killed during field firing practice at Warfusee. The distraught troops thought that Sammy would have to be buried in a foreign field, but Sammy's body was shipped back to England into the hands of P Spicer & Sons, Fine Art Taxidermists of Leamington. Thus Sammy's heroic war antics were recorded for posterity.

Initially Sammy was mounted in a glass case and was to be found in pride of place at the Drill Hall on Hencotes in Hexham. However, today this unusual War Memorial is to be found at the Fusiliers Museum of Northumberland in Alnwick Castle.

In his history of the war, John Buchan (author of *The Thirty-Nine Steps*) was succinct about the St Julien offensive:

> *The attack on St Julien prospered ill. The Northumberland Brigade had had no time to reconnoitre the ground, it was held up by wire, and it received the worst of shell fire. Its 1/6 Battalion managed to get 250 yards in advance of our front trenches, but could not hold the position. The Brigadier, General Riddell, fell at 3.30 and the brigade lost 42 officers and some 1900 men.*[33]

CHAPTER THREE

AFTER ST JULIEN
MAY AND JUNE 1915

Gas! Gas! Quick, boys! – an ecstasy of fumbling,
Fitting the clumsy helmets just in time,
But someone still was yelling out and stumbling,
And floundering like a man in fire or lime.

From '*Dulce et Decorum est*' by Second Lieutenant Wilfred Owen MC

Using the darkness of the night of 26 April, the dazed remnants of the Northumbrian Brigade retired from their hazardous positions to the relative safety of Wieltje, although even there they were within range of German artillery. The men were granted a much-needed rest day; the desperately tired Captain Bunbury recorded:

Many of the men and some of the officers seemed pretty badly shaken up with yesterday's and the previous day's ordeal and in many cases their nerves seemed all a jingle. We did not attempt to do anything with the men today beyond getting them to improve their dug-outs, for which they did not require much persuasion, as they were only too keen to make themselves as safe as possible from shell fire.[1]

As during the previous night, parties from all the battalions went out to continue the grim tasks of searching for wounded men and of burying the dead. Many bodies were found and buried where they lay. These included 7/2275 Private William Fox, aged 22, of Thorneyburn, Bellingham. Second Lieutenant Robert Allen wrote to his parents James and Elizabeth of Heathery Hall:

> *He was an excellent fellow, was very happy with his work and was very popular with his comrades. He died a brave and unselfish death while attending to the wounds of his comrade.*[2]

7/1981 Private John Thompson, aged 21, of Hexham, also died. Captain F. Robinson wrote to his father:

> *Private J. Thompson was killed yesterday morning while taking a man to the dressing station. He was a fine lad and a brave one at that. On the previous day he brought in wounded men all afternoon under heavy fire.*[3]

Captain Plummer wrote a further letter explaining that John was doing his duty as a stretcher bearer at the time of his death:

> *They have to expose themselves to a great extent whilst tending to the wounded and make good targets for the brutes called snipers, who do not refrain from firing on our wounded.*[4]

Today, along with many others of the Northumbrian Brigade who died on 25 and 26 April 1915, they are honoured by the daily ceremony at the Menin Gate Memorial, where the names of over 54,000 men who have no known grave are inscribed on the stonework of the monumental archway, which states: 'Here are recorded names of officers and men who fell in Ypres Salient, but to whom the fortune of war denied the known and honoured burial given to their comrades in death.' Although many of the dead were buried with great reverence in marked graves by their comrades at the time of their deaths, the sad truth is that the years of torrid warfare within the Ypres salient caused their bodies to be lost in the mire and destruction of the battlefield.

The men existed like troglodytes for the next few days, living in their dugouts while it was light, safe from the prying eyes gazing down from enemy aeroplanes.

Any sighting could call down harrowing shellfire. Then, as darkness closed in, they would emerge to man working parties, digging trenches, often within hearing distance of the enemy.

On 30 April, a working party from the 1/4 went out to Hill 60 (which at this time was still in British hands). They followed a circuitous route to avoid the Germans' favourite spots for dropping shells. To get there they passed a number of ruined chateaux, including Hooge:

Here the smells were something appalling and there were many scarcely covered copses of men and beasts. About here there had been a great deal of heavy fighting and the buildings were in a terribly shattered condition. Although I did not myself see it, several men of my platoon aver that we passed within a few yards of the body of a Canadian Sergeant who had been crucified to a door.[5]

After a day of shelling with ten men wounded, on the night of 29 April the 1/5 Battalion moved to an old line of British trenches near Zillebeke. Three days later, on 2 May, there was further savagery:

*Imagine a bright May morning and a platoon (about 55 men) busily engaged in washing, cleaning up, cooking and some sleeping. Suddenly a tremendous explosion, a deathly stillness as if all were paralysed, then fearful screams and groans and death gasps. What had happened? A high explosive German shell had fallen right into a wide part of the trench where many men had been. The sight of the wounded shedding their blood from gaping wounds and their agonising cries – one asking to be shot – would have convinced any humane man that war is an impossible way of settling national questions – or it will be in the near future. It was the 2*nd *May that this incident took place and this high explosive shell killed 7, wounded 18 – yet the day before 400 shells came over and dropped immediately behind this trench within 10 yards and no-one was hurt – but this one shell bursting right in the trench accounted for a total of 25 men. The trench after the dead and wounded were removed presented a ghastly sight – it was red with blood like a room papered in crimson while equipment lay everywhere.*[6]

Colonel Fielding of the Coldstream Guards was appointed Brigadier of the Northumbrian Brigade on 2 May, and that night they moved back through Ypres:

> *Travelling very slowly over roads which had been ploughed with shells, and on which they were still bursting every now and again, we made our way back, passing through the northern portion of Ypres and crossing a bridge over the canal. Everywhere we passed, the buildings had been wrecked by shells and the devastation wrought in this part of the country was awful, as seen even at night, while the sights and smells along the roadside were appalling; but it is marvellous how inured one becomes to this kind of thing, and takes practically no notice of them, except when a particularly powerful stench forces home the knowledge of its proximity.*[7]

On 4 May at 1100hrs, in a field at Droghlandt, Sir John French inspected and addressed the remnants of the Northumbrian Brigade.

Sir John French's Tribute to the Northumberland Infantry Brigade

Officers, non-commissioned officers, and men of the Northumberland Infantry Brigade. I want to say a few words to you this morning to tell you how much I appreciate the splendid work you have done this last ten days in the fighting at Ypres. When the Northumbrian Division came out here in the ordinary course to settle down at Cassel, it was expected to have some little time to pull itself together, as every large unit which comes to this country is obliged to have. But we had this treacherous attack under cover of asphyxiating gases, which no soldiers have used yet, and men who use them are not worthy of the name of soldiers. We had this villainous proceeding, and I was obliged to send you up to reinforce the troops there. That would have been a high trial for any body of troops, even for a regular division with years of training at Aldershot, troops that had been fighting before, the highest trial.

You met that call splendidly and the Northumbrian Infantry Brigade particularly distinguished themselves under the leadership of Brigadier-General Riddell whose loss we all deplore so much. He fell at the head of his Brigade while leading you to attack the village of St Julien. And though you established yourselves in the position, you had to retire afterwards, as you were not supported. Why, it is not for us to say. Even as it was, you occupied a line of trenches in advance of those that you left, so that you also took important ground yourselves.

Well, I think you deserve the greatest praise for this, and I wish every officer, NCO and man to accept the warmest thanks of the Commander in Chief of these forces for the part he took. I deeply deplore the loss of one of the most gallant officers that ever lived, and one of the best leaders.

In the special circumstances under which you were called up, it was particularly magnificent. And I think that the front that you all present is quite extraordinary after what you have gone through. Now you have paraded, showing a most soldier like front and apparently perfectly ready to go into action this afternoon if required. And for the whole of this I can only most heartily congratulate you and express my warmest appreciation of this conduct. When I am speaking of Territorials I am always reminded of the large body of Territorials who have shown such glorious and patriotic conduct. As they have, you took service in the Territorial Army for home defence. Immediately on coming out here you were called upon in a time of danger and emergency to take the place of trained troops in the breach. It is the highest example of patriotism. I must again say that that I heartily congratulate you for all you have done. And I am certain that if ever the Northumbrian Brigade is called upon again they will acquit themselves in the same glorious manner as they have during the last ten days.[8]

Sir John's sincerity was beyond question; those listening could tell that this was no required, formulaic speech:

It sounded far better than it reads in the Press report, as he spoke as though he really meant every word he said.[9]

When asked about this event, George Harbottle replied:

He addressed us and praised us for our bravery but I thought nothing about him at all. We just thought well he had come straight from his office somewhere back in the line. Praising us! We just accepted it! We did not want it rubbed in. That was the attitude we had about him coming there that day. That was the end of the battle of St Julien, but was for us only the start of months and years of similar conditions; although never again a situation as frustrating as that had been. 'A' Company revived with new recruits and officers later, but it never again could be the same fine company of comrades, highly trained and fit, that left Seaton Sluice on 20 April.[10]

On 5 May, the strength of the Northumbrian Brigade was enhanced by the addition of the 1/5 Battalion Border Regiment, a Territorial Force battalion which had been in France since October 1914 without seeing action.

On 12 May, Second Army Headquarters proclaimed that the designation of the Northumbrian Division had been changed. Henceforth it would be known as the 50th (Northumbrian) Division, and the Northumberland Brigade was designated 149 Brigade. Perhaps of more importance was that an officer and two NCOs from the brigade would be trained as bomb-throwers by instructors from 4th Division.

The enlarged 149 Brigade was asked to provide two parties, each of 300 men, to work during the night of 12/13 May. The 1/5 Border Regiment provided these parties from its four companies and men spent the darkest hours filling sandbags and forming barbed wire entanglements. Although they were under shell fire for the first time, they suffered no casualties.

In the early hours of 24 May the Germans launched an attack along a four and half mile front near Hooge, using chlorine gas once again, and succeeded in capturing the Bellewaarde Ridge and Mouse Trap Farm. This action was later designated *The Battle of Bellewaarde: 24-25 May 1915.*

From the previous night, 23 May, the battalions of 149 Brigade had been temporarily attached to the 4th Division, whose sector ran from west of Verlorenhoek in a north westerly direction to Turco Farm. This division held the line with 10 Brigade on the right and 12 Brigade on the left. As the battle opened, 11 Brigade was in reserve.

At the start of the German assault, the dispositions of the five battalions of 149 Brigade were:

At 1000hrs, the 1/4 were moved to the divisional second line, subsequently a half company was sent to the 2 Battalion Essex Regiment (12 Brigade) and one company to the 2 Battalion Royal Dublin Fusiliers (10 Brigade). These two battalions were holding the front-line trenches.

The 1/5 were distributed by company between 1/5 Battalion South Lancashire Regiment; 1 King's Own (Lancaster); 2 Battalion Essex Regiment and 2 Battalion Royal Irish Regiment (all 12 Brigade).

Until 0500hrs the 1/6 and 1/7 were in reserve west of Vlamertinghe, after which they marched to Reigersburg Camp and later crossed to the eastern bank of the canal. The 1/6 occupied a position near La Brique and the 1/7 a position astride the St Jean to Wieltje road.

The 1/5 Border was also distributed by company to 2 Battalion Royal Irish Fusiliers, 2 Battalion Seaforth Highlanders, 1 Battalion Royal Warwickshire Regiment and the 1/7 Battalion Argyll and Sutherland Highlanders (all 10 Brigade 4th Division).

So, as the Germans attacked, the 4th Division held the front line with the following disposition (from right to left) north of Verlorenhoek: the 1 Irish Fusiliers with 'A' Company of the 1/5 Border; the 1/7 Argyll and Sutherland and 'D' Company of the 1/5 Border; the 2 Royal Dublin Fusiliers; the 2 Royal Irish and 'B' Company 1/5 Northumberland Fusiliers; the 1 King's Own with 'B' Company 1/5 Northumberland Fusiliers; the 2 Essex with 'C' Company 1/5 Northumberland Fusiliers.

In the divisional second line (south west of Wieltje), the 1/4 Northumberland Fusiliers had on their left the 2 Seaforths to which was attached 'C' Company 1/5 Border. Next came the Warwicks with 'B' Company 1/5 Border followed by 1/5 South Lancs with one company of 2 Lancashire Fusiliers and 'A' Company of 1/5 Northumberland Fusiliers. Mouse Trap Farm (this position was at first called 'Shell Trap Farm' in the War Diaries of the units involved, but it came to be considered a name that augured badly, and was later altered to *Mouse* Trap Farm) was the centre of the 4th Divisional front, but after weeks of bombardment it had been reduced to a mound of rubble. Within these ruins, the Dublin Fusiliers had devised a weak defensive position, but the farm was separated from the enemy's front line by no more than thirty yards, so that when they discharged gas cylinders the Irish were enveloped immediately.

The 1/5 Battalion

The War Diary[11] of the 1/5 Northumberland Fusiliers tells the story:

At 2.30am the Germans commenced an attack with asphyxiating gas, the wind being favourable for its use against our trenches. This gas was accompanied by heavy shrapnel and high explosive shell fire with the result that portions of the trenches were practically demolished. The Essex Regiment ('C' Company 1/5) who were on the left of line held by the 12th Brigade endeavoured to disperse the gas by rapid fire but with little effect, although no doubt it saved many men from becoming asphyxiated had they lain low in the trenches. Directly the bombardment started, the company of the Essex, who had lain in support, advanced to the front-line losing several men in the advance, and two companies of South Lancs who had been held in reserve on the canal bank were ordered to move up into the second line. The King's Own ('B' Company 1/5 NF) succeeded in holding their line, although suffering heavily from the gas and accompanying shell fire ... Under the cover of the gas the Germans delivered an infantry attack against the Dublin Fusiliers and the Royal Irish ('D' Company 1/5 NF) on the right of the King's Own. The Dublin were forced to retire, with the result that the trenches occupied by the Royal Irish were enfiladed; large number of men being killed and wounded. The Irish were now compelled to evacuate their trenches, leaving many men behind suffering from gas poisoning, these men being either killed or taken prisoner by the enemy who swarmed into the trenches. From the trenches abandoned by the Irish the enemy directed their attack against the King's Own, who however, repulsed it, not, however, without losing several officers and men.

The narrative records that 5/2258 Company Sergeant Major James Allan and 5/2107 Private Joseph Scott showed conspicuous bravery whilst defending a barricade in the King's Own trenches. Company Sergeant Major Allan dauntlessly defended the barricade with a revolver having been mortally wounded in the back by a hand grenade; he was mentioned in despatches and is commemorated on the Menin Gate Memorial to the Missing.

The two companies of the South Lancs who had moved up to the Divisional second line had meanwhile advanced to the support line, the other two companies, which had been lying in reserve on the canal bank, advanced to the support line at 11am in the rear of the King's Own and Essex Regiment.[12]

As the South Lancashires moved up to reinforce the line, so did their attached company from the 1/5. As they made their way forward they passed an Advanced Dressing Station, where the results of the gas attack were horribly evident:

Propped up against a wall was a dozen men – all gassed – their colours were black, green and blue, tongues hanging out and eyes staring – one or two were dead and others beyond human aid, some were coughing up green froth from their lungs – as we advanced we passed many more gassed men lying in the ditches and gutterways – shells were bursting all around.[13]

Artist's impression of a gas attack
Author's Collection

Both sides maintained oppressive artillery fire until 1700hrs. At 2000hrs the Lancashire Fusiliers and the Warwicks attempted a counterattack against trenches taken by the enemy, but without success. Consequently, the King's Own and the Essex received orders to retire. During the night, the divisional second line, behind and parallel with the road from Wieltje to near Turco Farm, was re-organised as the new front-line. The Essex and Royal Irish moved back to a position in front of Irish Farm, presumably with their attached companies ('C' and 'D') from the 1/5.

Casualties throughout 24 May were heavy: 'A' Company (with South Lancashires): Other Ranks: 3 killed, 18 wounded and 12 missing; 'B' Company (with King's Own): Officers: 2 killed; Other Ranks: 5 killed, 31 wounded, 8 gassed and 13 missing; 'C' Company (with Essex Regiment): Other Ranks: 5 killed, 15 wounded and 13 missing; 'D' Company (with Royal Irish): Officers: 2 killed and 5 wounded; Other Ranks: 5 killed 11 wounded and 123 missing.

Many of those regarded as missing in the immediate aftermath later re-joined their companies; a number of them had been gassed and evacuated to hospital.

Captain Frederick Henry Lawson
1/5 Northumberland Fusiliers

Frederick was born in Newcastle upon Tyne in 1887, the son of Frederick and Eleanor Francis Lawson. He was educated at Durham Grammar School and served his articles with architects Newcombe and Newcombe, and afterwards with Mr Arthur Stockwell of Newcastle. He joined the Northumberland Yeomanry in 1907. However, in 1909 he was gazetted Second Lieutenant with the 1/5 Northumberland Fusiliers, rising to Lieutenant in 1910 and Captain in 1912. He volunteered for overseas service when the war broke out and disembarked in France in April 1915. He was killed in action on 24 May 1915, aged 28. He is commemorated on the Menin Gate Memorial to the Missing.

Second Lieutenant Frank Winfield
1/5 Northumberland Fusiliers

Frank joined the ranks of the 1/5 Northumberland Fusiliers at the outbreak of war and was gazetted Second Lieutenant. In early May he embarked for the Western Front. On 24 May he was wounded and taken prisoner. He died as a prisoner of war in hospital at Roulers (Roeselare) on 31 May. Frank is buried in Roeselare Communal Cemetery.

1/5 BATTALION NORTHUMBERLAND FUSILIERS
KILLED IN ACTION 25 MAY 1915

| 5/1490 | 5/1804 | 5/2272 | 5/2456 |
| Pte George Gibson | Pte Walter Pattison | Pte Matthew Hindson | Pte Thomas G Snowdon |

| 5/2653 | 5/2666 | 5/3212 | 5/2044 |
| Pte Edward Tait | Pte Anthony McMillan | Pte Frank Orr | Pte John Duffy |

| 5/2635 | 5/1437 | 5/2143 | 5/1899 |
| Pte George H Nixon | Pte Robert E Bell | Pte John E Wymer | Pte Henry Wilson |

The 1/4 Battalion

At 0500hrs the 1/4 advanced to number No. 2 Position, reported to 10 Brigade and subsequently moved to the second divisional line, west of the St Jean to Wieltje road, arriving at 1000hrs. As this position was jam packed with troops, they advanced to the support line at View Farm. 'C' and 'D' Companies manned a trench at Hill Top Farm. The whole area was under artillery bombardment; gas and shrapnel and high explosive shells were thundering down. 'C' Company was ordered to move to Shell [Mouse] Trap Farm, although fortunately they were prevented from reaching their destination: the farm was occupied by the enemy. Eventually, the battalion was ordered to support a counterattack which did not come off. Missiles were pelting everywhere and a gas shell fell into one of the trenches supposed to be sheltering the men from 'B' and 'C' Companies.

At dusk, 'B' company was moved to a trench running east of the St Jean to Wieltje road and south of Wieltje; 'A' Company and half of 'C' Company were ordered to the west of the road; 'D' Company were placed in support west of the road, although half of this company advanced to support the South Lancs filling a gap at Turco Farm. The War Diary records the following casualties: Officers: 3 wounded: Captain F. Robinson, Lieutenant R. W. Cranage and Second Lieutenant W. J. Bunbury; Other Ranks: 4 killed, 24 wounded, 9 gassed and 4 missing.

I had not long to wait at the dressing station before five motor ambulances arrived belonging to an American called Colby, who was running them at his own expense for the Belgian Army. Having heard that we had a number of casualties, and as there was not much doing on the Belgian front, he had brought his cars down on spec to see if he could assist our people. He soon had his cars loaded up, and taking me in his own car, we were taken to the Belgian Headquarters. There we were taken into the hospital, where they gave us some coffee, and the wounded men having been examined and where necessary dressed again, they sent us on again in some other cars to a place called Adinkerke, where we arrived about 7pm. Here we were most hospitably entertained by Lady Bagot who has a small mobile hospital of about 30 beds just outside the railway station, which she runs for the Belgians. Both Lady Bagot and the staff, which is English, gave us a great reception.[14]

The following is an extract from a letter from Private J. Moody published in the *Hexham Courant* on 17 June 1915:

On Sunday night, a terrific bombardment started and early in the morning [24 May] we got the order to leave our dugouts and advance. The Germans were using those gases so we had to use our respirators. I do not know how we would have come on without them, and we passed a lot of unfortunate soldiers making their way back, some very badly gassed. The effect of gas is too awful for words. The sweat was teeming down the men's faces and they were gasping for breath. Thanks to my respirator I was able to go on although I thought my head was going to split. As we advanced towards some trenches a German machine gun started to play on us and Lt Bunbury, one of our officers, was wounded. Wherever we crossed a field it was ploughed up by Jack Johnsons.

They were bursting all over and how we got so far up with so few casualties is little short of a miracle. When night fell we went forward again and took our place in the firing line. Things were pretty quiet just then, only a few stray bullets flying about, but we had to keep a sharp lookout as the German trenches were only 500 yards in front of us. We were only in the front line for two days and are now back in some reserve trenches not far from the front line. I expect we will be going further back for a rest shortly and will give you further news then.[15]

The trenches held by the 1/4 were shelled throughout 25 May and into the next day, during which parties of men were drafted to the Royal Engineers. Casualties for 25 to 26 May were: Other Ranks: 7 killed, 29 wounded and 1 missing. One of the men killed was 4/1983 Private John Robson of Hexham.

To date, 149 Brigade had been wholly engaged in a month or so of heavy fighting at close quarters with the Germans. Now they had to learn the art of holding the line, as well as all the skills needed for trench warfare. On 1 June, the 50th Division received orders from V Corps Headquarters: the elements of the Division were to be reassembled; 149 Brigade was brought back under divisional control at 0600hrs on 5 June. The powers that be then realised that it would be a shrewd idea to allow members of a relieving battalion to reconnoitre trenches before taking them over, getting together with men of the battalion being relieved to gather any useful information about their new position.

Meanwhile back in Northumberland, on 29 May 1915 the *Hexham Courant* printed the following extract from an article in *The Times*, a glowing tribute to the steadfast men of Northumberland:

The hardest task, perhaps, fell to the men of North England. The others, for the most part, had been some time in the field and had been broken in gradually to war. But these had arrived from home only a short time before.

The Northumberland men were employed in an attack on St Julien on the 26th. There was no time to reconnoitre the position; they got into wire and were faced with terrific shelling. Their 6th Battalion managed to advance 250 yards beyond our trenches, but they could not maintain their position and had to retire in the evening, Brigadier-General Riddell falling with many gallant officers and men.

Consider what is meant by the fight of these Northern Territorials. Men only lately out from home, most of whom had never before seen a shot fired in battle, were flung suddenly into the most nerve-racking kind of engagement. They had to face some of the worst artillery bombardments of the war and the new devilry of poison gas. There was no time for adequate staff preparation, the whole a wild rush, a crowding up of every available man to fill the gap and reinforce the thin lines. They were led by officers who a year ago had been architects and solicitors and business men. The result was a soldier's battle like Albuera* where we escaped the annihilation which by all rules was our due, by the sheer dogged fighting quality of our men and their leaders. The miners of the north are a sturdy race in peace both in work and sport. The Second Battle of Ypres has proven them to be one of the finest fighting stocks on earth.[16]

*The Battle of Albuera, the bloodiest battle of the Peninsula War, fought on 16 May 1811.

On the nights of 10/11 and 11/12 June, 149 Brigade relieved 7 Brigade (3rd Division) in the front line. The sector to be taken over was on the left of 150 Brigade and included the greater part of Sanctuary Wood and the ruins of Hooge on the Menin Road. So depleted was 149 Brigade that *all* of the remaining men were needed, with none in reserve, to replace the elements of 7 Brigade manning the front. The 1/7 were in nominal reserve with two companies in Zouave Wood and two in Sanctuary Wood. The 1/5 took over B1 and B2, the 1/6 B3 and B4, and the 1/4 B7 and B8. The 1/5 Border took over B9 and Hooge (which included B13 to B16 inclusive).

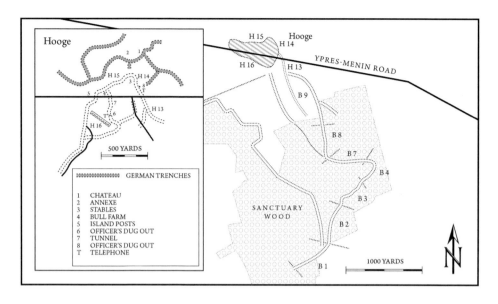

Hooge Defences, June 1915.

Hooge, on the main road beween Ypres and Menin, was at the heart of the Ypres salient and was the scene of fierce fighting in every year of the war. The chateau was eventually destroyed as was the adjacent village.

Hooge as seen at the end of the war
Author's Collection

First into the line were the 1/5 and 1/6; they were transported by bus to the edge of Ypres where they were met by guides from 7 Brigade.

The War Diary of the 1/5 Battalion describes the handover on the night of 10/11 June:

> *At 4.30pm (10 June) we suddenly received orders that we were to go into the trenches in the neighbourhood of Hooge. Colonel Cole and the company commanders had to proceed at once by bus to reconnoitre the trenches we were going to take over while it was light. The remainder of the battalion paraded and left in motor buses about 7pm. We disembarked just south of Ypres on the main road and marched into the town, where we met guides from the 1/4 South Lancashire Regiment. We left the town by the St Eloi (Lille) gate, crossed the railway (the Ypres-Roulers railway) and went across country to Sanctuary Wood. Our guides led us all right, but it came on to rain, was pitch dark and, what with the number of troops on the road and transport, we had numerous halts to let the rear catch up, and it was very late by the time we got to Maple Copse; there after some difficulty and a long wait, we found the company officers who took their companies straight off through the wood to the various trenches. It was a nasty job going up through the wood; there was a lot of bullets coming over striking the trees and ricocheting in all directions: one man was killed and several wounded. We took over the trenches at last: 'A' and 'B' Companies were in the front line, and 'C' and 'D' Companies in support trenches about two hundred yards behind in the wood. We found the trenches pretty fair on the whole, though rather swampy in parts. 'B' Company (left) were within one hundred and fifty yards of the enemy trenches, while on the right, opposite 'A' Company, the German trenches were out of view, over the ridge some five hundred yards away.*[17]

The 1/6 faced a similar journey on a very dark and wet night, with the relief completed at 0300hrs. Everyone waited anxiously for what dawn would reveal about their new position and the hostility they were likely to face:

> *It is surprising how one longs for dawn when occupying the trenches for the first time. Everything seems strange, and the artificial light supplied by star*

shells does not last long enough for one to get a good idea of the position you hold. There is a certain feeling of uneasiness until the first streaks of dawn enable you to take a cautionary peep over the bags and see for the first time the dark outline of the enemy's position. A general survey of your own position is also one's first thought, for knowing exactly where you are inspires confidence in no small degree.

The trenches were quite deep with a firing step in each bay; the parados and traverses required building up, lateral communications were exceedingly bad and dugouts or shelters of any description were conspicuous by their absence. A peep over the top revealed a great scarcity of wire in front of our position, and from B4 trench only ten yards separated our sap head from that of the enemy, and from some parts of B3 the enemy's trenches were invisible, so queerly did the line run.[18]

On the night of 11/12 June, the 1/4 and 1/7 along with the 1/5 Border moved up into the line. The 1/4 had a particularly torrid time in their approach, with delays caused by the battalion in front, wagons overturned in the road and guides losing their way; one company did not arrive that night. Three men were wounded.

Even amid the turmoil and crushing destruction of war, with mutilation and death always present, men would try to maintain some connection with the everyday. Some took pleasure in observing small details of the natural world that managed to survive in the desolate landscape. This touching passage is from the diary of an NCO from the 1/4 as he made his way forward to the trenches on the 11/12 June:

We left at 5.30pm. I had a rest until the battalion congregated. Saw the Marsh and Palmate Spotted Orchid, Water Forget-me-not, Water-Bird-Straw. On our march up we passed a plot of red and white Samfon [sic]. It was an awful distance and the trenches were in a pitch-dark wood. We were lost once or twice, and what with slipping about and falling down, and the pace that was set, everybody was fed up. It was turned 2am when we manned the trench.[19]

There's very little detail recorded about the 1/5 Border except that 'B' Company took over trench B9 whilst the remaining three companies manned Hooge defences, but they suffered a number of casualties during their time at the front, including Major A. F. Smith and four other men. The 1/7 relieved the Honourable Artillery Company with two companies placed in Zouave Wood and two in Sanctuary Wood. During the short nights, all the battalions were employed in restoring the trenches, especially Trench B9 and the Hooge Defences that they had taken over. Some of this work was supervised by the Royal Engineers. They excavated a communication trench from Hooge to the island posts, although sniping was a real problem during the day. The German snipers were masterly: any exposure of the head was met by the dull thud of a bullet on a sandbag or on flesh and bone. Many men were killed or wounded. The advantage lay with the Germans who were armed with rifles fitted with finely manufactured telescopic sights. The soldiers of 149 Brigade had no such weapons.

On 13 June, the 50th Division was informed that elements (7 and 9 Brigades) from the 3rd Division were to attack the Bellewaarde Ridge at 0415hrs on 16 June. The 50th (right) and 6th Divisions (left) were to assist by providing rifle and machine gun fire. From Hooge to the Ypres-Roulers railway at the north-eastern corner of Railway Wood, the German line formed a salient including Bellewaarde Ridge and Lake. This salient was the objective for 16 June, intended to deprive the enemy of an important observation post.

As the attack developed, 149 Brigade was to take the opportunity of advancing and improving its position about Hooge. On the day of the attack the Hooge defences were manned by two companies of the 1/7 who had replaced the 1/5 Border on the night of 14/15 June. Lieutenant Hugh Liddell wrote:

It was hardly a line at all, but a perfect maze. A division of ours was to make an attack yesterday and I was honoured by being placed in command of this section of trenches with my own company and half another company and four officers. My instructions were to defend this place at all costs and not to retreat at any price, even if everyone was wiped out. I was given this pleasant piece of news at 5.30pm [14 June], shown a rough sketch and told to go off and look around the trenches myself before taking the company in.

The way to the trenches was through a long communication trench which ran zig-zagging up a hill for half a mile or more. A lot of it was up to the knees in water and mud. Arrived at the company officer's dugout, the Captain in charge took me around. You cannot imagine what it was like. Tunnels and burrows running in all directions. Ruined houses, detached from the trenches, had to be defended. Places where you had to run like a scalded cat, and others which you had to wriggle across on your stomach. Dead men lying everywhere, some that had been there for weeks. German trenches never more than thirty yards away, and in some places only fifteen. You had to talk in whispers for fear that they would hear what you said. Many of the houses were at the point of collapse, and all were riddled with bullets and shell holes.[20]

Somehow the Fusiliers made it to their positions around Hooge, relieving the 1/5 Borders. The next day at 0600hrs the enemy bombarded them using everything they had, including trench mortars. Snipers were particularly tenacious that day: the 1/7's casualties were two dead, including Lieutenant Arnold James J. Trinder of 'C' Company – shot dead as he sat smoking at the bottom of his trench – and seventeen wounded.

Lieutenant Arnold James Trinder

1/7 Northumberland Fusiliers

Arnold was born in 1880, in Walton upon Thames, Surrey, the son of Arnold and Annie Elizabeth Chisholm Trinder. He was educated at Wellington College and was a popular member of Molesey Rowing Club. From school he joined his father's firm in London as a solicitor. In autumn 1914 he enlisted in the 28 Battalion, London Regiment, (Artists Rifles) and embarked for France, from where this battalion established an OTC. He was gazetted Lieutenant in April 1915 and joined the reserve battalion (2/7) at Blyth. He embarked for the Western Front on 4 May 1915 and was killed on 16 May, aged 34, on his first tour of duty at the front. Arnold is commemorated on the Menin Gate Memorial to the Missing.

About this time the noise of enemy mining operations was detected; they appeared to be heading towards one of the trenches in Hooge Defences with the intention of blowing up Bull Farm, a ruin in the front line. British soldiers could hear German voices at their feet, coming from underneath their trench. This German operation was verified by the Royal Engineers. As a result, the trenches in front of and on each side of Bull Farm were evacuated and machine guns trained on the farm from the rear in anticipation of the enemy advance after the explosion.

That night, the adjutant went forward to discuss the next day's attack by the 3rd Division, which was scheduled for 0415hrs, heralded by an artillery bombardment. Simultaneously, the 1/7 and other battalions along this section of the front were to open up with heavy machine gun and rifle fire at the enemy trenches. Depending on the progress of the advance, a decision would be made as to whether the 1/7 would advance and capture trenches that were in front of them, which assault would be led by Captain V. Merivale and Lieutenant W. J. Davis.

> *The bombardment started and gave the Germans a real bad time. Very soon on our left up went a white flag on a long pole. I reported over the telephone and asked for instructions. The reply was, 'Turn a machine gun on them'. Well, the white flag being no use, a lot of Germans left their trench, holding up their hands. They were soon knocked back into their trench again. Then a lot of them ran out and fled across country, and some London Scottish on our left jumped out and chased them with the bayonet. Altogether the Boches had an uncomfortable morning. Our people captured three lines of trenches and took between two hundred and three hundred prisoners. But the trenches in front of us were not taken; being so close to us our artillery could not shell them properly.*[21]

About noon, notice was given that another attempt would be made to take these trenches at 1530hrs and that an artillery bombardment of the lines would take place between 1500hrs and the advance. In order that the bombardment could take place, the men holding the front line would need to vacate the line – hopefully without the enemy catching sight of them.

I arranged with our people on either side to train their machine-guns on to No Man's Land in front of us whilst our trench was evacuated. At 2.50pm we started coming out, and ticklish work it was. We got out all right and had our wounded carried to a safe place behind, and then sat down to await developments. We had to do the observing of the artillery fire ourselves. Men were placed with periscopes at different points, and I hung on to the telephone myself, reporting as far as possible how our shells were falling.[22]

During the bombardment, there didn't appear any sign of life in the trench opposite, and at 1530hrs the evacuated Fusiliers began to return to the front line. However, by now the enemy were retaliating vigorously:

By now it was a far different matter, with shells and bullets flying as thick as snow-flakes – and the men, worn out and some of them in a state of collapse. It was a hard and anxious time while it lasted, but at length the trench was manned.[23]

The proposed second attack by the 3rd Division was postponed – all of the efforts made by the men from the 1/7 had been pointless. During this operation, the garrison of the Hooge defences had had a particularly rough time and the 1/7 had lost a significant number of men. One of those killed was 7/1396 Private George Borthwick, aged 19, of Ashington.

That night the two companies in Hooge Defences were relieved by elements from the composite battalions 1/6 and 1/8 Durham Light Infantry, from where they retired to Zouave Wood.

Those reliefs were late in arriving – about 2am next morning – so that I had not half enough time to get them in and my men out before daylight. I had to tell Lieutenant Ball to get our men out as best he could and I would follow on when I handed over to the new commander. Ball took the men out across country, as the communication trench was entirely blocked. After showing the captain around the defences and handing over to his care the German mine at Bull Farm, I followed suit myself and went back across country with a few stragglers I had collected.[24]

Eventually the remnants and wounded of the two companies from Hooge Defences reached the relative safety of the trenches in Zouave Wood. The officers saw to the needs of their men, and by and by withdrew to their dugout for some well-earned rest:

> *When Ball and I got into our dug-out in the wood, I do not think our own mothers would have recognised us. We had not had a wink of sleep for four nights and days, mud all over, clothes torn and every other imaginable sort of aid to disreputableness. We sat down, lit a candle and looked at each other, and started to laugh. I have had a good solid twelve hours' sleep since then, a wash and a shave, and am now ready to do it again, as it has its interesting and humorous side.*[25]

The next day, Divisional HQ sent orders that 149 Brigade at Hooge would be relieved by 7 Brigade (3rd Division) on the night of 18/19 June. Later, a secret message informed the 50th Division that it was to be transferred into II Corps; in exchange, the 46th Division filled the vacancy in V Corps. As a consequence, the 50th Division was going to take over the line held by the 46th Division opposite Messines and Wytschaete. The men of 149 Brigade marched to Ravelsburg on 21 June in blistering heat, and by 24 June had taken over the sector of the front line allotted to them. The 149 held the right-hand sector, with to their right 150 Brigade. Each brigade had two battalions at the front. The trenches in the new sector varied considerably:

> *Our trenches were of a breastwork type, and with small forts in the rear made quite a formidable garrison. There were a few dug-outs in the parados in the front-line trench, but they were in a bad state of repair, and it looked as if our spell here meant work with a capital W. Even some of the traverses were only two sand-bags thick and the parapet hardly bullet proof.*[26]

The Neuve Église sector, as it was called by the 50th Division, was very quiet and the men settled down to a routine which offered them a measure of rest. 'Quiet' can only be used in a comparative sense: no major attack was contemplated by either side, but the artillery of both were seldom silent; snipers were always on the lookout for the careless exposure of a head or body; trench mortar bombs would explode in the trenches and there was the continual menace of mining and sapping. A number of mines along the front were exploded. Every night there were working parties in No Man's Land carrying out the perilous job of wiring the front.

The War Diary of the 1/5 recorded on 24 June:

We lost a brave and valuable officer early in the morning in Captain W. G. Graham, who was sniped through the head whilst looking over the parapet.[27]

Captain William George Graham

1/5 Northumberland Fusiliers

William was born in Wallsend in 1887, the son of James William and Jane Graham. A pre-war Territorial Force soldier, he was gazetted Second Lieutenant in November 1913 with the 1/5 with whom he had previously served in the ranks. In Sept 1914 he was promoted to Lieutenant and then Captain in November 1914. In December 1914 he married Annie Evelyn Briggs and was the father of a daughter, Flora. He was killed by a sniper's bullet on June 24 1915, aged 25, shortly after being mentioned in despatches. William is buried in St Quentin Cabaret Military Cemetery. His headstone is inscribed:

THY WILL BE DONE

It appears that the new boys (of the 149) took to harassing the Germans in ways that were unlikely to result in any kind of peaceful co-existence. This included the killing of three German snipers by the 1/5 Border, deaths which resulted in heavy retaliatory fire on the area around RE Farm; two men were killed. Another method of upsetting the German applecart was the creation of a Heath Robinson searchlight which was used to illuminate enemy trenches during the night. Patrols in No Man's Land were now very much part of trench warfare, hurling bombs into the enemy's trenches and disrupting their working parties. Although this was usually a one-way fight, on the night of 8 July the enemy caused five casualties when they fired rifle grenades into trenches held by the 1/6. Amusingly, 149 Brigade's War Diary recorded, 'In one incident [a

German soldier] shouted across from D3: Go away you bloody Northumbrians; why don't you let us sleep!' On other occasions, signs were put up on the enemy's parapets: 'What do you bloody Northumbrians want here?' Another was evidently from a sportsman: 'Buck up Newcastle United!' [28]

Whilst in this sector the 1/7 received a draft of 114 men: 106 were from England whilst the difference was made up of men discharged from hospitals in France.

All things come to an end, and after a month in the Neuve Église sector the 50th Division was moved to Armentières. However, before this move further south, Major General the Earl of Cavan took over from Major General Sir W. F. L. Lindsay as Divisional Commander. Also, 149 Brigade received a new commander: Brigadier General H. F. H. Clifford, who succeeded Brigadier General G. Fielding.

CHAPTER FOUR

THE ARMENTIÈRES SECTOR

A flare went up; the shining whiteness spread
And flickered upward, showing nimble rats
And mounds of glimmering sandbags, bleached with rain;
Then the slow, silver moment died in dark.
The wind came posting by in chilly gusts
And buffeting at corners, piping thin
And dreary through the crannies; rifle shots
Would split and crack and sing along the night,
And shells came calmly through the drizzling air
To burst with shallow bang below the hill.
From *'A Working Party'* by Siegfried Sassoon

In the summer of 1915, the British Army Council called for the formation of a new, Third Army: more divisions of men, their training completed, were needed in France in preparation for scheduled advances. The generation of this new army was instrumental in the move of 149 Brigade (as part of the 50th Division) to the Armentières sector, where it was allocated to II Corps. In due course, on 15 July the 50th Division was informed that all three of its brigades were to move to the vicinity of this small town near Lille in northern France.

The existing positions held by 149 Brigade around the Ypres Salient (trenches

CI to CIV, positions SP4, NH Dugout and Souvenir Farm inclusive) would be taken over by the Canadian 1 Brigade. By this time, the 1/5 Battalion (Cumberland) Border Regiment had been attached to 149 Brigade. The relief began on the night of 14/15 July and continued over the next two nights.

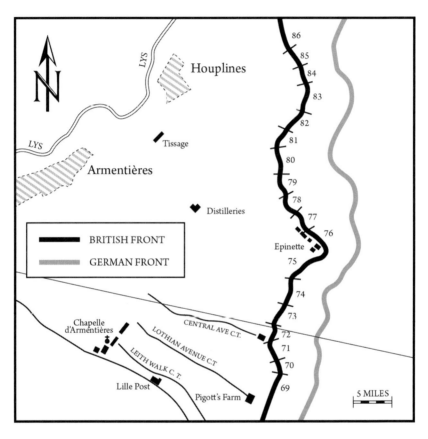

The Houplines and Armentières sector taken over by 50th Division

George Harbottle (1/6 Battalion) described the move from Belgium to France:

When we moved the few miles further south from Wytschaete, we had crossed the Belgian/France frontier, but were still in virtually undamaged countryside which had seen little of the war except for a few Uhlan patrols that had roamed the countryside in the early days of the German forward push in 1914. The farms were similar in construction but much cleaner and the population more friendly than further north. The French language of these Northern Frenchmen was very similar to that of the adjacent Belgians and very much easier to understand than Parisian French. Certainly the female side of the population were more 'come-onish' than their cousins further north.

Behind the Ypres area much of the administration was in Poperinghe. For the Armentières area the comparable town was Bailleul. This little town lay on the main road which ran from Cassel to Lille and from Bailleul going westwards you pass through Nieppe, and Armentières. Our 1/6 Battalion came into the district at Pont de Neippe, so called because it was the bridge over the River Lys and although little more than a straggling village it had nevertheless quite a bit of character about it.[1]

At 2000hrs on 16 July the brigade left Bulford Camp and within three hours had reached Armentières with the 1/7 and 1/6 going into billets in the Asylum, whilst the 1/4, 1/5 and 1/5 Borders proceeded to the trenches in relief of 80 Brigade; this was completed by 0240hrs the following morning. The War Diary[2] records that it was raining steadily as they moved into the trenches, relieving part of the 3 Battalion King's Royal Rifles and part of the 4 Battalion Rifle Brigade.

At Neuve Église and Armentières the trenches were splendid: they had been in existence for nearly a year, were very thick and deep, had lateral trenches running the full length in the rear, plenty of dugouts, and good communication trenches which made it possible to leave during the day and return to billets in the town. These trenches had trench boards to walk on, fire platforms to stand on, drains and sumps with pumps, shelters for lookouts with rifle racks, rubbish shoots, gas alarms, rifle batteries, loop holes, periscopes, etc, and war could be carried out in a comparatively safe manner. Dug-outs, like trenches, varied considerably. At Armentières they were all splinter proof and in some cases the officers' dug-outs were like little dwelling houses, fitted with beds, tables, chairs, pictures and stove.[3]

The weather that August was generally fine and warm, although there were frequent thunderstorms with torrential rain. Until the end of July it had been standard practice for each infantry brigade to spend up to sixteen days in a front line sector, but early in August this was reduced to twelve.

Breastwork Trenches, Armentières Sector, Summer 1915

The History of the 50th Division reported on the Armentières Sector:

The enemy was quiescent and was inclined to adopt an attitude of 'live and let live'. But that is not war, and it was necessary to remind him very frequently of the fact.[4]

How many men's lives were lost in trying to remind the enemy why he was there?

We got orders for a grand demonstration, to take place on the first anniversary of the declaration of war. Each machine gun was to fire one belt; each rifle ten rounds, each field gun three or four rounds. Then bayonets in the trenches were to be fixed and shown over the parapet, whistles blown etc, and in general the Hun had to be made to think that we were about to attack. I was very glad in view of this – which we felt sure would draw retaliation – to get my orders to proceed on leave in the morning.[5]

Accordingly, at 2000hrs on 4 August a gun from No 2 Mountain Battery opened fire with lyddite and shrapnel on the German trench opposite Trench 70, which was just south of the farm 'Grand Porte Egal'; the enemy had been erecting iron shields in a position clearly hiding something important. The infantry weighed in by opening up with rifle and machine gun fire, and during the ten minutes of bombardment they caused considerable damage to the German trenches. The enemy retaliated with artillery, machine guns, trench mortars and rifle grenades and, in turn, 149 Brigade responded with rifle grenades and bombs; during this pandemonium they also put an experimental trench mortar to the test, which proved to be rapid and accurate. The 1/4, who were manning Trenches 72 and 73 and the corresponding support trenches 72S and 73S, took a number of casualties, particularly from a stellar enemy sniper. One of those killed was Private Francis Riley from Hexham, a married man with four children.

4/1874 Private Francis Joseph Riley from Hexham (in the foreground)
To his right is probably 4/869 Sergeant Wilfred Marshall Henderson of Acomb.
Note the lack of steel helmets, which had not been issued yet.
Courtesy of K. P. Riley

His Company Sergeant Major, 4/32 John William Smith, wrote to his wife:[6]

Frank was seriously wounded in the head at about 8.30am on 4 August and died about half an hour later.

Captain Cecil George Arkwright also wrote to Mrs Riley:

He gave his life for his country, and I am sorry indeed to have lost him.[7]

During the day, the command of 50th Division was taken over by Major General Percival Spearman Wilkinson, replacing Major General the Earl of Cavan, who left in order to command the newly formed Guards Division.

We were in No. 78 Trench – the Germans had built a dummy hedge and it was necessary to find the reason why. Accordingly, on the night of the 23rd [August] Lt Winkworth, Sgt Coppick and Pte Longworth left our trench, word was passed down the line and all firing ceased, no flare lights were put up from our trenches. They would normally be out about half an hour, but an hour had passed and they had not returned. I was Sgt of the line from 9 to midnight and by 1.10pm I became anxious and was about to send out a search party when a sentry in a bay challenged a figure in front of his trench. It was Pte Longworth and he came in minus his hat or rifle with a revolver in his hand. He reported the Lt shot and lying between the lines in No Man's Land. The captain, myself and 5 bearers then went to his aid. We stumbled through our own barbed wire and then along a hedge, fell down an old trench and finally found the brave officer with the Sgt who had already carried him about 50 yards away from the dummy hedge to our own lines. He said they crawled up to the trench and the Lt had raised himself up to see better, but they had been seen and a machine gun sprayed them with bullets, one hitting Lt Winkworth in the elbow and passing into his stomach. We got him onto a stretcher and gave him 2 grains of morphine and carried him safely back to our own trenches. One or two bullets were fired at us, but we got back safely. The brave Lieutenant, a very good officer, died the next day.[8]

At 0930hrs the following morning, the enemy began to bombard Trench 80 with over a hundred whizz bangs and trench mortars. Luckily, no damage was caused and field guns and howitzers were used in reply, with many shells landing in the German trenches opposite Trench 79.

In early September, 149 Brigade was manning Trenches 67 to 73 inclusive and their corresponding support positions. On 6 September it was the turn of 1/6 Northumberland Fusiliers to relieve the 1/8 Durham Light Infantry. They occupied Trenches 67, 67 Close Support and 67 Support and Lille Post with the following dispositions: Trench 67 was manned with two machine guns, 124 other ranks and 5 officers. Position 67, Close Support, was manned by 32

Second Lieutenant Walter Winkworth
1/5 Northumberland Fusiliers

Walter was born in 1882, in Newcastle, the son of Walter Albert and Maria Louisa Munroe Winkworth. He was educated privately and at Rutherford College, Newcastle. He was employed as an electrical engineer. In August 1914 he enrolled at Leeds University OTC and was gazetted to the reserve battalion of the 1/5 Northumberland Fusiliers in early March 1915. He went to France with a draft of six new officers for the 1/5 Northumberland Fusiliers on 9 July. He was mortally wounded whilst in command of a patrol in No Man's Land and died the next day, aged 32, on 26 August 1915. Walter is buried in Bailleul Communal Cemetery Extension. He headstone is inscribed:

BE PREPARED

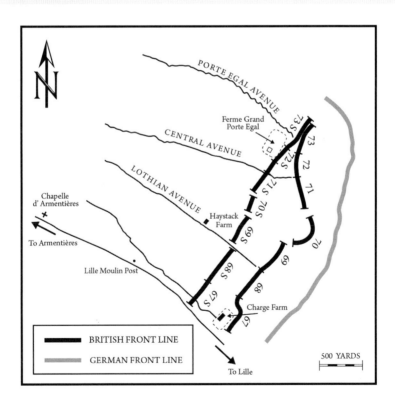

Trenches 67 to 73 and the support positions, September 1915

bombers and an officer, whilst 67 Support was manned by 57 other ranks, 1 machine gun and an officer. Lille post was manned by 37 other ranks, an officer and one machine gun. Relief was completed by 2140hrs. These dispositions illustrate the low strength of the battalion at this stage: fewer than 300 men. Apart from manning the trench the men were expected to work. For instance, 67 Close Support: construction of new grenade stores and repair of the parados which had completely collapsed. Initially the structure had been built between parados frames fitted into the ground. These were to be reconstucted using sandbags without frames. On 10 September the 1/6 Battalion was relieved by the 1/5 Northumberland Fusiliers, which was completed at 2253hrs without incident and the 1/6 returned to billets at the Asylum in Armentières. The following day this came under artillery attack.

Asylum at Armentières
Author's Collection

At the end of September, to the south of the Armentières sector, preparations were underway for what was intended as a major push by both French and British Forces, known collectively to the Allies as the *Third Battle of Artois*, whilst the Germans called it *Herbstschlacht* (Autumn Battle). The British came to refer to this engagement as the *Battle of Loos (25 September-13 October 1915)*. It was the biggest British attack of 1915, the first time they used poison gas – needs must when the devil drives – and the first mass engagement of New Army units. The offensive between La Bassée Canal and Loos began on 25 September in the wake of four days of artillery bombardment which expended over a quarter of a million shells. Following this, the battle plan called for the release of 140 tons of chlorine gas along the British front line. This was accomplished with mixed results: in places the wind blew the gas back into the British trenches. In the southern sector, the British made significant progress, but north of the Hulloch-Vermelles road they were less successful.

Despite having more ammunition and better equipment than before, the Franco-British attacks were contained by the German armies, apart from some local loss of terrain. British casualties at Loos were about twice as high as German losses. Elsewhere, at Champagne and Vimy Ridge, the French advance began well, but solid defence by the German Third, Fifth and Sixth Armies prevented them from making any long-term gains.

On 24 September all along the Armentières Front (the day before the opening of the *Battle of Loos*), they could clearly hear the artillery of the Third Army bombarding the Germans. On the next day, 149 Brigade were ordered to cooperate by posturing with fake attacks: as well as using artillery, rifle and machine gun fire, the individual battalions were ordered to burn piles of straw and phosphorus bombs in front of their trenches in order to deceive the enemy into thinking that a large-scale attack using gas was in the offing; this was to forestall any German Reserves being rushed southwards to the Loos battlefield.

So the 1/4, like many other battalions along the Armentières Front, were lugging bundles of straw up to the trenches during the day of 24 September. At first, the area was conveniently covered by a thick mist, but, as this burned off, alert enemy sentries were able to glimpse parties of heavily laden soldiers hustling forward from the support trenches to the frontline. Consequently, the Germans opened fire and seven men from the 1/4 were wounded. Further work was postponed until dark. During the night, the straw and phosphorus bombs were lugged out into No Man's Land in preparation for the next day's demonstration. Unfortunately the battalion on the right of the 1/4 set fire to their straw a little too early and soon the front was shrouded in smoke.

Today has been a joy day. At 2pm the artillery fired for an hour and a half, four thousand rounds, and eight hundred rounds of high explosive at a selected sector of the enemy's wire and trenches. At the same time hundreds of phosphorous bombs were thrown over our parapet and made a tremendous cloud.[9]

25 September was the day on which started the British advance at Loos. Attacks were made in several places in the line but just opposite us in Trench 75 we were to hold the attention of the enemy by a demonstration and so prevent any movement of troops to places where the attack was to be made in real earnest. At the same time, we were to be fully prepared to advance ourselves in case the neighbouring troops made headway. We did not relish our task at all, we were untrained in bayonet work and were physically unfit for advancing – nevertheless preparations were pushed forward. Our packs were taken to the reserve line, each man supplied with his day's rations and six sand bags and had to stand by in fighting order. During the night Sgt Townshend went over the parapet and turned the barbed wire trestles outwards towards the German lines. At the first streak of dawn bundles of straw were to be lighted and these had been previously soaked in paraffin and water. It was expected that they would give off smoke clouds under cover of which we were to deceive the enemy that we were leaving our trenches preparatory to our assault on their lines. At intervals, every bay was to open fire so as to give the impression that fire was being kept up so as to cover such movements. It was perhaps a well thought out scheme but the directing powers evidently did not allow for the intelligence of our own officers. Sometime before dawn it was observed by myself and others that the wind was blowing against us. Nevertheless, at the appointed moment the men detailed set fire to the straw and hence volumes of stinging choking smoke passed into our trenches – The Germans must have been intensely amused at us and our manoeuvre would most like have shown at once what we were studiously endeavouring to hide from them. The artillery kept up a brisk bombardment and our rapid fire was just feebly replied to, probably because the Germans considered it wise not to expose themselves when no danger threatened.[10]

Another instance of 'efficiency' occurred on 12 October, although in this case blame should not be attached to officers, so much as to the NCOs and men:

It had been arranged that Kitchener's artillery should bombard at 2.30pm and our bombers should throw gas bombs at 3.30pm, hence giving the Germans the impression that we were attacking. Surely this time we would ascertain if the wind was favourable.

At 2.30pm a salvo of shells went over us and at the same time gas bombs were thrown by some man in his excitement. Immediately the whole line started bombing and inside 5 minutes the artillery observation officer could not see 10 yards in front of him. One shell fell into the 1/7 Headquarters. Needless to say, our whole purpose was thus once more foiled, seemingly because sufficient care had not been taken to ensure the men knew exactly what purpose they were there for.[11]

An entry in the War Diary of the 1/6[12] on 28 August records that at 0510hrs a number of pigeons were seen flying from behind our lines to the German lines. Thirty minutes later three pigeons flew back from the German lines towards Armentières, and at 0700hrs two pigeons returned from Armentières and flew over the German lines. Suspicions were obviously aroused by this … a possible case of espionage?

Enemy prisoners were always in demand by Corps Headquarters so that they could identify the troops opposite the British positions. On receiving orders to provide such prisoners, the 1/6 thought up a scheme using a dummy figure clothed in khaki and provided with a rifle and bandolier. During darkness, the dummy was placed, face down, in No Man's Land as bait, looking just like a British soldier shot dead while on patrol. To lend more credibility, two Very (or Verey) lights were fired from a ditch close by, so as to draw enemy fire. They followed this by a cry and a groan in order to induce the enemy to believe that they had shot a member of a British patrol. From a nearby ditch, they kept watch on the 'corpse' from 0230hrs that morning, all day until 0100hrs the following morning. However, there were no takers; perhaps the lure of a British soldier with identification was not perceived as a prize. The men of 1/5 Border Regiment (attached to 149 Brigade) were regarded as distinguished patrollers; on the night of 27 September a patrol of ten of their NCOs, led by Captain R. R. Blair, came across an enemy patrol which they shot to pieces. They brought back the body of one soldier, which provided the necessary identification.

During the next night, Lance Sergeant William Tiffin and three men went out and brought in several articles, including a German postcard. Any intelligence, however trifling, was deemed valuable.

The army was continually supplied with new and improved equipment, and during September tubular pattern smoke helmets were issued and the old respirators withdrawn.

> *After the first use of gas in April and the makeshift respirators, there had been an issue of gas helmets. These were a hood of some medicated material; inserted in it were two large eye pieces. The bottom of the hood was tucked into the neck of your tunic. One soon used up all the air inside so they couldn't be worn for very long. In September an improvement on this was devised which included a mouth piece, which enabled you to get some air and so last inside the beastly thing for longer. Eventually the box respirators came out which were a great improvement and could be worn for quite a long time.*[13]

Furthermore, a certain number of steel helmets for experimental purposes were issued during September. At the outbreak of war, none of the combatants had issued steel helmets to their troops; soldiers went into battle wearing cloth, felt or leather headgear that offered virtually no protection from modern weapons. Soon it was seen that all of the armies were suffering a large number of soldiers with lethal head wounds caused by artillery shells. The French were the first to introduce steel helmets in the summer of 1915. British military designers, aware of the urgent need for safer headgear, studied the French design and found it to be too complex to manufacture and not strong enough for the job.

> *Up to this period our only head protection was our usual flat army cap. Now, however, both we and the Germans had been experimenting with steel helmets and the first ones started coming out. The German helmet fitted the head giving some cover to the neck and kept in position much better than ours. The wider brim that our helmets had gave some protection to the shoulders from shrapnel, but when in violent movement, such as an attack, they tended to slip about and needed readjustment from time to time, which*

was a nuisance. However, it was extraordinary how much safer one felt when wearing them, which had a distinct advantage.[14]

A British design, patented in London by John Brodie in August 1915, offered advantages over the French helmet. It was constructed from a single thick sheet of steel and resembled the medieval *sallet*.

Officers wearing the new style of Brodie helmet

The original design, Type A, was made from mild steel with a brim of 1.5 to 2 inches. Within weeks of the initial production, Type B was introduced with a harder steel containing 12 per cent manganese (steel from the Hadfield foundry). The helmet was virtually impervious to shrapnel striking from above and could withstand a .45 calibre pistol bullet travelling at 600 feet per second at a distance of 10 feet. It also had a narrower brim and a more domed crown. Further modifications were made throughout the war. It was not until the summer of 1916 that steel helmets were in general use.

As winter approached the rain came in, and the trenches in the Armentières sector became extremely unpleasant. It was difficult to drain them and in most areas men were forced to wade from place to place knee-deep in foul water. Furthermore, the sand-bagged breastworks began to crumble and it became increasingly difficult for any repairs to keep pace with their decay.

In late 1915, 149 Brigade consisted entirely of men who had enlisted as volunteers into the Territorial Force, which was governed by The Territorial and Reserve Forces Act 1908. As stated in Chapter One, this ruled that on offering his service the soldier 'shall be enlisted to serve for such a period as may be described, not exceeding four years, reckoned from the date of his attestation: and may be re-engaged within twelve months before the end of his current term of service for such a period as may be described not exceeding four years from the end of that term. Otherwise a man is discharged as time expired.

> *In October 1915, one of the senior NCOs in 'C' Company had become 'time expired'. He was a married man well up in his thirties and considered that he had done his bit, having been called up in 1914 and having served abroad throughout Ypres, St Julien and up to now. There was no conscription and there were still a large number of young men who had not enlisted. His view was that it was they, not he, who should be fighting. He therefore applied for a discharge and got it, which he was legally entitled to do. He quickly got a job in a munitions factory and was something of a hero among his workmates for what he had done already.*[15]

In response to Operation Order 53, 149 Brigade was relieved by 62 Brigade and moved westwards to a training site at Strazeele, which lies roughly half way between Bailleul in the east and Hazebrouck to the west. The 1/4 and 1/7 holding trenches 74 to 77 inclusive were relieved by 12 and 13 Battalions Northumberland Fusiliers on the night of 24/25 October. During daylight on 25, the 1/6 and 1/5 left Armentières making for La Crèche, and by 27 October all five battalions of 149 Brigade were in position at Strazeele training area, where the weather was miserable:

> *Rain, rain, rain – mud, mud, mud. This is what life is composed of at present. I can hardly get the men out for ordinary exercise, as it is no use wetting them*

to the skin when they have no clothes to change into. My company is billeted in two farms about half a mile apart, which is a nuisance. Frank Merivale and I live in one with half the company; Green, Barnard and Teasdale in the other farm with the other half of the company.[16]

The unrelenting rain necessitated training being carried out indoors, and at individual battalion level. During 5 to 7 November the various battalions received new drafts of replacements. (At this stage, virtually all of these were men from Northumberland. This would change as the years passed and conscripted men were sent wherever they were needed most.) The 1/4 welcomed Captain J. R. Robb of Hexham, whilst the 1/5 received 129 other ranks, the 1/6 received 2 officers and 101 other ranks and the 1/7 received 160 other ranks.

On 11 November, the battalions began digging dummy trenches which were designed to represent the German trench system opposite Trench 80. The map for this system of trenches was developed from aeroplane recognisance photographs, and the intention was that battalions should practise different plans for attack; during the week of 15-22 November, companies from the individual battalions executed close and open order drill and assaults on skeleton trenches, buildings and wire obstacles. On 16 November, the brigade received further batches of replacements: 38 other ranks to the 1/4, 48 other ranks to the 1/5 and an officer to the 1/6. By now, the men of the brigade had been issued with their new gas hoods, and on 25 November, a gas expert from the 2nd Army came to demonstrate their use by means of a deep trench filled with gas from cylinders. Over 1200 men passed through the trench, their helmets proving to be a great improvement on the old design.

At this time, certain changes took place within the 50th Division. Army Headquarters had decided that every division should have a designated Pioneer Battalion, which would be a divisional resource. This fell to the 1/7 Battalion DLI of 151 Brigade. Consequently, on 16 December, the 1/5 Battalion Border Regiment which had been attached to 149 Brigade was transferred to 151 Brigade, restoring its strength to four battalions.

Following this, the War Diary of the 1/5 Battalion recorded (16 December 1915):

We received orders that we were going to relieve the 9th Division in the Ypres Salient, an unpleasant surprise for everyone, as up till a short time ago we had been told that we were certain to go back to Armentières.[17]

Thus, by 17 December, 149 Brigade had left the delights of the Strazeele training area to return to the cauldron of the Ypres Salient.

At 09.30am we paraded and marched to Caestre, where we joined the 1/5 Northumberland Fusiliers and entrained for Poperinghe, the transport going by road. We proceeded shortly after midday to march to a wretched camp called Canada Huts. The camp consisted of more or less dilapidated wooden huts in a field, which we entered by a partially constructed sleeper track; but this suddenly came to an end, and after that we found ourselves literally up to our thighs in liquid mud.[18]

The Adjutant of the 1/5 Battalion recorded:

The mud around the huts was the worst I have ever seen – you literally had to wade to get into them and as we arrived just as it was getting dark, it took a long time to get settled in.[19]

CHAPTER FIVE

AROUND THE SALIENT

Some die shouting in gas or fire;
Some die silent, by shell and shot.
Some die desperate, caught on the wire;
Some die suddenly ...
From 'A Death-Bed' by Rudyard Kipling

They were headed for one of the most dangerous sectors on the Western Front, the notorious Hill 60. Today, Hill 60 is a World War I battlefield memorial site and park in the Zwarteleen area of Zillebeke, about three miles south of the centre of Ypres and directly on the railway line to Comines. Before World War I the so-called hill was known locally as *Côte des Amants* (French for 'Lover's Knoll'). I say 'so-called hill' because this piece of raised ground, a mere sixty feet high, is no more than the debris left from the building of the Ypres to Comines Railway in the 1850s. The excavated earth was dumped on either side of the embankment. On the west side was a long irregular mound that rapidly became known as '*The Caterpillar*' and a smaller pile of debris further down the slope towards Zillebeke was nicknamed '*The Dump*'. On the east side of the cutting, at the highest point of the ridge, lies the third mount known as '*Hill 60*'. Although this is a modest 'hill' by most standards, for those who occupied the 'heights' of Hill 60 it offered their artillery spotters an excellent view around Zillebeke and Ypres.

During the *First Battle of Ypres* in late 1914, Hill 60 was held by a depleted detachment of French troops. The summit was the object of frequent attacks and defensive action, and when British troops relieved the French in this area on the night of 1/2 February 1915 they found that the summit was held by the enemy.

In spring 1915, British raids on enemy-occupied Hill 60 were commonplace, initially by troops from the 28th Division and later by men from the 5th Division. Eventually, the British devised ambitious plans for the capture of this bête noire, involving the newly-formed tunnelling companies – despite being cautioned that holding Hill 60 after capture would be untenable unless the nearby *Caterpillar* were also taken. Nevertheless, by 10 April they had laid six mines. The attack began on 17 April with troops from the 5th Division capturing the 'hill' with comparative ease, and with only seven casualties.

However, as predicted, permanent occupation of this salient was a very costly affair. The Germans recaptured it during May 1915. On May Day, following a heavy barrage, they released chlorine gas at 1900hrs from positions about 100 yards from Hill 60, although the attack that followed was eventually repulsed. On 5 May at 0845hrs, when troops from the British 18th Division were holding the position, the Germans again discharged gas from two points opposite Hill 60. Within fifteen minutes, as the gas began to clear, the German 30th Division pushed forward, eventually taking the summit and all of the British trenches along the slopes of the hill. After a number of British counterattacks the Germans were forced back from the slopes but they managed to hold on to the crest.

This was still the state of play when, on 19 December, the 50th Division was due to take over positions from the 9th (Scottish) Division from Hill 60 to near the Menin Road … an area of constant skirmishing, raiding and mining by both sides. Even as 50th Division troops waited in trenches behind the 9th Division's position during the early morning before the relief that night, the Germans opened an artillery and gas bombardment along the north side of the Ypres Salient. Gas reached the 50th Division's positions. The War Diary of the 1/5 Northumberland Fusiliers recorded for 19 December:

We were woken up at 5am, by hearing rapid rifle fire and guns firing. Soon it was taken up all round, and it was evident that there was something on, as the fire became very heavy. Shortly afterwards we got a message telling us to 'stand to' and that the Germans were making a gas attack. Soon we were able to smell the gas, which was apparently coming from the north side of the Salient where the attack seemed to be taking place. The gas was not strong at Bedford House, and we did not put on our helmets, though our eyes were affected, probably by gas shells, and we put on our eye protectors.[1]

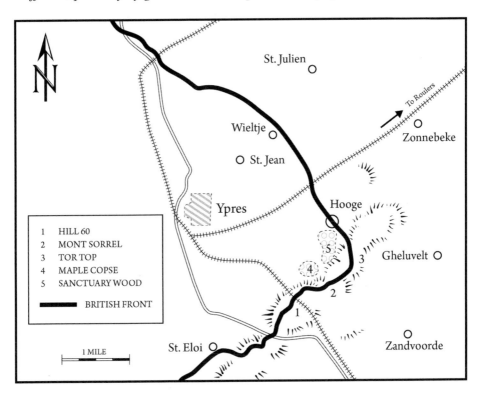

The 149 Brigade held a number of sectors on the south east segment of the Ypres Salient during the first six months of 1916

Throughout that day the Germans shelled the area around Bedford House indiscriminately, causing widespread damage. To everyone's relief, at noon 149 Brigade received orders to stand down. The early morning gas attack had been directed against the area held by the 6th and 49th Divisions who were holding the line in the neighbourhood of Potijze and Wieltje but it had not been followed up with an infantry assault. As evening fell, with the German bombardment hammering up and down the roads, the officers and men of 1/5 Battalion were beginning to wonder if the planned relief would take place. However, eventually the 1/6 Battalion relieved the 1/5 in Brigade Reserve, which released the 1/5 to move up and relieve the 8 Battalion Gordon Highlanders in trenches 36 to 38. This relief was complete by 2000hrs without any casualties.

All three brigades of the 50th Division were to go into the front line – 149 Brigade on the right, 150 in the centre and 151 to the left. The right subsector was immediately west of Hill 60. The relief of the infantry of 9th Division was completed during the following night with the 1/6 following the 1/5 Battalion into the line. From right to left the following dispositions were in place: 149 Brigade (1/5 and 1/6 Northumberland Fusiliers); 150 Brigade (1/4 East Yorkshire Regiment and 1/4 Yorkshire Regiment); 151 Brigade (1/6 and 1/8 DLI).

The 1/6 Battalion relieved the 7 Battalion Seaforth Highlanders in trenches 39 to 48 inclusive and at strongpoints R7 and R8, with 1/6 Battalion East Yorks on the left and 1/5 NF on the right.

The enemy in front of the 1/6 during the 22 December made their presence felt by spending the day sending over trench mortar rounds and grenades which were returned with interest.

On the night of 23 December, the 1/7 moved into trenches 36, 37 and 38 for a four-day tour of duty. Captain Hugh Liddell of 'B' Company, wrote:

It is 5.30am and during the last twelve hours I have seen enough in the mud and water line to write a book about. We left our billets in the ruined farm at 4.30pm yesterday, and although it is only about three miles to the front-line it took us four hours to get there. It was pitch dark, and, worse still, raining cats and dogs. The track we followed is simply strewn with shell holes and other pitfalls full of water. One has simply to crawl along, as the men are continually falling down, losing touch with the Company, etc. Added to this, of course, are the usual bullets and shells flying about, although they worry you far less than the other trouble. Half way here we got a good mouthful apiece of gas from a gas shell – it tasted neither very nice nor very different from what we have had on a previous occasion. About 8pm we completed the relief of the other people (1/5), and the first thing I found to cheer me up was twelve inches of water on the floor of my dug-out. The next excitement was in the telephone dug-out, where part of one wall fell in on my legs.[2]

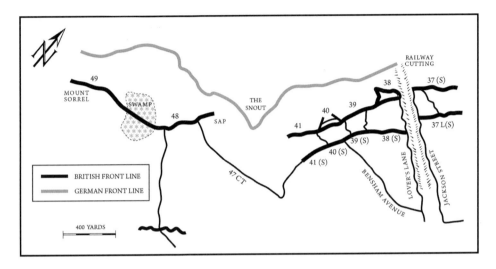

Hill 60 Trenches

The trenches were in no better state: they had been under constant bombardment; the damage caused by shelling had been exacerbated by incessant rainfall which caused miserably deep water underfoot, as well as weakening the earth walls. Hugh Liddell further reminisces:

It has cleared up a bit and I am getting rid of most of the water, and have every man on improving the trench. A big lump of parapet collapsed this morning, leaving us staring the Germans in the face. The same thing happened to their trench so we are quits. I hear that Walter Ball has three feet of water in his trench, so he is worse off than I.[3]

So, all four battalions of 149 Brigade spent their first Christmas on the Western Front on the notorious and inhospitable Hill 60 or its environs.

It was about Christmas 1915, and as usual had been pouring rain for days. We were holding the sector at Hill 60 – one company being to the north, and the rest being south of the railway cutting; and Battalion headquarters were at 'The Dump' just overlooking the cutting. There on the reserve slope of the little hill, we were protected from direct frontal fire, but could (and did) get it in the back from other parts of the Salient. As usual, also, in addition to 'the gentle rain from heaven', the Hun was raining shells, 'sausages,' 'rum jars' and 'minnies' on our lines; and of course – 'retaliation' napoo! [4]

The War Diary of 1/7 Northumberland Fusiliers records that on 23 December 1915 the battalion moved into trenches 36, 37 and 38 for four days. [5] During this tour of duty, the casualties were recorded as: Officers: 1 killed, this being Second Lieutenant Samuel Thornton Donkin, aged 21.

Second Lieutenant Samuel Thornton Donkin
1/7 Northumberland Fusiliers

Samuel was born in 1894, in Rothbury, Northumberland, the oldest son of Robert and Margaret Ann Donkin. Before the war he was in the Lothian and Border Horse. On 15 April 1915 he obtained a commission in the 1/7 Northumberland Fusiliers. After a period of time with the Reserve Battalion acting as Transport Officer, he disembarked on the Western Front on 4 May 1915. He was given the post of Bombing Officer. Aged 21, he was shot in the head by a sniper on Christmas Day while he made his way down one of the communication trenches. Samuel is buried in Railway Dugouts Burial Ground (Transport Farm).

Other Ranks: 1 killed and 11 wounded. The man killed was 7/2850 Private Matthew Hall, aged 29. Matthew had enlisted in December 1914 and had disembarked in France on 1 November 1915 with a draft of new replacements, joining his battalion at Strazeele. He was killed on Christmas Eve during the battalion's first tour of duty on Hill 60. He left a widow and at least two children living in Ashington, Northumberland.

The War Diary of the 1/4 Battalion, manning the front on Christmas Eve, recorded:

The trenches are perfectly appalling and the mud is indescribable. It was an awful existence during a tour of duty on the slopes of Hill 60. Mud, Mud, Glorious Mud, nothing quite like it for cooling the blood. Ankle deep, knee deep and sometimes waist deep in which men carried out an agonising existence during a tour in the front line, emerging like half drowned rats, covered in mud from head to foot, aching and shivering! The men were now plagued by the appearance of 'Trench Foot'. However, by use of whale oil massaged into the foot and the frequent changing of socks they reduced the agonies of the horrible complaint.[6]

On Christmas Day, the men of 149 Brigade – be it in the front line, in reserve or billeted some distance behind the lines – all units did their best to be cheerful.

The 1/6 Northumberland Fusiliers recorded that:

Christmas Day was cold, showery and muddy, but everyone seemed very cheerful in spite of it. Plum puddings from home gladdened the appetites of all ranks, and the officers had a turkey brought from Strazeele.[7]

The Adjutant of the 1/5 Battalion wrote on 31 December 1915:

Well! So ends, perhaps, the most memorable year in history – most of us, I think, hope that in this case history won't repeat itself![8]

Days into the New Year, the 1/6 relieved the 1/4 in trenches 39 to 48, 'A' Company in trench 40, 'B' Company in 39 and 39S, 'C' Company 41, and 41S, and 'D' Company in 47, 47S and 48. On 5 January, the enemy shelled these front-line trenches incessantly throughout the morning. The officers' dugout in Trench 48 was directly hit by an enemy whizz-bang, (the name derived from the fact that shells fired from light artillery travelled faster than the speed of sound: soldiers heard the typical 'whizz' sound of the travelling shell *before* the bang issued by the gun). Second Lieutenant Esmonde Richarde Burke White, age 33, was killed and Captain Temperley and Second Lieutenant Cooke wounded, severely reducing those in command of 'D' Company. In another incident, Second Lieutenant William Holmes Collinson was hit by a rifle grenade whilst in the communication trench between Trench 39 and 39S; he died within the hour. Three other ranks were also wounded at the time.

Second Lieutenant William Holmes Collinson
1/6 Northumberland Fusiliers

William was born in 1890, in Edmonton, Middlesex, the only son of William Rowley Field and Sarah Collinson. He was educated at Clare House School, Beckenham and Aldenham School, Hertfordshire. Before the war he was employed by Waterlow and Sons as a representative, and at the onset volunteered to join The Honourable Artillery Company as a private. He travelled to France with his battalion on 18 September 1914 and on 20 April 1915 he was gazetted Second Lieutenant with the 1/6 Northumberland Fusiliers and ordered back to England for training. Before this could happen he was instead sent straight to his new battalion because it had lost huge numbers of officers at the Battle of St Julien, 26 April 1915. On 5 January 1916, while in a communication trench between Trenches 39 and 39S, he was hit by a rifle grenade and died of his wounds, aged 25, within the hour. William is buried in Railway Dugouts Burial Ground (Transport Farm).

On 14 January four fledgling second lieutenants joined the 1/7 Battalion the day before it returned to Trenches 39, 40, 41 and 47 on Hill 60 for a four day tour of duty. One of these, Second Lieutenant Francis Buckley, described his journey to the front:

When it was beginning to get dark the battalion formed up in the road and the roll was called. At last we set off slowly, squelching through the mud on the wet roads, the rain pouring down unceasingly. We soon struck the pavé road that runs through Dickebusch, a long straggling village, still fairly intact and occupied by Belgian civilians. It was shelled now and again but not severely. When we reached this place, the battalion opened out considerably, platoons keeping 200 yards apart; a precaution necessary on roads that were periodically shelled at night. After plodding along for some time, we reached the Café Belge, a mere ruin now, but a well-known halting place for troops on the march. Here we turned off to the right and left the pavé road which runs on to Ypres, and after this the roads were much more difficult to travel. Shell holes were frequent and generally full of water, so that in the dark it was only too easy to stumble into them. 'Shell-hole on the right,' 'Shell-hole on the left,' 'Shell-hole in the middle,' 'Keep to your right' were being passed back continually. Progress was slow of course under these conditions and with heavy loads that we all carried. But it was all so novel to me that I had not a moment to feel dull or depressed. After a time, we reached the notorious 'Shrapnel Corner' and turned towards 'Transport Farm' for we were bound for the trenches of Hill 60. This place was famous for the British attack in 1915 and for the German counterattack with gas a little later on which was all too successful. It was also notorious for being one of the hottest corners of the British front. Owing to their vantage ground on the hill the enemy had little difficulty in sniping and shelling our trenches effectively.

As we approached Transport Farm I came for the first time under indirect rifle fire. A number of bullets fired at our trenches carried over and landed not far from the roads at the back. Though rather alarming in the dark to one unaccustomed to them, they seldom did much damage. Occasionally a man or two got wounded during these reliefs. Our company turned to the left again near Zillebeke railway station, and then struck off the road and reached the mouth of a communications trench which led after a hundred yards to the support trenches.[9]

Buckley goes on to describe the nature of the British and German front lines on Hill 60:

Whilst the German line ran solid along the top of the ridge, there were two complete gaps in the British fire trenches between Hill 60 and Mont Sorrel on the left. On paper, it looks as if there was nothing to stop the German from walking across and behind our lines whenever he chose. But I imagine that these empty spaces were covered by machine gun posts and that the artillery were ready to deal with any attempt of that sort. Another feature of the place was the awful nature of the ground outside the trenches. It was a morass filled with partially buried bodies – that is, partially buried by nature in the ooze and mud. During a dense mist about seventy identity discs were recovered from the ground behind our support lines. And it was worse in front between

*the opposing trenches. It was not likely, then, that the Germans would wish
to press us farther down the hill, at any rate for tactical purposes.*[10]

Typically, the time that each of the battalions of 149 Brigade spent at the front
on Hill 60 was four days between reliefs. However, even when not at the front,
men were required for working parties.

Buckley vividly describes life during his first tour of duty in mid-January 1916,
when the 1/7 Battalion were manning trenches 39, 40, 41 and 47 on Hill 60.

*'A' Company had two platoons in the front-line Trench 41, some 100 yards
from the enemy, and two platoons in a support line called '41 Support'.
The trenches themselves were well built and riveted with sand bags and
dry enough even during the wettest weather. We had in these days only
small shelters – the deep dugout was unknown. The three subalterns in 'A'
Company took turns at duty in the trenches, four hours on and eight hours
off, night and day. The duty consisted chiefly of visiting the sentries every
hour, and keeping a general look out, and seeing that the trench rules were
obeyed. A good deal of rifle fire went on at night. Sentries on either side
would exchange shots, and an occasional machine-gun would open out. At
close range the bullets made a curious crack as they passed overhead. Being
tall and having been warned of the efficiency of the German sniper, I had
to walk in most of the trenches with a bend in the back, which soon become
tiring.*[11]

On 16 January, the 1/7 Battalion had a particularly lively time whilst they
manned the trenches on the side of Hill 60. The scene is described by Second
Lieutenant Buckley:

*It was always said that the Germans got a fresh supply of ammunition at the
weekend, and Sunday was scarcely ever a day of rest. However that may be,
this Sunday was the worst day I had for some time. After sending over a few
small howitzer shells, the German field guns sent periodical showers of shells,
'whizz-bangs' we called them, on to the support trench and communication
trench. This went on all morning and whilst the shoot lasted they came over
in a perfect stream. After a quieter afternoon, a regular trench battle opened
out at night, rifle grenades and bombs being freely exchanged, and a number*

of trench mortar bombs – 'sausages and rum jars' – coming over from the enemy's trenches. Eventually our heavy guns opened out with lively retaliation and the enemy quietened down.[12]

Even though the Germans expended huge quantities of ammunition on 16 January, the War Diary of the 1/7 Battalion records that only one man was wounded. This was not always the case; as the battalions rotated during the manning of this dangerous sector there were many casualties.

On 31 January, the 1/7 Battalion took over trenches 48, 49, 50, A1, A2 and A3 on Mont Sorrel for three days. Mont Sorrel lay to the north of Hill 60. These new trenches were reported as a 'good set'. They were cut off from the brigade's trenches on Hill 60 by a swamp, through which ran a watery sort of ditch about four feet deep. In fact, this was the old front line, now waterlogged and quite useless. The ditch was not manned by day, but it was the responsibility of a patrol of bombers to pass along it at intervals during the night. Buckley, in his new position as battalion 'grenadier officer' or 'bombing officer', was responsible for these patrols, wading through the putrid water:

This was not a pleasant job, because you could not show a light and the mud smelt abominably. We were provided, however, with rubber boots reaching up to the thigh, so we did not get wet.[13]

Later during their stay in these trenches, the Germans erected a notice which proclaimed:

Attention Gentlemen!

(Then below, in German:)

If you send over one more trench mortar bomb you will get strafed in the neck.

Also in the trenches on Mont Sorrel were the 1/4, who reported that the enemy were very active with rifle grenades. As men of the 1/4 were retaliating there was a tragic accident: a bomb burst prematurely on 1 February, which killed Second Lieutenant John Robert Bowden Roberts. Four other men were badly wounded, of whom one died the following day. The enemy continued to be very active with grenades, and during the night of 2 February, 4/677 Private

Second Lieutenant John Robert Bowden Roberts
1/6 Northumberland Fusiliers

John was born in 1895 in Cullercoats, Northumberland, the youngest son of John Robert and Margaret Cecilia Roberts. He was educated at Newcastle Preparatory School, Charterhouse (1904-1910), and Pembroke College Oxford. He also trained at Inner Temple, London. He died of his wounds on 1 February 1916, aged 24, and is buried in Railway Dugouts Burial Ground (Transport Farm). His headstone contains the following inscription:

CHARTERHOUSE
PEMBROKE COLLEGE (CANTAB)
INNER TEMPLE
'DEO DANTE DEDI'

James Hedley ('B' Company) of West Woodburn was killed (see Chapter 13, *Aftermath*). The next morning 4/2825 Private Alexander Ure was also killed. Later in the week, whilst positioned in support near Bedford House, the 1/4 came under heavy artillery attack; Second Lieutenant Charles Gordon Sharp was wounded and died soon afterwards.

Second Lieutenant Charles Gordon Sharp
1/4 Northumberland Fusiliers

Charles was the youngest son of the Robert and Mary Sharp of Riding Mill, Northumberland. He was educated at Aysgarth School, Charterhouse, and Durham School of Science. At the onset of hostilities, he was working in the Belgiam Congo. Initially he joined the Anglo Belgian Corps but gave up his work to return home and enlist. He trained at the Inns of Court OTC and in April 1915 was granted a commission and joined the 1/4 Northumberland Fusiliers. He was posted to France on 15 September 1915. Whilst the 1/4 Battalion was in support at Bedford House they came under a heavy artillery attack and Gordon, aged 30, was wounded and died soon afterwards. He is buried in Vlamertinghe Military Cemetery

On 3 February the 1/5 moved into Trenches 48 (Glasgow Cross) to A3 inclusive, replacing the 1/7. All companies were in the front line, in trenches that were described as 'good' on the left and 'poor' on the right. On the following day these trenches came under enemy bombardment, during which a shell burst just outside the door of a dugout occupied by Captain Percival Donald Forrett who was killed and Second Lieutenant Frederick Charles Philips who was wounded. Unfortunately, Philips also died within the day, at No 10 Casualty Clearing Station, Poperinghe.

Captain Percival Donald Forrett
1/5 Northumberland Fusiliers

Percival was born in 1884, in Alfreton, Derbyshire, the son of Thomas and Isabella Forrett. He was educated at Chesterfield Grammar School and the University of London. From 1907 he taught science at Dame Allan's Endowed Schools, Newcastle upon Tyne. In 1910 he was gazetted Second Lieutenant from Durham University OTC. Further promotions followed: Lieutenant in 1911 and Captain in 1913. At the outbreak of war he volunteered for foreign service; he disembarked in France on 19 April 1915 and was badly gassed on 25 May 1915. He returned to the Western Front when passed fit for duty, but was killed by shell fire, aged 31, on 5 February 1916, whilst in the trenches. He is buried in Maple Cross Cemetery.

During this first week of February, while the men of 1/7 Battalion were in support positions – with companies in Armagh Wood, Square Wood, Railway Cutting and Sunken Wood – Buckley, Captain Welch and Lieutenant Greene were sent out to reconnoitre trenches north of Mont Sorrel which were on a mound called Canny Hill. (In Northumbrian, *canny* means pleasant, nice, (e.g. 'she's a canny lass'). The journey was full of incident: they crossed the swamp in daylight and were continuously harassed by the enemy. On 12 February, Buckley and his battalion moved up to take over trenches A4 to A11 on Canny Hill, near Sanctuary Wood for a four-day tour of duty. These front-line trenches were a quarter of a mile from those of the enemy but there were a number of signs that the Germans were busy digging a forward trench along a hedge about two hundred yards in front of the British trench, which was perturbing for the battalion's top brass. From the trenches on Canny Hill, Hugh Liddell describes events on 14 February:

> *Things have been humming. A general bombardment of our trenches started early yesterday and continued all day. It culminated in the blowing-up of two mines on our right. My trench is rather knocked about, but so far there are few casualties. I got to sleep about 1am and woke at 3 to find it snowing hard, just to add to our discomforts a little. It is impossible to see twenty yards across No Man's Land. The only thing we are sorry about is that the Germans did not attack us, as we were ready to give them what for if they came across.*[14]

The 1/4 was also in the Canny Hill sector. On 14 February the enemy shelled Hooge Ridge to the north of Canny Hill and during late afternoon moved forward to the area held by the Rifle Brigade, who managed to fend off the attack. During this advance the enemy bombarded the trenches held by the 1/4 and a number of men were killed, including 4/2796 Private James Grieve, aged 19, who had been in Belgium since September 1915. On the right of 149 Brigade's position, during the afternoon, the Germans succeeded in taking a few trenches held by the 17th Division. As the battalion's transport was passing along the Kruisstraat it was shelled ferociously and 4/849 Corporal Christopher Inglis, aged 22, was killed. Christopher hailed from the Falstone district of the North Tyne Valley. One of his officers wrote of him:

> *He was one of the coolest and most gallant of soldiers I have ever seen, and whenever the transport had a dangerous duty to perform he was the first to volunteer to carry it out.*[15]

The weather had turned very cold: snow and sleet billowed in an icy wind blasting all the way from Siberia. There was little comfort for the common soldier, as described by Captain Liddell during the battalion's stay on Canny Hill:

> *It is beastly cold I can hardly hold my pencil. How the men stick it I do not know, as many of them are practically out in it all the four days and nights They are as cheerful as can be though.*[16]

During that bitter night the 1/6 relieved the 1/9 DLI on Hill 60. On the following night the 1/6 supplied two officers and eighty men to the Royal Engineers for the reconstruction of X Trench. During this detail, Lieutenant Wilfred Hudson Bainbridge was wounded by a sniper's bullet to the head (see Chapter 13 *Aftermath*). Two incidents, illustrating that humour can be found even amidst horror, took place on 1 March, whilst the 1/7 were away from the front in a reserve position at Railway Dug-outs.

First:

I am living in a dugout which is tunnelled right into the middle of a railway embankment. It is all lined out with thick timber and the way in is by an underground passage some five yards long. I have a bed and a table, also two forms, so I am living in luxury this time. It is of course dark, and I have to burn candles all day long. There is a large pond outside my front door with bulrushes growing around the edge. There are waterhens and any amount of fish. This morning a large shell landed plump in the middle of it, the result being that the men are having fresh fish for dinner. Altogether this is a most desirable country residence, and the name of it is 'Shrapnel Corner'.

And secondly:

While the battalion was in reserve at the Railway Dug-outs, one of the tough 'old' bombers of 'A' Company thought to enliven the tedium of waiting by a little private sport. Observing a fine-looking duck on one of the ponds behind these dug-outs, he proceeded to stalk the bird, and drawing a bead on it with his rifle, fired. The fate of the bird is not recorded, but the bullet (I hope a ricochet) entered a dug-out occupied by heavy gunners. The next scene was an infuriated Sergeant Major of the Heavy Artillery in hot and angry pursuit of our hero, who thought it best to execute a strategic but somewhat rapid retreat towards the starting point. The situation was saved by the German gunners, who unexpectedly put down a couple of heavy shells between the pursuer and pursued. After this our sportsman returned to us at his leisure and without the loss of dignity. The moral of the story seems to lie in the occasional value of heavy guns for covering a retiring force.[17]

NORTHUMBRIAN TERRITORIALS
HILL 60 DECEMBER 1915–MARCH 1916

| 4/1128 | 4/869 | 5/1696 | 6/2289 |
| Pte Ernest Henry Robson | Sgt Marshall Henderson | Pte Thomas Watson | Pte Charles Lucas |

| 6/4849 | 5/3668 | 4/2573 | 7/2126 |
| Pte Adam Morrison | Pte Henry Taylor | Pte Richard Rigby | Pte William White |

| 7/1944 | 5/2355 | 4/2129 | 7/2222 |
| Pte Jacob Straughan | Pte John Colling Ward | LCpl Joseph Bell | Cpl Thomas Swan |

| 4/372 | 6/1492 | 7/2014 | 5/2482 |
| Cpl Robert Towler | Pte James Wood | Sgt Henry Hill | Pte Thomas Dickinson |

NORTHUMBRIAN TERRITORIALS
HILL 60 DECEMBER 1915–MARCH 1916

4/2043
Pte John W Fawcett

5/3124
Pte James Dunleavy

7/3120
Pte Christopher Foster

7/2336
Pte George Simpson

5/2678
Pte Charles Ions

4/2716
Pte William Watt

7/2850
Pte Matthew Hall

7/3069
Pte George Roper

4/849
Cpl Christopher Inglis

6/3528
Pte Anthony Batey

4/2796
Pte James Grieve

5/3706
Pte Douglas F Griffin

5/2187
Pte William Christie

7/1459
Pte George Curry

7/2869
Pte Charles Habberjam

4/1803
Pte Joshua Robson

On 2 March, after a heavy barrage, an attack by 76 Brigade managed to retake The Bluff (another artificial mound formed from the debris from the Ypres to Comines canal), which had been lost to the enemy on 14 February. Also captured were a series of trenches known as The Bean. The 50th Division staged a number of diversions by providing artillery support and extensive use of trench mortar bombardments on the enemy's trenches. At the time, the 1/7 held trenches 49 to A3 (Mont Sorrel) and were suffering appalling weather, with constant snow and frost causing misery for everyone. In retaliation for the bombardment, the Germans unleashed their own furious barrages. Casualties for this six-day tour of duty were: 1 killed and 9 wounded.

The War Diary of the 1/4 reports that during the night of the 6/7 March they returned to Hill 60. They found the trenches to be much deteriorated owing to the recent heavy snow and partial thaw which had caused the sides of the trenches to collapse in a number of places. On 9 March, these trenches came under heavy shelling and two sergeants were killed. One of these was 4/869 Sergeant Wilfred Marshall Henderson, aged 20, from Acomb (a village near Hexham), who was killed by a sniper's bullet. Wilfred had been a pre-war Territorial, and four fellow Territorials from Acomb were present at his interment in Railway Dugouts Burial Ground.

The enemy continued to bombard the 1/4, who were based in trenches in need of continuous repair. On 10 March, the War Diary records that four men were killed with a further thirteen wounded. One of these was 7/851 Private Archibald Bell of Falstone in the North Tyne Valley, aged 24.

The entire 149 Brigade was relieved by 151 Brigade on 14 March and moved away from the front for some well-earned rest. The 1/4, 1/5 and 1/6 moved by rail to Poperinghe whilst the 1/7 moved into D Camp near Ouderon. The Brigade's War Diary reports that casualties from 2 March were twenty-six killed and seventy-six wounded. After a series of inspections, including one of the 1/7 by Field-Marshal Douglas Haig, the men were given plenty of opportunity to rest. Drafts of new men arrived at Poperinghe: the 1/4 received one officer and forty-eight men, the 1/5 gained eighteen men and the 1/6 welcomed two officers and eighty men. After these days in relative warmth and safety, by 24 March the Brigade was back at the front. The 1/7 moved into trenches 37 to 47 on Hill 60.

Railway Dugouts Burial Ground (Transport Farm)
The resting place of many men from the 149 Brigade
Author's Collection

On March 25 the British exploded nine mines at St Eloi, south of Hill 60. The craters formed were then occupied by troops from the 3rd Division. In retaliation, the Germans bombarded the entire length of the front-line; from 1930hrs to 2200hrs they pounded the trenches and cuttings but the relief was not much delayed, and there were only two men wounded.

> *... unfortunate casualties were Second Lieutenant J. H. C. Swinney* [who was later killed at Wancourt 1917] *and 7/1251 Sergeant John William Dorgan, both good men and a loss to the battalion.*[18]

Swinney and Dorgan were in command of a team of sixty men charged with bringing up rations for the battalion, using the track of the light railway to walk to the front; Swinney was leading the column with Dorgan bringing up the rear. The Germans knew of this access route to the front and would blast it every now and then, which is what happened on this occasion. As the shells drew uncomfortably close, the men in the team lay down facing the side of the embankment for protection. Dorgan moved rapidly to the front of the column, adjusting the sandbags containing the supplies around the heads of his men, before joining Swinney on the ground. Unfortunately, Dorgan took a large shell splinter in the back of his leg and was evacuated to Hospital Farm where it was removed with anaesthetic, after which he was transported to a hospital in Newcastle under Lyme. Over the next three days the 1/7 took over fifty casualties – many more than the average (of about seven or eight) for a tour of duty of this length of time.

> *The whole of 'C' Company's batmen were killed by a shell and Second Lieutenant Roger Frederick Burt, a new arrival but an old friend, was also killed. Poor lad, he was always certain that he would be killed as soon as he got out to France! I saw in the trenches a pile of our dead, three or four deep, waiting removal to the rear.*[19]

Second Lieutenant Roger Frederick Burt
1/7 Northumberland Fusiliers

Roger was born in Worthing, Sussex, in 1896, the son of Frederick Melville and Sarah Murrell Burt. He was educated at Christ's Hospital School, West Horsham, and served in the OTC. Before enlisting he was employed at Hawthorn Leslie Ltd of Newcastle upon Tyne. He was gazetted into the reserve battalion of 1/7 Northumberland Fusiliers in July 1915, arriving on the Western Front on 7 March 1916. He was killed in action on 27 March, aged 20, and is buried in Railway Dugouts Burial Ground (Transport Farm).

The Soldiers Died in the Great War database records that eight men were killed on 27 March, including 7/1447 William George Robinson Laidler, aged 19, of Red Row, near Amble.

At 2345hrs on March 27, 149 Brigade was replaced at the front by 3 Brigade Canadian Infantry and days later, during the afternoon of 3 April, the 50th Division moved to man the front at Wytschaete. This sector ran from the neighbourhood of Spanbroekmolen (in the German lines) northwards in an irregular line across Vandamme Hill to the Vierstraat to Wytschaete Road, just south of Byron Farm, after which the line followed a north-easterly direction to just south of the eastern extremity of Bois Confluent. The 149 Brigade subsector was in the middle of the divisional sector, manning trenches H3 to L5. To the left was 151 Brigade and to the right 150 Brigade.

The men of 149 Brigade took over from 5 Canadian Infantry Brigade, who reported as they left that the Wytschaete sector was peaceful and quiet. Initial dispositions were: 1/7 H2 to K3 inclusive; 1/4 K2 to L5 inclusive; 1/6 two companies at RC Farm, one company at Siege Farm and one company at Watsonville Dugouts. 1/5 was in reserve at Locre.

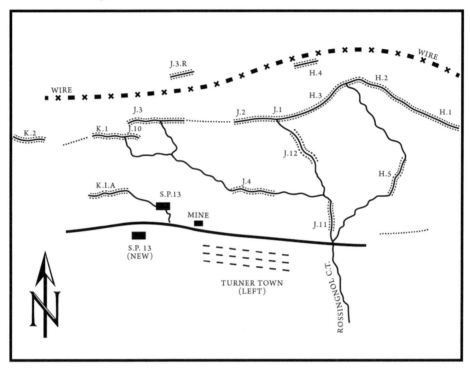

Wytschaete Ridge: Trench Map, April 1916

Next day we went forward to the new trenches. They were a change from those in the salient, and it was evident that there had not been much heavy shelling there. Instead of the high narrow trenches of Hill 60, they were mostly mere breastworks with little or no back protection. And the communication trenches were hardly deep enough to afford protection from sniping or indirect rifle fire. Fortunately, the Germans did not snipe these trenches. There were three gaps in the front line, and two small posts in No Man's Land. A long winding C T brought you from Battalion HQ, which was at Rossignol Farm about a mile from the front-line. The main feature of the landscape were the Wytschaete Ridge and Petit Bois – a thick wood on our left front. The

German trenches were not at first close to ours, and both their wire and ours was thick and solid.[20]

The sub-sector taken by the 1/7 displays one of the peculiarities of this sector: H4, a bombing post outside the front line but inside the wire, held only at night:

… but you only reach it by clambering over the top of the parapet after dark. The post was connected by a string to a sentry post in the front line. And various signals were arranged to warn the sentry in the front line as to what was going on, for example two jerks on the string: Man returning to trench; three jerks: Enemy patrol on right and so on.[21]

Another quirk of this sub-sector was a broken-down trench beyond the wire, called J3 Right, discovered by Captain Hugh Liddell ('B' Company) during one of his numerous forays into No Man's Land. Obviously it was difficult to approach owing to the mud and distance from the trenches, and dangerous because it might be attacked by enemy patrols. The 1/7 decided it was to be manned during the night.

Wytschaete village lay in the centre of the sector but behind German lines, with positions on Wytschaete Ridge allowing them to observe a significant proportion of the divisional front. As predicted by the Canadians, everything was reasonably quiet … until 9 April, when the enemy opened fire in earnest, hammering onto 149 Brigade's area from Petit Bois, situated to the rear and left of the German line. Behind their front line the Germans had installed a large number of trench mortars which they unleashed to give the men of 149 Brigade a blistering time. The day before, a dugout in the area occupied by the 1/4 had received a direct hit from a large artillery shell, killing two and wounding another four men. The two killed were 4/1490 Drummer Thomas William Cathrae of Hexham and 4/677 Private James Hedley of West Woodburn, whose brother had been killed on 1 February 1916. Both of the Hedley brothers were pre-war members of the Territorial Force.

The Petit Bois wood housed a range of guns of all sizes; their racket punctuated every day, the first barrage starting at noon and lasting ninety minutes. The cacophony of 9 April came from 5.9in, 4.4in shells and whizz-bangs, which hailed down on the 1/5 and 1/6 who had now taken up front-line duties. Casualties for the 1/6 during this tour of duty were: 6 Other Ranks and 1 Officer, who was Second Lieutenant Harry Laurie Benson, a popular officer whose loss was felt keenly by his battalion and friends including George Harbottle as shown by the extract from the 1/6 War Diary. Captain R. W. Nicholson and Second Lieutenant E. L. Bell were also wounded. George Harbottle wrote about his friend and was later to marry his sister:

Second Lieutenant Henry Laurence Benson
1/6 Northumberland Fusiliers

Henry was born in Newcastle-upon-Tyne, in 1890, the eldest son of Henry and Minnie Benson. He was educated at Aysgarth School and Charterhouse. Like his father he practised as a solicitor in Newcastle. At the onset of hostilities, he enlisted as a private in the 1/6 Northumberland Fusiliers, rising to Sergeant. He disembarked in France on 20 April 1915 and was engaged in the Battle of St Julien, six days later. In November 1915 he was wounded. Subsequently he was granted a commission. He was killed by shrapnel on 11 April 1916, aged 26. He is buried in Kemmel Chateau Military Cemetery.

Second Lieutenant H. L. Benson was one of our own having been promoted from the ranks. He joined the Battalion the day war broke out and, step by step, had risen to the rank of Company Sergeant Major of 'A' Company and was eventually commissioned in the field, coming back to his battalion as an officer. His death is keenly felt for Laurie, as he was affectionately referred to, was loved and respected by all who knew him, and his loss cast a gloom over the whole battalion, for his popularity was immense.[22]

Casualties for the 1/5 were even higher: Other Ranks: 9 killed. Day after day, the sub-sector held by 149 Brigade was battered by fire from a variety of armaments. One Geordie Fusilier from the 1/6 was heard to say, 'Ah wish they would hoy their bloody guns at us and be done wid!' Clearly, blistering showers of enemy shells couldn't dampen the soldier's mordant Northern humour! Mercifully, the tour of duty in the Wytschaete was a short one; on 25 April General Wilkinson handed responsibly for the three sub sectors to the 3rd Division. During this tour of duty, casualties for 149 Brigade were: Officers: 1 killed and 6 wounded; Other Ranks: 35 killed and 135 wounded. One of those killed was 4/1917 Private David Salkeld from Hexham, aged 24, a married man with a child. Captain Turner of 'A' Company wrote to his mother, in a letter dated 21 April 1915:

> *I am very sorry to inform you that your son was seriously wounded while out on a working party the night before last and died two hours later in the dressing station. He never regained consciousness after being hit and suffered no pain. He will be greatly missed by all of us. He was a good soldier always doing his work well and cheerfully …*[23]

The casualty returns for 1/6 for April 1916 reveal that over fifty men were wounded, but in fact well over 150 men were sent back from the front to hospital, presumably for various reasons: severe trench foot and pneumonia for example.

By 26 April, 149 Brigade had been relieved from front-line duties. The 1/4 and 1/7 were replaced by the 1 Northumberland Fusiliers and the 12 West Yorks respectively. However, each battalion was ordered to leave one company and three Lewis Guns in camps at Kemmel whilst the rest marched to the Corps rest area: the 1/5 to York Huts, Locre, and the others to a rest area between Metgren and Ballieul.

On 30 April, an alarm was sounded at 0045hrs heralding that the enemy intended to attack Kemmel, and in anticipation orders were issued for the Kemmel garrison and the battalions of 149 Brigade to move forward in support. At 0122hrs the enemy attacked at Spanbroekmolen but the assault was contained and 149 Brigade was ordered back to camp.

The weather was benevolently fine and warm as 149 Brigade enjoyed their rest period of training and recreation. The 1/7 won the brigade's football competition and were presented with a cup by Brigadier Clifford. By the middle of the month the garrison companies at Kemmel had returned to the fold. There were further alarms: for example, on 18 May a gas alert was sounded by the 9 Brigade (3rd Division) but this was later found to be a false alarm.

By the middle of May it was time for the 50th Division to return to the line, where eventually they took over trenches E1 to O4 from the 3rd Division. First to return to the front was 149 Brigade which took over the centre sub-sector from 9 Brigade. In each sub-sector two battalions held the front line, a third was positioned in Brigade Reserve and the other in Divisional Reserve. At the front, the 1/6 were on the right and 1/5 on the left for the first seven days, which was the norm in this sector.

As a 'welcome back' the enemy opened up along the whole of the front for two and half hours using virtually every weapon they had. Not surprisingly, the trenches were severely ravaged by this shelling, and sixty to seventy casualties were reported. During the night the Fusiliers, Divisional Pioneers, and Royal Engineers endeavoured to repair the extensive damage. The ten-week tour of duty was their second in this part of the line, and was standard trench warfare, including aggressive patrolling of No Man's Land. The War Diaries of 149 Brigade for June and July record the first instances of raids on the enemy's trenches since they arrived on the Western Front in April 1915.

German crew reloading a 25cm Minenwerfer

June was a hellish month along the whole front. North of the 50th Division the Germans shelled the Canadians north of Hill 60 – Mont Sorrel, Armagh Wood, Sanctuary Wood and Hooge; the smoke from bursting shells drifted ominously over the whole of the Ypres Salient. Along the 50th Division sector,

German artillery and trench mortars laid waste the British defences, wrecking trenches, causing lamentable injuries and death. When the positions of the enemy trench mortars were identified, they could be destroyed by the firing of a few rounds, but many of these retaliatory shells fell short, landing instead on British troops, causing the very damage they were aiming to prevent.

June was a particularly bad month for the 1/7: four officers and eleven men were killed. The enemy targeted the trenches, incessantly using trench mortars, a large *minenwerfer* (accurate short-range mortar) and howitzers. On 24 June, they zeroed in on trenches H2 and H3 so that the battalion suffered several casualties, including Second Lieutenant Hugh Vaughan Charlton.

Second Lieutenant Hugh Vaughan Charlton
1/7 Northumberland Fusiliers

Hugh as born in London in 1884, the eldest son of John and Kate MacFarlane Charlton of Knightsbridge, London and Newcastle upon Tyne. His father was a well-known artist. He was educated at the Mount, Northallerton, and Aldenham School. In May 1915 he joined the Durham University OTC and received a commission in the reserve battalion of the 1/7 Northumberland Fusiliers. He later disembarked on the Western Front, on 13 March 1916, and was killed by shrapnel from a direct hit from a short-range mortar on 24 June, aged 32. Hugh is buried in La Laiterie Military Cemetery. His headstone is inscribed:

ALSO TO HIS BROTHER
CAPTAIN J M CHARLTON
21ST NORTHUMBERLAND FUSILIERS
KILLED 1-7-16 LA BOISELLE

Later in the month, during the next tour of duty in trenches H2 to K1, the 1/7 the War Diary records: *We got a large deal of annoyance from large Minenwerfer and trench mortars which did a lot of damage to trench H2.*[24]

The casualties were Lieutenants Wilfred Jervis Davis and Charles Guy Arobiun Burnett and three Other Ranks killed, one of whom was 7/3453 Private Thomas Baulks of Ashington. The following day the enemy targeted Trench K1a. Second Lieutenant Arthur William Dale, in command of this trench, was badly wounded in the thigh by a large splinter of shell and died a few minutes later.

The reason for this notable increase in enemy activity was to keep the British Army occupied, preventing them from dispatching troops to support the French in the defence of Verdun. The Germans had launched a tremendous attack in February, but still had not succeeded in reaching their objectives.

In early July, 149 Brigade came out of the line, relieved by 150 Infantry Brigade for a few days, and moved to camps north of La Clytte. The Brigade War Diary on 4 July recorded that from 24 May the casualty figures had been: Officers: 10 killed and 16 wounded; Other Ranks: 45 killed and 319 wounded.

Second Lieutenant Frank Priestman Lees
1/4 Northumberland Fusiliers

Frank was born in Workington, Cumberland, in 1890, the eldest son of Herbert and Annie Lees. He was educated at the Friends School, Ackworth, and Leeds University. He was employed as a gas engineer. In September 1914 he enlisted as a private with the 16 Northumberland Fusiliers and was gazetted Second Lieutenant on 21 April 1915; he disembarked in France on 10 July 1915. He was killed by shrapnel on 17 June 1916 whilst on duty in the trenches, aged 26. Frank is buried at La Laiterie Military Cemetery. His headstone is inscribed:

> THAT THOSE THINGS
> WHICH ARE NOT SHAKEN
> MAY REMAIN

One of the officers killed was Second Lieutenant Frank Priestman Lees, aged 26, killed on 17 June. The following is an extract from a letter written by Captain Robb to Frank's father:

> *Whilst on duty in the trenches this morning Frank was hit by shrapnel and severely wounded on the left side. I was talking to him at the time it happened and no time was wasted in getting him to the dressing station, but the doctor could give us little hope and within two hours he passed away.*[25]

For the next few days, 149 Brigade supplied a number of men to working parties for various projects, from improving defences to burying signal cables. Nevertheless, there was some time for relaxation; at the Brigade Horse Transport Show on 7 July the 1/6 won the bulk of the prizes.

On 14 July, the brigade went into the line once more, this time south of St Eloi, trenches MI to O4. On 16 July 1916 the War Diary of 1/6 Battalion, reported:

> *At 12.20am an enemy patrol was observed to approach our bombing point in front of O4. The bombers fired on the leading man. The enemy then threw several time grenades – we retaliated and after a good deal of rifle fire the bombing ceased and the situation was quiet except for a German who was apparently suffering the effects of a bomb and his moans continued for over an hour. At stand to arms it was discovered that a German had been killed and lay not far from our bombing point. His body was brought in and it was discovered that he belonged to the 214th Regiment, 46th Division. His name was Willi Gierki and he was 18 years of age.*[26]

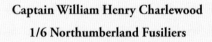

Captain William Henry Charlewood
1/6 Northumberland Fusiliers

William was born in Newcastle upon Tyne in 1893, the son of Henry Clement and Louisa Mary Charlewood. He was educated at Alnmouth Preparatory School, Sedbergh, and Selwyn College, Cambridge. He was gazetted Second Lieutenant in October 1914 and Captain on 9 May 1916. He disembarked in France on 20 April 1915 and was one of the few officers of the 1/6 Northumberland Fusiliers left after the *Battle of St Julien 26 April 1915*. During the night of 20/21 July, William led a patrol armed with a Lewis gun into No Man's Land to prevent the enemy from sending out working parties. At 0100hrs the patrol returned – with William mortally wounded. He died on the following day, aged 23, at No 2 Casualty Clearing Station, Ballieul. William is buried in Bailleul Communal Cemetery Extension. His headstone is inscribed:

VIRTUTE ET FIDE

On the following day, the British artillery concentrated on blasting through the enemy's wire. The resulting retaliation concentrated on Bois Carré, destroying the reserve ration store as well as the bomb store at Eastern Redoubt. As a result, eighty men from the battalion's new draft set about filling 2000 sand bags, to build parapets in Bois Carré communications trench.

That night, 149 Brigade was relieved by the 6 Canadian Infantry Brigade and moved to what was deemed to be a quieter part of the line near Wulverghem, below the Messines Ridge. They took over trenches 141 to D6 inclusive from the 61 Brigade. Major Cowen wrote:

After two months of continuous misery in the Salient we came to a health resort farther south. Here the trenches were good, standing on high ground they were dry, and the parapets were sound. Altogether a most agreeable change from anything we had as yet encountered. Our predecessors in this area had acted on the principle of 'live and let live,' and had ensured a peaceful and quiet time of it. Unfortunately the Northumberlands had had it well drilled into them that 'The chief end of a man' (as the shorter catechism has it) was to harry and annoy the Boche perpetually, to make his life a misery on all occasions, and incidentally kill as many as possible. All of this they proceeded to do as promptly and effectually as they could.

This was apparently not at all to the liking of Fritz and so one day a voice called over from the Boche trenches in accents full of pathos and with a plaintive tone of regret:

'I wish to God you **** Northumberlands **** would get out of this and let us have the **** back again.' [27]

Conditions in the trenches was aptly described by Lieutenant Buckley of 1/7 Battalion:

These new trenches were quiet enough, but the sniping of the enemy was far too good. I was nearly caught out before I realised the fact. I was looking over the parapet just in front of us with L.C. Austin when a bullet caught the edge of the sandbag along the top, stopping within a few inches of our heads. Of course, we dropped down quickly into the trench, but L.C. Austin waved his cap over the top to signal a miss. He told me, never do you let the German sniper think he had scored a hit.[28]

La Laiterie Military Cemetery
The last resting place of many from the 149 Brigade

During the first week of August the sector manned by 149 Brigade was taken over by 36th (Ulster) Division, which had had a hard time during the first days of the Somme offensive in July 1916. Although orders had not been issued, most of the officers had a good idea where they were bound. The Somme.

CHAPTER SIX

THE SOMME

By all of all man's hopes and fears,
And all the wonders poets sing,
The laughter of unclouded years,
And every sad and lovely thing;
By the romantic ages stored
With high endeavour that was his,
By all his mad catastrophes
Make me a man, O Lord.

From *'Before Action'* by Lieutenant William Noel Hodgson, MC

The first day of the Somme, 1 July 1916, is rightly infamous. The pitiful cries of dying men amidst the bedlam clamour of artillery have resonated over the years, and in the grim history of a grim war, it stands out as the bloodiest day. As the New Army attacked – and was cut down – on the Somme, the two battalions of 149 Brigade were manning a sector of the line near Locre, in Belgium. The 1/7 NF were in the right subsector whilst the left was manned by 1/4 Battalion. The 1/5 was in Brigade Reserve and the 1/6 in Divisional Reserve. The War Diary of the 1/4 Battalion recorded:

The enemy threw trench mortars at us in the early morning during a fog and caused casualties, 3 Other Ranks and 1 Officer, Second Lieutenant Scaife, who was wounded. The rest of the day was fairly quiet.[1]

In early August, the 50th Division, its infantry brigades and other elements, were informed that they were moving south for action on the Somme battlefield. The men of 149 Brigade boarded trains at Bailleul Station for Doullens, and over the next few days marched via Frenvillers, Naours and Pierregot to their destination: Hénencourt Wood, about four and a half miles east of Albert. At this time the 50th Division was transferred to the Fourth Army, III Corps. For the rest of August, 149 Brigade carried out training in preparation for a major attack to be launched by British troops on 15 September 1916, (now known as the *Battle of Flers-Courcelette, 15-22 September 1916*).

There is an interesting anomaly in the SDGW database: it records that on 3 September 1916, sixteen soldiers from the 1/7 Battalion were killed. All of these men are buried in either Mill Road Cemetery in Thiepval, or Connaught Cemetery in Thiepval or are commemorated on the Thiepval Memorial. There is no mention of these casualties in any of 1/7 Battalion, 149 Brigade or 50th Division War Diaries.

The War Diary[2] of the 1/7 Battalion NF states for early September: *The battalion remained in camp at Hénencourt Wood carrying out battalion, brigade and divisional training.* There is no mention of any casualties. The War Diary of 149 Brigade[3] states on 3 September 1916: *Divine Services. Night operations for Battalion scouts.* There is no mention of any casualties. The War Diary of the 50th Division[4] states for 3 September 1916: *50th Division in training.*

That these men were killed but not mentioned in the daily records suggests that they were probably some of the Scouts mentioned in the 149 Brigade's diary, and were either ambushed by the Germans or caught in an intense artillery barrage.

The attack on 15 September took place across an eight-mile front using twelve infantry divisions along with a small number of tanks and extensive artillery support. The artillery fired over 800,000 shells, a greater intensity than on 1 July, but less than on some of the other battles during the Somme campaign.

The front stretched from south of the village of Courcelette, west of the Albert-Bapaume road, eastwards to the south of Combles.

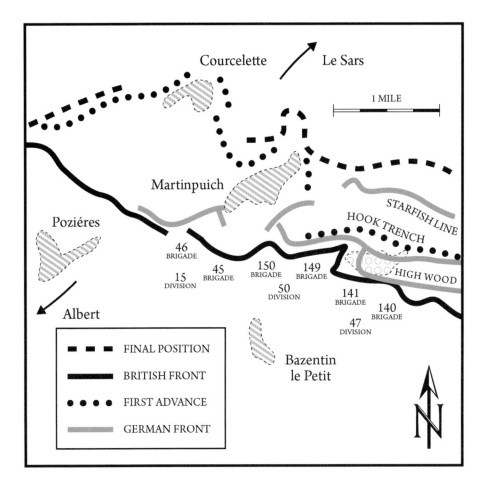

The Position of the 149 Brigade on the morning of 15 September 1916

This date is famous for the introduction of the tank to warfare, although this was a very primitive beast compared to those that we know today. By the day of the attack, Britain had built forty-nine tanks, but only fifteen of these managed to roll into action, at a speed of 1mph. Apart from the dangers of the raging battle, the tank crew faced extreme heat and high carbon-monoxide levels, together with metal splinters erupting from the tanks' armour, which was impervious to small arms and machine gun fire but susceptible to artillery shells. However, the tank was effective at crushing barbed wire and giving supporting fire to infantry. Further, on this first day their sinister appearance and size made them an effective psychological weapon.

An artist's impression of a Mark 1 Tank trundles across the Flers-Courcelette battlefield scattering the enemy. In reality, many failed even to reach the start line and many were ditched due to mechanical failure.

Author's Collection

The 50th Division's Sector was to the west of High Wood, (known to the French as *Bois des Fourneaux*). As we know, until September 1916 the 50th Division had not been involved in the momentous struggles on the Somme, but this was to change dramatically. Two of its brigades would be involved in the initial attack: on the right the 149 and on their left the 150 Brigade.

The preliminary bombardment began on 12 September, three days before the battle. By Thursday 14, the attacking units had taken up their positions as shown on the map on p.136. On the 149 Brigade front, the 1/7 NF were to be the vanguard on the left with the 1/4 on the right, nearest to High Wood. The sector allocated to 149 Brigade was a particularly difficult one as it formed the

In the background High Wood and in the foreground the terrain over which the 1/4 and 1/7 Northumberland Fusiliers struggled forward into withering machine gun fire. Now this blood stained land is planted with crops.
Author's Collection.

forward edge of a dogleg which flung back along the edge and around High Wood. None of the new tanks was allocated to this sector.

High Wood had been under attack by the British since a battle on 14 July 1916 (now known as the *Battle of Bezentin Ridge*), following which the wood lay undefended by the Germans for most of the day. Delays in communication and confusion, caused by orders and counter-orders from different British Corps Headquarters with overlapping responsibilities, led to the occupation of High Wood by the British being delayed, thus allowing German reserves

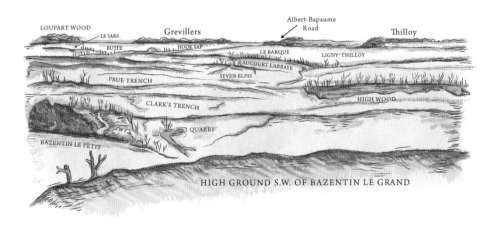

Scene of the attacks by the 50th Division, 15 September–14 November 1916
Chloe Rodham

139

to re-occupy it during their counterattack. Nonetheless, troops from the 7th Division managed to occupy the southern half of the wood, but with many casualties. Two cavalry squadrons advanced on the east side of the wood to Wood Lane, which ran from the wood to Longueval. However, the following day saw the evacuation of remnants of the 7th Division forcing the cavalry to retire since their flank was now exposed. The British and the Germans had jousted incessantly for control of the wood, but on 15 September it was in enemy hands. The responsibility for clearing the wood was allocated to 141 Brigade from the 47th Division.

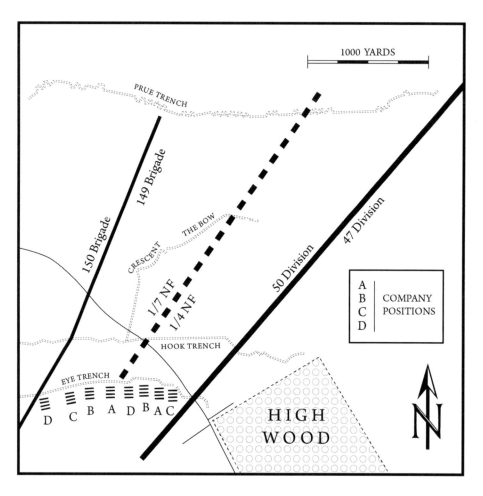

Details of the 149 Brigade attack on 15 September 1916.

Major F. B. Cowen of the 1/7 Battalion NF recorded:

While reconnoitering the assembly trenches for the attack in which the brigade is to take part in the course of the next few days, Brigadier-General H.F. Clifford was shot through the heart by a sniper, about 7.25am. This news was received with profound regret by all ranks for we could not possibly have had a better General. Lieutenant-Colonel Turner of the 1/5 Northumberland Fusiliers took over command of the Brigade temporarily until Brigadier-General Ovens joins on 14 September.[5]

By the night of 14 September, the two attacking battalions had reached the assembly trench – Clark's Trench – much aided by pitch darkness. From left to right the company designation for the 1/7 was: 'D' (Captain G. F. Ball); 'C' (Captain V. Merivale); 'B' (Captain E. Fenwicke Clennell and 'A' (Captain J. W. Merivale). On the left of the 1/7 were elements of 150 Brigade. To the right of the 1/7 was the 1/4 (nearest High Wood) with the following designation from left to right: 'D' Company (Captain H. H. Bell); 'B' Company (Captain L. D. Plummer); 'A' Company (Captain J. T. Henderson) and 'C' Company (Captain H. Cheesmond). On their right were elements of 141 Brigade.

Three objectives had been assigned to the 50 Division sector. First was the capture of Hook Trench which ran westwards from High Wood. Second was an advance of a further 500 yards and the occupation of Martin Trench, the Bow and part of the Starfish Line. Third was the capture of Prue Trench and a further section of the Starfish Line. The attacking front was initially 1000 yards wide increasing to 1800 yards as the successive objectives were achieved.

As mentioned, the position of the attacking battalions of 149 Brigade was ominous: earlier fighting had left a dogleg in the front, thus their position was 300 yards ahead of the 47th Division position (to the east). If for any reason the 47th Division's attack was held up, then the attacking Fusiliers would be exposed to murderous enfilading fire from the corner of High Wood, which would rake the ground between the wood and Martinpuich.

1/7 Battalion

On the left at 0620hrs the 1/7 NF attack got underway behind their creeping barrage; the companies swept forward in their four lines over the slightly rising ground which hid Hook Trench, their first objective. They took this without much difficulty, although with some casualties. Initially the two companies in the centre were held up by machine guns until these were taken out by the flanking companies. The plan required that the battalion would rest for ten minutes in Hook Trench, reorganising and fortifying the position, and then advance to the next objective in conformity with the barrage timetable. However, by this stage the attack uphill had had a disastrous effect on the formation of the attack. Companies and platoons were hopelessly intermixed. Nevertheless, the battalion was in contact on its left flank with 1/4 Battalion East Yorkshire Regiment, 150 Brigade, and on its right flank with its sister battalion, the 1/4 NF.

After the consolidation of Hook Trench, at 0718hrs, four lines of Fusiliers moved towards the second objective: Martin Trench. At this time the artillery barrages of both sides were in full destructive swing. One of the Company Commanders wrote:

> *The result was disconcerting in more ways than one. The ground was dry and had been pulverised by previous bombardments so that a cloud of dust and smoke like a London fog now appeared and hid all landmarks.*[6]

As the men advanced they lost direction and cohesion, and after advancing a few hundred yards it was decided to halt and assess the position: the two-remaining company commanders, Ball and Clennell, spread their map and used a compass to try and divine the direction of the sunken road and Martin Trench. They gathered up around forty men and resumed the advance, with Ball, who was on the left flank eventually spotting the trench – by luck it seems – only to be wounded in the ankle seconds later. Although tired by now, the men occupied the sunken road with considerable élan.

> *It is amusing now to recollect how the men rushed to the edge of the cutting, and then lost their balance and fell headlong down the steep sides, clinging on to and carrying down with them the amazed German garrison. We dealt with those of them that wished to resist, and accepted souvenirs from the rest, and started the business of consolidation in earnest.*[7]

Patrols were now sent out to left and right but were unable to get in touch with anyone. Following up, Captain Thomas (Trench Mortar Battery) arrived and set up his Stokes Mortar so as to cover Pioneer Alley, promising to annihilate any Germans who ventured down. Captain Fenwicke Clennell, at great personal danger, rescued the wounded Captain Ball. Using the cover of the smoke and dust fog, small fire trenches were rapidly dug on ground which was slightly higher than the top of the road.

At this point the prisoners were more numerous than the defenders and were sent back with 7/3584 Private John Martin, a diminutive – but astute – signaller:

He caused much consternation among his flock by deftly severing their trouser buttons before the journey began. It made an imposing procession – the prisoners with their hands deep in their trouser pockets, followed by Private Martin smoking an enormous souvenir cigar and mumbling, 'Ha way, you blinking buggers' … By this time the artillery fire had abated and the smoke and dust were rapidly clearing. An almost oppressive silence followed. The men rested, smoking cigars and eating 'Hindenburger Kake'. To the rear nothing could be seen, for it was rising ground. To the flanks, as far as we could see, the battalion had the world to themselves. In front, Starfish Line, Eaucourt L'Abbaye, Hexham Road and the Butte de Warlencourt looked peaceful and pleasant in the sunshine.[8]

Second Lieutenant Arnold Stroud
1/7 Northumberland Fusiliers

Arnold was the son of Mr J. G. Stroud and was educated at Tynemouth High School. At the onset of war, he was employed in the offices of the Liverpool, London and Globe Insurance Company in Newcastle. When the war began Arnold joined Durham University OTC and gained a commission in December 1915. He had only been at the front for a month before he was killed on 15 September 1916, aged 20. Arnold is commemorated on the Thiepval Memorial to the Missing.

Second Lieutenant John Ivor Grey
1/7 Northumberland Fusiliers

John was the son of John and Sarah Ann Grey of Acklington, Northumberland. He was educated at Morpeth Grammar School between 1906 and 1911. At the beginning of the war he was serving his apprenticeship as a mining engineer. He joined the 1/7 (Reserve) Battalion in August 1915 and embarked for the Western Front early in May 1916. He was killed on 15 September 1916, aged 21, and is buried in Bazentin-le-Petit communal cemetery extension.

By this time, it was realised that, on the right, the 47th Division's assault on High Wood had been held up, and the attack began to falter as the Germans raked heavy machine gun fire across the rows of advancing troops. Even those who managed to approach Martin Trench were held up by their own barrage. Several attempts were made to move forward but at this stage the battalion had lost a lot of men to artillery fire. Further ground was nonetheless won and eventually the remnants of the battalion moved forward to a sunken road, south of Bow Trench; under the command of Captain V. Merivale they were able to consolidate this position. Casualties were: Officers: 4 killed, 7 wounded. For Captain John William Meriville, see Chapter 13, *Aftermath*. Other Ranks: 40 killed, 219 wounded and 74 missing. See Appendix B for details. Amongst the other ranks killed were eighteen men whose names are found on the Ashington War memorial, including 7/2556 Corporal Ralph

Craze, aged 20 and 290805 Lance-Corporal Edward Chesterton, also aged 20. Edward Chesterton's number is distinguishable as resulting from the renumbering scheme of 1917. An explanation as to why he was renumbered is that by 1915, and throughout the remainder of the War, a man who went missing in action wasn't actually declared 'dead' until all avenues of enquiry through the Red Cross were exhausted; he would remain officially 'alive' until proved otherwise. A man would not officially be declared dead until at least six months had passed since his last known sighting – in this case 1917, by which time he had been renumbered.

1/4 Battalion

On the right, the position for the 1/4 was a difficult one. As mentioned, earlier fighting had left a dogleg in the front line. The 1/4 Battalion's position was 300 yards ahead of the battalion on their right flank (141 Brigade, 47th Division). If for any reason 141 Brigade were to be delayed in their advance, then the Northumberland Fusiliers would be exposed to enfilading fire from German strongpoints on the northwest corner of High Wood.

At 0620hrs the troops left the assembly trench to advance on their first objective, Hook Trench. By this time the Germans had observed two tanks on the extreme left of the brigade's front and as a consequence had opened up with a barrage just in front of their own front line, just seconds before the Fusiliers were due to advance. Just after 0700hrs a message was received from Captain Plummer, 'B' Company (Captain Lionel Davey Plummer was to die this day) on the left of the battalion's front that his men had captured Hook Trench with a minimum of opposition and that he was in touch to his right with Captain Henry Hogarth Bell of 'D' Company and also on his left with the 1/7. By now, wounded men were struggling back from the action.

Within twenty minutes the advance to the second objective was underway following a creeping barrage moving at 50 yards per minute. As the men left Hook trench it was occupied by a company of the 1/6 under Captain Trevor Carlyon Tweedy (who was killed during the fighting). A further company under Captain Cooke failed to make it.

LOCAL TERRITORIAL FORCE LOSSES:
MEN OF VALOUR IN ACTION AND PATIENCE IN SUFFERING

4/3447
Pte James Braddock

4/2104
Cpl Joseph D Cleugh

4/1821
LCpl M Martinson

200856
Pte Frederick Beattie

201038
Pte Edward T Bennett

4/3024
Pte Thomas Banton

7/3289
Pte Peter Stacey

4/2065
Pte George T Cockbain

4/1860
LSgt James W Cocker

4/4179
Pte John L Hart

7/2562
Pte George Edwards

4/1808
Pte Edwin Armstrong

5/7183
Pte W Errington

4/1000
LCpl Thomas Wilkinson

290713
Pte Thomas Vosper

4/2936
LCpl John A Jamieson

LOCAL TERRITORIAL FORCE LOSSES:
MEN OF VALOUR IN ACTION AND PATIENCE IN SUFFERING

4/1041
Pte William Irwin

4/3367
Pte John G Purvis

4/1724
Pte A Rutherford

6/1845
Pte Stanley Gray

4/2148
Cpl Robert Armstrong

7/3755
Pte Alfred Chisam

7/2051
Cpl Frank L Pringle

4/2235
Pte John W Thompson

4/909
Pte John E Newton

7/1502
Pte William Dumble

7/1207
Cpl Thomas O Austin

7/2072
Pte William Wilson

4/3311
Pte James Lisle

4/2273
Pte Alfred A Dodd

7/2348
Pte Robert Turner

7/3775
Pte Robert S Johnson

By 0743hrs it was known that the attack on High Wood had been held up, so 141 Brigade's reserve battalions were sent up to lend their weight to their attack because the right flank of 'C' Company (Captain Cheesmond) was severely exposed. In fact, the whole of 149 Brigade's attack was easily visible and was subjected to intense enfilading fire. To rectify this, elements of 141 Brigade tried to work their way along the western edge of High Wood; the 1/4 Battalion were ordered to assist this move by giving Stokes mortar and Lewis gun fire from Bethel Sap, a trench running at right angles to the battalion's jumping off trench on their extreme right. With no men available, Colonel Bertrand Dees Gibson (Commanding Officer of the 1/4) was unable to form a defensive flank on the right of Hook Trench. Second Lieutenant Wilson reported that the top of Bethal Sap and the right of Hook Trench were being swept by murderous machine gun fire from High Wood. Shortly afterwards Captain Dunsford of the 1/6 placed his company at the disposal of Colonel Gibson for the purpose of securing the right flank. Later, at 0945hrs, orders were issued by the 50th Division that Hook Trench was to be consolidated and strengthened as far as the divisional boundary with the 47th Division. This involved the strengthening of Bethel Sap and the securing of the dangerous position on the open right flank. An attack on this position by German bombers was repulsed by machine gun and Lewis gun fire and trench mortars.

At 1035hrs a company of the 1/5 under Lieutenant Daglish arrived to garrison Clark's Trench. Half of these men were sent to Hook Trench to bomb around Hook to the right and make contact with Bethal Sap. About an hour later the artillery heavily bombarded the north-west corner of High Wood, and as the 47th Division pushed forward the enemy were forced to retire; as they withdrew they were caught by machine gun fire and over a hundred prisoners were taken. Returning wounded soldiers were able to provide news about the attack on the second and third objectives. For instance, they reported that all the officers of 'C' Company had been wounded and that the ongoing attack on the second objective was being led by a corporal. Earlier reports suggesting that this had been captured proved to be incorrect.

At 1530hrs, Colonel Gibson moved forward to Hook Trench – which had been damaged by German shells – where he found men from all four battalions sheltering. His first action was to forge a strong connection on his right with the 47th Division. By dusk he had established that there were about a hundred men from 1/7 Battalion in the sunken road in front of his position. At 1930hrs, 151 Brigade were brought in to the advance, passing through Hook Trench to attack the second and third objectives, of which very little was known.

Captain Henry Hogarth Bell
1/4 Northumberland Fusiliers

Henry, was born in Hexham, the eldest son of Major George Henry Hogarth and Mrs Katharine Daubeney (formerly Bell) He was educated at Seabank, Alnmouth and Charterhouse, Godalming, Surrey. On leaving school in 1913 he obtained a commission in the Northumberland Fusiliers (Territorial Force). He was connected to the firm of Henry Bell and Sons Ltd, who had extensive interests in the Hexham area. He went out to France with his battalion in April 1915 and was mentioned in dispatches by General French. Previously wounded twice, he was killed on 15 September 1916, aged 20. He is buried in Caterpillar Valley Cemetery, Longueval.

Lieutenant John Angus Bagnall
1/4 Northumberland Fusiliers

John was born in Riding Mill, Northumberland, the eldest son of the late John Siddaway Bagnall and Alice Bagnall. He was educated at Colchester, Corbridge and Lorretto, Edinburgh. At the onset of war, he enlisted as a private in the 1/4 Battalion, but in November 1914 he received a commission in the same battalion. He embarked for the Western Front in May 1915. During the fighting on 15 September 1916, he was twice wounded before reaching the German line, but he gallantly went on and cleared the trench with a bayonet. While there he saw an officer lying wounded outside the trench. Although injured himself, he and another went out under heavy fire to bring in the wounded man. At this point he was hit again and was killed, aged 20. John is buried in Adanac Military Cemetery.

The Starfish Line (second objective) was taken by 0445hrs on 16 September, but the attack on the third objective (Prue Trench) failed.

During the afternoon of 16 September, the men of 149 Brigade were placed in Divisional Reserve and gradually the remnants of the battalions were withdrawn to Mametz Wood. The casualties for the brigade had been truly calamitous: there is scarcely a war memorial in Northumberland that does not contain the name of at least one Fusilier killed during this horrific battle. The 1/4 Battalion went into action with 22 Officers and 695 Other Ranks. Casualties were: Officers: 10 killed, 8 wounded: Other Ranks: 110 killed, 229 wounded and 143 missing. See Appendix B for details.

One of those killed was 4/20 Lance Sergeant Richard Brooks, aged 29, of Hexham, a married man with two children. Writing to Mrs Elizabeth Brooks, Captain Foster said:

> *The death of your husband is a great loss to his company. One of the best NCOs and one of the finest of my men … It was the NCOs on that memorable day that enabled the men to do their task, for when the officers fell early in the battle the NCOs carried on magnificently and ultimately gained their objectives.*[9]

Also killed were the Newton brothers – both privates – from Hexham: 7/909 John Edward, aged 21, and 7/3318 Ralph, aged 19, of Prior Terrace; they were two of four brothers who served (see Chapter 13, *Aftermath*). The Hexham War Memorial has the names of eighteen men killed during this momentous struggle. Further afield, on the Memorials of the North Tyne Valley, a further eighteen names are inscribed.   One of these is 7/2262 Private Alexander Hutton, aged 22 of Bellingham. Alexander Hutton is reported by the CWGC, inexplicably, as having died on 1 October 1916. In a letter to his mother, Captain Robert Allen, of the 1/4 wrote:

> *I am very sorry indeed to have to inform you that your son was missing after the action of September 15th when the battalion had so many casualties …*
> *I am afraid there is very little doubt that he was killed as the battalion have had no information of any prisoners being taken and the shell fire on the day was terrific. All the ground was searched on the 16th and 17th and all*

wounded brought in. I knew your son well and he was highly respected by all officers and men and will be a great miss to his company. I am afraid this is a very sad war and there are very few of the North Tyne lads left.[10]

IN LOVING MEMORY OF

ROBERT,

SECOND AND DEARLY BELOVED SON OF ROBERT AND ELIZABETH ARMSTRONG, THE OFFICE, WHITFIELD, LATE OF PARK END, WARK-ON-TYNE,

CORPL. 4TH N.F.,

Who was killed in the battle of the Somme, in France, on 15th September, 1916.

BORN 7TH MARCH, 1894; IN HIS 23RD YEAR.

" Greater Love hath no man than this : That a man lay down his life for his friends."

" Till the day breaks and the shadows flee away."

Death Card of 4/2148 Corporal Robert Armstrong
Author's Collection

Casualties for the other two battalions of 149 Brigade on 15 September were:

1/5 Battalion: Officers: 6 wounded; Other Ranks: 10 killed, 54 wounded and 8 missing.

1/6 Battalion: Officers: 1 killed, 8 wounded; Other Ranks: 279 casualties. For details see Appendix B. Many of those reported as missing would eventually be designated killed in action.

In the days that followed all the battalions provided working parties, their principal, mournful task being to bring in the dead and wounded from the battlefield. During the night of 21 September, 149 Brigade replaced 151 Brigade at the front again. Orders were received to attack the Starfish and Prue lines. However, by this time the enemy had retired and, thankfully, the assault was practically bloodless; a few casualties were caused by shell fire. The 1/4 and 1/5 occupied the Star Fish and Prue lines with 1/6 and 1/7 on their left; they established contact on both flanks. Thus, after a week of atrocious fighting they had reached the final objective of 15 September: Prue Trench.

The official despatches stated:

> *The result of the fighting of the 15 September and the following days was a gain more considerable than any which had attended our arms in the course of a single operation since the commencement of the offensive, and the 50th Division contributed its full share to its success.*[11]

Thus, by the evening of 22 September the men of 149 Brigade were holding the front line. Patrols ventured out towards Eaucourt l'Abbaye and established a line of posts 300 to 400 yards in front of Prue Trench.

Le Sars, October 1916
Author's Collection

By the end of September, the Allies had captured the high ground from Morval to Thiepval. The furthest advance into German territory was Gueudecourt, captured during the evening of 26 September. Nevertheless, north east of Martinpuich and Courcelette, the Flers Line – which ran in front of Eaucourt l'Abbaye and Le Sars – had still to be taken. On 29 September, the 23rd Division managed to capture Destremont Farm, south west of Le Sars. This was to provide great assistance for the attack on the Flers Line.

Four divisions were detailed to attack Eaucourt l'Abbaye along with the

German defences to the east and west of the village. Those chosen were from right to left, New Zealand, 47th, 50th and 23rd Divisions.

> *The 50th Division was well placed to carry out the attack though, as may be imagined, the infantry, after a fortnight of heavy fighting, were tired and badly needed a rest.*[12]

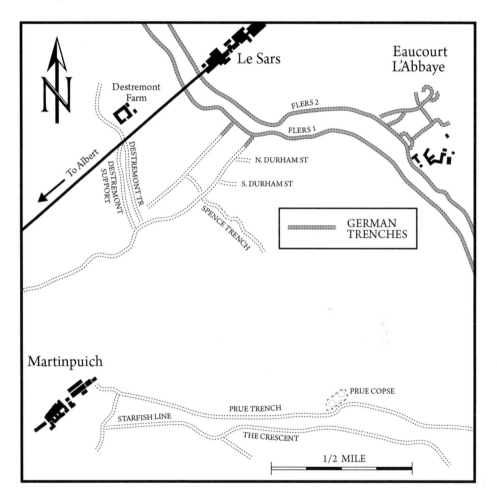

Attack on Eaucourt l'Abbaye, 1 October 1916

The attack was scheduled for 1 October, and was initially detailed to 151 Brigade, with 149 Brigade in support and 150 Brigade in reserve. However, early on 1 October the plan for the attack was modified. The original plan required that 151 Brigade would use its 1/6 Battalion DLI on the right, with 1/5 Battalion Border Regiment in the centre and 1/8 Battalion DLI on the left, with the 1/9 Battalion DLI in reserve. The reason for the change in plan was that it had become clear that two of these battalions (the centre and on the right) were low in numbers; because of this they were ordered to form up as a composite battalion. At this point two battalions from 149 Brigade were attached to 151 Brigade. One was the 1/5, ordered to attack on the left with the 1/4 in close support. The 1/7 were also in support of the attack on Le Sars. 7/7137 Private Gladden reminisced:

The enemy was to be taken by surprise. Guns continued to fire desultorily from both sides. Shells burst here and there but none near our trench. The old hands warned us about complacency. We were in support, to be sent for and used wherever needed, and the enemy could be expected to do all he could to prevent our taking a hand. Our static position was among the least enviable in an action of this sort. The logic of this discouraging advice was not lost upon us. We waited! [13]

During 30 September and the night of 30 September/1 October, the Divisional Artillery bombarded the enemy's front line and communication trenches. In retaliation, the German artillery fire was particularly heavy, especially between 1600hrs and 1900hrs on 30 September, after which it became intermittent. During the night, pioneers and infantry dug the jumping off trenches – North Durham and South Durham, Blaydon Trench and Rutherford Alley. Dumps of bombs, ammunition and water were built up.

Final orders required the attack to begin at 1515hrs with the infantry to attack in four waves. At zero hour, the advance began in impeccable order following a creeping barrage which was described as a perfect wave without any gaps. This was observed by an aviator:

At 3.15pm the steady bombardment changed into a most magnificent barrage. The timing of this was extremely good. Guns opened simultaneously and the effect was that many machine guns opened fire on the same order. As seen from the air the barrage appeared to be a most perfect wall of fire, in which it was inconceivable that anything could live. The first troops to extend from the forming up places appeared to be the 50th Division, who were seen to spread out from the sap heads and forming up trenches and advance close up under the barrage, apparently some fifty yards away from it. They appeared to capture their objective very rapidly and with practically no losses while crossing the open.[14]

At zero hour the 1/5 advanced on the left of the brigade front, obscured by the dense smoke of bursting shells as they disappeared over a slight ridge. Although the enemy artillery had retaliated promptly, nevertheless the attacking troops managed to pass through the barrage zone. By 1600hrs the front-line companies had reported the capture of the Second Flers Line, and had set about consolidating their gain against counterattack. Patrols were sent out towards a maze of trenches known as The Tangle, about 250 yards north of Flers Support, which an intelligence report had claimed were unoccupied. They soon found that this was not the case – their advance was met with swathes of bullets from enemy machine guns, and since the right flank of the attack was in the air, no advance was considered. On the right, the 1/6 DLI had met with stiffer resistance and had to be supported by the 1/9 DLI. It was during this assault that their commanding officer, Lieutenant Colonel Roland Boys Bradford, won his Victoria Cross.

Although the 1/4 were in support of the advance made by the 1/5 Battalion, there is no information in their War Diary on how they fared. During the night of 1/2 October, the 1/4 Battalion supplied carrying parties; during the same night the 1/7 Battalion moved up to Flers Switch and Spence Trench. Casualties for the 1/5 Battalion from noon 1 October to noon 3 October were: Officers: 2 wounded; Other Ranks: 2 killed, 73 wounded and 3 missing. Lieutenant Denys Armstrong died of his wounds on 3 October.

During the morning of 2 October, it began to rain again, with a number of heavy downpours throughout the rest of the day and into the next. Several of the freshly-dug trenches had no duckboards, so that men in those that had been hammered by artillery of both sides were soon floundering in thick, clinging mud which eventually became a soupy liquid. In these horrible conditions the 149 Brigade infantry, already exhausted, relieved the infantry of 151 Brigade. The 1/7 Battalion relieved the 1/6 and 1/9 DLI in the Flers Line; two companies to hold the front-line and two companies the support line. Second Lieutenant Albert Grey Straker was killed during the relief.

Second Lieutenant Albert Gray Straker

1/7 Northumberland Fusiliers

Albert was born in Blyth, Northumberland, the eldest son of William Potts and Ann Isabella Straker. He was educated at Blyth Secondary School and St Paul's, Cheltenham, and worked as a teacher in Blyth. He joined the Durham University OTC in May 1915 and was gazetted to the Northumberland Fusiliers in August 1915. He embarked for the Western Front in May 1916 and was killed, aged 23, on 3 October 1916, while holding the newly captured line between and in front of Le Sars and Eaucourt l'Abbaye. He was buried where he died and is commemorated on the Thiepval Memorial to the Missing. His colonel wrote, 'Albert was a willing and good officer and he worthily maintained the reputation of the battalion. I deeply deplore his loss.'

At daybreak on 3 October, a party of fourteen Germans approached the 1/7 Battalion's block on its right flank and surrendered to the bombers holding the post. The reason for their surrender? A desperate shortage of water. Further prisoners dribbled in during the day, eventually reaching thirty-eight in total. During the same morning, the 1/6 took over the line held by its sister battalion, 1/5 NF. The War Diary of the 1/5 reported:

Mercifully there was a thick mist which enabled them (companies) to get out without being seen, though the last company had a machine gun turned on it coming down Twenty-Sixth Avenue.[15]

The 1/4 Battalion took over the line held by the 1/8 DLI and 1/5 Borders. All of these changes took place in unrelenting rain and viscid mud underfoot. Men in the carrying parties were exhausted, delaying the relief till the middle of the morning. During the night of 3/4 October, the 23rd Division took over the front from the 50th Division. The men of 149 Brigade moved first back to Mametz Wood and later that day they marched to Albert, thence to Millencourt.

On returning from the front, General P. S. Wilkinson issued the following Order of the Day to his officers and men:

Nobody could be prouder than I at commanding such troops as you, the 50th Division. Within days of landing in this country you made a name for yourselves at the Second Battle of Ypres. Since that battle you have gained a great reputation on account of your magnificent defence of a portion of the Ypres Salient during the worst months of the year.

From the 15 September to the 3 October you have had another chance of showing your qualities in attack, and it is not too much to say that no division in the British Army has done or could do better. You have advanced nearly two miles and have taken seven lines of German trenches. Your gallantry and determination on every occasion since you joined in the Battle of the Somme have been worthy of the highest traditions of the British Army. I deplore with you the loss of many of our intimate friends and comrades. I thank you all for the excellent and cheerful way in which you have undertaken every task put to you.[16]

At Millencourt, all four battalions of 149 Brigade carried out refitting and reorganisation, then benefitted from a period of training interspersed with recreation and relaxation – for both the body and the mind. By the middle of October, the brigade was providing large numbers of men for working parties. For instance, on 16 October, the 1/4 Battalion moved forward to Mametz Wood (where they were accommodated in tents), supplying 500 men to work on the roads in the area under the direction of the Royal Engineers.

On 26 October, 149 Brigade was ordered to relieve 26 Infantry Brigade (9th Division). Dispositions for this relief were: 1/6 in the front line; 1/4 in support in Flers line; 1/7 in reserve in the vicinity of High Wood and 1/5 in reserve in the area of Bazentin-le-Grand. Enemy artillery was continuing to shell the front area, especially south of Eaucourt l'Abbaye. That same day, 149 Brigade received orders that an attack on enemy positions was scheduled for 28 October; this was later postponed until 30 October, and subsequently to 1 November. Nevertheless, the continuing relief of the battalions in the front-line continued, with the 1/4 replacing the 1/6 and the 1/7 moving forward to take up a position in the Flers Line. The enemy was shelling the area relentlessly. Although they made no assaults at the time, the casualty figures of 149 Brigade for the period 24 to 31 October illustrate the inexorable daily attrition faced by these units:

1/4 Battalion: Officers: 1 wounded; Other Ranks: 16 killed, 26 wounded and 3 missing. **1/5 Battalion:** Officers: 2 wounded; Other Ranks: 4 killed, 20 wounded and 2 missing. **1/6 Battalion:** Officers: 1 wounded; Other Ranks: 6 killed and 16 wounded. **1/7 Battalion:** Other Ranks: 8 wounded. These figures don't include those lost to sickness.

The Butte de Warlencourt overlooking the Somme Battlefield
Author's Collection

The attack proposed for 1 November was to be led by 149 Brigade, but because of the atrocious state of the battlefield it was delayed once again. The aim of this attack was to capture Gird and Gird Support Trenches, the Butte de Warlencourt and a quarry west of the Butte. Not surprisingly, the front line had become a hellish quagmire so thick and deep that any attack seemed impossible. Nevertheless the attack against the Butte de Warlencourt, an ancient burial-mound off the Albert–Bapaume road, north-east of Le Sars, was again scheduled for the morning of 5 November at 0910hrs. The Germans had constructed deep dugouts throughout the Butte and surrounded it by trenches and several belts of barbed wire, making it a formidable defensive position, *Gallwitz Riegel* (known to the British as the Gird Trenches). After the *Battle of Flers-Courcelette* (15–22 September) the view from the Butte dominated the new British front line and provided the Germans with very effective artillery observation.

As both 149 and 150 Brigades had been in the front line since 28 October they were exhausted; the attack would be carried out by 151 Brigade, consisting of Territorial Battalions from County Durham. During the night of 3/4 November, the latter brigade relieved 149 Brigade, who moved back into close support on the right flank. Operation orders for the attack stated that it was to be made by three battalions of 151 Brigade supported by the 1/4 and 1/6.

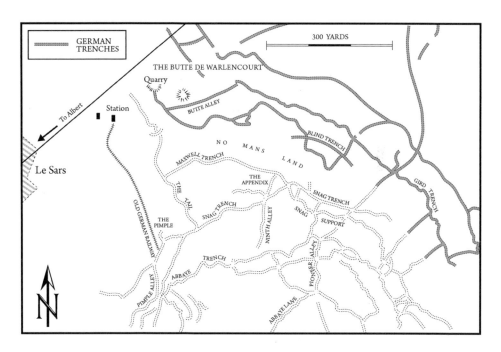

The 149 Brigade's Front, November 1916.

The mud, rendered even worse by overnight rain and thigh deep in places, was a formidable problem for the attacking troops. At zero hour the infantry scrambled their way out of their trenches, the first men out pulling up the men behind over the parapet to follow the creeping barrage. As the attack progressed a moderate German counterbarrage fell short of Snag Trench, but massed machine-gun fire began sweeping in from the flanks, taking many casualties as the British troops struggled through the mire at a walking-pace. Despite all of this they gained a number of their objectives, but during the afternoon the Germans retaliated strongly. They counterattacked the captured Gird Trenches and the Butte, and by 1500hrs the British had been forced out of Gird Trenches. Worse, during the next day the enemy continued their counteraction, and by 1300hrs had driven the remaining British troops back to their start line in Snag, Maxwell and Tail Trenches.

Another attack was ordered … but it was cancelled. The assault had cost the lives of 967 men. Although reinforcements had been in place and desperately needed, it had been impossible for the two battalions of 149 Brigade to move forward during the day as they were under a heavy, accurate curtain of fire that fell on the communication trenches and the whole of the forward area.

By 8 November the rain had at last eased off, and on 12 November, the Fourth Army Headquarters ordered a local attack by I Anzac Corps and III Corps on either side of the Eaucourt l'Abbaye-Le Barque road towards Gird Trench and Hook Sap. Hook connected the Gird Trenches with Butte Trench and formed a salient from which all of the ground opposite the 50th Division could be swept by cross-fire. This was just days before General Wilkinson (50th Division) was to hand over responsibility for his sector to the 1st and 48th Divisions. Since the attack of early November, the enemy had reinforced Butte Trench which ran from the quarry in front of the Butte in an irregular line to Hook Sap. The Sap, jutting into No Man's Land, was also strongly manned. Further, between the apex of the Sap and Gird Trench, the enemy had dug another trench parallel and in front of Gird Trench known as Blind Trench. Put simply, the front faced by the 50th Division was one from which it was possible for the enemy to send enfilading fire, from any point, against any attack from the British trenches.

Operation orders for an attack on Gird, Gird Support Trenches and Hook

Sap were issued by 149 Brigade HQ on 13 November. The 1/5 Battalion was to attack up to Hook Sap on the right and the 1/7 Battalion on the left flank was to capture Hook Sap, Gird Trench and Blind Trench. At the same time an Australian battalion would be advancing further to the right. There was no plan to attack the Butte. Meanwhile, the 1/4 Battalion was to be in support with two companies in Hexham Road and with two companies of the 5 Battalion Green Howards in the Flers Line; the 1/6 Battalion was to hold the front line from the left of the 1/7 Battalion to the brigade boundary on the left and support the attack with Lewis gun and rifle fire.

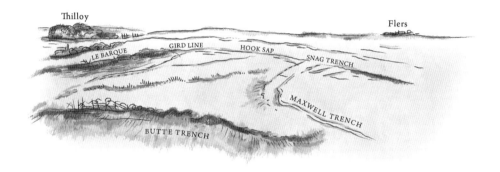

Scene of the attack on Hook Sap, November 1916, from the Butte de Warlencourt
Chloe Rodham

During the night of 13 November, the men of the attacking battalions assembled in Abbaye, Snag and Snag Support trenches. However, by this time torrential rain was again falling, reducing every trench to a morass. Buckley wrote:

Mud was everywhere, in parts up to the waist, and what was worse, the thicker, more tenacious kind that just covered the boots and clung in heavy masses. The exertion of forcing our way step by step in an already heavily burdened state during our various moves about this line remains in my mind as some of the most strenuous and exhausting times of the whole war.[17]

Dispositions for the attack at 0645hrs were: 1/5 Battalion: 'B' and 'D' Companies which formed the first two waves were in New Support Trench, 'A' and 'C' Companies were in Abbaye Trench; 'C' Company would form the third wave of the attack, whilst 'A' Company would occupy Snag and Snag Support Trenches. For the 1/7 'A' and 'B' Companies occupied Snag Trench with 'D' and 'C' in Abbaye; 'D' would occupy Snag when it was vacated by 'A' and 'B' Companies. The specific role for 'C' Company was for half of them to follow the attack of 'A' and 'B' to the final objective with water and bombs, whilst the other half remained in support.

> *This half company, I well remember, was inclined to congratulate themselves on their simple duties, but they poor chaps, had not reckoned with the intensity of the Boche barrage.*[18]

As dawn rose the Butte became visible to the left, followed by the British barrage which began at 0645hrs. In response, the sky 'was filled with pencils of golden rain' as all along the front the enemy fired Verey lights as an SOS. Coming to their aid, enemy machine guns opened fire from all directions followed by an intense, thunderous barrage.

> *An officer who was in the trenches south west of the Butte and saw the Northumberlands go forward, told me that he had never seen such a strange sight. The men struggled forward a few yards, tumbled into shell holes or stopped to pull out less fortunate comrades, forward a few more yards, and the same again and again. All the while the machine guns from the German trenches poured a pitiless hail into the slowly advancing line.*[19]

1/5 Battalion

Into this maelstrom, the men of the 1/5 left the relative cover of the trenches and advanced. As in many attacks of the Great War, keeping track of their progress was dangerous and unreliable; no telephonic communications were available so officers had to rely on runners carrying messages. On this day, by 0800hrs a message was received from Captain Gill ('D' Company on the right, who had been wounded) that his men had reached Gird Trench with only a few casualties. This was followed by news from 'C' Company that they, too, had gained their objective but that all of their officers were down. At 1000hrs, wounded men returning from 'B' Company reported that their company had reached its objective. This was followed by news from Captain Easton of 'A' Company: some of his men had reached Butte Trench. It appears that men from the 1/5 had joined up with Australian troops but the conditions were so grim that they were compelled to retire to Gird Trench, to consolidate a line for 500 yards astride the Eaucourt l'Abbaye–Le Barque road. It was not until late afternoon that more definitive news arrived: Second Lieutenant Armstrong, now in command of 'D' Company, sent word that about 150 men from 'B', 'C' and 'D' Companies werre holding roughly 100 yards of Gird Trench and had established a strong point.

1/7 Battalion

On the left it appears that the 1/7 Battalion also made progress. The War Diary reports that five minutes before zero hour the enemy opened intermittent rifle fire on their right, which may indicate that they had detected movement. Nonetheless at zero (0645hrs) the troops attacked punctually with the fourth wave encountering the enemy barrage before they reached Snag Trench. This barrage fell upon the first three waves of the attack as they left Snag Trench causing a number of casualties. Even so, and in spite of the clinging mire and falling comrades, they pushed on and were lost in the mist. An hour later, the wounded were staggering back, reporting that the attack had reached the enemy trenches. Slowly the mist dissipated and at 0900hrs Second Lieutenant Woods (of 'D' Company, who at that moment were holding Snag Trench, the front line) reported that he could see men from the battalion consolidating Hook Sap.

At about this time, Sergeant Dryden, who had been wounded, reported that his company had captured Hook Trench (it is now believed that this was actually Blind Trench). He went on to say that he had seen men on the left establish a post (No. 6); he also reported that Second Lieutenant Lawson had been killed as he led his men towards Gird Trench. Later, Captain Morris sent word that a wounded man had reported that his machine gun was in position at Post 7 and was still in action. Later still, it became clear that hand to hand fighting was in progress on the left. Men from 'D' Company, 1/4, began furiously to dig a new sap from Snag Trench to Hook Sap, but this work was halted at 1130hrs by vicious enemy machine-gun fire. By this time the 1/7 (on their left) had beaten off a counterattack. During the afternoon, the enemy continued to fight back so tenaciously that the positions held by the 1/7 were eventually overwhelmed, including Hook Sap. Communication between the attacking companies and headquarters was limited as it was well-nigh impossible for runners to pass between Snag Trench and Hook Sap without being taken out by murderous machine-gun fire or sniping. Hanging mist obscured the field and limited any observation. At 2300hrs there was an enemy offensive on both flanks by the three battalions of Guard Grenadier Regiment 5 and their Divisional Storm Company. During the night, an attempt was made to dig a communications trench from Pioneer Alley to the Hook but this was thwarted when the diggers were bombed from the apex of the Hook – indicating that the Germans had recaptured their end of the Hook.

By 2300hrs, Lieutenant Colonels N. I. Wright (1/5) and B. D. Gibson (1/4) had moved forward into Snag Trench. Their aim was to organise men for a fresh attack. For this they had available what remained of one company of the 1/7 and one of the 1/4 on the left, and a further company of the 1/4 and the remnants of 'A' Company 1/7 Battalion; all told about thirty men. Minutes after midnight (on 15 November) three bombing patrols set out, two to the left of Pioneer Alley and one to the right. Unfortunately, these patrols were spotted and subjected to heavy machine-gun and rifle fire, so were forced to return. The enemy opened up a heavy barrage. It was now evident that the Germans were holding Hook Sap – and with considerable strength.

The War Diary of 1/5 Battalion recorded:

> *The enemy are holding Blind Trenches and they somehow got in between us and our men, who must be in Gird Trench.*[20]

As the brigade's precarious position began to unfold, Snag Trench was consolidated for defence. All that morning the Germans shelled Snag Trench and Snag Support heavily. Both were extensively damaged. At noon, word was received from Second Lieutenant Armstrong that his position would soon be threatened from the left and the right and that he was short of bombs and ammunition. The 5 Battalion Green Howards supplied a carrying party of thirty-five men to try and rectify this. In the middle of the afternoon it was established that Armstrong and his men, including some from 1/7 Battalion, were still holding the Gird Line. Interestingly, the War Diary of the 1/7 Battalion records that the details of Armstrong's position were carried by a pigeon. That evening the positions in Snag Trench held by 1/5 and 1/7 Battalions were relieved by 1/4 Battalion East Yorkshire Regiment. Both battalions retired to the Flers Line where the 1/5 Battalion reported a roll call of 7 officers and 270 other ranks. Later, the East Yorks sent out two companies to take over Armstrong's position in the Gird Line which was completed by 1500hrs (16 November).

Throughout 17 November the Germans bombarded the front line and Hexham Road, intensifying just before 1700hrs when they attacked the East Yorks in the Gird Line from a number of directions: frontal, the north, along the trench from the west and (as the Australians had already fallen back in the face of a heavy attack) from the north east. As a result of losing their position in Gird Line, the 50th Division and the 2nd Australian Division were back where they started, in their original jumping-off trenches.

> *The only consolation that can be drawn from this heroic but tragic affair is that it may have created a diversion to our successful operations at Beaucourt. As an isolated operation, it was doomed from the start owing to the state of the ground and the exhaustion of the men who took part in it.*[21]

On the night of 17/18 November the remnants of 149 Brigade were relieved by elements from the 1st Division. By the morning of 20 November, the 50th Division was in III Corps Reserve around Albert, with 149 Brigade based in the town.

Casualties from the operations from 14 to 16 November 1916 were as follows: **1/5 Battalion:** Officers: 3 killed and 5 wounded; Other Ranks: 33 killed, 144 wounded and 85 missing. **1/7 Battalion:** Officers: 5 killed 7 wounded and 1 missing; Other Ranks: 19 killed, 95 wounded and 104 missing. **1/6 Battalion:** The severity of the German barrage (its accuracy having been helped by the German observers on the commanding height of the Butte de Warlencourt as an observation point) is demonstrated by the casualties taken by the 1/6

Battalion, whose role was to assist the attack with Lewis gun and rifle fire from the front line: Officers: 2 killed and 1 wounded; Other Ranks: 9 killed and 112 wounded. And the **1/4 Battalion:** Other Ranks: 16 killed, 56 wounded and 10 missing. For details see Appendix C.   To be accurate, one should note that the **1/4 Battalion East Yorkshire Regiment** attached to 149 Brigade suffered casualties, too. Officers: 1 wounded; Other Ranks: 37 wounded and 27 missing.

Second Lieutenant Thomas Nelson Melrose
1/5 Northumberland Fusiliers

Thomas was born at North Shields, the son of Thomas and Agnes Melrose. He was educated at Tynemouth Municipal High School. At the onset of war he was employed by Lloyds Bank in Wallsend, and he enlisted immediately. He was gazetted Second Lieutenant in March 1915 and embarked for the Western Front in June 1915. Thomas was killed on 14 November 1916, aged 23, and is commemorated on the Thiepval Memorial to the Missing

Second Lieutenant Dominic Roe Dathy O'Daly
1/7 Northumberland Fusiliers

Dominic was the son of Dominic and Harriet Elizabeth O'Daly, of Exmouth, Devon. He was educated at Handsworth Grammar and at Exeter College, Oxford, from where he was granted a degree in absence a few days before he was killed. He was a member of both Handsworth's and Oxford University's OTC. He obtained his commission in the 2/7 Northumberland Fusiliers in August 1915 and joined the 1/7 Northumberland Fusiliers in August 1916. Days before he left for France, Dominic married Eleanor Mary Nicholson, from Newbiggin-by-the-Sea. He was killed by a bomb, aged 21, on 14 November 1916, whilst leading his men in an attack across No Man's Land. His widow died on Boxing Day 1919 trying to rescue a dog that had strayed onto thin ice. Dominic is commemorated on the Thiepval Memorial to the Missing.

LOCAL TERRITORIAL FORCE LOSSES:
MEN OF VALOUR IN ACTION AND PATIENCE IN SUFFERING

5/2496
Sgt Archibald Buchanan

4/2786
Pte Harvey Mackey

290444
LCpl George G Shiell

290837
Pte Thomas Baron

240963
Pte George Hardy

292284
Pte Robert Gutherson

4/1618
Pte George W Boustead

240102
Pte George Gilbert

5/1642
Sgt Thomas Barras MM

242384
Pte Francis Young

5/6628
Pte Thomas Barker

290599
Pte George Avery

As winter descended on the Somme, 149 Brigade had seen its final involvement in the attacks of 1916. From its first outing on 15 September the brigade had advanced about three and a half miles through trench to trench fighting: no mean achievement, although all the battalions had suffered heavy casualties.

In Sir Douglas Haig's dispatches on 23 December 1916, he wrote:

The three main objects with which we had commenced our offensive in July have been achieved to date, at the date when this account closes: in spite of the fact that the heavy continuous rains had prevented full advantage being

167

taken of the favourable situation created by our advance, at a time when we had good grounds for hope to achieve yet more important successes. Verdun has been relieved; the main German forces have been held on the Western Front, and the enemy's strength has been considerably worn down. Any of these results is in itself sufficient to justify the Somme Battles. The attainment of all three of these affords ample compensation for the splendid efforts of all of our troops, and for the sacrifices made by our Allies.[22]

The terrain gained by the British had been achieved only at great sacrifice, and as the Allies bedded down against the gruelling winter, the Germans were busy. As the battle raged, German High Command ordered the development of a trench system at a significant distance behind the existing front: a heavily fortified defensive zone running from the Belgian coast to the Moselle. The Germans called this system the *Siegfriedstellung*, the Allies the Hindenburg Line; its most important section ran between Arras and St Quentin. The starting date for the retreat by the Germans was set for 16 December 1916 and was codenamed *Alberich*, after the malicious dwarf of the Wagnerian *Der Ring des Nibelungen*. The retreat was implemented in the light of the following order:

Der Gegner muss ein vollig ausgesogenes land vorfinden.

The essence of this? The entire zone between the old fighting line and the new was to be made into a desert.

This was all in the future; winter had now set in with bitter nights and frosty mornings. The men of 149 Brigade left the front on 19 November passing responsibility for its defence to 1 Infantry Brigade on the left sector and 145 Infantry Brigade on the right sector. Nobody was sad to see the back of the muddy and battered trenches, their communication trenches choked in places by rotting corpses. Further back they progressed by staggering and sliding over boggy ground, squelching through deep, cloying mud until they were out of range of the continuous fire of the enemy's field guns. With lightened hearts the men reached Albert, where the Brigade's Headquarters were set up at 88 Rue de Bapaume. After four days of bathing and refitting, working parties from the brigade set about clearing the rubble from the streets of Albert and helping at the local Royal Engineers' Depot.

On 1 December, 149 Brigade moved further east to a training area near Brestle. The 1/5 and 1/7 Battalions were billeted in huts, whilst – even in the depths of winter – the 1/4 and 1/6 Battalions were in tents. Here the battalions were trained in the handling of grenades. Even far away from the front, death lurked; whilst at the 4 Army Trench Mortar Training School at Vereaux en Amienois, 7/3391 Lance Corporal Robert Henry Duncan was accidently killed on 8 December 1916.

The Brigade kept Christmas Day in style: traditional turkey dinner, and the battalion's bands playing carols to keep the men's spirits up. Captain Hugh Liddell of 1/7 Battalion wrote on 24 December:

We are busy making the final preparations for our Christmas dinner. The men are going to get turkey, potatoes, vegetables, plum puddings, beer and a ration of rum; so, they will not do badly. I have been spending money like water these last few days as most of the business has been left in my hands. Sir Charles Milburn has sent £100, and there was a cheque from Lord Grey for £10 this morning. So, I think we shall manage all right. The Chaplain, Captain J.O. Aglionby and some men will go around the various billets singing carols.[23]

After this brief time of 'peace on earth', 149 Brigade received orders to return to the front on the night of 30/31 December, relieving 1 and 3 Infantry Brigades. In the following days, the battalions made their perilous way across the blighted landscape; Lieutenant Hugh Liddell of 1/7 Battalion wrote from near High Wood:

You cannot imagine what the country was like. Every square yard torn up by shell-fire. Not a house, and hardly a tree stump standing. When I say not a house, I mean there is not one brick standing where it was originally placed, as you can walk through the site of a village and never know it was there, except by the map. All the old Boche lines are covered with our camps, huts, etc. And we have railway trains running about where last summer the Boches used to roam.[24]

Dispositions for the relief were: the 1/5 replaced the 2 Battalion Manchester Regiment in the front line, right sector; the 1/4 replaced the 1 Battalion South Wales Borderers in support, right sector; the 1/7 Battalion replaced the 1 Battalion Cameron Highlanders in the front line, left sector, and the 1/6 replaced the 8 Battalion Berkshire Regiment in support, left sector. The weather on New Year's Day was described as 'damp and warm with showers of rain'.

> *The Germans opposite to our trenches were not disposed to be unfriendly about the New Year. On our left near the Butte they signalled to our men in the trenches before a trench-mortar bombardment started, as if to warn them to take cover. On the right, they were still more inclined to fraternize. Here both sides were holding trenches that would have become impossible if any sniping had been done. So, both our men and the Germans worked away at deepening their own trenches without molesting their opponents; although sometimes a crowd of men were exposed from the waist upwards at a range of about 200 yards.*[25]

This tacit, war-weary understanding – an example of trench war 'etiquette' that could and did arise when no battle was in progress – must have been welcomed on both sides. However, on New Year's Day events went further. A soldier from the 1/5 Battalion – after entreaties from the Germans – went out into No Man's Land and shared a drink with them. For this bravado he was later court-martialled for holding intercourse with the enemy. Throughout the day small parties of the enemy approached the British trenches, unarmed, but were warned off.

January 1917, and the days of the men of 149 Brigade were filled with patrol work, along with the maintenance of the front line when in the forward trenches, and the supply of working parties and training in the back areas. A number of Germans surrendered to the Fusiliers, including (on 17 January) a private from the 5th Guards Regiment.

Life in the trenches was taxing and unpleasant. An unknown officer in the Northumberland Fusiliers wrote in a letter dated 14 January 1917:

For an hour or two it was fine, but soon it began to rain and the water steadily rose. We couldn't make the pump work, and to make matters worse, I found a hole in my gum boot which rapidly filled with water. Fortunately, Fritz was in much the same plight and did not bother us. He was only about 200 yards away and almost any hour of the day we could see two or three of them standing about on the top. We did not snipe at them and they left us alone except to the extent of throwing some fish tail bombs near us, and we retaliated with rifle grenades. You have no idea of the state of the ground near these advanced posts. Wherever one looked, one saw the same endless extent of black mud and water, christened [sic] all over the place with the remains of old trenches and wherever one walked, one slipped or slithered about among the innumerable shell holes. Almost every day both British and Bosche lose their way and get into the enemy lines. Wandering about in the mud at night was rather an uncanny business as there were a great many dead bodies lying about, some already half sunk in the mud. The mud will have swallowed them all up before the winter is over.[26]

The same officer, in a later letter, recounted:

We found two men sitting in the mud four or five hundred yards from the ruins (Eaucourt l'Abbaye). Their gum boots had been sucked off by the mud, their feet had gone wrong and they were absolutely done to the world. They both went to hospital next day with trench feet.[27]

In early February, rumours were rife that the 50th Division was to move south to take over a portion of the French line. On the nights of 13/14 and 14/15 February, the division duly relieved the 35th and 36th Divisions in front of Belloy en Santerre and Bernary en Santerre to the south west of Péronne. Initially, 149 Brigade took up a position on the left with 150 Brigade on its right and 151 Brigade in reserve at Foucaucourt, with the 1/7 and 1/5 Battalions manning the front. The trenches were in a very poor state; some of the communication trenches were impassable. As soon as they arrived, work began to put this right. No infantry action took place while 149 Brigade were there, although both sides kept up intermittent artillery fire which occasionally led to fierce bombardments, the Germans employing a host of gas shells. As February progressed the frosty weather eased and once again the thawing trenches filled with mud. An officer with the 1/7 wrote:

> *We came out of the line last night. In the ordinary way we should have been relieved by 8pm. We left the trench at 3.30am (21 February) and it is now 2pm and I do not think we have got all the men out yet. You cannot imagine the mud. And no mother's son would recognise him. They are plastered from head to foot, and soaked through and through. There is such a maze of trenches about here (mile upon mile of them) that we are constantly losing people. They wander about for hours in the old disused trenches: and that is no joke with mud up to the knees and German shells chasing you all the time.*[28]

As the Germans were retreating to behind the Hindenburg Line, details of the brigade's next move emerged and on 5 March the 50th Division was relieved by the 59th Division, which was completed at 1000hrs on 9 March. The men of 149 Brigade took up position in the Warfusée area, where the various battalions focused on training in open warfare. By the end of the month the division was ordered to move up to the Arras region, where preparations were being carried out for the *Battle of Arras*, scheduled to open on 9 April. Accordingly, during the first week of April they moved forward until – on 8 April – they were positioned in the Avesnes area under orders to move forward at six hours' notice.

CHAPTER SEVEN

ARRAS SECTOR 1917

But with the best and meanest Englishmen
I am one in crying, God save England, lest
We lose what never slaves and cattle blessed.
The ages made her that made her from dust:
She is all we know and live by, and we trust
She is good and must endure, loving her so:
And as we love ourselves we hate our foe.

From *'This is no Case of Petty Right and Wrong'* by Second Lieutenant Edward Thomas

Died at Arras, 9 April 1917

On 4 April 1917, 149 Brigade received orders to move east to the Rollecourt area, and by 7 April they were stationed around Avenses, together with the other two brigades that formed the 50th Division. News of a successful attack along the Arras front on 9 April reached the 50th Division a few hours after it began, but it was not until 2330hrs on 10 April that 149 Brigade received orders to move forward to the Harbarcq-Wanquetin area. The next day, the 50th Division transferred from XVIII Corps to VII Corps and was instructed to relieve the 14th Division. The battalions of 149 Brigade were scheduled to be first into the front line: they moved forward just after 1730hrs through a landscape blanched by a heavy snowstorm:

We were yesterday billeted in a small village (Wanquetin), and suddenly received orders to move. We were on the road in about two hours' time, about 5.45pm. It started to snow, and snowed very hard indeed for about three hours. We passed through a very famous town [Arras] and after innumerable delays caused by indescribable traffic on the roads, we arrived in the present German trench about 3am. Things are going successfully. Prisoners are streaming in, and I can see from the battlefield how small our casualties have been.[1]

For some reason the men had been ordered to jettison their great coats, so were forced to rely on blankets for protection against the freezing weather; not surprisingly they were soon in a wretched condition. The route taken by 149 Brigade passed through Walrus, Dainville and Arras, then further east to the support trenches held by 42 Brigade (14th Division) south of Tilloy that straddled Telegraph Hill. The 1/6 Battalion took over the right portion of the line whilst the 1/7 took the left; the 1/5 were stationed in support in the old German front line. The 1/4 formed brigade reserve in Ronville caves. Apparently this relief was completed, without any incident, at 0335hrs on 12 April.

The front occupied by the 50th Division was on a ridge immediately east of the villages of Wancourt and Héninel. Through the latter village ran the Cojeul river which continued north east past the eastern outskirts of Wancourt where it took a sharp turn eastwards towards Guémappe, a fortified village. The left flank of the divisional front rested on the river east of Wancourt, the right was on the well-defined building known as Wancourt Tower, which stood on the ridge east of Wancourt and Héninel. Southeast, but outside the divisional right boundary, lay Chérisy. Directly ahead lay Vis-en-Artois. In German held territory, north of the Cojeul, lay Guémappe, from which enemy machine gun fire could enfilade the 50th Division front. The 56th Division held the 50th Division's right flank whilst the 3rd Division held their left. This sector had been taken as recently as 12 April, after heavy fighting, and the exact position of the front was not particularly clear, especially around Wancourt Tower. Patrols sent out from the 1/9 Battalion Durham Light Infantry (151 Brigade) to ascertain enemy positions were unable to reach Wancourt Tower because of the intense machine gun fire from Guémappe.

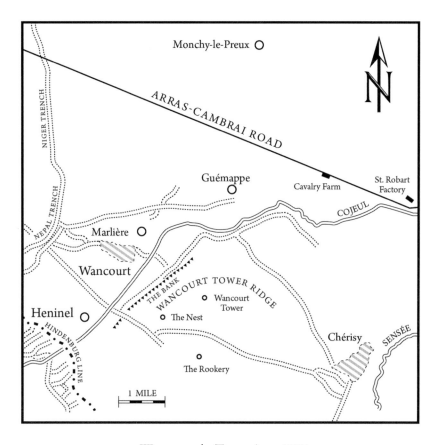

Wancourt, the Tower, Arras 1917

Orders were received that VI and VII Corps would begin a general advance on 14 April, and although orders were frequently being modified at the time, some even at the last moment, 151 Brigade advanced with 59 Brigade on its right. The attack involved the 1/6 and 1/8 Battalions Durham Light Infantry together with the 1/5 Battalion Border Regiment. In essence, 151 Brigade carried out its orders to the letter but later had to relinquish part of what they'd taken because the 56th Division hadn't succeeded in capturing Chérisy.

At midday on 14 April the 1/6 NF moved forward in artillery formation to the Brown Line southwest of Wancourt in preparation for a move forward at midnight to relieve the 1/9 DLI, who they wrongly believed held Wancourt Tower. However, on arrival they realised that the front line was actually some fifty yards short (west) of the Tower. They set about consolidating this position.

At daybreak on the following day, a bombing party of four men was sent out and managed to take the tower, a significant observation post. Predictably, by 1530hrs the Germans were observed digging a sap towards the tower in order to mount an operation to regain control. A platoon of Fusiliers moved against this sap and after a brief hand to hand skirmish the enemy were driven back, after which men were detailed to dig a communication trench from the battalion's line to the north of the tower.

During the day, the tower came under intense artillery attack and two enemy bombing sortées were repulsed. During this action, the 1/7 was in support, with two companies in Nepal Trench and two positioned along the bank east of the Cojeul; the 1/5 were in Niger Trench, the 1/4 were in Cojeul Switch.

Scene of the Attack on Wancourt Tower, Arras, April 1917
Chloe Rodham

On 15 April Captain Wilfred Joseph Bunbury of the 1/4 Battalion was killed. The 1/6 Battalion spent 16 April improving their position around the tower, but the 56th Division on the right were unable to dig a T Sap around the ruins as had been arranged. During the night of 16/17 April, the 1/7 Battalion were detailed to relieve the 1/6. However, at 2200hrs – during the early stages of the relief, and following an intense bombardment – the Germans attacked in force, overwhelming the garrison occupying the tower and retaking a small section of their original front line. The British came back in force with a bombing attack, but in the darkness – and being uncertain of where the enemy was – they failed to evict the German garrison. The remainder of the night was spent preparing for a stronger counterattack. The relief was cancelled. 'D' Company (1/7 Battalion), detailed to carry munitions forward to the front, suffered

Captain Wilfred Joseph Bunbury
1/4 Northumberland Fusiliers

Wilfred was born in 1882, in Winchester, Hampshire, the son of Charles Thomas and Harriet Emily Bunbury. He was educated at Beaumont College, Windsor, Eastman's School and Ushaw College, Durham, after which he was employed by Wise Speake, Stockbroker, Newcastle. In 1908 he married Dorothy Barbara Preston in Whitby and was the father of two daughters. At the onset of war he enlisted as a private with 1/4 Northumberland Fusiliers, and was promoted to Lieutenant on 27 December 1914. He disembarked with his battalion on 21 April 1915 to be wounded in action on 26 May 1915. During his recuperation he wrote *'Diary of an Officer with the 1/4 Northumberland Fusiliers in France and Flanders from April 20 to May 24 1915'*. After being passed fit for duty he was posted to the 1/4 Northumberland Fusiliers in March 1917. Wilfred was killed in action a month later, on 15 April 1917, aged 35. He is buried in Wancourt British Cemetery. His headstone is inscribed:

ON HIS SOUL
SWEET JESUS HAVE MERCY
AND GRANT TO HIM
ETERNAL REST

significant casualties: Officers: two killed, one wounded and one missing; Other Ranks: two killed, eleven wounded and one missing. The two officers killed were Captain James Herbert Cecil Swinney MC and Second Lieutenant James Archibald Mongomerie Miller.

On the morning of 17 April, the 1/7 Battalion were ordered to evict the Germans from their newly occupied defences. 'A' and 'B' Companies moved up to the place of assembly: a bank behind a ridge about 250 yards from the enemy. Men crawled by twos and threes over the open ground so as not excite suspicion, but even so it was remarkable that they reached the assembly point without being spotted. At 1153hrs, assisted on the flanks by bombers from the 1/6 and under an intense artillery barrage, the assault began. Even before the attacking troops had reached their objective, the enemy had retreated, although the 1/7 managed to take four prisoners. The whole of the front line was back in British hands; the Tower was occupied as well as a short section of trench north of it that had been used by the enemy as a bombing post. By evening the position had been consolidated and contact established with troops on the right and left flanks. That night both the 1/6 and 1/7 Battalions were relieved by the 1/5 Battalion. The 1/6 marched to gun pits north of Neuville Vitasse and the 1/7 to Nepal and Niger Trenches.

An officer of the 1/7 Battalion wrote on 18 April:

> *We have been in action and are now out for a bit. Things are going well for us about here, and the Boches are having a bad time. Prisoners are coming in every night, and also a lot of deserters; and we are hoping for great events shortly. The havoc about here is simply appalling, and one honestly feels sorry for the Boches. Some prisoners we took yesterday were nearly in a state of lunacy when we got them into our dugout. The CO went up to one to give him a cigarette, and he just shrank like a dog that expects to be kicked. There is no doubt they believe in many cases they will be shot when captured.*[2]

During the early morning of 18 April, whilst the 1/5 Battalion manned the front, a wounded prisoner was brought in who volunteered the information that the enemy were preparing to counterattack at 1400hrs with fresh troops; sure enough, at 1100hrs German infantry could be seen massing for an assault. Forewarned as they were, a barrage laid on by the divisional artillery completely dispersed these unfortunate troops.

By now the *First Battle of the Scarpe (9-14 April 1917)* had officially drawn to an end. The British had advanced four miles into enemy territory, capturing a large number of strategic positions, and were now commanding the heights looking eastwards.

During the next phase, known as the *Second Battle of the Scarpe (23-24 April 1917)*, the Allies continued to press the attack east of Arras. Their aims were to consolidate the gains made in the first days of the offensive, to keep the initiative, and to break through in concert with the French at Aisne. However, from 16 April onwards it was apparent that to the south, the French *Nivelle Offensive* on the Aisne was failing, and Haig came under pressure to keep the Germans occupied in the Arras sector to minimise French losses. The interim between the First and Second Battles of the Scarpe was of immense value to the Germans; it gave them time to bring up reserves and to recover from the temporary disorganisation from which they suffered during the first attack. It became increasingly evident that the next series of attacks would meet strenuous opposition. The going would be tough.

The first objective for the next advance eastward, on 23 April, (the 50th Division in tandem with the 30th Division on right and 15th Division on the left) was to occupy the whole of the ridge east of Wancourt Tower and a north-south line 1600 yards west of the ridge; this was known as the Blue Line. The second objective (the Red Line) was a southwest-northeast line from the southern end of the Blue Line to the bank of the Cojeul River, northwest of Vis-en-Artois and just short of the Rohart Factory. The attack was carried out by 150 Brigade with 149 Brigade in reserve at Ronville. The 1/4 Battalion were ordered to occupy the old German line north of Beaurains. Unfortunately, 150 Brigade were faced with furious German opposition and were unable to carry the first of the day's objectives, the Blue Line. There were over 1000 casualties. During the early morning of 24 April they were replaced by 151 Brigade; the 1/4 NF were attached to 151 Brigade, whilst the remaining three battalions of 149 Brigade moved up into support for the renewal of the attack.

'B' Company of the 1/4 was sent to the front line under orders from the 1/9 Battalion DLI on its right flank. They dug a new trench connecting with the DLI. Their left flank was in the air until the middle of the afternoon when they joined up with 1/5 Border Regiment. Four Germans were taken prisoner. However, 'B' Company were subjected to continuous and heavy shell fire and persistent sniping; Second Lieutenant Robert Johnson was killed, along with five other ranks, with 16 wounded. The remaining companies in the old British front line north of Wancourt were also hammered by artillery fire. At 1415hrs, 'B' Company sent forward one platoon to reconnoitre and capture an enemy trench astride the railway, which resulted in further casualties. Another platoon was sent forward under heavy artillery and machine gun fire to strengthen the garrison against counteraction. Further platoons from 'B' Company moved forward under the cover of darkness. 'A' and 'D' Companies dug a new support trench between the railway and the Cojeul river and occupied it. So, by the

Second Lieutenant Robert Johnson

1/4 Northumberland Fusiliers

Robert was born in Newcastle upon Tyne in 1892, the son of George and Margaret Johnson. He was educated at Rutherford College and was studying at Armstrong College when war broke out. He was gazetted to the 1/4 Northumberland Fusiliers on 22 August 1914 and served at a number of stations at home until posted to the Front in late September 1915. He was killed on 25 April 1917, aged 25. Robert is commemorated on the Arras Memorial to the Missing.

end of 24 April the Blue Line had been taken and during the fighting some 17 German officers and 793 other ranks had been captured. The following day 'B' Company was still facing shelling and sniping, and although things were not as bad as they had been on the previous day, there were nonetheless a number of casualties. During the night, the 1/4 Battalion was relieved and returned to the Harp (north section).

On the first day of May, 149 Brigade – as part of the 50th Division – were ordered to move eastwards towards the front. There had been some expectation that after the fighting of late April the men might be granted some rest, but their hopes were duly dampened and they moved to Souastre and Fonquevillers, followed by a march in fine weather on the next day to Mercatel. On 3 May, it became apparent that the First, Third and Fifth Armies were to mount an attack, now known as the *Third Battle of the Scarpe*.

After the British forces had secured the area round Arleux at the end of April they were determined to launch another attack east from Monchy to try to break through the *Boiry Riegel* and reach the *Wotanstellung*, a major German defensive fortification. This was scheduled to coincide with an Australian attack at Bullecourt, confronting the Germans with a two-pronged assault which British commanders hoped would force them to retreat further to the east. With this objective in mind, the British launched another attack near the Scarpe on 3 May. The brigades of the 50th Division were to be ready to exploit any success gained. However, neither assault was able to make any significant advance and they were called off the following day, with many soldiers wounded or killed. As a result of this failure the 50th Division were placed into Army Reserve and began to move westwards. By 5 May, 149 Brigade were based in the Pommera-Mondicourt area where they underwent extensive training – including live firing. The War Diary of 1/7 Battalion reports that six other ranks were wounded during rifle grenade training. During this time, the 50th Division was moved from Reserve Corps back to VII Corps.

On 15 May orders were received that over the next three days the division was to move to a forward area and that 149 Brigade was to be attached to the 33rd Division; all four battalions were billeted in the Boiry St Martin-Ayette area. From here, on the next day they advanced to St Leger and moved into a valley to the west of the village. Other elements of the 33rd Division attacked the Hindenburg Line as far as the Croisilles-Hendencourt road, attacking from Brown Trench and the Hump. They captured Burg Trench (the German front line) as far south as the Hump, then the support line to approximately 100 yards north of the Sensée river. There was no German counterattack, so the services of 149 Brigade were not needed.

During the night of 22/23 May, 149 Brigade relieved 19 and 100 Brigades in the right and centre sectors of the 33rd Divisional Front, from the Croisilles-Fontaine road to west of the Hump. The relief proceeded quietly and was completed by 0340hrs. Men from 149 Brigade worked with a pioneer battalion to dig new communication trenches and support line behind Lump Lane. Day and night the Germans bombed the brigade's front line trenches with fish tails (German trench mortar shells, eight inches long). During the next night, a number of German deserters from Reserve Infantry Regiment 226 surrendered to the 1/4; others gave themselves up along the section of the front held by the 1/5 Battalion.

There were plans to pursue a local operation – the 1/4 Battalion against the Hump – but for some reason they were rejected. On the night of 24/25 May the 1/7 relieved the 1/4 (right) and 1/6 relieved the 1/5 (left). Early that morning, before the inter-battalion relief had been completed, a German patrol attacked 'D' Company of the 1/4 behind their bombing block in Plum

Lane. The company fought back, and during the skirmish the bombing block was demolished by the battalion's own Stokes mortars. They went on to repulse the attack and set about constructing a new bombing block, but during this incident Captain Percival Elliott Cox was wounded, dying soon afterwards.

Captain Percival Elliott Cox

1/4 Northumberland Fusiliers

Percival was born in Newcastle upon Tyne, in 1891, the son of William Marshall and Margaret Hall Cox. He was educated at Rutherford School and Armstrong College, University of Durham, where he was a member of the University's OTC. Before the war he was a teacher at Walker County School. On 22 August he was granted a commission in the Northumberland Fusiliers. He disembarked in France on 1 May 1915 but was repatriated to the UK in early July 1915. He returned to the Western Front on St George's Day, 23 April 1917, but was killed in action, aged 26, on 24 May 1917. Percival is buried in Sunken Road Cemetery, Boisleux-Saint-Marc. His headstone is inscribed:

THY WILL BE DONE

One of the German deserters divulged that they were digging a tunnel underneath the British front line. Using the information given by the prisoner, a patrol went out into No Man's Land, where they found and entered the tunnel; it did indeed reach under the British line but it was empty and was not connected to the extensive German tunnelling system emanating from Tunnel Trench.

On 25 May, a patrol from 1/6 consisting of one officer (Second Lieutenant A B Gracie) and three men (Lance Corporal Lewis and Privates Harris and Carter) entered No Man's Land on the battalion's right with the orders that they were to get in touch with a neighbouring battalion. At about 0300hrs the patrol ran into an enemy machine gun post which opened fire, forcing them to disperse. Gracie and Carter managed to take cover in a shell hole, where they stayed undetected until later that night, when they managed to return to their lines. The other two, although wounded, also managed to make it to safety. At the same time, another two patrols from 1/6 were out in No Man's Land: the first patrol consisted of one officer and ten men from 'A' company, moving out from the right of the battalion front and maintaining contact with the other patrol. They, too, were discovered by the enemy before returning to safety. These forays confirmed that the Germans were holding Burch Support in strength – and that they were alert. They also pinpointed the position of an enemy trench mortar. The second patrol of one officer and nine men made their way along Plum Trench towards the enemy line. On reaching a spot about twenty yards from the enemy they discovered a party of twenty to thirty enemy soldiers working on their wire: too many to attack. The patrol retired a little way down Plum Trench and sent word back to the front line. The German working party was then dispersed by the safer option of rifle grenades and Lewis gun fire.

Working parties from the 1/4 (4 officers and 120 men) and 1/5 (3 officers and 90 men) were detailed to carry ammunition up to the front line for the 33rd Division, which launched an attack against Tunnel Trench; 149 Brigade wasn't needed for this attack. During the night of 26/27 May they were relieved by 19 Brigade, moving back to Moyenneville. Two days later the brigade marched in beautiful sunshine to Monchy-au-Bois via Ayette-Douchy, south of Adinfer Wood, where they rejoined the 50th Division. Training continued in good weather involving a practice attack on Quesnoy Farm in cooperation with a contact aeroplane supplied by the 8th Squadron Royal Flying Corps. Oddly, during this time of training, the death of Lieuenant Clive Montagu Joicey was reported in the St George's Gazette[3] as 'killed in action' on 5 June 1917. This is supported by a number of other databases. A letter from a brother officer said:

I was with Clive an hour before he was killed. He was on my left about 120 yards further down the trench. I found him as cheery as ever, his old self, and a good man to do with when going over the bags. I heard afterwards he led his company to the first objective, cheering his men on to the last, when he was killed instantly by a shell. His company did gloriously and took all objectives and I know that this was due largely to Clive's great dash and fearlessness.[3]

Parties of officers were allowed to visit the site of the division's struggles on the Somme, particularly the ground around Bazentin and the Butte de Warlencourt. It was not all work for the men: a series of sporting events were organised. The 1/7 won the Brigadier's Cup which had been donated by Brigadier General Hubert Conway Rees for the highest aggregate points at the Brigade Sports.

However, by 15 June the 50th Division were needed at the front, taking over from the 18th Division in the left sector of the VII Corps front, facing Chérisy. By the night of 18 June, 150 and 151 Brigades had taken over the front line; 149 Brigade relieved 54 Brigade as Brigade Reserve. The divisional front was approximately 3000 yards long, and was 1000 yards west of the German-held villages of Fontaine-les-Croisilles on the right and Chérisy on the left. The German trenches were about five hundred yards west of the two villages but were difficult to observe because they were dug on the reverse slope of the ridge west of the Sensée Valley. On the right flank was the 33rd Division with the 56th Division on the left.

During the night of 23/24 June, 149 Brigade relieved 151 Brigade, near Heinel. Dispositions were: 1/5 in the front line, Jackdaw and Bullfinch trenches and their close support trenches; 1/6 in support trenches Egret and Loop and their support trenches; 1/4 and 1/7 in reserve. They immediately set about improving these trenches, while carrying parties brought drums containing chemicals up to the front. Unfortunately, the last of these parties came under a vicious artillery bombardment and one of the drums received a direct hit: one officer was killed and thirty other ranks gassed.

On 26 June, along the 149 Brigade front, more than four hundred gas drums were projected into the enemy's front line trenches. This attack caught the Germans unaware and caused significant casualties; the next day a ribbon of stretcher bearers could be seen ferrying men from the area. A later report stated that twenty-five of the enemy were killed in one dugout. Although two of the drums accidently burst in the Fusiliers' trench, no casualties were recorded. Following up on the gas attack, elements from 150 Brigade captured an enemy-held position, Fontaine Trench, taking prisoners and machine guns. However, as a result the enemy retaliated with extensive artillery barrages and air attacks against the 149 Brigade front and communication trenches, causing damage that needed extensive repair.

In preparation for the gas attack some of the forward positions held by 149 Brigade, in particular Dead Boche Sap and Cable Trench, had been evacuated. These were quickly taken by the enemy but were subsequently recaptured by means of a bombing attack. During the darkness of 26/27 June the brigade was labouring hard to consolidate these outlying positions and to dig a new trench from Wren Lane towards Cable Trench. On the next night, the brigade carried out a series of inter-battalion reliefs: the 1/5 replaced the 1/6 in the front line. All of this was carried out under an avalanche of enemy fire.

The next night (28/29) the enemy attempted to raid a sap in the left of the sector held by 149 Brigade. They were driven off in disorder and a German officer (from Infantry Regiment 145) with a number of men were killed and a prisoner taken. At 0300hrs a German soldier approached the block in Durham Lane and was subsequently wounded and taken prisoner. He was interrogated, revealing that he was an Alsatian who served with the First ERS Battalion, Infantry Regiment 173. He also conceded that he and fifteen others had been attached to the front line regiment to replace men disabled by the gas attack. Casualties for 149 Brigade for June were low: four killed and twelve wounded.

After June, there were no major attacks along the Arras front. Nonetheless, life out there was strenuous; both sides' artillery were active almost constantly. Time was spent with perpetual patrol work, punctuated now and again by a raid against enemy positions. On top of this, the Fusiliers toiled nonstop, restoring defences at the front and digging new trenches. Towards the end of July, a new offensive was scheduled by the Allies, east of Ypres; there was the need for diversionary raids across the whole of the Western Front in order to keep the Germans busy and guessing.

From 1 to 4 July, 149 Brigade took over a portion of the line between Swallow and Pelican Lanes held by 150 Brigade: on 1 July the 1/4 relieved the 1/4 Yorkshire Regiment in the newly acquired section of the front; the 1/7 would replace 1/4 in the support role. Later that night the 1/7 relieved the remnants of the 1/6. On 2 July, the 1/5 replaced the 1/6 – now in support trenches – who would take up position in Brigade Reserve. Some time on 3 July the enemy attempted a small scale attack on the left of the divisional sector; there was no assault against the subsector held by the 149, although Wren and Jackdaw

Trenches were pummelled by an intense barrage. In retaliation they bombarded the German-held Bottom Trench with gas shells. An inter-battalion relief took place during the night of 5/6 July, during which there was concentrated artillery bombardment. In retaliation, the brigade's trench mortars, hidden by a smoke screen, targeted Narrow Trench and dugouts in the vicinity of Chérisy, causing serious destruction.

The 149 was replaced in the line during the night of 10/11 by 150 Brigade and moved into Divisional Reserve, south of Neuville Vitasse, where they were billeted in huts. They resumed training over the next seven days, then returned to the front, replacing 151 Brigade on the nights of 18/19 and 19/20 July. Dispositions on 20 July were: 1/4 in Vis sector (right); 1/7 in the Guémappe sector (left); the 1/5 were in support in Egret and Lion Trenches and their support trenches, with one company in Marlière; 1/6 were in reserve north of Neuville Vitasse. By night, working parties from these battalions were labouring, digging new trenches.

During the early hours of the morning of 23 July, on the front held by the 1/4, there was an enemy raid following a zealous barrage (consisting mainly of fish tail bombs). Their objective was to capture Posts 1 and 2. They tossed bombs into the communications sap connecting Post 2, then skirted round the post and entered the sap about twenty yards in from the post. Hand to hand fighting and local bombing forced the enemy back. It turned out that the raiding party was from Infantry Regiment 458; they left two men dead in the sap and a number of others in No Man's Land. Casualties for the 1/4 were: one man killed: 202229 Private Frank Burditt, and two others wounded.

Four days later, a small group of ten to fourteen Germans attempted to raid Post 6 in the Vis sector (right) held by the 1/5. They were observed approaching up the valley from the north. As they came in range, the garrison opened up with rifle fire, killing their officer. At this point the rest of the raiding party dispersed and retreated eastwards. The officer's body was identified as being from the 2 Battalion Infantry Regiment 458. The rest of the month was spent in inter-battalion reliefs. At the end of the month the 1/6 was manning the Guémappe sector; the 1/5 the Vis sector, 1/7 were in support and 1/4 in reserve. Casualties for 149 Brigade were: Officers: seven wounded and two missing; Other Ranks:

thirteen killed, seventy-six wounded and two missing. The brigade received some replacements: twelve officers and fifty-eight men.

In the early days of August, men from 149 Brigade raided the enemy trenches a number of times. During the night of 2/3 August, two officers (Captain J.D.S. McCubbin and Lieutenant H.D.K. Davies) with thirty-six men from the 1/6 Battalion left Thorn Post to raid The Gun Pits; the aim was to take a prisoner for identification. The raiding party crossed the old site of Lanyard Trench and by 0130hrs had safely reached the enemy wire which was one concertina thick; they managed to cut a four foot gap undetected, then crept in a further seventy yards where they searched for forty minutes but found no-one. Before they made their way back to safety, they used Bangalore torpedoes to destroy a section of the enemy's wire. This was followed the next night by another excursion: a party of twenty-six men from the 1/5, under the command of Lieutenant H.E. Merritt, attempted to raid an enemy sap. Again, the objective was to take prisoners for identification. The party returned empty-handed after traipsing round No Man's Land for two hours; it appears that they had lost their bearings and had been unable to find the enemy's position.

Even as 149 Brigade were relieved by 150 Brigade on the night of 2/3 August, a third raid was attempted on the Gun Pits in the early hours by men from the 1/6. The raiders left Thorn Post and ventured into No Man's Land. On reaching the wire they were detected and fired upon by machine guns; again, they were forced to return empty-handed. On being relieved, the brigade moved to the south of Neuville Vitasse where the individual battalions were billeted in huts, tents or bivouvacs. Once again, training was the order of the day, in sultry weather with heavy thunderstorms.

While 149 Brigade was based at Neuville Vitasse the 50th Division was transferred from VII Corps to VI Corps, and after eight days 149 Brigade went back up the line, replacing 151 Brigade in the right sector of the divisional front during the night of Sunday 12 August, with 150 Brigade on their left. Dispositions were: 1/4 right; 1/7 left; 1/5 in support and 1/6 in reserve. Further inter-battalion reliefs followed until, at the end of August, 149 Brigade was relieved by 150 Brigade, which was completed by 0600hrs on 29 August. The 1/7 and 1/5 Battalions were billeted in huts north west of Mercatel, whilst after spending one night in tents the 1/6 moved to a newly built camp a quarter of a mile north west of Boisleux-Saint-Marc. The 1/4 moved into Shaft Line (the old Hindenburg Line) in order to provide working parties for the Royal Engineers. Casualties for August were: Officers: one wounded; Other ranks: seven killed, forty-three wounded and three missing.

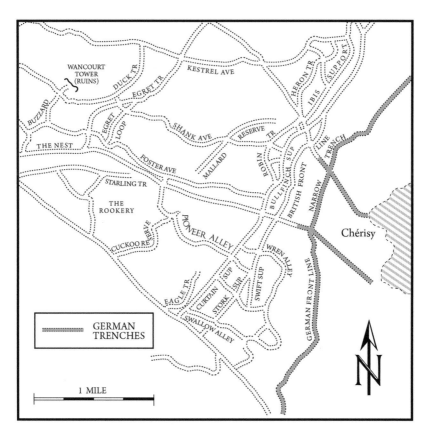

Attack on 15 September 1917 on Narrow Trench, Chérisy Sector, Arras

On 6 September, 149 Brigade relieved 151 Brigade in the Vis-Guémappe sector with the following dispositions: 1/4 at the front in Vis subsector; 1/7 at the front in Guémappe subsector, 1/5 in support and 1/6 in reserve. To mark the anniversary of the attack in 1916 on Martinpuich and High Wood, the 50th Division launched a local attack on 15 September consisting of three phases, all carried out by 151 Brigade:

Phase 1: A raid on Narrow Trench and Narrow Support Trench by three companies of the 1/9 DLI lasting thirty minutes, to begin at 1600hrs.

Phase 2: A raid on a different section of Narrow and Narrow Support Trenches by one company of the 1/8 DLI lasting twenty minutes, to begin at 1940hrs.

Phase 3: A gas attack using Liven's Projectors at 0440hrs on 16 September.

To assist these raids the right-hand battalion of 149 Brigade Front (1/4 Battalion) fired coloured lights to confuse German signals. They also manipulated four groups of collapsible dummy figures (Chinese attack), 150 yards east of the end of Shikar Avenue: they raised and lowered the dummies from the front-line trenches to simulate troop movement.

Elements of a Chinese Attack
Chloe Rodham

During Phase 1 there was an intense barrage of smoke, thermalite, lachrymatory high explosive and shrapnel shells, machine gun and trench mortar fire on the enemy front, during which the dummies were raised as obfuscatory coloured lights lit the sky. Within ninety seconds the enemy were trying to 'kill' the figures and were bombarding the ends of Shikar and Kestrel Avenues and the 1/4 posts along the battalion front, from which the garrisons had been withdrawn. At 1640hrs the figures were lowered – undamaged. Casualties were: Lieutenant James Hope-Wallace killed and one man wounded.

Lieutenant James Hope-Wallace

1/4 Northumberland Fusiliers

James was born in Kensington, London, in 1872, the eldest son of John and Mary Hope-Wallace. In 1900, he succeeded his father as owner of the vast Featherstone Estate in Northumberland. He married Ursula Mary Addlington in November 1905 and was the father of two daughters. James joined the 1/4 Northumberland Fusiliers just after the outbreak of war. He was gazetted as Second Lieutenant in September 1914 and disembarked for France on 29 June 1916. Weeks before he was killed he returned to the UK to attend the memorial service of his brother officer, Clive Montagu Joicey. James died from wounds caused by a bursting shell on Saturday 15 September 1917, aged 45. He is buried in Hibers Trench Cemetery, Wancourt.

During Phase 2 the dummy figures were once again raised as the artillery and machine gun barrage opened, with more confusing coloured lights. An intense enemy barrage fell within two minutes on the brigade's front line, with Ape Support, Bison Reserve and the Cojeul Valley trenches being shelled vigorously. At 2000hrs the figures were lowered; by this time they had suffered some damage. Casualties for 149 Brigade were two men wounded.

Following Phase 3, the enemy retaliated until 0500hrs with artillery and trench mortars. A further inter-battalion relief followed on the night of 17/18.

The same night at 3am fifty cylinders of gas were projected over German lines. This gas attack cost the Germans dear, probably more than the two raids, for next day they were seen burying or removing large numbers of the men caught in the gas cloud. My own observers reported 200 gas casualties and the total number reported reached a figure between 300 and 400.

German casualties were easily distinguished, as the Germans removed them in blankets slung between two men on a pole. Besides, as it happened the gas cloud drifted north and caught the Germans during a relief nearly half a mile away from the scene of the two raids. For example, the Germans were burying dead all day in the neighbourhood of St Roharts Factory, which is some distance from Chérisy.[4]

The German report of this operation showed that they had failed to realise the nature of the attack.

The War Diary of the 1/7 Battalion Northumberland Fusiliers reported on the raids:

All three phases were successful; prisoners were taken and heavy casualties inflicted on the enemy and much damage done to their trenches and dug-outs. A dummy tank and dummy figures for drawing the enemy fire were used with success.[5]

The enemy's official version of what happened on September 15/16 tells a different story, one much more suited to German propaganda:

Western Front (German Official 16.9.1917)

South east of ARRAS enemy artillery activity increased in intensity. Under cover of a smoke cloud the English attacked in the neighbourhood of Chérisy on a front of 1500 metres. Tanks and flame projectors cleared the way for the assaulting troops, but our excellent resistance by the artillery and machine gun broke down the attack. In those places where the enemy penetrated into our lines they were ejected in hand to hand fights by our infantry. Towards evening the enemy again attacked at the same point. This undertaking failed and was driven back with great loss.[6]

During 21 September 149 Brigade, in the left sector of the divisional front, were relieved by 150 Brigade and moved into a divisional reserve area. The 1/5 and 1/7 Battalions were billeted in York Lines, a new hutted camp, spending their time in training, whilst the 1/4 and 1/6 Battalions were billeted in Durham Lines Camp from where they provided working parties under divisional command.

Orders were received that the 50th Division was to be relieved by the 51st Division on 6 October. Before that, on 28 September, 149 Brigade were back in the line to replace 151 Brigade in the right subsection (Chérisy). Dispositions were: 1/4 front line right; 1/7 front line left, 1/5 in support and 1/6 in reserve. Casualties for September were: Officers: two killed and four wounded; Other ranks: six killed and thirty-two wounded. Fortunately, the brigade received a generous batch of replacements of 8 officers and 603 other ranks: 174 to 1/4; 29 to the 1/5, 164 to 1/6 and 236 to 1/7.

On this section of the Western Front, men faced an exhausting daily dance with death and destruction. Incidents took place hour by hour; night after night they faced trench mortars, artillery barrages and machine gun fire. And there were accidents. The War Diary of the 1/7 Battalion on 25 July records:

> *CSM Ernest Cook (fatally) and 2 further NCOs and 1 man were accidentally wounded by the fuse of a German shell whilst collecting salvage.*[7]

October began with 149 Brigade at the front, although after their first day the enemy's artillery was fairly quiescent. Relief of the 50th Division by the 51st Division began on 4 October, when 149 Brigade marched to Courcelles. The weather changed for the worse: they faced rain and high winds, but training began nonetheless.

On 16 October, the various elements of the division began to board trains for the Zeggers Cappel area, just south of Dunkirk. After many moves eastwards, on 23 October orders were received that the 50th Division was to relieve part of the 34th Division in the front line. This fell to 149 Brigade, with 150 Brigade in support, and was achieved by 25 October.

CHAPTER EIGHT

THE AFFAIR AT HOUTHULST FOREST
AND THE WINTER OF 1917/1918.

I, that on my familiar hill
Saw with uncomprehending eyes
A hundred of Thy sunsets spill
Their fresh and sanguine sacrifice,
Ere the sun swings his noonday sword
Must say good-bye to all of this;
By all delights that I shall miss,
Help me to die, O Lord.

From *'Before Action'* by Lieutenant William Noel Hodgson

In the early days of October 1917, 149 Brigade was manning the Chérisy Sector area of the 50th Divisional Front, which was held by the 1/4 (right) and 1/7 Battalion (left). The 1/5 Battalion was in support, whilst the 1/6 was in reserve at Henin. In command of 149 Brigade from 2 October was Brigadier General Edward Arthur Puis Riddell DSO, replacing Brigadier General Hubert Conway Rees who was on sick leave in England. At the same time, orders were received that the 50th Division – minus its artillery – would be relieved; throughout the 4-6 October, 153 Infantry Brigade (51st

Highland Division) would relieve 149 Brigade. Within days, orders were issued at divisional and brigade level that all elements should prepare to leave the Courcelles area, and that the division was to be transferred from VI Corps to II Corps. Travel arrangements for 149 Brigade were that HQ, the 1/4 and 1/5 Battalions together with the 149 Machine Gun Company and 149 Trench Mortar Battery would take the train at Miraumont and travel to Cassels in Belgium. On the same day, the 1/6 and 1/7 Battalions entrained at Bapaume and travelled to Esquelbecq. After leaving their transport, all units marched to billets in the Arneke area. By 20 October, the 50th Division had been transferred from II Corps to XIV Corps (5th Army), and 149 Brigade had moved eastwards to the Proven area. All the battalions were billeted west of Proven with the Brigade HQ situated at Poona Camp.

On 22 October orders were issued that the 50th Division should make preparations to relieve a section of the 34th Division at the front, north east of Langemarck, with a view to taking part in an offensive (part of the action now known as the *Second Battle of Passchendaele*). Consequently, on 23 October all units of 149 Brigade travelled by rail from Proven Station to areas south-east and south-west of Boesinghe. The Brigade HQ was positioned at White Mill, near Elverdinge, whilst the 1/6 and 1/7 billeted at Marsouine Camp east of the Yser Canal; the 1/4 were at Hulls Farm and the 1/5 at Saragossa Camp. Reconnaissance of the front which the brigade was to take over had been conducted on 22 October.

During October 1917 the *Third Battle of Ypres* was entering its final stages. On 9 October, the Fifth Army had attacked between Houthulst Forest and Poelcappelle, while the Second Army tried to advance along the Passchendaele Ridge. These attacks were a disaster: they failed miserably to capture any of the major defensive positions remaining in Houthulst Forest. The *First Battle of Passchendaele* followed on its heels, on 12 October. Again, the exhausted and battered infantry – lamentably supported by inadequate artillery preparation – met with disaster.

It was a case of too much ventured and nothing gained. This led to another attempt on 26 October: the *Second Battle of Passchendaele,* the primary aim being to capture the remnants of Passchendaele village.

The Canadians spearheaded the attack across sodden, squelching ground and ultimately managed to capture a further 500 yards of enemy-held territory. On the left, the Fifth Army was required to make another desperate assault on the dark and brooding Houthulst Forest, the nemesis of 149 Brigade.

On the night of 24/25 October, 149 Brigade replaced both 101 Infantry Brigade (34th Division) and 104 Infantry Brigade (35th Division). The battalions destined for the front were the 1/4, 1/5 and 1/7. The 1/4 relieved 11 Battalion Suffolk Regiment, 101 Brigade, at the front from map reference V.7.b.70.60. (Schaap-Balie 1/10,000 map sheet 20 SE and SW) to Turenne Crossing (exclusive); the 1/5 took over the front from Turenne Crossing (inclusive) to Aden House (inclusive) from the 11 Battalion Suffolk Regiment, 101 Brigade, and the 1/7 the front from Aden House (exclusive) to Colombo House-Six Roads at U.6.b.90.45.(Schaap-Balie 1/10,000 map sheet 20 SE and SW) from the 20 Battalion Lancashire Fusiliers, 104 Brigade.

Francis Buckley Original Drawing
Author's Collection

Initially each battalion would man the front using one company. However, even *reaching* the front was a monumental task using the duckboard tracks of Railway Street and Hunter Street:

We left camp near Pilkem in the late afternoon of 24 October, and passed by 'Iron Cross Roads' to "Hunter Street", a duckboard track which came to an end a mile short of Egypt House, a pill box which was to be Battalion Headquarters. From the end of this duckboard track we passed along a track through mud marked every twenty yards by whitewashed posts. I was detailed as whipper-in to the battalion and so was the last man.[1]

Egypt House, 1918

After blindly following the figure of the man in front for what seemed an endless age, we had the order passed back to leave the track and shelter near some pill boxes on our right. This was because the track in front was receiving an unhealthy amount of attention from the Boche guns. This we did, and men grouped close together under the lee of these concrete shelters looked for all the world like swarms of bees. After about fifteen minutes I noticed men moving off again, and so once more we took the track.[3]

The men clearly found this part of the journey both dangerous and tortuous, but their situation became even grimmer as the duckboards came to an end:

Just as I was beginning to wonder how much further we had to travel, we reached the end of the duckboard track. And here our previous troubles were as nothing compared with those that assailed us, as we dragged our loaded carcasses through mud from post to post, a few yards at a time. Time and

196

again men got stuck in this horrible slime and I saw more than one grown man in tears. One case I well remember; it was one of many. A man stuck fast. Corporal Henderson and I got hold of him and dragged him out, but he only stumbled forward a few yards and then gave up. We pulled him out four or five times, but had at length to leave him to get along in his own time, as we were getting out of touch and far behind the rest of the column.[4]

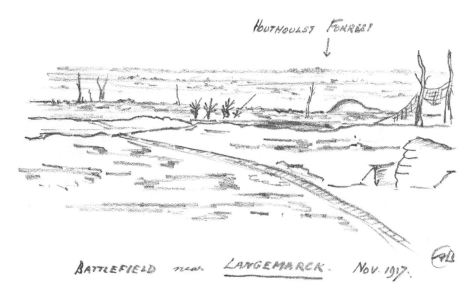

Francis Buckley Original Drawing
Author's Collection

Even now the enemy continued to shell the area as the weary men lumbered on:

As we caught up again with the main body, we found 'D' Company clustered around the pill boxes at the crossroads near Egypt House. And I heard that a shell had caught the head of this company, killing the Company Sergeant Major and several of Company Headquarters men, and wounding Captain R.A.('China') Brown, the officer in charge of 'D' Company.[5]

Captain Brown was replaced as commanding officer of 'D' Company by Lieutenant W.H. Fisher.

> *The so-called front line was a series of shell holes with maybe one or two men in each shell hole. They were not linked – all separate.*[6]

Orders were received that units from XIV Corps in conjunction with units from XVIII Corps on the right and the French First Army on the left would renew the stalled Allied advance on 26 October 1917; specifically, this meant that the attack would involve the 50th Division with the 57th Division on its right (4/5 Battalion Loyal North Lancashire Regiment) and the 37th Division on its left. On the 50th Division's front the attack was carried out by troops from 149 Brigade. This advance was drawn up to use three battalions: the 1/4 on the right, the 1/5 in the centre and the 1/7 on the left, with the 1/6 in reserve. The 1/4 Battalion Yorkshire Regiment (150 Brigade, 50th Division) was also to be placed at the disposal of 149 Brigade in case of an emergency.

Each of the three attacking battalions was to attack on a three-company front. Each company was to attack on a single platoon frontage, one platoon in each wave. The fourth company of each battalion would form the battalion's reserve. The orders stressed that the platoons would leapfrog one another and that special parties should be detached as necessary to deal with each strongpoint occupied by the enemy, which once taken would immediately be prepared for defence against counterattack. The offensive was to move forward under the cover of a creeping barrage, a standing barrage, a back barrage, a distance barrage and a machine gun barrage. The creeping barrage was planned to begin at eight minutes before zero hour and would advance at the rate of one hundred yards per eight minutes throughout.

The weather remained atrocious on 25 October and the Germans continued to bombard the back areas with shells; the 1/7 Battalion's HQ at Egypt House came in for particular treatment. Towards midnight, officers laid out tape lines at the jumping off points. Lieutenant H. Richardson laid the line for the 1/7 Battalion, whilst that for the 1/5 Battalion was laid out by Second Lieutenant Young, from Turenne Crossing to Arden House.

On the right (the 1/4 Battalion) the plan for the attack was modified twice within a matter of twelve hours. First, an inspection of the ground over which the troops were to attack found that there was room for only a two-company frontage, rather than three as planned. Later, when the tape was laid by Second Lieutenant J. A. Burton, it was found that there was actually room for only *one* company to attack. As a result, orders were modified to a *one* company frontage, followed by one company in the rear on the right and one to the left. Pieces of tape were used to mark the battalion's boundary.

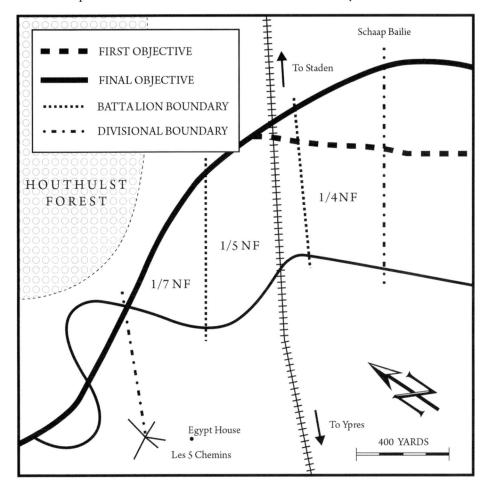

Attack on 26 October 1917

Zero hour was fixed at 0540hrs on 26 October. The waiting, always hard on the men, was made far worse by torrential rain which began to fall at 0300hrs and persisted at intervals through the day during the attack, further drenching the sodden landscape. Nevertheless, at 0540hrs the troops, already soaked to the skin, scrambled to their feet and moved wearily forward.

1/4 Battalion

On the right, the arrow of three companies, as described above, advanced in good order and were clear before the enemy laid down its barrage. They made a measure of progress until they were held up by severe machine gun fire from 'huts' (concrete pill boxes) about 150 yards to the east, which were full of machine guns and which had effectively been left untouched by the artillery barrage. The 1/4 Battalion's War Diary states[7] that the *British barrage consisted entirely of shrapnel which was quite useless against the line of concrete huts which was the battalion's first objective.* Even though the barrage travelled at a modest one hundred yards in eight minutes, the swampy ground was so badly cut up by shell fire that, not surprisingly, the troops were unable to keep pace with it. Further, more boggy ground to the right of the huts meant that it would be fruitless to make any attempt to outflank them on that side. Eventually the attack stalled about eighty yards in front of the first objective, and the men were forced to go to ground, finding shelter wherever they could. Every movement became an invitation for lethal sniping and machine gun fire from the concrete huts ahead of them. Meanwhile, two platoons of the reserve company moved into the battalion's original line and consolidated this position. Under orders, the advanced positions gained were eventually abandoned after dark. During the night of 26/27 October, the battalion was relieved by the 1/4 Battalion Yorkshire Regiment, the exhausted men making their way east using Railway Street (duckboard track).

Second Lieutenant David Arthur Smith
1/4 Northumberland Fusiliers

David was born in Ancroft, Northumberland, the youngest son of David and Mary Smith. He initially enlisted in the Durham Light Infantry and was promoted to Sergeant on 16 January 1915. After serving twelve months at the front he returned to England to take up a commission. He was gazetted into the Northumberland Fusiliers in August 1917 and disembarked on the Western Front on 18 September 1917. Aged 26, he was killed in action on 26 October 1917 and is commemorated on the Tyne Cot Memorial to the Missing.

Preliminary casualties for the attack were: Officers: 2 killed, 1 died of wounds, 5 wounded and 2 missing; Other Ranks: 36 killed, 156 wounded and 64 missing. In the months to come, many of these 'missing' would be assumed 'killed in action'. See Appendix D for a fuller list of casualties.

Second Lieutenant David Lindsay Young
1/4 Northumberland Fusiliers

David was born in Newcastle upon Tyne, the son of Lindsay Smith and Ruth Ester Young. He was educated at Mill Hill School, London, and subsequently articled to a leading firm of chartered accountants in Newcastle. He initially joined the London Rifle Brigade, and subsequently was granted a commission in the Northumberland Fusiliers. David was killed in action on 26 October 1916, aged 24, and is commemorated on the Tyne Cot Memorial to the Missing.

1/5 Battalion

In the centre, two companies of the 1/5 went forward; again, the going was formidable:

You were just sitting on the edge of this shell hole with your feet in the water. When the whistle went and you went forward it was a toss-up whether your legs would come or not! The ground was yellowy green, soft quicksand. I got one leg in there and two fellows got hold of my rifle and pulled me out. You were plunging forward – you couldn't walk – there was nothing to be seen, your mind and thoughts were on the ground you were struggling across, wanting to avoid quicksands. There wasn't any cover. The shell holes were full of water, I wasn't going to bury myself. It was raining all the time; if you sat on the edge of a shell hole, if you didn't slide down the water came up to meet you. I don't suppose you had more than about 12 inches of soil going about the top. We couldn't walk across the water. You were struggling on – all you did was to go forward. There was a whole roof of shells and God knows what going on top of you. Machine guns whistling past your ear, whizz bangs – God, there was everything! You could see them dropping. If a chap got badly wounded and got in one of these shell holes he was finished. There was hardly anyone left when we got to the wire. You were no further forward – it was worse than a stone wall. There was no hope of getting through. We just thought, 'God, we've got here! How are we going to get back? [8]

On the right, 'C' Company was held up about seventy yards east of the assembly positions by heavy machine gun fire from the 'huts'. The left company ('D' Company) succeeded in gaining a footing on Hill 23, but could not advance further because of heavy machine gun fire from the woods on the left. The two reserve companies were badly cut up by shell and machine gun fire. Eventually, at about 1500hrs, the battalion was compelled by heavy losses to fall back on its original position.

Preliminary casualties for the 1/5 Battalion were: Officers: 1 killed, 7 wounded and 4 missing, including the Roman Catholic Chaplain, The Reverend P. Looby; Other Ranks: 60 killed, 149 wounded and 230 missing. Again, in the months to come, many of these 'missing' would be assumed 'killed in action'. See Appendix D for a fuller list of casualties.

Under cover of darkness, the battalion was relieved by elements of the 1/4 Battalion Yorkshire Regiment and moved back to Rose Cross Camp where, to add further misery, they were shelled by the Germans. One of the Nissen huts was hit causing further casualties: seven other ranks were killed and fifteen were wounded.

1/7 Battalion

On the left, the 1/7 Battalion attacked with 'A', 'B' and 'D' Companies.

Our barrage was a hopeless failure: only shrapnel was used, instead of bursting overhead, as we expected, it burst at least four hundred yards in front of us and behind the line of German machine gun posts. It was worse than useless as it simply served to give the alarm. Until then everything was perfectly quiet, but immediately our guns started, the Boche sent up coloured lights and their barrage came down. [9]

As the men advanced they faced a deathly wall of enfilading machine gun fire:

The Boche machine guns started almost at zero; a single gun started over on our left and traversed towards our right and was very soon joined by other guns along the line. Most of the fire we noticed came from the rising ground on our left and from the forest.[10]

A minute later, the enemy laid down a reversing creeping barrage on the front line: Cinq Chemins – Angle Point – Aden House, which raked backwards towards the stumbling, advancing troops.

The two companies 'A' and 'D', on the flanks of the battalion's front, advanced up to 200 yards. However, 'B' Company in the centre was immediately held up by heavy machine gun fire from the 'huts' in front. Eventually, the men from this company were able to surround the line of 'huts', but in doing so many men were killed or wounded. At this point a platoon from 'C' Company was sent up to help 'B' Company, followed soon afterwards by another platoon to help 'A' Company, who by this time were also held up by machine gun fire along with precise sniping from their right flank. 'D' Company on the left managed to reach their objective but were constantly harried by snipers and machine gun fire from the forest. With the help of the platoon from the support company they struggled on under heavy machine gun fire but with serious losses, inflicted especially by fire from a well-armed enemy trench that

Houthulst Forest
from the south
Author's Collection

Pill Box in Houthulst Forest
Author's Collection

remained untouched by the British barrage. Second Lieutenant R. Thompson, unflinching, led his men forward in an attempt to capture this impediment to their advance, but he was killed, as were most of his men.

> *Of fighting in the true sense of the word we had none. Most of the Boche we saw were beating it back (from their advanced positions I suppose). It was simply a slaughter by machine gun fire, shell fire and sniping from the forest. When daylight came and I saw in what a hole we were, I never thought we could get out alive.*[11]

Second Lieutenants J.H. Shaw and A. Temperley on the right pressed forward in an attempt to keep in touch with the left flank of the 1/5. However, in doing this their command suffered many casualties and a further platoon from 'C' Company was dispatched forward to help. Shaw was killed and Temperley was wounded but for a while he continued to lead his depleted platoon. Temperley was finally taken out by a sniper as he crossed the German wire, and within minutes Second Lieutenant A. P. Strong was also down. By now, all four officers and most of the NCOs from 'A' Company had fallen, so the remnants of this company – fearing a counterattack – were forced to fall back to a line with 'B' Company, which had still been unable to advance and was suffering atrocious casualties, including Lieutenant S.D.S. Tucker and Second Lieutenant F. A. Brown.

The No.3 platoon from 'C' Company, sent up to support the attack, lost all their officers and many of their men and was of little use in helping the beleaguered remnants of 'A' Company. By now the centre and right companies were rudderless, unable to hold their ground; nonetheless, orders were issued to those who remained to consolidate a position as far as possible in front of the starting line as they could, which seems to have been an advance of about 150 yards. Consequently, the right flank of 'A' Company on the left of the battalion front was now unprotected and had to push back its flank to get in touch with the left of 'B' Company. Almost immediately, the Germans reoccupied the forward positions they had briefly lost. By this time, as many as possible of the wounded had been brought in.

At midday, a runner from 'D' Company HQ was sent forward to Captain J. Affleck to report that the remnants of the battalion were back at the starting line: the attack was a failure and he was to retire. Not surprisingly, the runner was killed and the orders were never received. In any case, such was the position of Affleck and the nine or ten men that remained, it would have been suicide to retire while it was light.

The Germans commanded the air:

> *Our own aeroplanes were more than discreet during the attack, and after a hurried survey of our position left the enemy in complete and undisputed possession of the air. The German airmen flew very low, firing at our men with machine guns, one even waving a hand, to which we made no response, being too fed up, wet and cramped to care much what we did.*[12]

The men stranded on the battlefield lay where they could find some meagre level of safety, in shallow shell holes, pooled with filthy, stagnant water. Unable to move, they had only the comradeship of the few around them, not knowing how many others were still alive. They were prey to incessant snipers:

> *I repeatedly saw the German snipers from the forest pick off our wounded as they endeavoured to crawl back to our lines. During the whole day, it was sheer suicide to show the least sign of life; bullets were clipping the sides of our shell hole most of the time. Two of my men in a shell hole nearby, too shallow for comfort, endeavoured to deepen it by lying on their backs in turn and pushing the earth out with their feet. Although I warned them to keep down, they either did not hear or else heeded not; and one of them was shot three times by a sniper – the third shot killed him.*[13]

The afternoon brought no relief as the enemy planes returned, trying to improve the accuracy of their machine gun fire on the soaked and bone-weary survivors who littered the battlefield. Their misery was compounded by the enemy artillery coming into action. Death lurked everywhere.

> *After several long shots, the range was shortened and a shell dropped fair in the side of the crater (just behind my own) sheltering the Lewis gun and its surviving team of two. It passed between the two men and buried itself deep in the mud and burst. But instead of finishing us all only one man was hurt by a splinter, which passed through his helmet and just penetrated his scalp.*[14]

At dusk, Captain Affleck set about understanding 'D' Company's position. He had no idea where his men were – or indeed where the rest of the battalion lay. His limited view was that 'D' Company was in a shallow basin and from it he was unable to gather the whereabouts of the rest of the battalion which, unbeknownst to him, had by now withdrawn to the start line. He could see that immediately to the front was a piece of rough ground with scrubby trees enclosed by a wire fence, which was part of the forest. He came quickly to the conclusion that to spend another day in this depression, dominated by the weaponry in the forest, would be suicidal. At nightfall he issued the following orders:

> *I told Corporal Henderson, my last NCO, to gather all the walking wounded he could find and get back to Company Headquarters to inform Fisher where I was and that I was out of touch on both flanks and that I would push on with what men I had to get on to the higher ground and to send up Doucet's platoon* [sic – he was unaware that Doucet and most of his men had already been killed, early in the attack] *to fill in the gap on the left.*[15]

Lieutenant Frederick Anderson Brown

1/7 Northumberland Fusiliers

Frederick was born in Newcastle, the only son of Frederick and Mary Brown. He was educated at Allan's Endowed School. On the outbreak of hostilities, he enlisted as a private in the Royal Army Medical Corps. Subsequently he was commissioned into the Northumberland Fusiliers. Posted to the Western Front, he was wounded in November 1916 and following convalescence he returned to the front in July 1917. He was killed in action, aged 21, on 26 October 1917. He is buried in Poelcappelle Military Cemetery.

As the NCO left, Affleck abandoned his trench coat and other things he deemed unnecessary and slithered through the mud on his right. Near the road he found the remnants of his right section: three men sheltering under their ground sheets. Further up the road he came upon a wounded 'B' Company man with a badly fractured knee, lying full length in the mud:

He was fully conscious and I crawled alongside and had a few whispered words with him. He said he thought the attack had failed and that 'B' Company had retired. I told him who I was and promised to fetch him when darkness descended (it was then just dusk). He was a brave lad; I was afraid he might cry out when I left him, but he never made a sound. I am glad to say that we got back to him all right, and he reached England safely, minus a leg.[16]

Lieutenant James Angus Scott
1/7 Northumberland Fusiliers

James was born in Ryton on Tyne, the son of William and Ellen Scott. He was educated at Mill Hill School, London. At Mill Hill he was a member of the OTC. He was given a commission with the Northumberland Fusiliers when he was seventeen. He embarked for the Western Front in March 1917 and was killed in action, aged 19, on 26 October 1917. He is commemorated on the Tyne Cot Memorial to the Missing.

Within yards of this wounded man, Affleck came across a belt of strong wire which was protecting the enemy position behind it. He went back and tried to strengthen his own position using such men as remained. As the moon was rising, he withdrew his men back to the starting point, where he set about burying the dead, including his friend Doucet, and getting what was left of his bedraggled men under cover before dawn.

After all our preparations and hopes for our innings on the great battlefield of Flanders, to end in this way – failure, and with nothing more to show for it but a big casualty list.[17]

Casualties for the 1/7 Battalion were: Officers: 9 killed, 1 wounded and 1 missing; Other Ranks: 43 killed, 150 wounded and 53 missing. As ever, in the months to come, many of these 'missing' would be assumed 'killed in action'. See Appendix D for a fuller list of casualties.

At midnight, the battalion was relieved by the 1/5 Yorkshire Regiment and moved back to Marsouin Camp. Even as the survivors were licking their wounds the camp was attacked by enemy aircraft and more of them were hit, including Quartermaster Captain Robert Patrick Neville and one other rank killed, with a further eighteen wounded, of whom five subsequently died.

Captain Robert Patrick Neville
1/7 Northumberland Fusiliers

Robert was born in Dublin in 1871, the son of Richard and Anne Neville. Aged 14, on 4 November 1885 he enlisted into the Northumberland Fusiliers. Over the next 25 years Robert rose to Sergeant and saw service with 2 Battalion, and subsequently with 1 Volunteer Battalion Northumberland Fusiliers, in Ashanti, Sudan, Crete and South Africa. On 15 October 1896, whilst based in Singapore, he married Annie Fox O'Hara; they went on to have at least five children. In 1911 he joined the permanent staff of the 1/7 Northumberland Fusiliers, based at their headquarters in Alnwick. At the outbreak of war he mobilised with his battalion and arrived at the front in April 1915, serving as quartermaster until January 1917 when he was invalided to the UK. After a period in hospital and some time with the reserve battalion, he returned to the front in May 1917. In the King's Birthday Honours list of 1916 Robert was awarded the Military Cross for bravery and conspicuous gallantry in the field, and in the New Year Honours List of 1917 he was promoted to Honorary Captain. Later that year, on 27 October, he was severely injured by the explosion of a bomb dropped by an enemy aeroplane and died from his wounds. Patrick is buried in Solferino Farm Cemetery.

Francis Buckley records:

Those who knew him, and his work in France, will need no reminder of the many things he accomplished for the comfort of both men and officers alike when in the front line trenches and when in the comparative security of 'reserve'. Many were the consultations he held with the M.O. as to matters which would tend to the welfare of the men, and many a man will recall, with grateful remembrance, the wonderful soup which he managed to brew and get conveyed to the trenches at Hill 60, at Sanctuary Wood, Mount Sorrel, and other unhealthy parts of the 'Salient' where it was served piping hot, and where, no doubt, it played a notable part in maintaining the remarkable record of fitness which the battalion showed throughout the whole winter of 1915-16.

… his beloved battalion, and his country, were deprived of the life and the services of so true a gentleman and so gallant a soldier.[18]

1/6 Battalion

Even though the 1/6 was in reserve, based at Pascal Farm, the battalion saw some of its men involved in the day's action. 'D' Company, under Captain K.M. Drummond, was sent up to support the 1/7 on the left, and a platoon from 'A' Company under Lieutenant E.L.Bell was ordered to assist the 1/5 in the centre. The War Diary records: During the 26 October, the battalion suffered about twenty casualties from shell fire. Lieutenant Stanley Dawson Simm Tucker was killed.[19]

Lieutenant Stanley Dawson Simm Tucker
1/6 Northumberland Fusiliers

Stanley was the son of Mr and Mrs Thomas Tucker of Gateshead, County Durham. He was educated at Aldro Preparatory School and Eastbourne College where he was a member of the OTC. On the outbreak of hostilities, he was farming in Australia, but returned in February 1915 to England to obtain a commission. In May 1917 he embarked for the Western Front. Although wounded twice during the attack, he continued to lead his men towards the German line until he was mortally wounded, aged 29. His commanding officer wrote: 'We fought a hard fight at [location censored] but paid a heavy price particularly in officers who all led their men gallantly. Your son in particular showed the utmost bravery, as I knew he would having formed a very high opinion of him.' Stanley is commemorated on the Tyne Cot Memorial to the Missing.

Although the rest of 149 Brigade was relieved before midnight by two battalions from 151 Brigade, the 1/6 remained overnight in shell holes (around Pascal Farm) and next day helped in organizing the evacuation of the wounded. Before it could withdraw, the battalion suffered a further thirty casualties from shell fire.

The ill-prepared attack of 26 October by the intrepid men of 149 Brigade was summed up in the following:

The rain had, however, done its deadly work, for all the gallant fellows could do was drag themselves along through the thick clinging mud and water at a much slower pace that the barrage, which soon got ahead. Then from the pill box and shell hole murderous fire was poured upon them. Many fell dead; some of the wounded fell into gaping holes of water and were drowned; fortunate were those who escaped, but on went the survivors.[20]

On 9 November, the 50th Division was relieved by the 17th Division and began to move westwards from the horrors of the front. By 13 November, 149 Brigade was billeted in the Serques area, where training had started which continued until 8 December, when the 50th Division held a sports day before beginning to move back eastwards on the following day. Their orders were to take over the Passchendaele front from the 33rd Division.

Although the *Second Battle of Passchendaele* had been over for more than a month, heavy guns from both sides continued mercilessly to pound the front and back areas. It soon became apparent that both sides were exhausted ... incapable of further attacks. Both reverted to trench warfare.

The Passchendaele front ran just east of and including Passchendaele and south of the ruined village. Initially, 150 Brigade held the line with 149 Brigade in support in Potijze and 151 in reserve at Brandhoek. The front line consisted of a series of manned posts: those east of Passchendaele were described as 'not so bad' but the line south of the village was atrocious. The terrain between Passchendaele Ridge and Potijze was:

... so terrible and the signs of battle so horrible, as to scar the minds of all who passed that way.[21]

The state of the ground and its hazards were described in his diary by an officer moving up to support positions at Seine, nearly a couple of miles south west of Passchendaele:

Our first journey into this sector was a strange and eerie experience, though we reached our position without casualty, and without much shelling. To those officers who had recently just joined us, it must have been an uncanny breaking in for they were suddenly transported from conditions of civilisation

NORTHUMBERLAND TERRITORIALS
WHO HAVE FALLEN IN THE HOUR OF BATTLE

45002
Pte Frank Newton

240979
Cpl John W Hadaway

242491
Cpl John A Nunn

291703
Sgt George T Thompson

205130
Pte Edwin Jevers

18/1390
Pte Henry Brunton

25/1060
Pte John E Leonard

291907
Pte James W Turnbull

261017
Pte Robert Hall

260164
LCpl Robert Brown

240295
Pte George A E Wilson

261017
Pte James Hutchin

242178
Pte William J Dalgleish

240362
Pte Thomas D Woods

290501
Pte T H Weightman

21/762
Pte George Parker

to conditions and environments totally different from any they had ever before
seen, or been able to conceive – conditions where there was nothing anywhere
to suggest life in any form or civilisation in any degree.

*Passing the White Château on the outskirts of Potijze, we proceeded along the
Ypres-Mooslede road until at length we came to a notice board bearing one
word, Frenzenberg. It was geographical interest only, for not a trace of the
village remained. The very ruins were indistinguishable from the rest of the
clay. The road along which we passed was in fairly good condition, thanks
to the work of various labour units continually employed upon it. It was
an important one, for except when the visibility was very good, motor and
horse transport took up supplies almost as far as the Ypres-Roulers railway.
On either side was black waste. The ground had been so churned up that
no green thing remained; everywhere were shell holes, mud and water;
wreckage of every description was strewn about. Occasionally we came upon
the wrecked vehicles which had fallen a prey to enemy shelling, and had been
swept off the road and abandoned. Frequently we came upon sadder sights:
the badly mutilated and rotting bodies of horses and mules – servants of
man, whose innocent lives he had taken to further his own ends. Here and
there along the route a trench board track led off from the left side of the road
into the mist and obscurity. Occasionally a pill box which had weathered the
storm, loomed into view. The only sign of life in this region of death were
weary parties, scarcely recognisable as human beings, slowly making their
way down from the line. Our guns, of all calibres, were barking viciously on
each side of us.*

*When we had almost reached the point where the road meets the railway
we turned to the left down a plank road, known as the Mule Track. For
some distance, we followed roughly the line of the railway, and then deviated
slightly to the left. We were now proceeding straight for the Passchendaele
Ridge though, owing to the mist, we could not see it. Everywhere the scene
was grim, black, charred and most unnatural, and the strange appearance of
everything was accentuated by heavy black clouds which lowered overhead,
and cast a peculiar light over the landscape. The ground was patched here
and there with islets of ground mist and the higher ground to the east of us
was quite hidden from view.*[22]

After arriving at Seine, the support position, the officer set out to investigate the approach to the front line before darkness:

In front of us was a slight valley which at one time had been wooded, but which now resembled the rest of the countryside, being nothing more than mud and water with charred and very shattered logs lying about. One or two still stood erect like large daggers pointing to the sky, but most were pounded up with the clay. The valley was entirely under water, but we discovered a somewhat precarious trench board track across it. The ground rose steeply and here and there we saw one or two pill boxes. To our right was a rising expanse of mud; to our left was lower ground consisting also of mud and much water. There seemed to be an almost entire absence of landmarks in the drab landscape. To find one's way in such a region would be bad enough in daylight; but by night – impossible – unless there were special methods of guidance.[23]

It was as many records would portray: blood, mud and desolation – conditions redolent of medieval carnage – warfare at its most terrible. Passchendaele during the winter of 1917-1918 demanded endurance and courage from British soldiers living in conditions so appalling that it took every ounce of their determination simply to survive.

Each infantry brigade did a revolving four days: four in the front line, four in support, four in reserve. On the night of 16/17 December, 149 Brigade (without the 1/7) relieved 150 Brigade at a front which ran from Tiger Copse (exclusive) to a road (D6.5 7.5) and included Passchendaele village and the highest part of the ridge, a front of 1600 yards. This front line was in effect a scattering of manned posts. On the right was the 49th Division and the left the 14th Division. Dispositions were right 1/6, left 1/5 and 1/4 in support; the 1/5 The Border Regiment (from 151 Brigade) was in reserve. This relief was completed without incident during a period of mild weather, albeit that the ground was still heavy and sodden. However, the next night there was a hard frost, which meant that the hitherto impassable terrain between the two front lines became navigable for an enemy attack. The War Diary of the 1/5 Battalion for 18 December records:

'B' Company, the centre company, captured 14 prisoners (including an officer) and three machine guns. A party of about 20 of the enemy attempted to approach our post and the NCO opened fire with Lewis gunfire and headed the officer off. The prisoners were identified as from 1st Machine Gun Company, Infantry Regiment 160. First identification of 15th Division on the Corps front.[24]

Between 12 and 23 December the 1/7 Battalion, based at St Jean Camp, was supplying daily working parties on the Light Railways. Three companies were based with the 6 Canadian Rail Transport Company, whilst one was based with the 269 Railway Company Royal Engineers. Following this assignment they received a letter of thanks from the Canadian Engineers for the work they had done, in which the Canadians said they were sorry indeed that they were leaving them. For a few days the battalion was billeted in Ypres, in the cellar of a convent. Interestingly, the convent traced its roots back to a Benedictine house in Brussels, founded in 1665 by Lady Mary Percy, Countess of Northumberland; it housed Irish nuns who were still in residence at the beginning of the war.

Ruins of the Irish Nuns' Abbey, Ypres.
Author's Collection

214

The soldiers of 149 Brigade went back into the front line on the night of 27/28 December, relieving 150 Brigade. During the day, the left post held by the 1/7 was attacked by the enemy who attempted to surround it. They were engaged by the post garrison: one German was killed and an NCO was wounded and taken prisoner. He died of his wounds the following day. These Germans were identified as men from 3 Company, 1 Battalion Infantry Regiment 68. To ring out the old year and ring in the new, the Germans severely bombarded the front.

Casualties for December were: Officers: 1 wounded; Other Ranks: 14 killed and 80 wounded. However, in December the brigade received a large draft of new recruits: 6 Officers and 241 men, the bulk going to the 1/5.

New Year's Day 1918 found 149 Brigade in the front line with 1/7 right and 1/4 left, with 1/6 in support as a counterattack battalion based in the Hamburg area, and 1/5 in reserve at Potizje. The brigade supplied three hundred men for work duties with the 6 Canadian Railway Engineers Company. That night the brigade was relieved by 151 Brigade and moved westwards away from the horrors of the Passchendaele Ridge with the knowledge that the 33rd Division would be taking over their responsibilities. The battalions were transported by rail and bus to the Poperinghe area and, in the case of the 1/4 and 1/7 Battalions, further west to Watou on the French border. Safely installed in the Watou district, the men of 1/7 sat down to a long-awaited Christmas dinner, a pleasant break from the interminable training.

> *The men had their Christmas dinner today, and I think they all enjoyed themselves. Each man had a 1lb of pork, 1/2lb of plum pudding, a bottle of Bass, apples, oranges, cake and as much French beer as they wanted.*[25]

Following this period of training in relative luxury, on 26 January the division moved east, back to the front line. Three days later, 149 Brigade took over the right sector at Passchendaele from the 33rd Division. Dispositions: the 1/5 replaced the 1 Battalion Middlesex Regiment (left) and the 1/6 replaced the 4 Battalion King's (Liverpool) Regiment (right). The 1/7 was in support at Hamburg. Each night, one company of the 1/7 provided parties for carrying rations and supplies up to the front.

February marked a time of great change for 149 Brigade and for the whole British army. There were two prevailing schools of thought: the 'Westerners', primarily the upper echelons of the military, insisted that Germany could only be beaten by driving them back to Berlin. The politicians, that is to say Lloyd George and Lord Milner, were 'Easterners', who believed that beating Germany's allies would result in an overall German defeat. Lloyd George did not have enough political clout to remove Haig from his command, but he used his Machiavellian skills to manipulate conditions which caused great hardship to Haig and to the army.

On 3 November 1917, the War Office revealed that the number of fresh recruits that Haig was likely to receive to top up and maintain his divisions in 1918 would be far below the number he actually needed. The War Office estimated that the current deficit of 75,000 men would expand to 259,000 men by late 1918; Haig's staff projected this at nearer 460,000.

In essence, Lloyd George wanted to retain troops in Britain, preventing Haig from 'misusing' them on the Western Front in what he perceived to be a waste of resources. In the event, Army Command asked for 615,000 men to maintain formations in the field. To this request only 200,000 were made available, and it quickly became clear that up to 100,000 of these were simply not fit to serve.

After much deliberation, the army's leadership came up with two possible answers to this problem: either to disband fifteen divisions, or to reduce each division from twelve battalions to nine. At this juncture, with extraordinary lack of tact, Lloyd George agreed with the French, on behalf of the Army, to extend the front under British control by twenty-eight miles.

All of these machinations went on with the full knowledge that the war on the eastern front was over, freeing up a further fifty German divisions to face the unprepared, undermanned and demoralised British Army. (All of this was to come to the boil on 21 March 1918 when Germany attacked along a forty-three mile front in a calculated attempt to win the war before the Americans arrived in force.)

Within 149 Brigade it fell to the junior battalion, the 1/7, to take the brunt of this reorganisation. Their future role was to be the Divisional Pioneer Battalion for the 42nd (East Lancashire) Division, a Territorial Division commanded at that time by Major General Arthur Solly-Flood. In some brigades, proud battalions with hard won traditions were disbanded. This was the fate of the 16 Battalion Northumberland Fusiliers (96 Brigade, 32nd Division). However, at least these Fusiliers were to remain Fusiliers: 'A' Company was detailed to the 1/4 Battalion: 'B' Company to 1/5 Battalion, 'C' to 1/6 Battalion and 'D' Company to the 1/7 Battalion. On 10 February, the 1/7 Battalion left Alnwick Camp, Potizje, and 149 Brigade for pastures new.

On the previous day, the slimmed down 50th Division, with its three brigades each consisting of three battalions, handed over part of their front line to the 29th Division and took over a sector from the 66th Division. The new sector comprised the portion of the Passchendaele Ridge from the Zonnebeke-Moorslede road (inclusive) northwards for 1200 yards. Using the new three-battalion system, the front was manned by one battalion rather than two. Another battalion was in support in the Seine sector, and in reserve was the third battalion at Potizje. Initially the 1/4 Battalion was at the front between 9 and 12 February.

Taken from the War Diary of the 1/4 Battalion Northumberland Fusiliers:

At 5pm on 9 February relieved the 2/6th Battalion Manchester Regiment (66th Division) in the front line. It consisted of a line of posts on the forward slope of the Broodseinde-Passchendaele ridge. This line was held by two companies: 'A' on right holding 6 posts and 'B' on the left holding 7 posts. Each post was held by 1 NCO and 3 men during the day and 1 NCO and 6 men by night. Reliefs were carried out before dawn and after dark. The men during the night would work on wiring the front of these posts; carrying up their own materials, the wire was put up 75 yards in front of this line of posts. Once completed the belts of wire were 10 feet thick and knee high. Each company managed to put up 80 yards of wire during this tour at the front. The main defensive line was on the reverse slope of the Broodseinde-Passchendaele ridge which consisted of a line of strong points and was held by 'D' Company. One platoon was left at Daring Crossing in reserve. The main work for 'D' Company was the improvement of the support posts. Parapets and barricades were strengthened and draining and sanitary arrangements *were made.*

One Company, 'C', was held in reserve in the vicinity of Daring Crossing at the disposal of the battalion commander for counter attacks on any part of the battalion front. This company carried rations and materials to the other three companies and provided daily parties for salvage work.

At night patrols were sent out with the objectives of locating the enemy and reporting on the state of the ground in front of our line. On the night of 9/10 February these patrols reconnoitred as far as a line 100 yards in front of our line and on the night 10/11 February up to a line drawn through the eastern edge of Dairy and Daisy Woods. No enemy were encountered and the ground was found to be very cut up by shellfire and waterlogged.[26]

Casualties were reported as: Officers: 1 wounded; Other Ranks: 3 killed and 4 wounded.

Revolving battalion reliefs followed until 20 February when the 50th Division was replaced by the 33rd Division, and by 23 February, 149 Brigade was located in the area around Wizernes. Although it was not yet confirmed, the 50th Division had finally seen the back of the Ypres Salient. As usual, training began, which continued to 7 March, when orders were received that the 50th Division was to be transferred to 5 Army. At first, they moved to the Moreuil region, but on 11 March they were moved again to the Proyart area. The 149 Brigade was based at Mézières, south of the Somme, and were now in Army Headquarters Reserve, at twelve hours' notice to move in the event of emergency. They did not have long to wait ...

CHAPTER NINE

GERMAN ADVANCE ACROSS THE SOMME, MARCH 1918

How long, oh Lord, how long, before the flood
Of crimson-welling carnage shall abate?
From '*How long, oh Lord?*' by Captain Robert Palmer (d.1916)

During 1917 the British Army had been perpetually on the offensive at *Arras, Messines, Passchendaele* and *Cambrai,* taking a desperate and worrying number of casualties. Nonetheless, in early 1918, the Prime Minister committed the British Army to extending the length of its front line, assuming duties hitherto undertaken by the French; this was an extra responsibility of twenty-eight miles, from St Quentin to Barisis.

To say the least, the French defensive positions had been seriously ill-maintained. Indeed, in places they were non-existent. To make a bad situation worse, the British High Command had instigated a new doctrine, 'Defence in Depth', which required all levels of command to master and instigate fresh training systems. This strategy was designed to delay rather than prevent the advance of an attacker, buying time and causing maximum enemy casualties by yielding ground, rather than defeating an attacker with a single strong line. The system relies on the attack losing momentum as it moves forward; the defender yields lightly defended territory in an effort to stretch the attacker's logistics. Once the attack has lost its momentum, defensive counterattacks can be mounted on the attacker's weak points. Below is an illustration of a typical divisional set-up manned by the new nine battalion system.

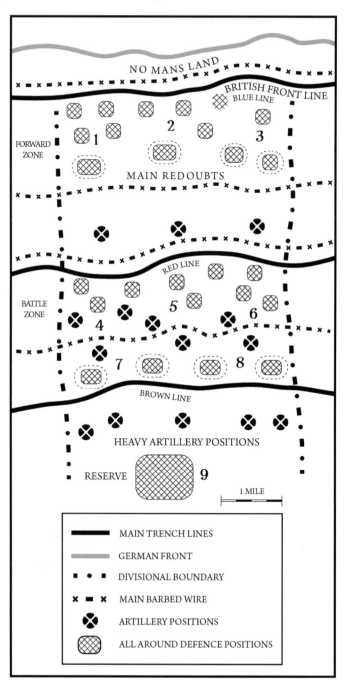

The Forward Zone would contain a number of highly defended redoubts which were not physically connected but which would allow lines of interconnecting killing zones between them if the weather were clear. The Battle Zone would be more stringently defended and would be where the main fighting would occur if the front line were threatened. Further behind the system the Green Line would form the last system of defence.

At home, the War Cabinet imposed two further constraints on the British forces, the first of which was to limit the level of reinforcements to the army, which compromised the BEF operational effectiveness. Secondly, they called for the reorganisation of divisions by reducing the number of their battalions: 115 infantry battalions were to be disbanded as the fighting strength of each division was reduced from 12 battalions to 9. This task was completed by 4 March and it affected both the morale and the fighting efficiency of each division. Meanwhile, even as these taxing changes were being implemented, British Army Intelligence was gleaning troubling information about the build-up of German forces. It seemed that a big attack was in the offing.

During 1917 the British had inflicted major, although not terminal, damage on the German Army, and as early as November 1917 the German High Command had decided that they must *attack* rather than simply *resist* their enemy. They perceived that after the rigours of 1917 the British Army would be exhausted … and therefore vulnerable. Furthermore, the window for an attack in the spring of 1918 should be well before the Americans could enter the fray with any force. In the Germans' favour was that the war on the Eastern Front was all but over (it was formally ended by the Russians at the *Treaty of Brest-Litovsk* in March 1918), therewith releasing a large number of fresh German troops to transfer to the Western Front.

They spent a long time in assessing where the attack should be made: Flanders, around Arras? Verdun? Either side of St Quentin? They drew up plans for each of these locations, but in January 1918 the area north and south of St Quentin was selected for the attack. The Germans concluded, rightly, that the British-held positions stood on ground favourable for attacking infantry, that defences were weak or non-existent and that the defenders were spread too thinly to give any effective resistance; at many points along the front they outnumbered the British by four to one. The date of the battle, known as the *Kaiserschlacht* (Kaiser's Battle), was set for 21 March 1918, by which time the Germans had developed infiltration techniques by which highly mobile units could penetrate gaps in the newly extended and unfinished British defence system. Strongly held points could be mopped up later. This attack across the old Somme Battlefield was known as the *Michael Offensive*.

Lightly armed German Stormtroopers moved rapidly through the Allied lines, often under the cover of a dense fog

At 0440hrs on 21 March, along a dark and murky forty-three mile front, the calm of early morning was shattered by an immense barrage from over a thousand artillery pieces of various sizes. For the next five hours the Germans systematically destroyed, using high explosive and gas shells, command posts, communication and heavy gun positions far behind the British front. Later, the onslaught concentrated on the garrisons of the British outpost line and their forward defences. At 0940hrs, following a shorter barrage of the British forward lines, a flood of German infantry surged forward led by an élite core of Stormtroopers. Shrouded by dense fog, they rapidly overran many of the forward positions of the British outpost line and pressed on, picking their way around points of resistance. By the afternoon it became clear that to the south of St Quentin the British had suffered severe losses; that night, orders were issued for a limited withdrawal – which within days became a major retreat.

The 50th Division received warning orders at 0430hrs on 21 March from Fifth Army Headquarters. At 0530hrs, 149 Brigade HQ at Mézières was notified: be ready to move within a few hours. Nevertheless, with everyone waiting round apprehensively, it was not until the evening that the brigade (now just three battalions, the 1/4, 1/5 and 1/6) left their billets near Le Quesnol on the east side of the main road between Amiens and Roye. By nightfall the men of 149 had reached Brie by train, from where they were dispatched on foot to Caulaincourt and the Green Line. The 50th Division was ordered to support the 66th Division (XIX Corps).

The XIX Corps sector was contained by two river valleys, the Omignon to the south and the Cologne, which flowed into the Somme at Péronne, to the north. The front was defended by two infantry divisions, the 24th (right) and the 66th (left). The opening bombardment on the XIX Corps was relentless and devastating. On the 66th Division front the first waves of the enemy's 25th and 208th Divisions soon broke through the Forward Zone from Grand Priel Woods in the south to Templeux le Guérard in the Cologne Valley. The 4 Battalion East Lancashires, who were dug in in front of Hargicourt, were swiftly trounced by attacks from both flanks. Similarly, the 2/8 Lancashire Fusiliers to the north of Hargicourt were bulldozed aside. By 1030hrs, as the fog lifted, German infantry had reached the forward edge of the battle zone at Brosse Wood.

The men of 149 Brigade had orders to assemble on the Green Line (or rear zone of defences) which ran from Villevecque to Boully, covering Fléchin, Bernes and Nobescourt Farm. Tired and hungry, the men marched from Brie to the Green Line, although they made slow progress: thick mist, darkness and heavy traffic on the road all caused delays.

As dawn crept in they reached their position; burdened by their heavy packs, the men were bone weary. By 0800hrs on 22 March the Green Line was occupied along the Divisional Front with the following dispositions: from right to left 149, 150 and 151 Brigades. In front the line was well wired but the trenches – one could hardly call them that – had only been dug to a depth of one to two feet. The men of 149 Brigade manned the line with the 1/4 Battalion on the right, which covered Caulincourt and the 1/6 on the left, a frontage of more than 2000 yards which ran from the crossroads one mile south-west of Villevecque to Poeuilly (inclusive). The 1/5 formed the reserve at St Martin, whilst the Brigade HQ was based in Tertry. Also in the line was the 149 Machine Gun Company, with two guns held in reserve.

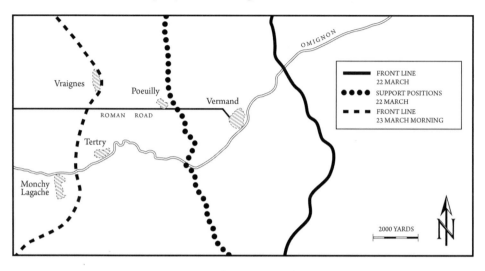

German positions on the morning of 23 March 1918

The 1/4 were on the extreme right of the 50th Division's front with men of the 24th Division on their right flank. In front of the Green Line, a defensive front was held by the 16th Division, although as the enemy pressed forward just after midday they retired in fairly good order. The enemy quickly occupied the villages of Vermand and Soyecourt.

The 1/4 Battalion

The Germans attacked 149 Brigade's position late in the afternoon, although the exact time is unclear: The War Diary of the 1/4[1] reports the time as 1600hrs, that of 149 Brigade as 1500hrs and the divisional diary states 1745hrs. At whatever time, German hordes attacked in eight waves providing an easy target for rifle and machine gun; nonetheless, on the 1/4's front, the enemy managed to secure the high ground overlooking the village of Poeuilly, only to be driven back in a later counterattack.

South of the Omignon the enemy stormed through the left of the 24th Division and forced their way over the Caulaincourt-Beauvois road, west of Trefcon. A little later they were able to penetrate the left of the sector held by the 1/4, so a company from the 1/5 under Lieutenant J Leech was placed at the disposal of the 1/4 to reinforce their right flank. Number 2 Wood was regarded as key to the integrity of the brigade's right flank, and this was held with a 'refused flank' that bent back in a north-west direction from the village of Caulaincourt.

It was on the Green Line that we joined the battle with the enemy, and the fight waged fiercely through Friday afternoon. Casualties, especially amongst officers, were heavy from the first, the Commanding Officer, Lieutenant Colonel William Robb being wounded and all the company commanders killed or missing. The story of Captain W. B. Hicks and 'A' Company will be told later; suffice it to say here that on Friday evening they were regarded as missing, probably captured. Captain T. W. Gregory, of 'B' Company, was wounded, but continued to fight; was wounded again in several places, and died in the Field Ambulance in the neighbouring village of Tertry. Captain A. Findlayson of 'C' Company was wounded in the arm, but refused to go back, fighting with a number of his men from behind the shelter of a broken wall in the village. It is feared that this officer, an unyielding, indomitable Scot, fell at the spot from which not even wounds could dislodge him. Equally gallant, scarcely varying in a word, is the story of Captain King, of 'D' Company, another officer that never came back. Second Lieutenant Chevreau, a Franco-British officer, holder of the Croix de Guerre, was in charge of an advanced position with a platoon of 'B' Company. He and his 34 men fought until they were reduced to 8, of whom several were wounded. Though badly wounded himself he continued to fight, in order to cover the escape of his wounded men to the Aid Post. He gave no ground to the last and died at his post. Lieutenant [T.C.] Lund was wounded in two places, treated at the Aid Post and not seen again. Second lieutenant [J.W.] Cockburn was wounded at the opening of the action. Second Lieutenant [T.] Tibbs was missing, being last seen heroically defending his position.[2]

With both flanks exposed, the 1/4 was forced back to Caulaincourt, leaving the 1/6 in place and unaware that the 1/4 had retired. During this action Captain Thomas William Gregory, aged 23, was killed.

Captain Thomas William Gregory
1/4 Battalion Northumberland Fusiliers

Thomas was born in Newcastle upon Tyne in 1894, the son of William Nottingham and Anne Elizabeth Gregory. At the onset of hostilities he was a student at Armstrong College, Newcastle, and was also a member of Durham University OTC. Immediately he was granted a commission into the Northumberland Fusiliers. Thomas departed for France in May 1915 and was severely wounded 4 July 1915. After being passed fit for duty, he returned to the Western Front on 4 October 1916. Following this he returned home sick and whilst in England was promoted captain. After convalescence, he returned to the front in early September 1917. He was killed on 22 March 1918, aged 23. Thomas is commemorated on the Arras Memorial to the Missing.

A number of men from the 1/4 Battalion won the Military Medal for their actions on 22 March 1918:

30/253 Lance Sergeant Arthur William Peters

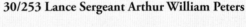

On the 22nd March, at Caulaincourt, this NCO, from a forward position, protected the flank of the neighbouring Company and harassed the enemy in his advance. He held his ground although almost surrounded and when his task was accomplished extricated his platoon with great coolness and skill. During the whole of the time the Battalion was in action he set an example of courage and cheerfulness in difficult circumstances.

46793 Corporal James W. Keen

On the 22nd March, at Caulaincourt, this NCO, although twice severely wounded, rallied and reorganised the men to cover the retirement of part of the Regimental Transport. He refused to leave his post until ordered by an officer to proceed to the dressing station, which he reached with the utmost difficulty.

21/16 Private Edward Alcock

On the 22nd March, at Caulaincourt, this man volunteered to accompany his platoon Sergeant in re-occupying a trench. He showed great bravery in remaining alone in the trench whilst the rest of the platoon was rallied and brought back.

200550 Private William Heron

On the 22nd March, at Caulaincourt, this stretcher bearer worked with the utmost gallantry, attending to the wounded without regard to danger or fatigue. Subsequently throughout nine days of fighting he continually exposed himself to heavy machine gun fire and shelling carrying on his duties as stretcher bearer for long periods without rest.

200037 Private David Foster

On the 22nd March, at Caulaincourt, under heavy fire, he carried his Commanding Officer, who was severely wounded, to a place of safety, a distance of 600 yards. Throughout a week of continual fighting and movement he showed himself a thoroughly reliable soldier, and utterly regardless of personal danger. On several occasions, his example of coolness and courage helped to steady his comrades. (see also p. 243).

The 1/6 Battalion

To begin with, the 1/6 were able to hold their ground; it was reported that they took a number of prisoners, many of whom had pockets stuffed with English cigarettes. As the battle progressed it became obvious that something was amiss on the battalion's right: the 1/4 had retired. Soon they observed that a large force of the enemy was massing at Soyécourt, although the Boche did not attempt any more frontal attacks but were content to send out strong patrols along the valley south of Poeuilly and also towards their refused flank. The War Diary of 1/6 Battalion records:

Capture of prisoners were made in these neighbourhoods. Some of these

> *prisoners readily surrendered and appeared pleased to be thus easily out of the war.*[3]

At midnight, the 1/6 were sent orders to retire from the Green Line at 1400hrs (on 23 March) and move to a position between Tertry and Vraignes-en-Vermandois, east of Estres-en-Chaussée, about two miles to the rear.

The 1/5 Battalion

At 1445hrs on 22 March, the 1/5 sent 'C' and 'D' Companies forward from their position in reserve to report to the front-line battalions. As previously discussed, one of the counterattacks originated from St Martin and drove the enemy over the Caulaincourt-Poeuilly road with the cooperation of the 1/6 and retook most of Caulaincourt. However, the enemy were steadfast; a second counterattack was needed to help restore the situation. Casualties for the day were: Officers: 1 killed and 2 missing; Other Ranks: 70 killed, 33 wounded, and 35 missing. The officer killed was Second Lieutenant John McIntosh of Hexham.

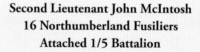

Second Lieutenant John McIntosh
16 Northumberland Fusiliers
Attached 1/5 Battalion

John was born in Hexham, Northumberland, in 1886, the son of Angus and Ellen McIntosh. In 1900, after leaving his job as a blacksmith, John enlisted in the 19 (Queen Alexandra's Own Royal) Hussars. He served in South Africa and rose to the rank of Company Sergeant Major. At the onset of hostilities, the Hussars went out to France with the British Expeditionary Force, *The Old Contemptibles*. He was involved in the drastic fight during the retreat from Mons and was the proud holder of the Mons Star. In early 1917 he reluctantly accepted a commission with the 16 Battalion, Northumberland Fusiliers. When in early 1918 the 16 Battalion was disbanded he was posted to the 1/5 Northumberland Fusiliers. He was killed on 22 March, aged 32, when his battalion mounted a counterattack to restore the 149 Brigade's position on the Green Line. John is commemorated on a special memorial in Trefcon British Cemetery, Caulaincourt.

It was a nerve-racking thing when they attacked you. They used to come like a house, like bonded together. Our idea of attacking was extended order – a good bit between each man – so that if a shell burst it would only maybe take one man, it might take two. The Jerries came across like the side of a house, heavy, and they used to fire off the hip. The leading man, I suppose, trying to put the wind up you. But that didn't take much effect; I mean the thicker they were together the more the bullet would take two men instead of one.[4]

As the general withdrawal was in progress, on 23 March further orders reached the Divisional HQ from Corps HQ that the 50th Division was to continue to retire to the line of the Somme Canal. Each of the three brigades made an initial withdrawal to the line Le Mesnil-Athies at the discretion of their commanding officers. From this line, the withdrawal to the Somme Canal was to be carried out under divisional orders. The men of 149 Brigade were to cross over by the bridge at St Christ. Ignorant of this withdrawal, at 0630hrs, in thick mist, enemy forces launched an attack against the now vacant Green Line, preceded by violent artillery fire. On realising that the fox had already left the henhouse the enemy pounded on, engaging the retiring battalions in numerous rearguard actions which at times were desperate. The fighting of 23 March is succinctly recounted by the War Diary of the 1/6 Battalion NF [5]:

The retirement from the Green Line was carried out in perfect order along the whole battalion front and at 4.30am the troops arrived on the new ground and, after being supplied with hot tea and rum from the battalion's cookers, commenced digging in a line of posts running south from the Mons-en-Chaussée-Vermand road. In a couple of hours our troops had dug in sufficiently to secure the line and dispositions were made to hold it. At 8.30am, however, operation orders were received to commence a retirement at 9am to which the whole line would conform. By the time those orders could be repeated to the companies, the front line had become involved in close contact with the enemy who advanced in large numbers and in mass formations. The 150th Brigade on our left counterattacked along their front and commenced a retirement. On the battalion front 'A' and 'C' Companies were too involved with the enemy to get clear and three platoons of 'A' Company and part of 'C' Company were unable to free themselves and were afterwards regarded as missing. Lieutenant [C.A.] Balden with part of 'A' Company was last seen fighting in a hand to hand encounter with the enemy. Lieutenants [G.A.]Oswald and Hamilton were both seen wounded and were afterwards known to be missing. In the meantime 'B' Company covered the retreat of the remainder of the battalion and fought a brilliant rear guard as far as Mons where it was relieved by another company. The whole retirement again was carried out in perfect order, although the enemy pressed forward with machine guns, artillery and aeroplanes and kept up a gruelling fire from all three weapons. In this retirement, Lieutenant S.J. B. Stanton was wounded but was able to continue with the retiring forces. Second Lieutenant Milligan was also wounded and carried down with the retirement. The line of retirement was due west. It was a brilliant, summer-like day with hot sun and as the battle went on hour after hour unceasingly, with the enemy artillery becoming more and more pressing, the fatigue of marching and fighting was more and more felt.

At 12.30pm Brie was reached, the troops being in good order and passing through a covering force from 8th Division. In and around Brie enormous fires were burning and ammunition dumps which could not be removed [were] blown up. Hut camps and aerodromes on the east side of the Somme Canal were also burning during the retirement. From the Green Line the battalion had fought and retired a distance of 10½ miles in eight hours, the greater part being covered in extended order over open country and with rear guard actions taking place from time to time to relieve enemy pressure. At Brie the Battalion less 'D' Company, which occupied trenches on the west bank of the Somme canal, rested east of Villers-Carbonnel. Later the battalion moved up to support 'D' Company commanded by Captain [K.M.] Drummond.[5]

The 1/5 Battalion

By 1130hrs on 23 March the 1/5 had been outflanked, which prompted its retirement to the Somme Canal. For a time, the battalion dug in on a line south east of Athies but eventually Battalion HQ with 'C' and 'D' Companies crossed the Somme Canal at St Christ at about 1500hrs. 'A' and 'B' Companies were somehow detached during the withdrawal and were unable to join them until early on the morning of 24 March. West of the Somme Canal, 'C' and 'D' Companies dug and held a line of trenches.

The 1/4 Battalion

At 0900hrs on 23 March the 1/4, led by Captain T.A. Lacy-Thompson and based at Monchy-Lagache, were marched back to Devizes. They crossed the Somme Canal at St Christ and took up a position commanding the bridgehead, which 'C' Company held until relieved by troops of the 8th Division:

The whole line was withdrawn, under cover of darkness, to Merancourt, where we provided the men with hot tea and food, and later through Devizes to the river at St Christ. Considerable fighting took place here on the Saturday night, the enemy making repeated and desperate attempts to gain possession. On one occasion, he actually succeeded in getting across, but thanks to the excellent work of 'C' Company (amongst whom Corporal Steele may be named) was destroyed or driven back by concentrated rifle and Lewis gun fire.[6]

During the action of 23 March, two men from the 1/4 carried out acts of gallantry for which they were awarded the Military Medal:

202750 Corporal Theophilus Steele

On the night of 23rd March 1918 when his company was holding the bridge over the Somme at St Christ, this NCO covered the bridge with his Lewis gun and held back the enemy until compelled to withdraw owing to his gun being out of action. His example and leadership throughout the nine days of fighting were magnificent. He brought his gun back intact when the battalion was relieved.

201975 Sergeant William Mowles

On the 23rd March at St Christ bridgehead, this NCO, while acting as Company Sergeant Major, rendered invaluable service in rallying and encouraging his men for a counter attack. The success of this effort was due in considerable measure to his energy and courage.

The 149 Brigade Diary reports[7]:

> *The withdrawal to the west bank of the Somme Canal was begun at 11am*
> *covered by the 1/5 Battalion holding Ennemain and the high ground to the*
> *east of the village with one Company. This rear-guard was heavily engaged,*
> *but held its ground whilst the whole Brigade* [this is slightly at odds with
> the narrative from 1/6 Battalion - A.G.] *crossed the St Christ Bridge and*
> *took up positions from Cizancourt (exclusive) to Happlincourt (exclusive),*
> *order of battle right to left, 1/4, 1/5, 1/6, with two remaining machine guns*
> *in the line.*

Having been relieved by the 8th Division, the 50th Division saw little actual fighting on 24 March; 149 Brigade passed a day of relative peace as the battalions fell back to Foucaucourt. By 1700hrs they were taking up a line, one thousand yards in length, from north to south of Assevillers including the eastern portion of the village: the 1/5 were on the right, the 1/6 on the left and the 1/4 in reserve. The Brigade HQ was at Estrées. Here the 22 Entrenching Battalion was attached to 149 Brigade.

> *Our position on Sunday 24th was on a slight rise between St Christ bridgehead*
> *and Misery but we were withdrawn to Foucaucourt during the morning for*
> *a brief rest. Here a dramatic surprise awaited us, for Captain* [W.B.] *Hicks*
> *and over 90 men of 'A' Company joined us. They were as reinforcements from*
> *the dead. On the Friday afternoon, they had been cut off from the rest of the*
> *battalion, but refused to surrender. A diversion by some other British force*
> *(presumed to have been cavalry) weakened the enemy circle. Hicks and his*
> *gallant men immediately seized the opportunity, fought their way out, and*
> *escaped to the south near Nesle.*[8]

However, after the withdrawal to Foucaucourt, at 2030hrs 149 Brigade was placed at the disposal of the 66th Division. The 1/6 Battalion came under artillery attack and Captain Kearsley Mathwin Drummond was severely wounded by a bursting shell, dying later that day. At 2230hrs both the 1/5 and 1/6 Battalions were ordered eastwards: the 1/6 moved to the north, the 1/5 to the south, of Barleux. At this highly fluid juncture, the 1/5, minus one company, was attached to 24 Brigade, 8th Division. Later they were ordered to return to 149 Brigade at Assevillers. By this time a large enemy force had crossed the Somme Canal at Éterpigny and were attempting to occupy high ground north of Barleux. In response, the 1/6, together with a company from 1/5 and the 1/6 Battalion Cheshire Regiment (118 Brigade, 39th Division) took up a position on this high ground to cover the retirement of the 66th Division. The enemy was swarming in from the south-west. During the night, the 1/6, acting as a rearguard, fell back on Assevillers, but by 0100hrs on 25 March they were back in their original position in front of the village. The disposition at this time was from right to left 1/5 DLI, 1/7 DLI, 1/4 NF, 1/6 NF with the 1/5 NF in reserve in Assevillers. All of these battalions were under the command of 149 Brigade.

Captain Kearsley Mathwin Drummond MC
1/6 Battalion Northumberland Fusiliers.

Kearsley was born in Newcastle upon Tyne in 1885 the son of Professor David and Margaret Horsley Drummond. He was educated at a preparatory school in Newcastle and from 1899 at Repton School. He enlisted in the 1/6 Northumberland Fusiliers and was gazetted second lieutenant on 12 September 1914. He embarked for France in May 1915, but within two months was severely wounded. After recuperation Kearsley returned to the Western Front in January 1917 and remained there till June 1917. He was promoted to captain in March 1917. He returned to the front again in September 1917, only to die of wounds on 24 March 1918 aged 32. Kearsley is buried in Rosières British Cemetery. His headstone is inscribed:

SON OF SIR DAVID DRUMMOND

NEWCASTLE UPON TYNE

To the left of this line-up, elements from the 66th Division were manning the front which, at 0930hrs on 26 March, was attacked by the enemy. They were forced to retire, leaving the left flank of 149 Brigade horribly exposed. Two companies of 1/5 counterattacked and were able to restore some order on the brigade's left, but the 66th Division continued with their withdrawal.

Consequently, the composite 149 Brigade was compelled to withdraw to a line stretching from Rosières-en-Santerre to Vauvillers (both inclusive), with the 8th Division on the right and the 66th Division on the left. As they retreated, 149 Brigade left a rearguard of one company of 1/5 NF and one company of 1/5 DLI on high ground 1000 yards east of the main defensive line. This rear-guard was heavily engaged in turn, but at 1300hrs they were still holding their own. By 1600hrs the 66th Division was again in trouble and the enemy managed to drive them out of Framerville. The 1/4 counterattacked and captured all but the eastern portion of the village.

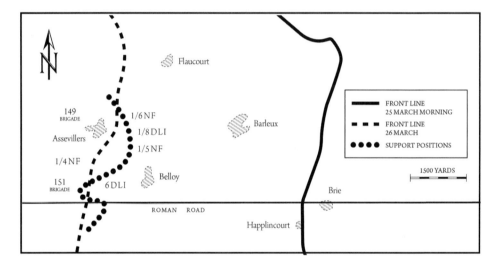

Position of 149 Brigade, 25 March 1918

On Tuesday 26 there was another vigorous fight at Vauvillers and neighbourhood with several spirited counterattacks led by Captain Lacy Thompson, whose work during these days defies description. To the deep regret of all he was wounded, as was Captain L.G. Thomas, of Trench Mortar Battery (acting as infantry at this time with our battalion). Second Lieutenant [W.] Anderson, who had done conspicuously good work, was also a casualty. General fighting followed, ranging over the country from Rosières to Harbonnières.[9]

The following narrative about the 1/6 Battalion was written after the war by an unnamed member of the battalion:

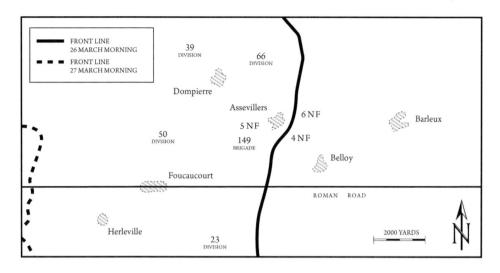

149 Brigade position, 26 March 1918

At 7.30am [26 March] *the enemy attacked again. A storm of machine gun bullets swept the 1/6 Battalion and the troops of 66th Division, and once again hordes of Germans flung themselves on the thin lines of British soldiers. The 1/6 Battalion stood fast, but alas, the 66th Division was compelled to fall back. In justice to the Lancashire men it must be said that their retirement was not due to the lack of courage. They had fought desperately through the whole attack since 21 March and were reduced to a mere remnant. They had lost almost all their officers, and their companies were about the strength of an ordinary platoon. But the River Somme, which runs here from east to west parallel with, and about four miles to the north of the Amiens-Vermand road, was between the 66th Division and the troops on the left, and there seems little doubt that a sudden advance of the enemy along the Somme valley, due to a British retirement north of the Somme, was the cause of the 66th Division falling back.*

To hold Assevillers was now hopeless. At 9am orders came to withdraw to a line between Rosières and Vauvillers, and the battalion accordingly retired. A pause was made in Foucaucourt after the first stage of retirement, which took place over rough country, much broken by wire and old trenches. Rolls were called and stragglers re-joined their sections, and in perfect order, although much reduced by casualties, the battalion took up a new position.

As the battalion passed through Foucaucourt, huts and stores were blazing. If the place could not be held, at any rate nothing of value was to be permitted to fall into the hands of the enemy. At Foucaucourt cross roads, two runners had been left with a message for all officers who had not yet passed through. Later in the day the writer learned that these runners had waited at the cross roads with the military policeman on duty until the Germans were entering the village a couple of hundred yards away. The policeman then ordered the runners to leave. When they came away the policeman remained. He was standing at his post as cool and calm as the constable who stands at the foot of Northumberland Street. Shells were bursting around him, and the approaching enemy were but a stone's throw from him. Apparently, he had no orders to quit his post and he stood fast.

In the new position between Rosières and Vauvillers all was quiet on the immediate front of 1/6 Battalion ... darkness came on and the 1/6 took over advanced posts with other troops of the 50th Division on the right and left. The night passed quietly.[10]

Ruins of the church at Assevillers
Author's Collection

This account of the events of 27 March is based on those found in the War Diary of the 1/6 Battalion:

The enemy did not get in touch with our outpost line till 8am when he was seen moving across our front in force in direction of Rosières which was being heavily shelled and the 8th Division front attacked. This attack was beaten off. Large numbers of enemy were seen massing on our front and Lieutenant Brownrigg and a party of NCOs and men attacked and captured a party of 16 Germans who had forced their way between the battalion's left and the right of the 1/5 NF.

Enemy directed main attack on 66th Division's front north of Vauvillers and at 12 o'clock a telephone instruction was received to retire. Carried out a retirement in conjunction with the 1/5 NF on the left ... A few minutes later a telephone message was received cancelling [the] retirement and ordering a counterattack. The troops were already moving along the whole front and had reached the line of the Rosières-Proyart light railway, with the enemy attacking in force and bringing up machine guns ... Colonel Anstey (50th Division) rode onto the ground ordering troops back to fight at the call of their officers. Battalion HQ, Composite Company and 'C' Company (Captain Davies) of the 1/6 NF, parties of the 1/4 East Yorks and Entrenching Battalion formed up on the line of the Rosières-Proyart light railway under the command of Lieutenant Colonel F. Robinson. The counterattack was launched with the greatest courage and determination, and the enemy were driven from the ridge, Colonel Robinson leading the attack, in doing which he was shot down, badly wounded.[11]

The baton was then taken up by the Adjutant, Captain Armstrong, who was also severely injured within minutes, following which Lieutenant A. W. Leech took command.

The counterattack had succeeded brilliantly, and a further attack on Long Trench and the enemy machine guns which were playing havoc along our front was ordered. Part of Long Trench and two enemy machine guns were captured together with parties of the enemy.[12]

Troops from the 8th Division, along with a party from the 1/4 East Yorkshire Regiment (150 Brigade) supported this counteraction and were able to supply small arms ammunition to the men of the 1/6, who by now were scrabbling for bullets. The enemy at this time appeared to be in retreat; the new line was consolidated and linked to that of the 8th Division.

> *An enemy attack developed from the direction of Vauvillers on our left flank, and the left was driven in the direction of the Gillaucourt-Rosières railway. Thereupon orders were given for troops holding Long Trench and forward positions to form a defensive flank to the 8th Division … This line held under pressure. The enemy did not press any more attacks and practically all the ground won taken during the counterattacks was successfully held. All wounded officers and men were evacuated.*[13]

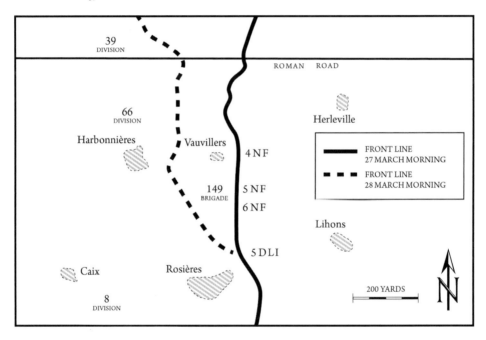

Position of 149 Brigade, 27 March 1918

However, the cost had been high: Lieutenant Colonel Robinson, Captain Armstrong, Captain Davies and Second Lieutenant Brownrigg were all wounded. Casualties in other ranks were extremely high, including the wounding of Regimental Sergeant Major Colin Finch. In the evening the 1/6 Battalion front was relieved by troops from the 8th Division and the 1/6 moved to the south of Harbonnières so that the battalion could reorganise under Captain Leathart. They were later joined by Lieutenant Leech with the remnants of his attacking force: some twenty men.

Both the 1/4 and 1/5 Battalions were involved in counterattacks during that day. The 1/5 reported that they had suffered a ferocious onslaught and had fought back; that night the final line was in front of Guillaucourt, with part of 149 Brigade concentrated on the Harbonnières to Weincourt road. In the case of the 1/4, the battalion held its position at Vauvillers until noon when they were compelled to withdraw as both their flanks were exposed. During the afternoon, Brigadier General Edward Riddell personally led the counteraction. Unlike the 1/6 Battalion, the diary of which is full of detail, very little information is available about the exploits of the 1/4 and 1/5.

> *Thus ended the 27 March, for ever memorable in the annals of the 50th Division and all its units as a day of hard fighting and magnificent courage. Every available man had been rushed up to fight and at one time the only troops General [E.P.A.] Riddell (149 Brigade) had at his disposal for counterattack was a scratch collection of Brigade staff, cooks, grooms, batmen and signallers.*

> *For the enemy, the 27 March was in several ways a blow to his ambitions, for north of the Somme our line had begun to stabilise, the Seventeenth German Army was worn out and could get no further, and was being successfully counterattacked: all three German armies had suffered enormous losses and all that German General Headquarters could do was reinforce the Second and Eighteenth Armies in a final attack on Amiens.*[14]

Early on the morning of Thursday 28 March, the Germans broke through at Warfusée and Bayonvillers and then crossed the river Somme at Cerisy. This created a critical situation resulting in the 8th, 50th and 66th Divisions retiring during the night to a line Vrély – Caix – Guillaucourt – Wiencourt – Marcelcave – Villers Bretonneux. Initially, 149 Brigade was commanded to hold the line from Rosières along the light railway line to Harbonnières (inclusive) with units of the 50th Division Royal Engineers together with two battalions of the 8th Division towards Proyart. This allowed the 39th Division to retire through Harbonnières. After this, 149 Brigade fell back to a line Caix-Guillaucourt, so that at 0800hrs the battalions' dispositions were: 1/6 at Caix, 1/5 at Guillaucourt with the 1/4 on the right of 1/5. The 1/7 DLI stood between the 1/4 and the 1/6. The 22 Entrenching Battalion was ordered to the right bank of the Luce river south of Guillaucourt. At 1000hrs the Germans attacked in a south-easterly direction and broke through the line at Guillaucourt. The 1/5 Battalion[15] reported that they fought back but there is no written evidence to support this claim. The two companies of the 22 Entrenching Battalion (attached to 149 Brigade) that had not retired to the Luce were called upon to confront the enemy.

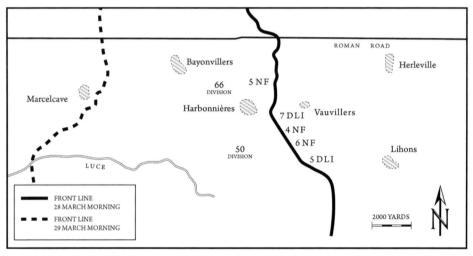

Position of the 149 Brigade, 28 March 1918

A glance towards Guillaucourt showed me the Boche infantry eight hundred yards away. He was coming our way and would soon reach the crest overlooking Caix through which troops of all sorts were now passing. Below me, to the south, under the shelter of one of those remarkable steep-sided banks which abound in this country, were the 22 Entrenching Battalion calmly eating their dinner and, as is the custom of the British soldier at meal times, quite oblivious of what was happening around them. I galloped to them shouting, 'Fall In'. Fortunately, the men were in extended order in a long line at the bottom of the bank with the officers in a group. I shouted the order to fall in into two ranks, and told them it was a race for the crest of the hill. As they climbed up the steep sides of the bank, away behind me, near Harbonnières,

I heard the sound of a hunting horn. It was General Jackson, the Divisional Commander, blowing his 'pack' to him. 'Forrard away' and up the hill and over the crest went the Entrenching Battalion and back into Guillaucourt went the Bosche [sic]. For the time being Caix was saved.[16]

Even this gallant effort was of little significance as by now the 39th and 66th Divisions were withdrawing towards Cayeux-en-Santerre, forcing 149 Brigade to retire to the line Caix-Cayeux, where they were able to hold the Caix and Cayeux bridgeheads. The War Diary of 1/6 Battalion records:

These positions were held till 4pm when the left flank was driven in, leaving 'A' Company (Captain Leathart) in an exposed position. Fortunately, the men from 'A' Company were able to effect a safe withdrawal.[17]

The remnants of 149 Brigade marched through Beaucourt, Mézières-en-Santerre and on to Moreuil. Here they billeted for the night of 28/29 March, trying to get some well-earned rest. At this point, the British front line south of the Somme ran from Mézières to Ignacourt and Hamel.

The following day, Friday 29 March, was Good Friday. The men of 149 Brigade together with the 1/4 Battalion East Yorkshire Regiment (150 Brigade), the 1/5 Battalion DLI (151 Brigade), the 22 EB and the 149 Machine Gun Company – all under the orders of 149 Brigade – were moved in the morning to a wood astride the Amiens-Roye road, a mile south of Demuin, in support of the 20th Division.

Three or four hours – rather less than more – in the barns at Merville-aux-Bois, and the battalion were once more into the line. They marched back over the Avre to a position in front of Domart, between Demuin and Hangard. They were now commanded by Captain E. L. Dobson, who had re-joined from a Corps School.[18]

Elsewhere, we know from the 1/6 Battalion War Dairy[19] that they marched from Moreuil to a position due south of Demuin and advanced in artillery formation to Point 90 on the Amiens-Roye road, where the enemy was attacking in force. Early in the afternoon the 1/6 moved to secure a wood about 500 yards to the east, covering the forces on their right as they retired, after which they returned to Point 90. At 1600hrs the 20th Division failed in an attack on Mézières and the division was forced to fall back onto the line of the Demuin-Moreuil road, leaving149 Brigade's right exposed.

Barricade at the entrance to Merville-au-Bois
3.5 miles west of Moreuil

In response, the units of 149 Brigade launched a series of attacks: the attached 1/4 East Yorks drove the enemy from the high ground north of Maison Blanche with the support of the 1/6 Battalion, while the 1/5 DLI, also attached, captured a wood immediately north of Villers-aux-Érables. These localised assaults bought time for the 20th Division to reform in its new line. At 1900hrs 149 Brigade (plus attached troops) began to withdraw to the north of the Amiens-Roye road in order to join up with the 20th Division, now on the right of 149 Brigade. That night the brigadier of 149 Brigade was instructed to hand over all his remaining troops to the command of 20th Division, upon which the brigade was ordered to rendevous to the north west of Rifle Wood in support of the line taken up by the 20th. Early in the morning of 30 March, the Germans once again attacked towards Moreuil, and at 0600hrs orders arrived from 59 Infantry Brigade (20th Division) for part of 149 Brigade (the 1/5 and 1/6) to take up poistions in defence of Rifle Wood (south of the Amiens-Roye road). In spite of this, by 1100hrs the Germans had managed to take the wood.

They were swiftly evicted. At this point the 1/6 War Diarist remarked that the battalion's strength was only 120 men: fewer than a single company. [19] Knowledge of the exact whereabouts of 1/4 Battalion is somewhat sketchy, but their involvement on 30 March is not in any doubt. Private William Robson and Private David Forster were awarded Military Medals for their actions on 30 March:

200666 Private William H. Robson

On March 30th, between Demuin and Domart, the senior officer of the Battalion being severely wounded, Pte Robson dressed his wound, and under terrific machine gun and shrapnel barrage, emerged from cover and crossed open ground carrying the wounded officer on his back. Owing to the intensity of the fire he was obliged to leave the officer temporarily but returned with the stretcher bearers in time to cooperate in a further and successful effort to bring the officer to safety.

200037 Private David Foster

On March 30th, 1918, near Demuin, the senior officer of the Battalion being wounded in the leg and left behind in the course of retirement, Pte Forster returned through a heavy barrage of shrapnel and machine gun fire and succeeded in carrying him to a point where stretcher bearers could attend him.

Captain [E.L.]Dobson, who did finely in his responsible position, was hit during a severe fight on Saturday 30 [March] and was rescued under circumstances which demand space in this little account. A rectification of the line on a small scale had to be effected just as Captain Dobson was wounded. His right thigh was shattered, and he was carried some distance, but owing to his weight had to be temporarily left behind. When the battalion formed up anew he was 400 yards out in front under heavy fire. Private W. Robson and Private Armstrong volunteered to attempt to rescue him. Private Armstrong was hit, and they had to return. Second Lieutenant Gwylon Davies then went out, but was also hit and had to return. Second Lieutenant the Reverend W.E.Pearson and Private David Foster made a third attempt, reached Captain Dobson safely, and carried him back to the shelter of our own lines.[20]

During 30 March, Captain James Cunliffe Leask, aged 42, of the 1/5 was killed.

Captain James Cunliffe Leask MC
1/5 Battalion Northumberland Fusiliers

James was born in Dublin in 1876, the son of Robert and Anna Leask. He married Mary Anderson in Dublin in 1901 and was the father of two children. He arrived in Newcastle in 1912 and joined the Territorials as a second lieutenant in 1913 and was subsequently promoted to captain. He won his Military Cross for leading a brilliant attack on the village of Deniun in late March 1917. James was reported missing on 30 March 1918 and was officially presumed to have been killed on that day, aged 42. James is commemorated on the Pozières Memorial to the Missing.

The citation for his Military Cross stated:

For conspicuous gallantry and devotion to duty, in leading a counterattack through a village. After severe fighting he successfully cleared the village and enabled a force to be extricated, thus greatly assisting the withdrawal that was in progress. He behaved with gallantry and skill.

The War Diary for the 1/6 NF[21] records that the battalion was ordered by Brigadier General Hislop of the 59 Infantry Brigade to take up a position at the road junction running south from Hangard to the Amiens-Roye road in anticipation of orders to counterattack in force towards Demuin. No orders were forthcoming. Instead the Germans instigated a withering attack on Rifle Wood and the 20th Division front; by early afternoon they had managed to force the 20th Division and some French troops to withdraw, including the 1/4 and 1/5 NF. They crossed the River Luce to take up a position at Domart.

Private Joe Pickard of the 1/5 was severely injured on 31 March, Easter Sunday, when his battalion came under an intense box barrage of enemy shells:

> *He boxed us and started to 'harrow' the box – like harrowing a field – searching the box with shells. The first lot was alright and it was coming through for the second time when I got hit. I remember seeing this big black cloud go up the side of the ditch. When I came to myself I was lying on my back up the road amongst a lot of dead Frenchmen. There was a Frenchman, he was just like a pepper pot hit about the head. I jumped straight up – I went straight down again and I thought, 'Well the leg's away!' I found out where I was hit, tore my trousers down. I thought, 'Well, if I stop here it is either a bullet or a bayonet!' They wouldn't pick you up you know, couldn't afford it, they were travelling fast. I got me [sic] first aid packet out and all there was in there were a lot of gauze, a little tube of stuff and a big safety pin – that was our first aid. I tore the trousers down: I was hit underneath the joint of the leg and I tied it on there. The piece of shrapnel had cut the sciatic nerve, chipped both hip joints, smashed the left side of my pelvis, three holes in my bladder and I lost my nose – a bloody right mess ... I knew there was something the matter with my face – I was bound to – I knew the blood was running. I never bothered about it. Well I mean in a case like that you think whether you want to live – and to hell with what you look like.*[22]

Joe began to crawl painfully down the road on his hands and knees. Fortunately, he was spotted by a Red Cross van that carried him to a derelict farmhouse where he was left for dead: his wife was informed of his death and the number of his grave, and was offered condolences from the King. Meanwhile, he had been found and transported to Rouen Hospital where he underwent a series of operations. Eventually he was evacuated to the Third Western General Hospital in Neath where he stayed until January 1919.

> *... so one day as the sister was standing at the table and we were just chatting away I said, 'Have you got a mirror, Sister?' She said 'Yes'. I said, 'Do you mind if I have a loan of it?' I said, 'Give us a loan of your scissors.' I cut all the blinking bandages off to have a look at it. The nose was off to about halfway up the bridge. She was a bit dubious about it and said, 'What do you think about it?' 'Well,' I said, 'What can I do – it's off, it's gone – you don't think I'm going to travel up the line to look for it.'*[23]

By now, the 1/6 – together with the 1/5 DLI (attached to 149 Brigade) with small detachments of Cornwalls, Somersets and the 25 Entrenching Battalion – were guarding the bridgehead at Hangard. They soon realised that the flank of the 1/5 DLI was exposed and vulnerable, but attempts to sort this out met with failure. Worse still, the 1/6 came under attack by their own artillery. At 2000hrs orders were issued for the 1/6 to take up a new position covering the bridgehead at Hourges which they accomplished within the hour; later the 18th Division came forward from Domart under the impression that the bridge was in the possession of the enemy but at 2300hrs they withdrew, leaving the 1/6 to guard the bridge.

At the close of fighting on 31 March, the British line ran from Moreuil Station to Hangard and to the line west of Warfusée-Abancourt.

After ten days of continuous fighting, the 50th Division was relieved on 1 April, although 149 Brigade, (with a strength of only about 400 of all ranks) still attached to the 20th Division, was dug in on the crest of a hill 1200 yards north-west of Domart. They held this position until 1800hrs when they were relieved by men of the 41st Division and marched to Longeau, where they were billeted overnight. The next day, 149 Brigade boarded a train at Saleux, (south west of Amiens) to travel to Rue and subsequently to Douriez, in the Pas de Calais region, near to the Montreuil area where 50th Division HQ had been established. At last some rest and restructuring was possible. New recruits were introduced to their duties, filling the vast and tragic holes in the brigade's strength.

The War Diary of 149 Brigade for 31 March recorded the following casualty figures: Officers: 6 killed, 32 wounded and 12 missing; Other Ranks: 69 killed, 415 wounded and 515 missing. Many of those missing would in time be classed as missing, killed in action. Details are in Appendix E.

The Reverend R. W. Callin of the 1/4, who was with his battalion throughout the retreat across the Somme, recorded:

Apart from heavy casualties, the worst feature of the Somme fighting retreat was undoubtedly the incredible fatigue and lack of sleep. Men simply could not keep awake despite the danger, and the slightest respite found them in deep slumber. Any bed was a good bed – a heap of stones by the roadside, a ditch, an open field, a sloping bank. Cold and hunger were forgotten in Nature's overwhelming clamour for sleep. Passing through Moreuil on the eve of Good Friday, men dropped asleep on doorsteps for three of four minutes at a time, walked a few yards further, slept on another doorstep and so on … Physically the men had come to the very end of their tether, and only sheer willpower kept them going. It was not so much a question of muscles being tired – though they were very tired – as of the very bones being sore, and all reserve force being utterly used up. Nevertheless, what that willpower could do, the enemy learned at his cost. Despite the fatigue, despite the demoralising effort a retreat was bound to have, this black fortnight was illuminated by instances of individual bravery of the highest traditions of the Fifth Fusiliers and the British Army: whilst the set teeth and bulldog tenacity of the battalion as a unit, contesting each mile of ground, holding on to the last moment, counter-attacking when hopelessly outnumbered, robbed the enemy of his vital élan, made him hesitate when hesitation meant failure, and contributed a full quota to the fighting which robbed him of the prize for which he strove so much.[24]

If the German offensive on the Somme were to be judged on whether it achieved its initial objectives, the verdict would be that it was a substantial failure. General Erich Luddendorff's major aim had been to win the war before the Americans could fully be integrated into the war effort, by smashing through the British lines and rolling them up northwards. The capture of Amiens would have severed the major arterial supply route from the coast to Paris.

German staff officer Colonel Wetzell had predicted the results of the offensive in November 1917:

It must not be forgotten that in a successful offensive, the attacker will be forced to cross a difficult and shot to pieces battle area and will get gradually further and further away from his railheads and depots, and that, having to bring forward masses of artillery and ammunition columns, he will be compelled to make pauses which will give time for the defender to organise resistance. Too optimistic hopes should not be conceived, therefore, as regards the rapidity of the breakthrough attack on the Western front. If our foes act only in a more or less planned and rapid manner, as we have done so far in spite of the most desperate situations, they also will succeed in bringing our offensive to a stop after a certain time.[25]

Early successes against Gough's unprepared Fifth Army reassured Ludendorff that the German advance on Amiens, intended to force a wedge between the French and British armies, would succeed. In the event his army failed to secure Amiens with its important railhead, although only because these two allies managed to hang on by the skin of their teeth. The Germans did gain 1200 square miles of ground, but it contained no strategic or tactically significant features; it was a wasteland, ravaged – ironically – by their own forces *(Alberich)* as they retreated to the Hindenburg Line early in 1917. What the Germans had taken was essentially a salient which in the coming months was vulnerable to attacks from the south by the French and from the north by the British. (Indeed, as soon as the Allies had built up enough strength they would make a move, but that was not until 8 August 1918.)

By the end of March 1918, the British army was buckling; it was on the ropes but the Germans had failed to deliver the knockout blow. The British had suffered some 178,000 casualties with a further 92,000 by the French: a total of 270,000. The Germans had lost 239,000. However, of more importance was that the Germans had used up a significant proportion of their finite resources of raw materials ('finite' because of an effective naval blockade). The Allies had also used up huge quantities, but enemy submarine warfare had been brought under control so that fresh supplies could now get through by sea; materials could be replaced in a short time.

However, as for 149 Brigade … their thoughts were concentrated simply on surviving the German advance. The war went on.

CHAPTER TEN

OPERATION GEORGETTE:
GERMAN ADVANCE IN FLANDERS, APRIL 1918

For all we have and are,
For all our children's fate,
Stand up and take the war,
The Hun is at the gate!

From Rudyard Kipling's '*For all we have and are*'

The spring advances on the Somme and at Arras had been a frustrating failure for the Germans. However, General Erich Ludendorff had more missiles to his arsenal: the next blow would be struck in Flanders where there were strategic targets just a few miles behind the British Line. One of these was the vitally important rail centre at Hazebrouck, a mere twenty miles east of Armentières. Hazebrouck, with its network of railways, linked the channel ports with all the important parts of the northern front. The proposed subsequent capture of Dunkirk, Calais and Boulogne, a matter of fifty miles away, would strike a cataclysmic blow to the British Army, severing its lifeline to Britain. These were the prizes on offer to the Germans. As spring passed and the low-lying wetlands of the area began to dry out, an advance looked distinctly interesting. The original German plan for the region was codenamed 'George', but when Ludendorff's staff came up with a scaled down version it was known by its diminutive – '*Georgette*'.

Georgette, scheduled to begin on 9 April 1918, would use seventeen divisions of the German Sixth Army to bulldoze into the junction of the British, Second and First Armies between Armentières and La Bassée Canal. They planned to charge forward directly towards Hazebrouck rail complex by way of Bailleul. On 10 April, if all went according to plan, the German Fourth Army would advance against the Messines Ridge, south of Ypres, with the aim of capturing the prize of Mont Kemmel. The general intention was to encircle the army at Ypres.

The front line ran from Givenchy to the Ypres-Comines Canal and was held by the following Divisions in this order: British 55th, Portuguese, British 40th, 34th, 25th, 19th and the 9th. With the exception of the 55th and Portuguese Divisions, all had seen action on the Somme less than a month beforehand. In reserve were the 50th, 51st, 49th and 29th Divisions, the former two of which had also seen action on the Somme. Haig planned that the sector should follow the flexible defence system, although here the Battle Zone must be held at all costs.

Portuguese troops manning the front line
Author's Collection

The weakest part of the chain was the undependable Portuguese Corps (*Expedicionário Português*), under the control of the British First Army in the Laventie Sector. It had been in position in this area for the whole of the winter months of 1917, manning a seven-and-a-half-mile sector divided into four brigade subsectors. Portuguese morale was low, in part because they were unaccustomed to the atrocious northern weather, but also – worse – there was a growing sense among the soldiers that there was no good reason for them to be in France at all, although it must be said that a number of their units were very aggressive in raiding the German lines. In early April the incipient unrest manifested itself in indiscipline; a number of cases were reported, and by 4 April the exhausted men of the 7 Infantry Battalion mutinied, refusing to return to the front after a few days behind the lines. This incident prompted the decision to pull the Portuguese troops from the front and replace them with British units. On 6 April, the Portuguese 1st Division was duly withdrawn and replaced by the 55th (West Lancashire) Division, extending its lines southwards to take up part of the sector; the Portuguese 2nd Division, holding twice its normal frontage, was to be relieved on the fateful 9 April by two British Divisions, one of which was the 50th Division.

By 4 April 1918, the 50th Division was part of XI Corps, centred on the town of Robecq, with 149 Brigade billeted in the Gonnhem and L'Eclême areas. On the following day the 50th was ordered to move to Estaires and join XV Corps of the First Army; it was out of the skillet and onto the hotplate for 149 Brigade. On their arrival north of La Bassée Canal, the depleted battalions were replenished with large numbers of reinforcements, the majority of whom were all but boys, practically untrained without any war service at all, along with a number of old soldiers – even some 'Old Contemptibles' who had fought at Mons. There had been a great selective clearing of the depots in England: Class B men, earlier deemed unfit for service, were reclassified as Class A and duly sent to the front as rank and file soldiers. Of course, it was much harder to replace the senior officers and NCOs killed on the Somme.

One of the young, inexperienced new recruits propelled to the Western Front after the offensive of 21 March was 66633 Private Albert Edward Bagley, aged 18, who was called up on 13 September 1917. He was to write extensively about his experiences at the time. After landing at Boulogne on 1 April, the youngsters destined for the Northumberland Fusiliers spent three days at Étaples before travelling towards Estaires. Bagley was posted to 1/6 on the afternoon of 5 April. He and his pals were regaled with stories about the bad times the 'old uns' had come through … and what was brewing for the future.

Orders were received for the relief of the weak 2nd Portuguese Division – who were holding the Front four miles east of Estaires, between Neuve Chapelle and Fauquissart – to have been completed by 11 April.[1] This was allocated to the 50th Division and as a consequence 149 Brigade moved to Merville on 8 April. Their sister brigade, the 151, was to be the first to the front in the relief of the Portuguese, and had moved into billets in Estaires.

Grand Rue, Estaires, in early 1918
Author's Collection

At this time Estaires was a busy little town hardly touched by the war and still full of civilians, with shops and estaminets doing good business with the military. All of that was to change dramatically on 9 April at 0400hrs, when the Germans opened a tremendous bombardment along a line opposite Béthune to Armentières. Shells rained on Estaires and nearby La Gorgue and soon buildings were crashing down into the streets. Fires raged throughout a town full of French families.

Grand Rue, Estaires, after the German bombardment
Author's Collection

On 9 April, the Portuguese front was held by its 4 (Minho) Brigade in the north; its 6 Brigade was in the centre and its 5 Brigade in the south; in reserve was 1 Brigade. The Germans discharged a catastrophic barrage on this section of the front using 1700 artillery pieces, and the Portuguese artillery responded immediately with its own 80 guns. Three hours later, at 0700hrs, eight German divisions swept in two implacable waves onto this weak front. The 35th Infantry, 42nd Infantry, 1st Bavarian Reserve and 8th Bavarian Reserve in the first wave, and the 8th Infantry, 117th Infantry, 81st Reserve and 10th Ersatz in the second wave: a behemoth of 100,000 men against 20,000 demoralised Portuguese defenders. Apart from some limited vigorous defence by the 2nd Division, in essence the Portuguese ceased to exist as a fighting unit on 9 April.

At 0500hrs on 9 April, 149 Brigade, billeted in and around the villages of Le Sart, Arrewage and Caudescure, west and northwest of Merville, were placed on 'stand to' to be prepared to move at one hour's notice. Orders followed at 0730hrs to advance and concentrate at Chapelle Douvelle. The plans for 151 Brigade's relief of the Portuguese had been cancelled and they had moved instead to a series of defence posts south of the River Lys where they would engage with the Germans at noon.

At 0730hrs, Second Lieutenant W.A. Kipling of the 1/4 was ordered to recon-noitre the route that his battalion would use to pass through Merville, which had been blasted by enemy artillery fire. By 0945hrs the 1/4 had set off, but even by the time they'd reached the outskirts of the town they'd already sus-tained a number of casualties. They paused and allowed the 1/5 to pass, after which they made their way through the badly damaged streets. It must be said here that the narrative of these days is quite difficult to follow because there is no extant April War Diary for 1/6 Northumberland Fusiliers.

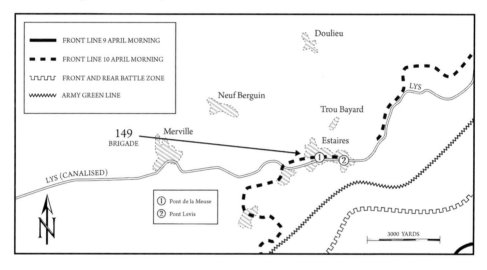

Position and Movement of 149 Brigade, 9 April 1918

As the three battalions moved forward to face the Germans, the enemy artillery was shelling along the whole sector, not only on the front but also onto the back areas:

We had been marching for about four hours and were just having our fourth ten minutes' rest, when we noticed a funny singing sound, and on asking one of the old 'uns, he informed us that it was a shell, and that if we kept quiet we would hear it burst. A few seconds passed and we could hear a dull thud and boom, as this shell burst in a town about three or four miles away, we had passed through earlier in the morning. I cannot explain what sort of feeling passed over me when I knew that a shell had actually passed over me and when I realised that we were getting near 'there'.[2]

At 1000hrs, news reached 50th Division HQ that the Portuguese were under concentrated attack and that the Germans had broken through along the whole length of their line. Soon afterwards the men of 151 Brigade found that Portuguese soldiers were passing through their lines as they retreated, some without their weapons. This position was the new front line and by noon they could see the enemy. During an afternoon of zealous and bitter fighting the brigade was slowly forced back to the Lys and Lawe Rivers.

As the 1/6 drew close to Estaires:

> To our great surprise, coming down the road in the opposite direction were Portuguese soldiers with no war equipment, and in their bare feet, but some still possessed their rifles and bayonets. Of course, naturally, this set us wondering why they should be coming dressed in this fashion, but however, our thoughts were set at rest within a very few short hours.[3]

The main German thrust along this section of the front was by means of two rapidly advancing columns, the first heading for the bridges over the River Lys and the second coming from Le Drumez with the intention of rolling up the outpost of redoubts and securing the crossing of the River Lawe near Lestrem.

On reaching their assembly point, the 1/4 were dispersed to take up concealed positions in nearby farms. At 1315hrs orders were issued at 149 Brigade HQ for the 1/5 and 1/6 to move to Trou Bayard and take up a series of defensive positions.

> Some of the 'old sweats' must have got rather bored with this state of affairs, for I noticed that one by one they were disappearing over the parapet. A few minutes elapsed and they commenced to reappear, some with what appeared to be coloured tablecloths slung over their backs. On jumping back into the trench, they commenced to open the various bundles, and to my surprise, I saw they contained all manner of articles, such as knives, forks, spoons, loaves of bread, pink little cigarette packets, clocks, watches and pictures were amongst the curious collections. One of them informed me that they had obtained these goods from houses a few yards in front of us. The cigarettes were eventually handed out to all of us – on receiving my share I was as pleased as punch and looked to obtain a light![4]

At this juncture the 1/4 came under direct orders of the 50th Division and were instructed to stay where they found themselves, regardless of the developing situation. Soon afterwards they were placed at the disposal of 151 Brigade and, as ordered, moved towards the water tower in Estaires. On reaching the outskirts of the town, the four companies moved off the road and were deployed in artillery formation pushing forward to take up positions in farms along the north side of Estaires to await further orders. 'D' Company was dispatched to guard the railway at Beaupré; the other three companies were ordered to dig in around strongpoints near the water tower (north of the main Estaires to Neuf Berquin road). This had been completed by 1700hrs. Earlier in the day (1430hrs) 149 Brigade HQ had been set up at Pont de Poivre alongside that of 150 Brigade. The advancing Germans reached the Lys near Nouveau Monde at around 1500hrs and swiftly set up machine guns which raked the positions on the northern bank. About fifteen minutes later the 1/5 and 1/6 moved into a position to support the line held by 150 Brigade. Their explicit orders were to counterattack any part of the front line that was breached. The overall thinking at this time was that the line of the Rivers Lys and Lawe was to be held at all costs. The 1/6 moved to the left to protect that flank (east). They were also detailed to send patrols towards the stream that ran northwards towards Stenwerck, to ascertain whether the Germans had already crossed the River Lys higher upstream, and to protect the division's left flank.

At 1545hrs a message was sent from the HQ of the 50th Division to 151 Brigade that the 1/4 were moving up to provide support and, explicitly, they were to be available to counterattack if the enemy made a breakthrough along this sector. The 1/4 moved immediately, arriving at a position on the northern outskirts of Estaires and within the hour were placed under the command of Lieutenant Colonel G.O. Spence of the 1/5 DLI.

Sergeant Thompson (1/4) was sent forward with five men to reconnoitre a route towards Pont de la Meuse and to establish contact with elements of the 1/5 DLI. At approximately the same time, Second Lieutenant A.N. Lawson (1/4) was ordered to lead a patrol of ten men to review the position at Pont Levis and also to make contact with elements of the 1/5 DLI. Captain J.V. Gregory (the officer commanding the 1/4) also agreed to send a further platoon which met up with Sergeant Thompson's patrol. The remainder of 'A' Company led by Lieutenant W. H. Nicholson were to garrison and strengthen the defences of a house on the north side of the river bank between Pont de la Meuse and Pont Levis.

40355 Private T. Collingwood

Collingwod of the 1/4 Battalion won his Military Medal for conspicuous bravery and devotion to duty on 9th April 1918 near Estaires. He made repeated journeys as Company Runner to Battalion Headquarters through very heavy shell and machine gun fire, working gallantly until completely exhausted.

By now there was concern that the enemy may have crossed the Lys using the bridge at Bac St Maur, east of Estaires, although there was no evidence that this had happened. At the same time 238009 Sergeant J. Wigham led a platoon equipped with two Lewis Guns over Pont Levis to the south bank of the Lys, reporting to the 1/5 DLI. With Lieutenant W.H. Nicholson (1/4) in charge, a series of defensive positions were set up on the south bank covering the approaches to the bridge.

All of this involved furious fighting, as described by the Reverend Callin:

Two advanced positions in particular were of the highest value – Pont Le Meuse and Pont Levis, the crossings across the River Lys. Dispositions were accordingly made in conjunction with a Durham Light Infantry Battalion and fierce fighting took place for these important points, fighting in which the youths from home, conquering inexperience and the first fright of battle, vied with our veterans in tenacity, resolution, and faithfulness. The machine gun fire was deadly, the flat open country being fatally adapted to this modern weapon. Nevertheless, the spirit of our men was seen in the desperate efforts they made to reach their positions, the grip they kept on them, and the effective check they imposed on the enemy's advance. Second Lieutenant [A.N.] Lawson (rejoined from leave) was wounded near Pont Levis and presumed dead, but after weeks of waiting we learned that he had been picked up by the enemy and was in a German hospital, making a good recovery from severe wounds. Second Lieutenant [J.C.] Napier was also wounded in the neck, but managed to reach a British hospital. Captain J. S. J. Robson MC (rejoined after long absence on special work), in a desperate attempt with a small party to strengthen our position after Lawson had fallen, was himself wounded.[5]

The Reverend Callin wrote that Second Lieutenant Charles Davison (affectionately known by all as 'The Prince'), following the loss of Second Lieutenant Lawson, led a reinforcing party to relieve pressure on the defenders at Pont Levis.

This was one of the fights which do not lend themselves to picturesque description, and scarcely figures in newspaper accounts. But, it was a quiet deadly struggle through daylight and dark to secure possession of a position of great strength. No effort was spared by the enemy to prevent our reinforcing it, and by sheer weight of numbers and intensity of fire he meant to throw us right away from it. So, the deadly trial of strength continued until by the mere weight of the attack we had to modify our positions.[6]

Second-Lieutenant Charles Montague Davison
1/4 Northumberland Fusiliers

Charles was the eldest son of Charles Newton and Louisa Christina Davison. He was educated at the Royal Grammar School, Newcastle, where he was a prefect and awarded colours in both football and rugby and was a member of the school's OTC. In March 1917 he was gazetted to the 1/4 Northumberland Fusiliers, and went out to France in May 1917. On 10 April he had been ordered to assess the situation at Pont Levis, but before he could reach his objective he was mortally wounded. He died, aged 19, in a Casualty Clearing Station on the 10 April 1918. Charles is buried at Haverskerque British Cemetery. His headstone is inscribed:

I HAVE REDEEMED THEE
I HAVE CALLED THEE
BY THY NAME.

By 1900hrs the situation on the south bank of the Lys had deteriorated badly. At Nouveau Monde the enemy had established machine gun posts in houses, from which they were able to enfilade these garrisons. Major General Jackson, the 50th Division Commander, ordered 151 Brigade to withdraw to the northern bank of the River Lys, and the Royal Engineers to destroy the remaining bridges over the river. By now the Germans had brought their field guns forward and were systematically smashing up the bridgehead garrisons at point blank range.

The Pont de la Meuse was successfully destroyed, but not Pont Levis; this was a disastrous failure, blamed on the detonator wire having been severed by enemy fire. At 1910hrs, the 1/5 were ordered to take up positions in strong points near Trou Bayard and to meet up with the 1/4. Towards midnight, 149 Brigade HQ were told that the Germans now held the Bac St Maur-Croix de Bac road (running northwards from Sailly sur la Lys) and that they had crossed over the canalised part of the river. They were now on its northern bank and were a threat to the left flank of the forces defending Estaires. During the night – which was described as 'relatively quiet' – rations were delivered, the men fed and watered. Thus, the first day of fighting at Estaires had ended. Reported casualties for 149 Brigade on the day were comparatively few, given the intensity of the fighting.

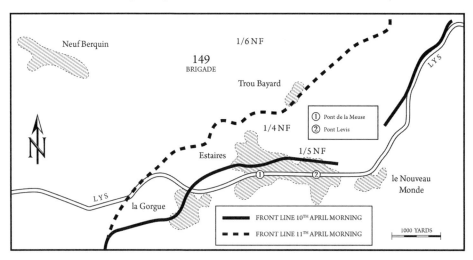

Position of 149 Brigade on the mornings of 10 and 11 April 1918

The original British line which had run from Givenchy to Bois Grenier was now in tatters and as darkness closed on the battlefield the line ran roughly from Festubert, Le Touret, Le Cason, Vielle Chappelle, Pont Rigneul and round the north of Lestrem. The men of 149 Brigade held various sections of the line to the east of Estaires and on to the west of Sailly sur la Lys. The line continued to Croix au Bac, north of Fleurbaix and on to just north of Bois Grenier. In fact, a spectacular dent had been driven into the original British line along a ten-mile front. The next day would involve 149 Brigade in ferocious combat.

Very early in the morning of 10 April – around 0200hrs – orders were issued for an alignment of the divisional front. 50th Division HQ received directions at 0330hrs that the new dispositions had to be carried out before dawn; 151 Brigade would hold from Lestrem Bridge (exclusive) to Pont Levis (exclusive), 149 Brigade from Pont Levis inclusive to the Lys opposite Rue de la Lys, with one battalion in the front line and two in reserve. A misunderstanding occurred between 149 and 151 Brigades with the result that Pont Levis – the remaining bridge over the Lys – was left unguarded overnight. At 0540hrs the 1/4 were instructed to send two platoons to take up position at Pont Levis alongside the 1/5 DLI. Captain J.S.J Robson of 'C' Company set out with the two platoons to help strengthen the defences of the bridge, but as they moved forward they faced pitiless machine gun fire across the open ground, during which Captain Robson was wounded. Private Foster Parkin of the 1/4 was awarded the Military Medal for his extraordinary courage on both 10 and 11 April:

204604 Private Foster Parkin

For conspicuous bravery and initiative on 10th April 1918 near Estaires. He pushed ahead with a Lewis gun in a most daring manner, and covered the advance of his Company with enfilade fire. Later in the day he shot down a low flying enemy aeroplane. On 11th April 1918 he remained behind, covering the withdrawal of his Company with Lewis gun fire until he had exhausted his ammunition, when he successfully brought his gun out of action.

Subsequently a third platoon from 'C' Company (1/4) was brought forward as reinforcement. Once again it came under heavy fire. The War Diary records that Second Lieutenant Davison, who had accompanied Second Lieutenant W.F.R.Essex, was wounded whilst reconnoitring the situation at Pont Levis.

Although the 1/5 put up bold resistance at Pont Levis, by 0730hrs elements from the German 35th Division had bludgeoned their way across the Lys and into Estaires. The remaining companies of the 1/4 had been ordered to make their way to Ferme Quennelle (on the road from Estaires to Trou Bayard) just west of a strongpoint known as Newport. Although they were expected to move before dawn, their orders were not received until it was light; the Battalion HQ and 'B' Company had been held up. 'B' Company eventually occupied a position near Pont de Poivre adjacent to Harlech strongpoint and made contact with a company from 1/6 Battalion commanded by Captain Stafford. They set about organizing a defensive position to the rear of Harlech and on the opposite side of the Trou Bayard Road. A patrol ventured out in front of the position and could see immediately that the Germans were trying to move machine guns forward in order to attack them. By now, further enemy troops were swarming across Pont Levis; they captured the position at Ferme Quennelle and were able to hammer their way into Estaires where they soon occupied most of the buildings on the north side of the main street. At this point the commanding officer of 149 Brigade entrusted the 1/6 with a counterattack, which was covered by all the artillery available: four howitzers and twelve 18-pounders. All available machine guns at Trou Bayard cooperated by providing covering fire as the Fusiliers deployed under the trees near Trou Bayard with their right flank on the Estaires to Neuf Berquin road.

Sadly, because we have no April War Diary for the 1/6, details of this gallant counterattack are few; in the 1/6 War Diary for May there is a letter dated a few weeks later, written by the Officer in Charge, addressed to Brigade HQ:

3 May 1918: Owing to the exceptional volume of the heavy casualties suffered by this Battalion lately, which include the Commanding Officer, Adjutant and Intelligence Officer, great difficulty is being experienced in obtaining authentic data for the continuous history of operations in which this unit has taken part by the War Diary in question. Major J. G. Leathart, at present at Le Touquet, is the only surviving officer who can supply certain necessary facts, and as he will not be returning to the battalion until the end of the present week, I fear that it will not be possible to submit the War Diary for April at the stipulated time. It will be forwarded at the earliest possible moment.[7]

The 'earliest possible moment' would never come to pass: the next tour of duty for the 1/6 was on the Aisne where they suffered catastrophic and irredeemable casualties, as did all units of 149 Brigade.

Private Bagley played his part in the counterattack of 10 May. He recalled that, after a rest stop, the men fell in on the nearby road where they were ordered into what felt suspiciously like an attacking formation, a notion confirmed within minutes. After walking in single file for about a mile they were ordered to swing round so that they were once more spread out in line abreast. Bagley and his colleagues soon realized that they were at the front of a brigade attack with the rest of the division acting in reserve.

This, unfortunately, must have been according to plan, for it so happened that walking in this direction we were presently met with such a fusillade of machine gun bullets that it fairly took our breaths away, and momentarily brought us to a standstill, but a word from our Sergeant behind sufficed to make us continue our advance. The rain of bullets did not slacken however, in fact it seemed to increase, and either by instinct or by madness we all bent our heads forward as one might do if walking in the face of a downpour of rain. How many minutes passed under these conditions I cannot say but it suddenly altered by the Sergeant behind us who shouted, 'Look out lads, there's the buggers, give them hell.' On looking up I saw Germans by the ton so to speak, some kneeling and some standing, all trying to outdo their name in the matter of firing as many bullets as possible per second. The shout of the Sergeant must have put some life into our rather numb bodies, for we started off at a run yelling at the top of our voices. Being somewhat nervy I bent my head as I ran for I didn't relish the idea of watching closely how quickly I could run the distance between me and the gentlemen of the guns. Just then the yells on my side increased in volume and on looking up for the cause, saw that the Jerries were getting up and down a guy for all they were worth [sic]. This put added life into us and we increased our yells and speed, feeling inwardly as if we had got the war won. All of a sudden, the flying Jerries disappeared in thin air to be replaced by more bullets flying. They had merely fallen back to a trench and were as safe as houses whilst we were in the open. At this, every man jack of us pulled up and threw themselves flat on the ground and opened fire. Each side was now blazing away at each other, regardless that each round costs about two pence.[8]

Private Bagley went on to relate the following incidents from the fighting:

Poor boy! He was groaning something awful. Looking into his face I saw he was a boy called Phillips whom I knew fairly well while in training in England. Just then a corporal came up, and hearing the boy groaning said, 'Come on lad, do you want the Jerries to get you, come on, buck up!' All he replied was, 'Oh mother, mother!' till he was calling at the top of his voice. His condition got worse, until at last, he fell back – all over within 2 min of receiving the fatal bullet. The corporal and I lifted him gently and laid him under some hawthorn trees close by, and covering him over with a groundsheet …[9]

The soldier who had just been killed was 66406 Private Edgar Phillips, aged 25, of 'B' Company. He was the son of John and Edith Phillips of Stoke-on-Trent, and is commemorated on the Pleogsteert Memorial to the missing.

Nonetheless, the 1/6 advanced resolutely, forcing their way through the houses and gardens north of the main street of Estaires. They encountered the enemy, who by now were holding the cemetery and the approaches to Pont Levis, and were faced with savage fire, but on they went, clearing the Germans from large parts of the town, forcing the enemy back to within two or three hundred yards of Pont Levis. By 1030hrs these resolute Fusiliers had managed to make contact with elements of the 1/5 DLI who were holding the river bank at Pont de la Meuse (east of Pont Levis), where the 1/6 were able to set up machine gun posts in some factory buildings. From these positions, the gun crews were at first able to concentrate fire on the approaches to the river, to great effect. However, these posts became increasingly untenable: by late afternoon the Germans were concentrating artillery fire onto the positions. One by one they were destroyed, and their guns lost. It was a gallant stand to the end, but one with little hope of escape or survival. One of the casualties of the day's fighting was Lieutenant Stanley Morpeth.

Lieutenant Stanley Morpeth
1/6 Battalion Northumberland Fusiliers

Stanley was born in Newcastle in 1896, the eldest son of Joseph and Margaret Morpeth. He was educated at Newcastle Modern School. When war broke out he was serving his articles with Dickinson, Miller and Turnbull, solicitors. Following his intermediate examination, he volunteered for service and obtained a commission in the 1/6 Northumberland Fusiliers in August 1915. He went to the Front in June 1916 and was wounded in November. When passed fit for duty he returned to the Front on 27 July 1917. He was reported missing on 10 April 1918. It transpired that he had been wounded and captured. Until the middle of October he was in a hospital near to the front, after which he was transferred to a hospital in Ozersk, West Prussia, arriving there on 17 October 1918. During his journey he contracted influenza which developed into pneumonia. Stanley died on 20 October 1918, aged 22, and is buried in Poznan Old Garrison Cemetery. His headstone is inscribed:

QUIT YOU LIKE MEN
BE STRONG

Under the cover of their determined assault on the factory buildings, the enemy were able to push more troops across Pont Levis, and this in spite of dense machine gun fire from Trou Bayard being directed onto the bridge. Ever more enemy troops pushed forward, although they were taking a lot of casualties. They succeeded in working their way back into the northern part of the town, making the positions held by the 1/6 indefensible, forcing them to withdraw to the area round the water tower. As the day progressed, the enemy became once more entrenched in Estaires.

At 1600hrs the Germans attempted an advance, behind a heavy bombardment, towards Trou Bayard but eventually this was halted by intense machine gun fire from Pont Poivre. This attack forced the 1/5 to withdraw, leaving the left flank of the 1/4 exposed. 'D' Company (in reserve for the 1/4) were sent up to help. They later reported that they had dug in between the crossroads at Trou Bayard and Cul de Sac Farm, although while doing so they had lost quite a few men. As evening fell, the enemy maintained their pressure on the line held by 149

Brigade and at 1900hrs the 1/6, owing to having so many dead or wounded, had to evacuate part of Estaires. The defences still held, but they were creaking.

As darkness engulfed the battlefield, the 50th Division line ran from Lestrem on the right to Beaupré along the Estaires Road to Trou Bayard and on to La Boudrelle. Wyrall notes that the possession of La Boudrelle on the night of 10 April may be open to doubt.[10] Officially the Battle of Estaires ended on the night of 10 April, but men in the line would argue that the fighting was unrelenting throughout the night and into the next day.

The Germans thrust forward again on 11 April, attacking savagely along the entire length of the front, and in places they made some progress. Between Givenchy and the River Lawe British resistance held, but between Locon and Estaires the enemy were able to advance westwards towards the prize of Hazebrouck. At Estaires the troops of the 50th Division, tired and reduced in numbers by the exceptionally heavy fighting of the previous three weeks, threatened on their right flank by the enemy's advance south of the Lys, were heavily engaged. After holding their position with laudable grit during the morning, they were slowly pressed back in the direction of Merville.

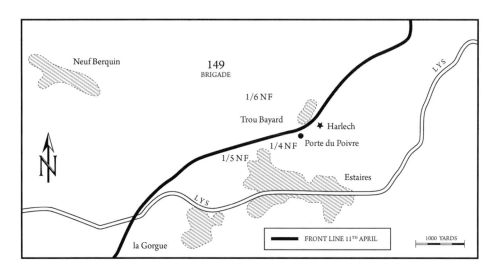

Positions held by 149 Brigade on the morning of 12 April 1918

By 0200hrs on Thursday 11 April dispositions for 149 Brigade were that it held a line running from the Estaires to Neuf Berquin Road to just west of Trou Bayard. The 1/5 held the right sector with 1/4 the left sector including Trou Bayard. The 1/6 were held in reserve. As dawn broke the 50th Division were holding the Front Line (151 Brigade on the right, 149 in the centre and 150 on the left, the most westerly). The Germans eventually overran the defensive positions at Trou Bayard held by the 1/4 Battalion at about 0700hrs. Two Fusiliers from the 1/4 Battalion won Military Medals in recognition of their acts of outstanding bravery on this day.

235022 Lance Corporal Herbert Hunter

For conspicuous bravery and devotion to duty on 11th April 1918 near Trou Bayard. When the position was obscure he twice went forward from Battalion Headquarters to ascertain the exact position of the front line, and under heavy machine gun fire brought back very valuable information, which cleared up the situation and enabled the Commanding Officer to fill in a gap.

201913 Private Bob Fletcher Pond

For conspicuous bravery and devotion to duty on 11th April 1918 near Estaires. Private Pond, who was a Company Runner, repeatedly carried messages under extremely heavy fire. He was eventually severely wounded in the right arm while carrying a message from a detached flank. He nevertheless delivered his message before reporting his wound, and was the means of preventing a platoon from being completely surrounded.

On the 50th Division's left, the Durham Battalions of 151 Brigade were under intense pressure, and after a preliminary bombardment the Germans were able to exploit a gap between the 1/5 and 1/6 DLI, pouring troops into the area. The 1/5 DLI were forced back, unable to maintain contact with 1/5 NF of 149 Brigade, which allowed the Germans to hammer their way along the road leading to Neuf Berguin. At 1100hrs the 1/6 NF (in reserve) were ordered forward to establish a line running northeast from the Estaires-Neuf Berguin road. However, after three hard hours their advance had made little headway because they met with such severe opposition. It was also reported that a section of men from 149 Brigade were holding out at Trou Bayard. Who these men were and what happened to them is unknown.

Men were now scattered all over the place; Lieutenant Alex Thompson of the 1/6 NF recalls:

So sudden and intense was the fire that our troops were compelled to lie flat on the road on which they were marching – there being no ditches or other cover available – and no movement could take place so long as the enemy machine guns were allowed to remain in position. I hastily collected some twenty men and advanced across an open ploughed field for 400 yards to the outskirts of the village. On reaching the first outbuildings I had only four men left, but by making our way through and around the houses we cleared the village of the enemy as far as the road junction – an advance of some 1,000 yards. Being such a small party and in danger of being captured we returned – with difficulty.[11]

This fearless counteraction allowed the Royal Engineers to further develop the defensive system east of Neuf Berguin; by 1400hrs it was already in use by forces defending against the enemy who were pressing from every direction.

The volume of firing got so fierce that at last flesh and blood could not stand against it any longer. As if by some instinct every man threw himself down flat, burying his face in the soil as best he could for protection. I was lying flat and wondering how long I would be like this, for the soil was sticking to my lips, and I felt a tickling sensation under my face. Raising my head as high as I dare I saw that the tickling was caused by a beetle worming its way, between my face. [sic] Oh! How I wished then that I was a beetle, or at least could be so small, so that it would be near impossible for a bullet to hit me. The bullets flying over my back, about a foot and a half from the ground, brought me back to the reality of things.[12]

Bagley went on to describe – and then defend – the seemingly 'cowardly action of running away … when given the order to retire':

An order was given to retire, as the Germans on our right flank were advancing in a circle and we were in danger of being surrounded – we had enough to do to watch those straight in front! Well, it took no second telling for our chaps to fall back as the strain of facing the machine-gun fire had almost upset all mental balance. Instead of being a 'retire' it developed into a race of who could put the most distance between Germans and ourselves in the least time. Of course, all did not run at first, but when one saw your own men going back like mad, it stood to common sense it was no good you trotting back then firing a few rounds, then back further, then firing again and so on – which is what is meant by 'retiring'. A lot of the chaps were taking their equipment off and throwing it away, thus enabling them to run faster. While jogging over the rough fields I reasoned out with myself that if the bullet was coming at me it would hit part of my equipment and thus perhaps lessen its bad intent on my poor body. I suddenly remembered that the rifle in my hand was useless, so dropped it, but of course that was justified.[13]

Bagley explained his apparent weakness:

First of all it was through one or two bolting, as they did, that gave the others the idea that the game was up, and further, when a chap sees another flying, he doesn't see why he should stick it when the chap next is clearing off! Then again, ninety per cent of our men were just boys like myself, all between the ages of 18 and 19, and this was only their third day in action and about their tenth day in France altogether from when they landed from England. And lastly, during the last three days they had been facing war as many another soldier in France had not experienced who had been hardened to it gradually by spells in the trenches and out again, whereas these boys, as I have said, had only been in the firing line three days, and at this period of war it was about the worst to experience, for we were up against an army which had men of two or three years' experience and also boasted the flower of the German army, and moreover, a victorious army, for they had advanced a considerable distance when it came for us to be thrown against them.[14]

This surely highlights the terrible state of the British Army after several years of war; nearly all men of a suitable age and strength had already been called up and used. When the legal age of men being sent abroad to fight fell to eighteen years, the conscripts were boys, not men. Within days of landing they were marching out to face machine guns and shells. Furthermore, if this account describes the overwhelming fear of a few young soldiers, there are many other tales of heroism gallantry and courage. Indeed, Bagley himself went on to earn the Military Medal. Lieutenant Alfred John Field, 1/6 Battalion, was killed in action on 11 April whilst Lieutenant Arthur William Leech, 1/5 Battalion, was seriously wounded, dying the next day.

Lieutenant Alfred John Field
1/6 Northumberland Fusiliers

Alfred was born in Tynemouth, Northumberland, in 1883, the second son of Alfred and Anne Amelia Field. He was educated at Newcastle and was a partner in the firm of Alfred Field and Sons, explosive merchants. He had served five years in the Volunteer Battalion Northumberland Fusiliers. He enlisted in the 1/6 Northumberland Fusiliers as a private and was granted a commission in the Fusiliers in July 1915. In September 1916, Alfred married Mary Staniland. He travelled to France in November 1917 and was the battalion's bombing officer. Alfred was killed in action on 11 April 1918, aged 35, and is commemorated on the Ploegsteert Memorial to the Missing.

Lieutenant Arthur William Leech MC
1/5 Northumberland Fusiliers

Arthur was born in Woodbridge, Suffolk, in 1884 the youngest son of George and Celia Leech, and was educated at Woodbridge School. At the beginning of the war he was engaged as a war correspondent by the Daily News. In May 1915 he was given a commission with the 1/6 Battalion Northumberland Fusiliers. He embarked for the front in February 1916, returning to the UK, ill, following the Somme campaign. He returned to France in August 1917, but was wounded on 11 April, dying the next day from his wounds, aged 34. Arthur is buried in Longuenesse (St Omer) Souvenir Cemetery

The 1/4 were under pressure: the Germans were striking from all directions. By 0700hrs they had captured the extreme right of the previous night's position at Trou Bayard and by 1400hrs the divisional line was being forced back to the west. At 2000hrs it appeared that the line was holding, but three hours later, after a conference between the commanding officers of the 149, 86 and 87 Brigades, orders were being issued to fall back to a line Vierhouck-Neuf Berquin road with 149 Brigade to hold the section of this line including Vierhoek to the crossroads on the Neuf Berquin to Vieux Berquin road, just south of Pont Rodin. These orders stressed that the retirement was to begin at 0230hrs on the following morning, 12 April.

On the night of 11 April, the British line at Merville ran roughly north-south about two miles east of the town. In the Divisional History, Wyrall[15] speculates about what would have happened if the Germans had maintained their thrust forward during the night of 11 April; the outcome might have been disastrous for the British. He points out that there is strong evidence that on entering Merville, the discipline in the German ranks disintegrated: they began to plunder and loot, as they did during the Somme Offensive. However, this was a brief respite for the British; official despatches record that at 0800hrs the enemy attacked again, with newfound fury, on a front extending from the south of the Estaires-Vieux Berquin area.

So, before dawn on 12 April, 149 Brigade withdrew to its new position. The brigade marched in three sections: the first was the 1/4 and 1/5 under Lieutenant Colonel Irwin forming the flank and advanced guards; the second was the 1/6 and a smattering of 1/4 under Major Temperley and the third was a reinforcement battalion, under an officer commanding Corps Troops.

By 0200hrs the 1/6 had entered Vierhouck and had formed a defensive flank along the road (north easterly direction) to Pont Rondin, the line looping south of the village around its western edge, and at 0630hrs 149 Brigade reported that they had crossed the road and had encountered only limited opposition. Dispositions were: the Reinforcement Battalion on the left with the 1/5 to its right extending to the Neuf Berquin-Vieux Berquin road. However, they couldn't make contact with the 29th Division on their left. By noon the enemy had made a half-hearted attempt to test these defences, without success, but nonetheless the line was worryingly frail and every available man was fed into the line to plug the wide gaps.

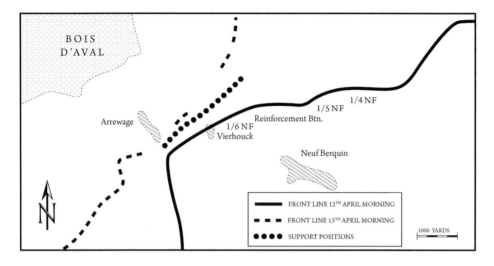

Position of 149 Brigade, 12 and 13 April 1918

Yard by yard, the remnants of 149 Brigade were pushed back. Retreating men took shelter wherever they could. The fighting was now between groups of soldiers who had no idea where they were. They had no inkling of the bigger picture. Random skirmishes punctuated the day – counterattacks with very little chance of success. Men strove simply to survive, often without leadership.

Lieutenant Alex Thompson of the 1/6 found himself with a group of men completely cut off from the rest of his battalion. They were occupying some slit trenches, in front of which was a thick hedge which was soon taken by the enemy, supported by machine guns and trench mortars.

Our position seemed hopeless, but I knew there were no troops in reserve to our position, so I issued an order that the position must be held at all costs until further orders. Early in the morning of 13th April the enemy sent several aeroplanes over us and a concentrated bombardment was thus accurately directed on our positions. Infantry attacks were driven back with heavy losses. After a short while my last remaining Lewis gun was destroyed by shell fire. I ordered all men to lie flat in the shallow trench and one man was instructed to keep watch and pass the word along the trench when the next infantry attackers were within 40 yards of the trench. When this happened all the garrison opened rapid fire, the result being that the enemy imagined that we were more numerous than we really were, and each time the enemy were driven back with heavy losses. These tactics of bluff were repeated throughout the day. Bombardments and infantry attacks continued throughout the whole day and so intense and accurate was the fire that even wounded men and stretcher bearers were shot down – not one wounded man left the trench without being killed.[16]

Relentless enemy attacks slowly drove back most of the neighbouring troops around Thompson's precarious position and his men were left isolated.

At 3.30pm, a large body of enemy infantry appeared on the road on high ground some 200 yards to our rear and these men gradually closed upon us. After firing in three directions with the few men I had left the Grenadier Guards on my right did the only thing possible in the circumstances and surrendered. I and the two remaining men with me (one wounded) then laid down our arms and left the trench full of dead. The two men with me were prepared to fight on for a few seconds longer, but it was obvious that no good purpose could be served by three more lives being lost when the position was already captured.[17]

Lieutenant Thompson was now a prisoner of war, but Private Bagley was still at liberty, constantly driven back by the thrust of the enemy to new, hastily-dug positions. At some point Bagley and a small party of the 1/6 found themselves stranded with the enemy on all sides:

All our fellows were trying to settle in our own minds what was the best thing to do. I saw an officer crawling towards our hole, and as he passed the various posts he gave them instructions. He told us it was hopeless to try to do anything against the Jerries. We had to vacate our position, one at a time, and make a dash for freedom.[18]

Some of the men at this point decided that they had had enough of the fighting, especially as by now the Germans had spotted them and had opened fire.

Bagley continued:

To my horror, I saw a lot of men taking off their equipment and then jumping up, holding their hands up and advancing towards the excited Germans. I was not of the same mind. Getting out of the hole, I said to my pal, 'Come on, mate! I'm not sticking here, let's make a bolt for it', and commenced to run down our line to the right – as that was the only possible 'exit'. The firing from the left was getting worse, so I intended to shelter at the next hole until it died down. On jumping in, I found a man lying, half in and half out of the hole. Looking closer I saw it was an officer; also, underneath him was another officer practically invisible. I was shocked to see the top man was no other than Lieutenant Waggott. His trench coat was badly torn and saturated with blood, but he was quite dead, which rather unnerved me, when I had been under him the day before.[19]

Second Lieutenant Garibaldi Matthewson Waggott was one of the officers posted to the 1/6 Battalion Northumberland Fusiliers in February 1918 when the 16 Battalion Northumberland Fusiliers was disbanded. Another casualty was Lieutenant Edgar Watson Stiles.

Lieutenant Edgar Watson Stiles
1/7 Northumberland Fusiliers, attached 149 Brigade

Edgar was born in Doncaster in 1881, the youngest son of Matthew Henry and Alice Stiles. He was educated at St Cuthbert's College Worksop and London University, matriculating in 1900. He was an articled solicitor initially in Doncaster and later with Mr T. C. Smith of Berwick upon Tweed. Subsequently he went into practice on his own. At the beginning of the war he was Sheriff of Berwick. He was given a commission in the Northumberland Fusiliers in the middle of 1915 and embarked with a draft of recruits to France in March 1916. He remained in France until he was wounded, dying of his wounds on 13 April 1918, aged 36. Most of his service at the front was with a Trench Mortar Battery. Edgar is buried in Lapugnoy Military Cemetery.

For conspicuous bravery and devotion to duty in action on 12 April, 66633 Private Albert Bagley was awarded the Military Medal.

Many of those taken by the Germans would find that life did not become any easier; the fight to save one's life on the battlefield became a struggle for survival within the German Prisoner of War system. Many died from their wounds, others from hunger and illness, in conditions made intolerable by the cruelty of their captors.

During 13 April, orders were received that the remnants of the 50th Division were to be pulled back to La Motte-au-Bois; the men of 149 Brigade were billeted 2000 yards west of La Motte. A number of the senior commanding officers, including Brigadier General Riddell of the 149, were withdrawn to Divisional HQ to rest, although the ordinary tommy still had a lot to do. Men had been scattered during the fighting; some were unable to return to their units.

Somewhere in the outpost line, Private Bagley was still under fire when at 1000hrs the outposts were fired upon from a house directly opposite and the line was swept by machine gun fire. Eventually he fell upon a well-made trench manned by Australians and Machine Gunners. Here he was well fed and to his surprise was even given some cow's milk. He spent the night there, and on the following morning he attached himself to this unit. Late in the afternoon they spotted the enemy advancing on the trench, but they stopped and dug in for the night when still a hundred yards away. During the next day the British line was bombarded, followed by an advance:

The greater part of the day passed quietly, till about half past five in the afternoon, when, suddenly we were surprised to see the Germans mount their parapet and start towards us. Immediately we were on the alert, fingering our trickers [sic] and waiting for the officer to give the word, but no sound came from his lips. We were getting up to fever heat, wondering what was going to happen. Just then, the officer said in a quiet voice, 'When I give the word, no-one except the machine gun must fire.' This did not give much satisfaction, but it somehow broke the tension. When the Jerries were barely fifty yards away the word came slowly, and what a relief it was. The Sergeant was working the gun, and he seemed very calm as he slowly turned the gun from left to right. On looking to see the result, I was amazed to see that almost every fourth man went down. Still they came on, and then the gun slowly started on its return journey, and still almost every fourth man was going down, it was as if watching some machinery working. The Jerries were still advancing, but somehow did not quite look quite so determined, and as the gun commenced again to mow from left to right, they seemed to waver. Then we could hear the officers ordering them to advance, at least, I imagine so from the tone of the voices. The Jerries then halted altogether, still the voices urged them on, when suddenly, as if by instinct, they all turned and commenced to bolt. At that, we opened fire with our rifles to help them along, and it did make them move. Straight over their own trench they went, and on; getting smaller and less in numbers till finally, very few were left to disappear in the distance altogether. Like children, we cheered ourselves almost hoarse.[20]

That night the Australians and 235 Brigade Machine Gun Corps were relieved. Before he left, an officer gave Bagley a note to take to his battalion's commanding officer to cover him for the two days he had spent with the Australians.

On 14 April, the remnants of 149 Brigade assembled at the footbridge a mile south-west of La Motte-au-Bois and began to dig trenches on the Bois des Vaches position on the northeast side of the wood (about two miles south of Hazebrouck). On the right were 150 Brigade with Australian forces occupying the reserve line on their left. In front of the Australians were the 5th Division. At this time, the fighting strength of 149 Brigade was ten officers and four hundred other ranks. The digging continued over the next few days, then at noon on 15 April orders were received that the 50th Division should move to the Wittes-Aires area, leaving 149 Brigade in place under the temporary command of Captain Tweedy. Late on 17 April, 149 Brigade was ordered to re-join the 50th Division which was now situated in the Rincq-Mametz-Rebecq area, west of Hazebrouck, where the training and reorganisation of the remnants of its battalions began.

We came out of the fight broken, exhausted, but with high morale. This time the enemy had been held quickly and securely. New hope and confidence throbbed in every heart. We were in the mood for inspiration, and the inspiration did not fail us. As we withdrew from the battle we were met by Lieutenant Colonel B. D. Gibson, fully recovered from his illness of September 1917, full of vigour and radiating will-power; accompanied by the friend and helper of all, our Second in Command Major J. Ridley Robb. What their personalities meant to us no pen can describe, but they were felt at once and were our re-creation.[21]

The town of Bailleul had fallen on 15 April. Nevertheless, the British managed to blunt the German attack on Hazebrouck, one of the Germans' principle objectives. In March, a number of divisions had been recalled from Italy, Palestine and Egypt; these men were quickly fed into the line, which stalled the German juggernaut. The advantage had passed from the attackers to the defenders. Once again, the battle was won by British resolution. However, further north the Germans who had taken Messines Ridge now threatened the Ypres Salient.

The War Diary for 149 Brigade [22] recorded the following casualties for April 1918: 1/4 Battalion: Officers: 1 killed and 5 wounded; Other Ranks: 16 killed, 203 wounded and 122 missing. 1/5 Battalion: Officers: 1 killed, 4 wounded and 5 missing; Other Ranks: 30 killed, 143 wounded and 339 missing. 1/6 Battalion: Officers: 1 killed, 9 wounded and 3 missing; Other Ranks: 27 killed, 249 wounded and 204 missing. As was usually the case, many of those recorded as missing would later be declared killed in action. A more detailed casualty list is in Appendix F.

After Lys, 149 Brigade was amply supplied with a draft of over 2,200 men, including 59 officers, who were allocated to the three battalions. Predictably, many of the ranks were young and green, arriving fresh from their Training Battalions. Their new arena was that of the French Sixth Army on the Aisne Front.

CHAPTER ELEVEN

ANNIHILATION UNDER FRENCH COMMAND
MAY 1918

Boom of thunder and lightning flash –
The torn earth rocks to the barrage crash;
The bullets whine and the bullets sing
From the mad machine-guns chattering;
Black smoke rolling across the mud,
Trenches plastered with flesh and blood –

From '*Chemin des Dames*' by Second Lieutenant Crosbie Garstin

In late April, the five British divisions were posted to the French Sixth Army on the Aisne, to what at the time was regarded as one of the quietest parts of the Western Front; the Germans even dubbed this sector the 'sanatorium of the west'. These divisions were the 50th, the 8th, 21st, and 26th, subsequently reinforced by the 19th Division. Orders were received on 25 April, and within 24 hours the men of the 50th Division began to make their way east.

Every one of the divisions had been severely tested in March and April – on the Somme and near Armentières – and had suffered grievous losses; they were in serious need of respite from the incessant danger and misery of their earlier posts. However, as will be recounted later, it seems that they marched out of one kind of hell straight into another. Trained soldiers, NCOs and officers were in short supply. This was summed up by Major General Sir Edmund Guy Bainbridge, commander of the 25th Division:

These reinforcements, largely composed of the nineteen-year-old class, who had been training for the last nine months in England, were most excellent material, but absence of older men suitable for promotion to NCO rank was, in some units, a serious disadvantage. A proportion under nineteen years of age were wisely kept back for another two or three months of training. It is a thousand pities that they should have been sent from England at all. Owing to age and physique, some of these immature boys were quite incapable of carrying the weight and doing the work required of an infantry soldier in the line: their presence in the ranks rendered them a danger to their units. To use them at the time was only a waste of those who might later on, with proper training and physical development, have become valuable reinforcements for the Army.[1]

This was an opinion with which Brigadier General Edward Puis Arthur Riddell, commanding 149 Brigade was in total agreement.

Since the middle of April, the 50th Division had been in training and reorganisation in the Roquetorie area. On 26 April, the men of 149 Brigade boarded railway carriages at Pernes travelling via St Pol, Noyelles-sur-Mer and Abbeville to an overnight rest camp. The following day they continued their journey in a circuitous route around Paris, then Pontoise to Fère en Tardenois where they left the train and marched six miles to Coulonges-Cohan, where they set up their HQ. Their training area was at Cohan, where from 30 April they began drilling in earnest. Five days later they were scheduled to go into the line, replacing the 51st French Division. By now the 50th Division had set up its HQ at Arcis-le-Ponsart.

The French had captured the *Chemin des Dames* in October 1917, following their victory at the Battle of Malmaison (*Bataille de la Malmaison 23-27 October 1917);* the defeated German forces had retreated from the *Chemin des Dames* and moved north of the Ailette river valley. The French Sixth Army held

Chemin Des Dames: The Californie Plateau and view towards Reims.
Author's Collection

a sector of fifty-five miles, from Noyon in the west to a position three miles north of Reims in the east. This army was the responsibility of General Denis Auguste Duchêne, a rebarbative man by all accounts, reputed to be perpetually ill-tempered and foulmouthed.

General
Denis Auguste
Duchêne

As mentioned, the sector taken over by the British Divisions of IX Corps had been very quiet for a long time; indeed, the French and German troops had settled into a placid *modus vivendi*. They were to find that many of the trenches were in a serious state of disrepair. Like the British system for defence, this previously held French sector consisted of a Forward Zone, Battle Zone and Rear Zone (Green Line), with an ample number of gun emplacements. The Forward Zone contained a number of strongpoints along the length of the British sector. The Battle Zone was a mile to the rear of the forward positions and it comprised a number of defended strong points based on small hills.

These were used as battalion and brigade headquarters and allowed for a clear field of fire for interlocking machine guns. The Rear Zone was located south of the Aisne river and canal; this defensive zone contained a large sequence of trenches with limited organised operational systems.

The sector held by the 50th Division was 8,100 yards wide, with a No Man's Land of 2000 yards or slightly more; the headquarters were based in Beaurieux, a village north of the river Aisne. This sector was divided into three sub-sectors, each held by a brigade, together with a machine gun company.

Operationally, each brigade had one battalion in the line, one in support and one in reserve. Brigadier General Riddell, in command of 149 Brigade, wrote of the dispositions of the 50th Division:

The sector was a most interesting one, bristling with tactical problems. In the right (149th Brigade) and centre (151st Brigade) sub-sectors, the ground formed a very gentle, uniform glacis slope from the Bosch lines down to the river Aisne with seven steep sided, thickly wooded hillocks which arose abruptly from the surrounding plain to an average height of sixty feet … A clear view of the right and centre sub-sectors could be obtained, as far as and including the Bosch front line and close support trenches; but the remainder of his trench system was lost to view in the woods as it disappeared behind the ridge (parallel to our front line) on which he had his front line system. From this ridge the Bosch could see every movement in our front and support lines especially in the right sector, [i.e. 149 Brigade] where movement along the trenches by day drew the fire of his snipers. Thus, it was extremely difficult to conceal the positions of our posts; a difficulty greatly increased by the fact that the trenches were dug in chalk against the whiteness of which our khaki clad men stood out in vivid contrast … The left sub-sector [held by the 150 Brigade] had one outstanding feature: the famous Californie Plateau. Rising to a height of 350 feet above the plain, with perhaps half a dozen bricks to mark the site of the once beautiful village of Craonne, this extraordinary plateau stood out seared and naked with its almost precipitous slopes disappearing as they fell to the thick woodland which carpeted the plain in every direction.[2]

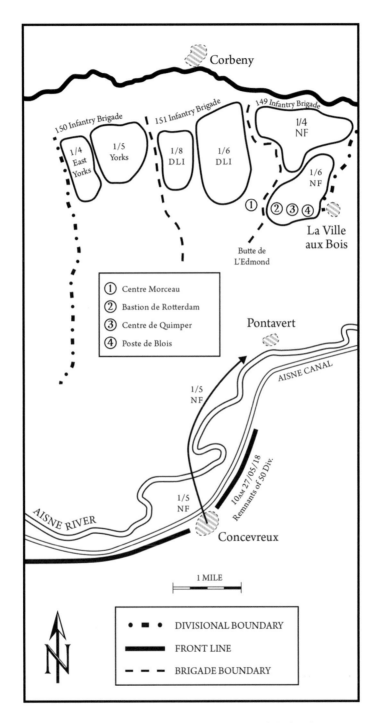

Corbeny

150 Infantry Brigade

151 Infantry Brigade

149 Infantry Brigade

1/4
East
Yorks

1/5
Yorks

1/8
DLI

1/6
DLI

1/4
NF

1/6
NF

① ② ③ ④

La Ville
aux Bois

Butte de
L'Edmond

① Centre Morceau
② Bastion de Rotterdam
③ Centre de Quimper
④ Poste de Blois

Pontavert

AISNE CANAL

1/5
NF

10AM 27/05/18
Remnants of 50 Div.

AISNE RIVER

1/5
NF

Concevreux

1 MILE

N

• ▪ •   DIVISIONAL BOUNDARY

FRONT LINE

‒ ‒ ‒   BRIGADE BOUNDARY

50th Division's dispositions on the eve of the battle

The sector to the right of 149 Brigade, held by elements of the 8th Division, was very different; it formed a right-angled salient projecting into the German positions. It was flatter territory, consisting of an Outpost Line some 1,000 to 1,500 yards in depth, as well as a Battle Zone 1,500 to 2,000 yards deep. The front line was some 7,500 yards long.

There existed even at this late stage in the war significant differences of opinion about how to hold back the German juggernaut. At the end of 1917, General Phillipe Pétain, Commander in Chief of the French Armies, laid down a new set of principles for defence. He felt strongly that the Allies needed a greater degree of flexibility. In his view, it was no longer a good idea to pack the Forward Zone with men; the front line should be held lightly, with only enough manpower to slow down the initial onslaught of the attacking enemy. The Battle Zone was to be the area in which to engage and contain the enemy, and was designed to ensure that it could not be reached by the attacking troops until they had already been delayed, and was as far back as possible to deny them any significant artillery backing.

However, support for this defence system was far from unanimous. One of Pétain's detractors was Duchêne, who was also in command of the British IX Corps. He advocated passionately that the defensive battle must at all costs be fought in the Forward Zone without giving up any French territory. Because of Duchêne's patriotic insistence that any territory gained at the cost of French blood should never be given up, Pétain reluctantly approved the retention of the *Chemin des Dames* as a line of resistance, with the proviso that none of the divisions of the Sixth Army placed in reserve was to be brought north of the Aisne.

Duchêne's reasoning for holding the *Chemin des Dames* – so called because it was a route once used by the daughters of Louis XV from Paris to the Château de Boves, the home of a friend – was purely emotional; he simply could not stomach the thought of ground in his sector being sacrificed. For him, it would be the equivalent of surrendering Fortress Verdun. Furthermore, in Duchêne's opinion the resolution of the British Expeditionary Force had been wavering in recent months … the French couldn't rely on the British.

However, the real weakness of the *Chemin des Dames* defence was that it lacked any depth, whereas five miles to the rear the Aisne river and canal formed a considerable natural boundary. The British commanders, free from the symbolic necessity of holding on to the *Chemin*, were quick to point out the shortcomings of the current defence arrangements. They favoured using the Aisne as the main line for defence; the ridge would then become a line of outposts and the sector would be ideal for deploying a defence in depth. However, Duchêne was not a man disposed to taking advice from subordinate commanders – especially British Commanders, whom he despised.

The difference of opinion between the French and British about the defence of the Aisne sector came to a head on 15 May at IX Corps Headquarters. All the divisional commanders of troops in the front-line made a collective protest to Lieutenant Colonel Sir Alexander Hamilton-Gordon, the commander of IX Corps, who was a dour man, thought by many to be weak and indecisive. They pointed out that what they were being asked to do was contrary to what all divisional commanders had been taught in the last two months – to evacuate the forward zone, out of trench mortar range. These protests were communicated to Duchêne, who replied, 'You English have learned up north how to retreat – I will teach you how to stand.' This left Hamilton-Gordon in an invidious position. Although he was in command of IX Corps, it was a relatively small and weak force, under a French commander of higher rank on French soil. There was very little he could do other than accept the line of command, as had his subordinates. Had he but known it, time was running out: within days the Germans would launch a momentous attack; one which would punch a great hole through the Anglo-French line.

Following the German attack in northern France known as the *Battle of the Lys*, code named *Operation Georgette*, Quartermaster General Erich Ludendorff had been planning an attack across the *Chemin des Dames*, an assault that would be named after the famous Swedish-born, Prussian General, Gebhard Leberecht von Blücher. Their aim was to smash through the Allied defences and press forward towards the Marne Valley and Paris. The German high command anticipated that this thrust towards the French capital would cause the French to panic and transfer all their reserves from the Flanders region, thus dividing the Allied armies. Ludendorff would then be free to implement his main line of attack against Haig's forces in the north.

These plans would require absolute secrecy so that maximum operational surprise could be achieved. A thirty-five-mile front from Soissons to just north of Reims was selected for the attack, scheduled for 27 May 1918. Ludendorff entrusted this major advance to two armies: the Seventh Army under Generaloberst Max von Boehn (whose troops would undertake the main thrust of the attack) with support on its eastern flank from the First Army commanded by General der Infanterie, Fritz von Below.

The Seventh Army was made up of six corps. Facing the British front of three weak divisions were two of these: the first was under the command of General Richard von Conta (IV Reserve Corps) and the second under General Graf von Schmettow (LXV Corps). In all, along the front, forty-one German infantry divisions faced nine weak divisions from the French Sixth Army as well as the three divisions from the depleted British IX Corps.

The build up by the Germans for the offensive was meticulous. All movements took place under cover of darkness. The terrain was also helpful, since the area between Laon and the front line was in places heavily wooded and the trees were by now in full leaf, providing ideal cover for dumps of ammunition and other supplies. Even nature was with them: the mating calls of thousands of frogs in the Ailette valley drowned out any noise. The clatter made by the movement of vehicles to the front was painstakingly reduced: the wheels of all vehicles were well greased and covered with leather; iron rimmed wheels were padded with wool or rag, and artillery pieces with loose parts were wrapped in straw. Horses' hoofs were padded. Secrecy was such that no labels or distinguishing markings were attached to vehicles moving along the roads and railways.

Ludendorff knew that his artillery was key to the success of this operation and he relied on the experience of Oberst George Bruchmüller who had been in charge of artillery during the earlier German offensives in March and April. A collection of 5,263 guns of various calibres were to be used against 1,422 Allied guns. This difference in firepower was the most extreme of any of the battles during the war. It was planned that in the first ten minutes all elements of the

German artillery would fire only gas shells, to create panic and to demoralise the besieged defenders, after which a mixture of gas and high explosive shells would target French and British artillery positions. Trench mortars would be concentrated on the front-line. The German artillery barrage was designed to last for two hours and forty-five minutes, the shortest but most potent of all the German offensives of 1918. Days before the start of the battle, confidence in the German camp was high. Major General von Unruh, Chief of Staff of von Conta's IV Reserve Corps, had carried out a detailed assessment of the sector occupied by British troops and helped plan the assault on the Californie Plateau. In an audience with Ludendorff he was asked what he expected would be the extent of the advance on 27 May. He predicted that the Germans would reach the Vesle River some twelve miles to the south, capturing the *Chemin des Dames* and the Aisne Valley.

On 25 May a raiding party from the 1/8 Battalion DLI (151 Brigade) penetrated the German positions and brought back a wounded prisoner who provided invaluable information about the forthcoming assault. The following day saw warnings of the attack being sent out from 50th Divisional Headquarters to its three brigades, to the effect that they suspected that the Germans were planning an advance on the morning of 27 May with a preliminary bombardment at 0100hrs, followed at 0430hrs by an infantry assault supported by tanks.

On the morning of 27 May, all three brigades of the 50th Division were manning the front line in the following order from left to right: 150 Brigade (with the French 22nd Infantry Division on its left), 151 Brigade, 149 Brigade. To the right of 149 Brigade were elements of 23 Brigade, 8th Division. The 149 Brigade held the front with a series of outposts, with the main line of resistance based approximately 1500 yards to the rear.

> *The 151st Brigade on my left and the 8th Division on my right had adopted the same system, except that their piquets* [i.e. outposts] *were smaller and more numerous – a difference in dispositions which, I am sure, tends toward weakness and lack of control. However, on these adjacent fronts the outposts were smaller and more numerous. This made the line weaker as it was much harder to control from the battalion headquarters.*[3]

285

During their brief occupancy of their sector 149 Brigade had been toiling flat out, building four fortified redoubts, which formed impressive obstacles 500 and 700 yards behind the battle zone. Each of these redoubts was manned by one company of the support battalion (the 1/6 Battalion on the day) as well as having four machine guns and two heavy mortar teams. These weapons had been cleverly positioned to provide direct fire over the battle zone if needed. Furthermore, on slightly rising ground, two anti-tank guns had been placed behind the redoubts. Riddell recorded:

> *The units on my right and left had no strong line to correspond to this reserve battle line, although they did have machine gun posts.*[4]

Riddell and Major General Henry Jackson GOC (50th Division) met at 1800hrs on 26 May and they determined that 149 Brigade was required:

> *… to fight it out to a finish on our Battle Line. No outside help could reach us in time. Brigades were to bring their reserve battalion* [for 149 Brigade this would be its 1/5 Battalion] *to the north bank of the Aisne and use it for counterattack. The arrival of French Divisions in time would depend entirely on our ability to hold the Bosch north of the Aisne.*[5]

Concerning this method of defence, Riddell had severe reservations:

> *We know from experience in this war that an attack in force will invariably overrun a weakly held position to a depth of two to three miles, if well supported by artillery. In spite of this accepted principle we had no garrisoned defensive zone south of the Aisne.*[6]

Nevertheless, each division in the line was allowed to call up a brigade from the 25th Division, if the necessity arose.

During the morning of 24 May, the 1/4 had relieved the 1/5 in the front line. Two companies occupied the outpost line which was effectively the old front line. Another company manned a line of posts and trenches along Route 44, the Reins to Laon road. The fourth company with the Battalion HQ was in residence at the most northerly redoubt in the Battle Zone, Trench de la Plaine.

The War Diary of 1/4 records: *This was a rather difficult relief but was carried out successfully and completed by 3am.*[7]

The 1/4 received news of the forthcoming German attack on 26 May at 1930hrs. They set about preparing defensive positions, including the outpost line falling back to the trenches along Route 44. Sentries were left to monitor these outposts. Brigade HQ issued orders that as soon as the attack began, artillery and Stokes mortar fire would cover the outpost line and the wire entanglements of No Man's Land. On seeing the enemy, the sentries were to fall back after they had fired their SOS signals.

The German assault began as anticipated.

1/4 Battalion

An entry in the War Diary of the 1/4 Battalion written at 1300hrs on 27 May 1918 records:

The enemy put down an extraordinary intensive barrage on the whole of the Forward Area, composed of high explosive and gas mixed. All troops were standing to in their battle positions and many casualties were caused through the shelling. At 3.45am the enemy attacked along the whole line on the battalion front, they apparently came from behind the Ouvrage de la Carrière in a south-easterly direction almost parallel to Route 44. The survivors of the outpost line withdrew to the line of posts where Lewis Gun and rifle fire broke up the attack and drove back the enemy.[7]

The events of the early hours of 27 May were recorded by the Reverend Wilfrid Callin, Chaplain to the 1/4:

Sunday was a day of glorious sunshine and beautiful calm. Over the whole area a great quiet prevailed. Some of us have long been suspicious of such calmness, as a sure sign of some further frightfulness being prepared in secret by the Hun. And signs had been given that something was afoot. His famous red aeroplanes – the stormy petrels – had been seen for a day or two; new guns had been ranging; convoys or motor lorries had been reported near his lines. What this denoted became definitely known on Sunday evening. Prisoners had given the information that at 1am, Monday 27th, the enemy intended to attack in great force. The last needful preparations for battle were completed, and the Fourth, inspired by Colonel Gibson, waited the fateful hour. At something past eleven o'clock on the Sunday night our own guns began – anticipating the Hun by a hundred minutes, and helping to disorganise his concentrations. But on the stroke of 1 o'clock the whole front from Soissons to Reims broke into flame and we knew for the third time in ten weeks we were up against the real thing. Within fifteen minutes it was obvious that the Hun had an extraordinary concentration of guns of every calibre, and that the bombardment had been organised beforehand in most thorough and accurate fashion. A big proportion of gas was used, about four varieties being distinguished in the later French and British reports. The whole line was deluged with shells, and the front trenches especially must have been reduced to a pulverised mass. For two hours and a half this continued; then lifted further on as the infantry and tanks attacked at 3.30am. There ensued a fight that had epic qualities. Standing in the ruins of their defences, the Northumberlands awaited the onslaught – waited and met it with rifle and Lewis gun fire until the grey hordes broke and stayed their course, tanks and men alike, overwhelming in numbers, they pounded on again and our men were pressed back to their second positions, fighting as steadily and effectively as their depleting numbers permitted. Another battalion came to help, and the wood in front of Pontavert became a perfect hell.[8]

At first, 149 Brigade held back the German assault, aided by their careful preparations. Their withdrawal from the outpost and the bombardment of the old front line by the divisional artillery caused the Germans to modify their tactics. Stiff resistance by the Fusiliers occupying the defences along Route 44 ruled out a direct attack, but they were eventually enveloped by German troops from both flanks because the brigades on the left and right proved to be less resilient. The 1/4 demonstrated that the concept of defence in depth carried out by well drilled troops worked well; many men survived the preliminary bombardment due to their early withdrawal, unlike other sectors whose defenders suffered many casualties as a consequence of not withdrawing troops from exposed positions. By 0400hrs the Germans had overwhelmed the stout resistance, although it took three separate attacks. The final assault involved the use of four tanks which eventually forced the survivors of the forward companies into the Battle Zone. Those from the left forward company were either killed or taken prisoner – as they tried to withdraw they found the enemy behind them, having flanked from the right.

Shortly afterwards the Germans attacked the Battle Zone with the tanks that had penetrated the line to the north, continuing their advance. At this point the commanding officer of the 1/4, Lieutenant Colonel Bertrand Dees Gibson, evacuated his Battalion HQ back to the line of redoubts at Centre Marceau. The main line of the German assault came from the direction of Ville-aux-Bois on the right, the area occupied by the 8th Division. Here the 1/4 and 1/6 (the 1/6 being the support Battalion) were surprised to find that the Germans were able to attack them from the rear.

Thus, by 0445hrs any resistance in the Battle Zone had been overcome by a rapidly advancing enemy. At Centre Marceau, telephone communications with Brigade HQ was still in operation, and at 0500hrs Gibson informed Riddell that he was holding on to the line of redoubts with forty men, but the situation was desperate. Riddell recalled this conversation:

I told him to hold out to the last and that I would order a company of the 1/5 Northumberland Fusiliers in reserve to retake Temple Farm and help his left. I can remember his brave, firm voice now as he said: 'Very good sir, Good bye.' I suppose he knew that there was no chance. The man on the spot, if he is a good man, always knows best. I heard afterwards he was shot in the head while cheering on his men in a final effort. A splendid death for a splendid man.[9]

By 0530hrs the enemy had taken the redoubt line from the right and rear. At this point Gibson and a few men fell back to the Butte de l'Edmond where this pitifully small force, by now joined by a party of the Divisional Machine Gun Battalion, made another stand. Here Gibson was killed.

The War Diary records:

From this time the 1/4 Northumberland Fusiliers ceased to exist as a fighting force.[10]

Lieutenant Colonel Bertrand Dees Gibson
1/4 Battalion Northumberland Fusiliers

Bertrand was the only son of Colonel Wilfred and Ann Gibson of Ruradean, Hexham. Born in January 1876 at Maidens Cross, he was educated at Ushaw College, Durham. He qualified as a solicitor and went into partnership with his father in 1899. He practised in the Hexham and Haltwhistle Courts and acted as solicitor to Hexham Farmers' Protection Association. Bertrand married Margaret Elizabeth (née Jackson, of Stainton, Yorkshire) in the summer of 1907. He was a sporting polymath, one of the finest lawn tennis players that Tynedale had produced. He captained Northumberland at hockey, and played cricket and rugby for Tynedale.

Bertrand joined the pre-territorial, 1st Volunteer Battalion of the Northumberland Fusiliers in 1900. He spent time at the School of Musketry at Hythe and was appointed instructor of musketry for the battalion. At the onset of hostilities he was promoted to the rank of major. He travelled to France with his battalion in April 1915 and saw action within days at the Battle of St Julien, during which the battalion commander was wounded and Bertrand assumed command. In the summer of 1915 he was gazetted to lieutenant colonel. Bertrand earned his DSO in January 1917 for his courageous fighting on the Somme in September 1916. By July 1917 Bertrand was in hospital in Wandsworth, suffering with nervous exhaustion, but on reporting fit for duty he insisted that he rejoin his battalion at the Front, which he did in April 1918. Bertrand was awarded the Croix de Guerre avec Palms, posthumously, in recognition of his leadership on 27 May 1918, the day he died, killed by a sniper's bullet. The Divisional History recorded that 'Lieutenant-Colonel Gibson was a Territorial Force Officer of great experience and reputation, a fine soldier and was greatly beloved by his Battalion.' The Reverend Callin wrote of Lieutenant Colonel Gibson:

Thus the Battalion lost its Commanding Officer, a man revered and loved by all. All nerve and will, he died fighting to the last, the very incarnation of courage. A born leader and a superb soldier, he had joined the Fusiliers in the early Volunteer days, finally becoming Commanding Officer in the summer of 1915. His name will be ever remembered by those who knew him as one of the straightest, strongest men we have known.

Bertram is buried in La Ville-aux-Bois Cemetery. A wife, a son and a daughter survived him. His wife had the following inscribed on his gravestone:

IN GLORIOUSLY PROUD MEMORY
OF MY BELOVED HUSBAND
"UNTIL"
QUO FATA VOCANT

The Reverend Callin wrote:

Draw a line from the front of the wood eastwards to the Bois des Buttes and you have roughly the line on which the Fourth fought its last battle as a battalion. The enemy came on in great force diagonally from the right, between Ronnteaux and the line running Ville-aux-Bois/Bois des Buttes, so getting in behind the battalion and working towards Craonne. Thus they were completely cut off. Out of the mêlée only a few emerged. Marshall came down gassed and after a certain rest and treatment at Concevreux, returned to the fight with Major Robb's party, Napier (barely recovered from his wounds) came down badly gassed and had to be sent to hospital. Captain Gregory, the adjutant, was wounded and reported to have been left in the marshes, but by the almost super human courage of two men, Hunter and Coghlan, was carried out and eventually reached hospital, wounded in three places. Captain Benson of the Trench Mortar Battery, having made his way to the forefront of the fight, led an attack on a German tank, but was killed in the effort. Colonel Gibson fell, shot through the head as he was directing the last defences. With the enemy on every side, the River and canal both behind them, the survivors, on the exhaustion of ammunition, were taken prisoner.[11]

By 0900hrs the remnants of 149 Brigade had retreated in the direction of the Aisne river and canal between Chaudrades and Concevreux, where the brigade set up its new HQ. The brigade major, Captain H. W. Jackson, along with Major Ridley Robb of the 1/4, quickly organised a plan of defence. Jackson later wrote to Riddell, who had been wounded on 27 May, describing the last-ditch attempt to guard the bridges over the Aisne:

Well, you will remember the perfect stream of men coming along the canal bank from the direction of Pontavert. I stopped these men at the bridge – there were no more than 2% of NCOs and no officers. I suppose I collected 200 in due course – formed them up in two ranks and told them off into two sections and platoons on the canal bank. There were men from 8th Division, 149 and 151 Brigades and other details. I explained the situation to all men as best I could, formed four composite platoons and placed them in position. My greatest difficulty was having no officers and I remember having to go to the extremity of drawing my revolver on two men who tried to go back. … The danger came from the right flank as the Boche had taken Pontavert, gained the crossing there over the river and canal, and was working south-west on the south side of the canal, the time being 9.30am. Major Robb (1/4 Northumberland Fusiliers) came up about that time. I handed over to him and said I was going to the left to find out what was happening, find Major [I.] Tweedy (Commander 1/5 Battalion Northumberland Fusiliers) and establish a brigade headquarters in Concevreux. Just as I was going off, a major of the Worcesters came along the canal bank in a car! Apparently, a battalion of the Worcesters – 25th Division – was coming up to help us. We discussed the situation to the accompaniment of a few 'pings' from a Boche sniper's rifle. I said I thought two companies should counterattack along the southern bank of the canal with the blowing up of Pontavert bridge (about 1,200 yards away) as their objective, as I was convinced that only a few Boche had crossed the canal up to that time, but it was certain that the 8th Division (who I think were responsible) had failed to blow the bridge. Also touch had to be gained with the 8th Division. The Worcesters did eventually go up to our right flank but were too late to achieve anything in the form of a counterattack.[12]

Major Robb held the position along the Aisne Canal until 1300hrs when his composite force was ordered to withdraw to conform to a line held by the 3 Battalion Worcestershire Regiment. The following men from the 1/4 were awarded the Military Medal during the Battle of the Aisne:

200832 Private Stephen Robert Futers   **204568 Private John Daykin**

For gallantry and devotion in duty on the morning of 27th May 1918, on the south bank of the Aisne Canal near Concevreux. These men volunteered to carry messages to a unit of the 25th Division over open ground and exposed to heavy machine-gun fire. Pte Futers volunteered to deliver the message in the first instance, and succeeded in doing so, but on his return journey he was wounded in the back and was unable to deliver the reply. Pte Daykin then volunteered to take a second message, which he managed to deliver, and succeeded in bringing back a reply. Both these men were exposed to very heavy machine-gun fire throughout their journey.

200091 Corporal John Edward Mogerley

On the 27th May 1918, this NCO was detailed to find out where small arms ammunition could best be dumped for the battalion. He went from Le Fait Farm to Wireless Station Concevreux under very heavy machine-gun fire. He received his instructions from the Commanding Officer and made a most gallant effort to get the ammunition up to the battalion, but was turned back by an officer. He again returned to find the battalion, but found they had moved. He ascertained their line of retirement and in spite of heavy machine-gun fire he found a suitable place for a dump and the ammunition was picked up by the battalion.

200489 Private John James Knot

On 27th May 1918, on the road between Le Fait Farm and Ventelay village, the transport was being heavily and accurately shelled. One shell landed on a limber, and the driver and mules were all wounded and the rear half of the limber destroyed. Pte Knott salved the rear half of another damaged limber and hitched it on. He mounted the wounded mules and drove them through Ventelay still under heavy shell fire, until they collapsed.

John Knot was also awarded the Distinguished Conduct Medal.

200490 Sergeant John Kelly

On May 27th 1918, near Révillon, this NCO assisted in organising Lewis gun teams for the purpose of retarding the enemy's advance on Fismes. He displayed the utmost coolness under fire, and his example and leadership on several occasions prevented premature retirement on the part of young and inexperienced soldiers. Later in the day, near Glennes, he took up a position with two Lewis guns in a wood commanding the enemy's approach until almost surrounded, inflicting heavy loss on the enemy and considerably delaying their advance. The courage and tenacity shown by this NCO was beyond praise, and rendered great service in difficult circumstances.

Also for his gallantry **Lieutenant Colonel Bertram Dees Gibson DSO** was posthumously awarded the French decoration, the Croix de Guerre with Palms:

This officer was in command of his battalion, which was holding the front-line trenches on 27th May 1918 in the Aisne sector. He continued to send information of the enemy's advance until his Headquarters was completely surrounded. He then collected all available men of his Headquarters party, and although attacked on three sides it was due to this officer's personal example that the enemy were delayed in their advance for a considerable time. He was shot through the head and killed whilst standing on the parapet to get a better view of the enemy, who at this time were advancing up a communication trench.

1/6 Battalion

Lieutenant Alan Ryder Hall
1/6 Northumberland Fusiliers

Alan was the last surviving son of the late Mr Hall and Emma M Hall of Tokyo. He was educated at Richmond School, York, and Drexel College, Philadelphia. At the onset of war Alan held an appointment in Japan. Alan was a well-known member of the Yokohama and Kobe Athletic Clubs. On returning to England in March 1915 he joined the Inns of Court OTC. In August 1915 he received a commission with the 1/6 Northumberland Fusiliers and embarked for the Western Front in October 1915. On 30 May 1918, Alan volunteered for patrol duty. His patrol encountered a party of the enemy who were holding a wood, to whom he refused to surrender and whilst withdrawing with his sergeant he was killed, aged 30. During the fighting on the Somme he was mentioned in despatches. Alan is commemorated on the Soissons Memorial to the Missing.

At the onset of the German assault on 27 May, the 1/6 were in support, positioned in a line of redoubts approximately 500 yards behind the Battle Line. The four redoubts – Bastion de Rotterdam, Centre de Quimper, Poste de Blois and Centre Marceau – were held by two companies from the battalion, with four machine guns and two heavy trench mortars in emplacements that could fire over the battle line. The two remaining companies were based in trenches and dugouts next to Lieutenant Colonel Eric Temperley's Headquarters at P C Kleber. These positions were pulverised during the preliminary German bombardment, as were those of the other units in the front line. By 0500hrs German *Sturmtruppen* and tanks were advancing on Centre Morceau, which (as mentioned above) was held by a mixture of troops from the 1/4 and 1/6 Battalions.

At 0530hrs Temperley ordered a counterattack with his reserve company. They managed, with great courage and élan, to evict the enemy from the Bastion de Rotterdam, but by this time the Centre de Quimper had fallen. Meanwhile, the German *Sturmtruppen* had worked around the redoubts which they eventually captured from the rear. A large number of men from the 1/6 were taken prisoner, including Eric Temperley and seventeen other officers; Temperley who had embarked in France on 20 April 1915, was repatriated on 25 December 1918 and died at the age of 83 in 1986.

Captain Joseph Garrard, who served as a company commander with the 1/6 and had been with them on the Western Front since the catastrophic *Battle of St Julien* in late April 1915, wrote to General Edmonds in 1935 about his experiences during the *Battle of the Aisne*. He was commenting on a draft copy of the Official History and in particular the role of the 50th Division. He wrote:

> I am pleased to note the mention in the draft of tired British Divisions and also of imperfectly trained recruits, and feel some satisfaction that these statements will be put on record.[13]

Although he expressed his high regard for the generals and battalion commanders under which he served, Garrard voiced concerns about the lack of preparations made in his sector before the attack:

> There appeared generally a distinct lack of co-operation between infantry and Machine Gun Corps. They were miles apart metaphorically as far as operations were concerned and the latter seemed to be satisfied if their crews knew where their SOS lines were, which from my point of view seemed hopeless and useless, I being on the spot as it were.

At the commencement of the German attack the Machine Gun Corps (two teams) had totally expended their ammunition and were useless to me. I chased them back to their next positions, which they did not know.[14]

Garrard went on to say that there appeared to have been no measures to counter the advance of four German tanks in his sector; no armour-piercing shells had been issued to either the infantry or the machine gunners.

He concluded:

The morale of the German troops was not very great even with the bolstering up that their victories in March and April might have given them and if the British troops had only been in better condition and a little more set, a different tale would have been told. It was a very unsatisfactory business, rotten in fact, yet taking everything into account no faults could be found anywhere and everyone did one's best, poor as it was.[15]

1/5 Battalion

On 27 May the 1/5 were in reserve, based at Conccvrcux, south of the Aisne. They were under the command of Major Ivan Tweedy. At first glance the battalion's strength was relatively healthy.

The War Diary records:

Strength of battalion at 30 April was 37 officers and 936 other ranks. However, many of the new recruits were young recruits, many only eighteen whilst many of the officers had been drafted from Irish regiments. A significant amount of time would be needed to weld these men into a cohesive fighting unit.[16]

One of these new recruits was 61704 Private Robert Percy Williams, a lad from the heart of Wales who was aged only eighteen when he was sent to France and posted to the 1/5. During the fighting on 27 May he was captured and was to spend the rest of the war as a prisoner. Robert later told the story of his time on the Aisne front:

61704
Pte Robert Percy Williams
Courtesy of D. Blanchard

We were sent into a quiet sector, which we had taken over from the French near Reims, a place called Fismes. We were just manning the lines, we didn't do anything, we thought we were just there to get acclimatised because the French told us that nothing had happened in the sector for a couple of years. There was a bit of shell fire and a man called Sutton, [75247 Private Arthur Sutton, who died 15 May 1918], *a chap from Wakefield, was killed. He was the first of our young boys to die, then a lad from Accrington was killed. But Sutton was a friend of mine, I'd met him in Doncaster when we were in the KOYLI's, then we were transferred to the Northumberland Fusiliers. We were in 'C' Company, and he was in my platoon, when a shell fell only fifty yards away and they told me, "Poor old Sutton's had it!" I was very upset and depressed.*[17]

The War Diary[18] records that on 13 May the 1/5 had relieved the 1/6 in the support area and dispositions were: HQ: PC Kleber; 'A' Company in the vicinity of Ville-au-Bois; 'B' Company in the Centre de Quimper; 'C' Company in Centre de Marceau and 'D' Company in Trenches Lefeuvre and Dardenelles.

On 27 May, despite being in reserve trenches, the 1/5 also were under artillery barrage at 0100hrs, although not to the extent of the front line battalions. Williams recalled:

I was in a dugout in the third line trenches when an officer came around and said that there might be action tonight. I'd not been under bad shellfire before and I was shaking and was almost sick with fright as we waited, just waited until all hell broke loose. When the guns opened up, the noise was deafening, the shells falling, causing tremendous explosions and destroying not only the trenches above our heads but the stairs leading down to us. We were told to leave our dugout and we scrambled into a trench that had been practically destroyed. Gas shells had been falling all night and saturated everything, covering our masks with a sulphur film. You couldn't see. I had stomach ache. I felt faint and sick and had to spew up, forcing me to take the gas mask off and vomit as best I could, trying not to breath in.

Casualties were being suffered and between the din we could hear them shouting for stretchers bearers. I thought 'Oh my God, I'm going to die, I am going to die!' We did not know what was happening, not fifty yards either side of us.[19]

The intense German barrage had caused appalling damage to trenches, to communications and to the morale of the men, many of whom had only been in France for a few weeks. Williams continued:

Then Corporal Collins came along. He was panicking, he'd seen tanks, he said that the Germans had broken through and we were surrounded. Every man for himself, everything has collapsed … he said there was no chance, we must get out of it, otherwise we shall be captured. As I stumbled from the trench I dropped my rifle, it was panic, the noise was terrible. I was weighed down by my pack, by fifty rounds of ammunition strapped around me, by my entrenching tool, the earth was blown up all around and I couldn't see. Then a shell burst close by, shrapnel wounding me in the leg. It wasn't bad, we had puttees on, but I saw my leg was bleeding.[20]

At 0240hrs the 1/5 were ordered to move forward to a position south east of Beaurepaire Wood. As they moved northwards they were shelled heavily and it was not till 0400hrs that they eventually reached their new position, in open ground adjacent to the village of Pontavert. This movement of reserve troops was totally against what officers like Riddell believed in, in that it committed his reserve battalion into the battle too early. Across the whole front this type of decision appears to have been made on an ad hoc basis with no inter-brigade communication. By this time all the front-line positions had been overwhelmed and in many instances the second line positions had also been taken before the reserve battalions could be brought into play. In Riddell's view, the better approach would have been to form a line along the banks of the Aisne river and canal and await the arrival of battalions from the 25th Division, the reserve division.

Riddell had always been aware of the defensive value of the Aisne which was mentioned in his post battle report, in which his frustration and anger are barely disguised:

> *Most undoubtedly, the position south of the Aisne was infinitely stronger than that held north of the river and should have been regarded as our main line of resistance … and considered our positions north of the river in the light of outposts. I wish we had done so – but we were under orders of the French Army and needs must obey.*[21]

Thus constrained, the 1/5 were fed into the battle just as the defences at the front line and the battle zone were being smashed by the sheer force of the German advance. At 0515hrs, 'C' (left) and 'D' (right) Companies were ordered to man the intermediate line between Butte de l'Edmond and the Bois des Buttes under the command of Lieutenant Colonel Temperley of the 1/6. These orders did not arrive until after 0600hrs; the Butte de l'Edmond had already fallen. As the two companies moved forward they were met by a fearsome barrage. 'C' Company were unable to occupy the Butte de l'Edmond-Bois des Buttes line as they came under vigorous machine gun fire. As a result, the remnants of both companies made a stand in trenches south of the Butte de l'Edmond. From this position the troops put up dogged resistance, wiping out most of the attacking Germans. However, it was not long before German troops advancing from the Bois des Buttes were behind the trenches occupied by 'C' and 'D' Companies. Many Fusiliers were taken prisoner, but a few under the command of Major J.C. Leatheart of the 1/6 managed to fight their way back to join the troops holding the Aisne. 'A' and 'B' Companies, commanded by Major I.Tweedy, were ordered to advance to the trenches adjacent to Brigade HQ at Centre d'Évreux and to check the enemy advance on Pontavert. As the enemy had already captured the woods to the north, this wasn't possible; they came under a furious barrage and took many casualties. The line fell back towards Chaudardes on the north side of the Aisne river and canal. By 1430hrs the remnants of the 1/5 had withdrawn across the Aisne to Concevreux, but by this time the Germans had also crossed the river and

canal. One of those who died during the fighting of 27 May was 23/683 Private Harry Vipond Allan, aged 20, from Ashington, who initially enlisted in the Tyneside Scottish and after being wounded on the Somme, was subsequently posted to the 1/5 NF. Harry is buried in Marfaux British Cemetery.

The Reverend Callin described the Fusiliers' withdrawal on 27 May:

A few of us remained in Concevreux during the morning to deal with what wounded we could. Fifty or sixty perhaps passed through our hands and were sent to hospital at Meurival – on stretchers, on doors and on barrows. Nicholson (who had been acting as Liaison Officer with the brigade) came in with a very nasty wound in the thigh, but as cheery and as indomitable as ever. The last we dressed was our Regimental Sergeant-Major, [G.D.] Fewster, very badly hit indeed; what happened to poor Fewster after he left us we do not know. When he had gone Lieutenant Playford (Doctor), the Rev Coyle, (RC Padre) and I decided to leave – Sergeant Hall and two men remaining to fire the stores that could not be removed. I caught the transport at the top of the hill and from there watched as the Boche crossed the valley towards us. Though it was after midday, he was putting up his Very lights to show to his people behind where his advanced positions were located. His machine gun posts could be clearly distinguished and his lines of men by roadside, hedgerow and dyke.[22]

By this time Riddell had been badly wounded:

It was all hands to the pumps now. Martin still had thirty men and officers of his staff about him. We ordered everyone to turn out, and climb out of the dugout to join the 1/5th. It was quite clear, with a bright sun. Shells were bursting all about us and machine gun bullets flipped the leaves and smacked into the trees. We could hear the Lewis gun of the platoon of 1/5th Durham Light Infantry 'rat tatting' away behind us, showing that they were holding on, but to the north of me I caught sight of a few Bosches close to hand in the bushes. Martin and I with Leatheart of the gunners ran on towards the 1/5th NF. We had only gone a few yards when a shell burst to our left; I felt a terrific blow to my face, and saw Martin roll over. I went to him. He was quite dead. I walked on half dazed, with a great hole in my face into which I could put my hand, but I did not feel much pain.[23]

Major I. Tweedy took over command of the remnants of 149 Brigade. In the afternoon this force took up a position on the heights between Meurival and the Roucy-Ventelay road. This they held until 2300hrs when a message was received that the enemy had occupied Ventelay and were advancing towards Romain; this movement would cut off Tweedy's force.

Corporal Adolf Hitler of the 16 Bavarian Infantry List Regiment recalled his time at the Battle of the Aisne:

We set off for the second offensive in 1918 on the night of the 25 [May]. On the 26 we spent the night in a forest, and on the morning of the 27 we prepared for duty. At 5 o'clock in the morning we departed. The day before, during the afternoon, we received reinforcements for the big offensive at Chemin des Dames ... on 28 May alone fifty-nine men were killed in action. The high losses were in no small degree due to the inadequate time allowed for integrating reinforcements into the regiment.[24]

Eventually, orders were received that the remnants of the 50th Division were to amalgamate under the command of Lieutenant Colonel Kirkup, with the aim of defending a line along the south bank of the Ainse, but by 1430hrs on 28 May they were compelled to retreat when the enemy outflanked them on both sides. Their next position was in an existing trench system on the forward slope of a hill south of Concevreux, but the enemy's artillery rapidly zeroed in making it untenable. The next withdrawal was to Hill 200 south of Ventelay. As evening approached the line held by the remnants of the 50th Division ran from La Faite Ferme (a mile north of Ventelay) to a point northwest of Le Grand Haneau, where French reinforcements were coming into line to connect with the 197 French Division. The 8th Division were on the right. However, by dusk the Germans had pushed forward to Courlandon.

Scanty as were our numbers, separated as each action was, a steady fight was carried on. The main body – if such a small force can be called a main body

– under Major J. R. Robb, fought tenaciously as they slowly gave way before this enemy – fighting, bluffing, retiring, reorganising and fighting again. On Monday [27 May] night at La Haie Farm they were almost cut off and had to retire across country on a compass bearing through fields and woods. Tuesday night was spent at Ville-en-Tardenois. Wednesday with a junction of some of the sections through Romigny and Jonquery to Baslieux. Here a composite Brigade was formed under Major Robb's command, with Captain David Turner in charge of the 149 Company. They returned to a line near Romigny. The difficulties faced by the slender force were enormous – difficulties of numbers, morale and liaison. It speaks volumes for the fine leadership of Major Robb that so much was done. He and his indomitable officers were the soul of the fight. At Romigny we lost Captain Turner … He spent the night with his men at Ville-en-Tardenois but was defending Romigny village on the Thursday morning.[25]

By 30 May a significant German victory seemed inevitable. They had captured over 50,000 Allied soldiers and over 800 artillery pieces as they advanced to within thirty-five miles of Paris. In spite of their early success, the advancing army was nonetheless beset with problems, including supply shortages, fatigue, lack of reserves and many casualties. Further, they faced counterattacks and stiff resistance from the newly-arrived American Divisions, who engaged them at the *Battles of Château Thierry* and *Belleau Wood*. On 6 June, after many Allied counteractions, the German advance halted on the Marne, short of its major objective, Paris. *Blücher* had ended in failure, as had the *Michael* and *Georgette* offensives of March and April 1918.

The *Battle of the Aisne* turned out to be the swansong of the three proud Territorial Battalions of the Northumberland Fusiliers. The 1/4, 1/5 and 1/6 Battalions of the reconstituted 149 Brigade had arrived on the Western Front in late April 1915; they had suffered the *Battle of the Somme* (March 1918) and *Lys* (April 1918). Thus far, numbers in the depleted battalions had been made up with soldiers from all parts of Britain, but the ravages of 27 May proved to be the end of the line.

It appears that it was impossible to find troops to replace the men lost at Aisne. During the days that followed, the remnants fought as the 149 Battalion, rather than 149 Brigade, a composite unit commanded by Major Robb of the 1/4. The 1/4 and 1/5 Battalions each consisted of only one company, whilst the 1/6 had two companies, each of 130 men. However, by the first week in July, orders were received to reduce these three to cadre training battalions, each with a strength of sixty-two men: officers and other ranks. The surplus men and officers were posted to other battalions of the British Army. Eventually these cadre battalions were billeted near Dieppe. Subsequently the 50th Division and 149 Brigade were reconstituted – but they lost their identities. On 11 July, General H.C. Jackson addressed the remnants of 149 Brigade:

I do not refer to the Cadre Battalions but to you men who are going down to the Base and who will be sent to other units. I want to say how sorry I am to lose you all. I know how you feel, especially you men who have served three years or even longer with one battalion. Your Battalions have become your home and I sympathise in having to leave your friends and associations.

It has been my privilege to command you over three months, and I have made friends whom I will be very sorry to lose. It has been your lot to have been in three severe actions during that time, and you have proved to be good soldiers, whom I am sorry to part with. But under the present conditions we have no choice in the matter.

When you get to the Base you will be given many opportunities for training. I want you to make the most of such training. Learn to kill Boche. Many of you have killed your Boche and you know what a serious thing it is to miss the enemy. It means that a Boche is left alive, who has no right to be so.

Within about a fortnight's time, we will be entering into the fourth year of the war, and killing Boche is the only way to end the war. Therefore learn never to miss a target.

Again, I say how sorry I am that you have to be broken up but my good luck goes with you, where ever you go.[26]

The sole surviving battalion, 1/7, now serving as a pioneer battalion with the 42nd (East Lancashire) Division saw action until the Armistice on 11 November 1918. As for Major General Denis Auguste Duchêne, the architect of this military disaster: he was relieved of his command by order of the French Prime Minister, Georges Clemenceau, on 9 June 1918, during a political crisis in Paris. However, he was allowed to remain in the army, and on 16 June 1920 he was made a Grand Officer of the *Légion d'honneur*.

The War Diary of 149 Brigade for May records the following casualties:

1/4 Battalion: Officers: 2 killed, 5 wounded and 16 missing; Other Ranks: 3 killed, 40 wounded and 535 missing. See Appendix G for details.

Captain David Thompson Turner
1/4 Battalion Northumberland Fusiliers

David was the eldest son of William Murdoch and Hebron King Turner, of Haydon Lodge, Haydon Bridge, Northumberland. David joined the 1/4 Battalion at the outbreak of war and embarked for France in April 1915. He was wounded at the battle of St Julien. He was again wounded at Neuve Eglise in 1916. For his gallant work at St Julien he was mentioned in dispatches by General Sir John French. In command of the depleted 149 Company, David was killed on 30 May 1918, near Romigny, aged 28. He is buried in Chambrecy British Cemetery. His headstone is inscribed:

GREATER LOVE
HATH NO MAN THAN THIS.

1/5 Battalion: Officers: 3 killed, 2 wounded and 11 missing; Other Ranks: 10 killed,101 wounded and 338 missing. See Appendix G for details.

1/6 Battalion: Officers: 6 wounded and 15 missing; Other Ranks: 14 killed, 56 wounded and 530 missing. See Appendix G for details.

In the days following the battle, men who had managed to survive emerged and reported for duty. Most of those recorded as 'missing' were later found to have been killed in action. The rest had been taken as prisoners of war; many of these would die in German hands.

Captain Neville Marriott North
1/5 Battalion Northumberland Fusiliers.

Neville was the only son of Harry and Frances North, of South Africa. He was educated at Bedford Modern School and Leeds University. He was gazetted to the 1/5 in September 1912 and proceeded to France in April 1915. He was wounded in May 1915 and again in July when he was invalided to England, having been awarded the MC for gallantry and devotion to duty. He returned to France in November 1915. In September 1916 he was wounded for the third time and once more invalided back to England. He returned to duty on 20 April 1918 and was reported missing and presumed dead on the 27 May 1918, aged 28. Neville is commemorated on the Soissons Memorial to the Missing.

Arthur Conan Doyle reported on how the Germans treated their British prisoners:

So rapid had been the hostile advance that the dressing stations were captured and many of our doctors and wounded fell into the hands of the Germans to endure the fate which these savages so often reserved for the brave but helpless men who fell into their power.[27]

A specific act of barbarity was witnessed by Private Joseph Hodgson of the 1/4:

At the same time as I was taken, one of our lads was buried in the trench with his head and shoulders sticking out. Ten minutes or a quarter of an hour after the men in the trench had surrendered one of the Germans threw a hand grenade at this man and killed him. I do not know to what unit this German belonged.[28]

One of the many captured on 27 May was Private Percy Williams:

By this time the gas had lifted and I could see the Germans running across, scores of them, I was so confused, you see, and the noise had left me all of a muddle. I didn't know where I was. Then I turned and saw this German with his fixed bayonet standing over me. He shouted 'Halt, halt, halt', and then he motioned 'or else' and grabbed me … There was absolute panic. We could see the Germans in their grey uniforms, with their fixed rifles and bayonets. You must remember that we were nearly all boys of eighteen and we were up against seasoned veterans … we were lads of eighteen, just boys.[29]

Initially, Percy was sent to Güstrow prisoner of war camp. Many of those captured would spend over six months in squalid conditions, short of food and medical supplies. In many cases, Red Cross food parcels would never reach their intended recipients; they were stolen to feed, through the black market, the local population and camp guards as the Allied blockade of German ports intensified causing widespread shortages. In other cases, prisoners were believed dead and were therefore unknown to the Red Cross and did not receive any aid. Many were living on the meagre prison rations alone, and had lost nearly half their body weight by the time they were liberated.

We couldn't believe our luck that after all this time the war had finished and we should go back to England. But so many of the men were ill, a lot of them were dying from the influenza epidemic. The clothes used to hang off them and their faces were thin. Their arms were thin, their legs were thin, they were not in a position to work, they could hardly stand, some of them. There were men of all nationalities in the camp – French, Belgians, there were some Russians, great big fellows who were now all skin and bones, scores and scores died and we had to dig the graves. In Bremen there was an Australian called Wheatley, he was a big chap, six footer, an engine driver from Sydney, and he was in the next bed to mine. One day I asked the German orderly where Wheatley was and he said he was 'kaput, kaput'. He'd died and they'd buried him already. That upset me terribly. He'd been a prisoner for a couple of years and was as thin as a rake, he'd lost all his colour, coughing all the time. In the end he couldn't breathe. He looked desperately ill – no resistance.[30]

QUO FATA VOCANT

WHITHER THE FATES CALL

CHAPTER TWELVE

THE PIONEER BATTALION

Four days the earth was rent and torn
By bursting steel,
The houses fell about us;
Three nights we dare not sleep,
Sweating, and listening for the imminent crash
Which meant our death.

From *'Bombardment'* by Second Lieutenant Richard Aldington

The dearth of fresh soldiers at the front – as outlined in Chapter 9 – persisted. As we know, after much deliberation the Army proposed two possible solutions: either to disband fifteen of its divisions or to reduce each division from twelve battalions to nine. It was the latter, after a great deal of argument, that was chosen.

Within 149 Brigade it fell to the junior battalion of the Northumberlands, the 1/7, to bear the brunt of this reorganisation. Their role was to be the Divisional Pioneer Battalion of the 42nd (East Lancashire) Territorial Division, commanded at that time by Major General A. Solly-Flood. They were part of I Corps, First Army. As such they were directly under the command of Divisional Staff and were no longer part of any brigade structure. The three brigades of their new division were 125 Brigade (1/5, 1/7 and 1/8 Lancashire

Fusiliers), 126 Brigade (1/5 East Lancashire Fusiliers, 1/8 and 1/10 Manchester Regiment) and 127 Brigade (1/5, 1/6 and 1/7 (Manchester Regiment).

> *The whole Division had hitherto been drawn from the East Lancashire area – Manchester, Oldham, Bury, etc – and looked upon us as intruders. The Northumberlands were of course not the people to let slip so admirable an opportunity of accepting a feud: and in October 1918 we committed the unforgivable sin of winning the Divisional Association Football Cup, which completed their unpopularity.[1]*

The First Eleven, 1918.
Author's Collection

The 1/7 began their move to their new role of Divisional Pioneers with the 42 Division on 10 February 1918, taking with them a draft of forty-four men newly arrived from England. Their journey started from Alnwick Camp in St Jean, near where the 1/7 had fought their first battle in April 1915. The name of the camp was taken from the town in Northumberland, known for its extraordinary castle, in which the battalion's pre-war headquarters had been situated. One can only imagine the depth of feeling as the men of the 1/7 parted; no-one could have doubted that in many cases it would be 'adieu' rather than 'au revoir' to men who had been companions, friends and perhaps even family. From Alnwick Camp they were transported by light railway to St Lawrence Camp, near Brandhoek. Two days later they travelled by motor lorry to Fouquereuil west of Béthune to take up duties. Initially the Northumberlands were tasked with helping the pioneers of 6th Division who were holding the Front Line between Cambrin and Loos. 'A' Company laboured with the 170 Tunnelling Company of the Royal Engineers, 'B' Company worked with the 428 Field Company of the Royal Engineers, 'C' Company laboured in the village of Philosophe, whilst 'D' Company worked in and around Vermelles. This work continued till the end of the month.

Vermelles 1918
Author's Collection

During our stay of about a week at Philosophe, the village was quiet. [Philosophe was a small colliery village, home from home, no doubt, for many of the men] *But one night the German guns sent over a perfect stream of shells just over the tops of the cottages for about twenty minutes. About a week later, after we left the village, it was completely knocked to bits by the enemy's 10 inch howitzer shells.*[2]

At about this time the battalion received a draft of 116 men from the disbanding 16 Battalion Northumberland Fusiliers. Major J. S. Macleod was posted from the 8 DLI to act as second in command, together with four new officers: Captain C. F. Eayce, Lieutenant A. Nattis and 2nd Lieutenants A. E. Dodd and F. W. Ridley.

On 7 February 1918, under the new scheme, the 16 Battalion Northumberland Fusiliers was disbanded, and the four companies departed from their camp at Elverdinghe to join the various battalions to which they had been allotted.

> *'D' Company was detailed to the 1/7 Battalion and the march was commenced in low spirits, our last parade as a battalion, and the severing of many friendships, being all too fresh in our memories. As the day wore on, and the miles dropped behind us, our spirits improved, and soon the 'company' was singing lustily, and facing the future with that cheery optimism which distinguishes the British soldier all the world over.*
>
> *We were now nearing our destination and in the distance could distinguish what appeared to be some sort of signpost, which on closer acquaintance proved to be a signpost indeed in the shape of Major [V.] Merivale MC, resplendent in a white sheepskin, waiting to give us a hearty welcome and guide us to the camp. Here we found everything ready for us, tea prepared, blankets issued, and all arrangements made for our comfort. We now learned that the 'battalion' was at Fouquereuil, and that we were to spend the night at the camp and join it next day.*
>
> *Next morning we completed our journey, arriving at Fouquereuil about midday, when the 'company' was handed over to Lieutenant-Colonel Hugh Liddell MC. Immediately all doubts as to our reception vanished. From the very first we were made most welcome, all ranks from Lieutenant-Colonel Liddell MC downwards seeming to forget that we were of another battalion and only remembering we were of the same regiment. We very greatly appreciated this and when 'D' Company, as was inevitable, was broken up and absorbed by the companies of the 1/7 Battalion, the quick way in which all settled down showed the good feeling which existed.*[3]

After the merging of the men from 16 Battalion NF, at the end of the month the original 'C' Company was broken up and the men re-allocated to the other companies; the original 'D' Company was renamed 'C' Company. Thus the 1/7 became a three-company battalion.

The 42nd Divisional History lists the strength of 1/7 Northumberland Fusiliers

(Pioneers) on 1 March as 43 officers and 945 other ranks. At the beginning of that month, the Battalion Headquarters of the 1/7 was situated at Béthune, but on 6 March they moved to Lapugnoy, east of Béthune, where they took over billets vacated by the 1 Monmouths. The plan over the next few days was that each company in turn would be withdrawn from their working duties for training, reorganisation and integration into the 42nd Division. As they toiled the companies were shelled incessantly. On 22 March, the War Diary records that one Fusilier was killed and another four were wounded whilst working with 428 Field Company, the Royal Engineers.

Lieutenant Athelstan Sylvester Kenshole Webb
1/7 Northumberland Fusiliers

Athelstan, known as Jack, was born in Leicester in 1896, the only son of Harry and Elizabeth Webb. He was educated at Leicester Grammar School and Hanley Castle, Malvern. Before the war he was employed in fine art insurance. In October 1914 whilst underaged, he enlisted in the Leicestershire Regiment but was quickly transferred to the Inns of Court OTC at Berkhampstead. He was given a commission in the 1/7 Northumberland Fusiliers and transferred to the Front in July 1916, aged 19. In November 1916 he was invalided home suffering with shell shock and during his convalesence was promoted to Lieutenant. Jack returned to active duty with the 1/7 in November 1917. He was wounded by shrapnel on 21 March 1918, dying from his wounds on the same day, aged 21. Athelstan is buried in Achiet-le-Grand Communal Cemetery Extension. His headstone is inscribed:

IN MEMORY DEAR

Before dawn on 21 March, after a colossal bombardment, along a forty-three-mile front from east of Arras to the south of St Quentin the German army launched 150 well-trained divisions against a force of fifty shattered, exhausted and disorientated British divisions. This was following a well-developed plan to exploit the weakest points in the British Line: *Operation Michael*.

On the morning of 23 March, the 1/7, with the infantry brigades of the 42nd

Division, were transported in a fleet of buses and lorries through St Pol and Doullens and onwards towards Ayette, a village eight miles south of Arras and eight miles north-west of Bapaume. At Ayette the soldiers were faced with a sorry drove of refugees: women, children and old men, many of whom related tales of German savagery and rapacity. Two brigades bivouacked in Adinfer Wood whilst the third brigade took up a position along the Ayette–Douchy road facing south-east, with two of its battalions manning an outpost line on the Ablainzevelle-Moyenneville Ridge. The 1/7 spent a chilly night bivouacked in Adinfer Wood; fires were forbidden. To make things worse, the incessant shrill piping of green woodpeckers kept many men awake.

On the next day at 0500hrs the 1/7 moved forward towards Logeast Wood where they took up positions along an outpost line from Logeast Wood to Courcelles-le-Comte and began to dig in. At 1300hrs reports were being received that the enemy – supported by tanks – had captured Achiet-le-Grand, and at 1400hrs the battalion moved off in artillery formation with orders to strengthen the British line southeast of Achiet-le-Grand. Here, under direct orders of 127 Brigade, the 1/7 began to occupy and improve a position west of the railway. However, by midnight they had moved back to the Logeast Wood-Courcelles line, which after two hours they vacated, handing the position to 127 Brigade who had retreated from their front line east of Achiet-le-Grand.

At 0300hrs on 27 March they moved eastwards to Ablainzevelle and by 0700hrs were bivouacked west of Essarts-lès-Bucquoy. In the early evening they were on the move again and by 2300hrs were occupying a trench line Douchy-lès-Ayette to Quesnoy Farm. The next day the 1/7 moved up to a number of support positions on high ground north-north-west of Bucquoy and by midnight were in the front line relieving the 2/5 Battalion West Yorkshire Regiment. In the darkest hours of the night of 30 March the men of the battalion, by now utterly exhausted, were relieved by the 10 Battalion Queens (West Surrey Regiment); they trudged into reserve at Fonquevillers, arriving six hours later on 31 March after a very eventful journey. The village had been badly knocked about in 1914 and the only places left were cellars.

An incident also of a disagreeable kind occurred near the end of our journey. Between Gommecourt and Fonquevillers we had to halt, until the trenches allotted to us had been located. At this point the road was packed with troops returning from the line; and some battalions brought their cookers here, so that the road was crammed almost tight with men and transport. For a long time nothing happened, but eventually a German field battery fired several rapid salvos of shells enfilading the road. Fortunately, the greater number fell slightly wide of the road, but a few men in one of the Manchester battalions were hit. It was, however, a lucky escape.[4]

During the period of the German Offensive in March, the War Diary of the 1/7 reported two officers wounded. One of these was Lieutenant Johnson who was in charge of 'A' Company at the time. Six men had been killed, forty-eight wounded and twelve were missing. One of these killed was 203053 Private Isaac Fisher, aged 24, of Ashington, (left) who had been part of the original draft that arrived in France in April 1915. Mr and Mrs Fisher of 27 Katherine Street, Ashington, were to visit their son's grave at Bac du Sud Military Cemetery in November 1922.[5]

April Fool's Day found the battalion at Fonquevillers. During the evening, the 1/7 moved to the front at Bucquoy relieving the 10 Queens; 'A' Company (Captain Francis Buckley) on the left and 'B' Company (Captain J. Affleck, a veteran of Houthulst Forest) on the right with 'C' Company in reserve.

We were also given a route, but in the darkness, it was difficult to find, and it led to a curious incident on our journey forward. We assembled the company ['A' Company] on the road outside Gommecourt and made towards the village as fast as the crowded state of the road would allow. Happily, we were not shelled here, but there were signs on the road that others had not been so fortunate. When we reached Gommecourt, a mere ruin now of broken trees and buildings, we were clear of the press of transport and troops. We turned south east hoping to strike a tramway running towards Biez Wood. Nothing, however, could we see of the tramway, and we could only push on, hoping to find it. After going awhile, we certainly seemed to be reaching a rather queer place, for we saw our men setting out wire, and a rather scared little man appeared out of the darkness and told us that 'Jerry was over there,' pointing down the road. We did not stop for this, but when a German Verey light shot up almost under our noses, we decided that we had indeed come too far, and that it was time to turn back. This we did without waste of time and retraced our steps to Gommecourt. I was expecting any minute to hear a machine gun open on us down the road.[6]

As a result of this terrifying experience the battalion followed a route they knew and after a long march they met the Essarts to Bucquoy Road. As they pressed on they could hear the continuous clamour of field batteries firing on the enemy's front, without German reply.

Even though the 1/7 were much delayed, the guides were still in position near Bucquoy and were able to lead them through the north end of the village to the trenches, which consisted of an old German drain which was about six feet deep and very straight. It ran parallel to the east side of the village and extended a further 200 yards from the outskirts. The trench lay on a slight hill whose crest was 200 yards further on. They could glimpse Logeast wood to their left, but there was no sign of the enemy.

It was too dangerous a place for substantial blazes – too much smoke – so the tired and hungry Fusiliers cooked a meal over discreet fires of fine wood splinters. With the onset of daybreak it was easy to see that the Queens had not been very meticulous in their housekeeping. All of the reserve ammunition (well over 5000 rounds) lay in mud-covered piles, so the men buckled down to clearing the trench of mud, salvaging and cleaning the ammunition. All through the morning it was obvious that the Germans did not know the position of the 1/7 as three of their aeroplanes constantly flew low over the area firing random bursts from their machine guns, hoping to goad their enemy into movement. German artillery was pounding the village behind the Fusiliers. Luckily the German gunners left their trench alone; the drain had no traverses (it ran in a straight line rather than zig-zagging) so a well-placed shell would have blown them to pieces. During the afternoon a German messenger dog was captured near Bucquoy bearing a message which translated as: *The affair of Bucquoy is off for the present, as we do not know where Tommy is.*[7]

Later in the day the enemy were observed digging a line of posts running in a north-south direction, 400 yards east of the front line. That night, Second Lieutenants J. Dodds and J. H. Edmunds took out a party of twenty men in order to secure a prisoner if possible. At this point, details in the descriptions of the raid are inconsistent:

The War Diary[8] states that *…the patrol engaged the enemy on the ridge and captured a wounded prisoner, reportedly from 119th Regiment, 17 Division.*

The War History of the Seventh Northumberland Fusiliers recounts that:

> *… the prisoner was captured without firing a shot and surrendered without a struggle. It proved to be a useful capture, for it showed that a fresh German Division had arrived opposite our Front.*[9]

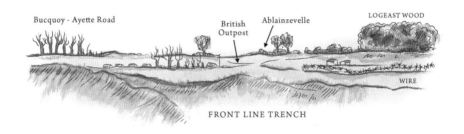

The Front at Bucquoy 2 April 1918
Chloe Rodham

For this daring raid, Second Lieutenant Dodds was awarded the Military Cross. In a statement to his company commander on returning from the raid with a captured German NCO, Dodds reported:

> *We left the lines at 8.45pm and got to the wire (one hundred and fifty yards ahead), and then started crawling along. We got to a position about fifteen yards past the wire and stopped to listen. I saw the prisoner coming along towards the wire about fifteen yards away. I think he was coming to examine our wire. When I was twelve yards from him, I sprang up and rushed at him and covered him with my revolver. He surrendered to me without a struggle. We saw German patrols going about no-man's-land in large numbers; and we also heard parties working or digging in front.*[10]

315

From their trenches at Bucquoy, during the night of 2 April the 1/7 were able to observe elements from the 32 Division under Major General C.D. Shute make a counterattack towards Ayette. Using three companies of the 15 Highland Light Infantry they stormed the village, helped by the 16 Lancashire Fusiliers on their right. The 5/6 Royal Scots moved forward in support and sappers from the 206 Field Company followed closely and consolidated the new positions. The Germans were driven as far back as the old hangers of the aerodrome at Moyenneville.

At 0200hrs on 4 April the 1/7 Northumberland Fusiliers were relieved by the 1/7 and 1/8 Lancashire Fusiliers (42nd Division) who were instructed to extend the flanks of the front line. At this stage, the three companies of the 1/7 were attached to the three brigades of the 42nd Division to carry out any duties that were needed and to act as a local reserve if required. The 1/7 HQ was moved to Fonquevillers. The next morning the Germans heavily bombarded Fonquevillers and the surrounding area using gas and high explosive shells, and in the afternoon they launched an attack on the British front east of Bucquoy and succeeded in capturing part of Bucquoy village.

After serving at the front for a number of days, the men of the 1/7 were dog tired and suffering from a lack of good food and sleep, as their commanding officer knew:

> *I hope to get the battalion out of the Line tomorrow, and I am afraid to think what they will be like. They have been fighting and digging for over a fortnight under the worst possible conditions, and they are so weary that I hardly know how they will walk out of the line.*[11]

During the night of 7/8 April, the 42nd Division was relieved by the 62nd Division with the positions of the dispersed companies of the 1/7 taken up by their fellow north-countrymen: the 9 DLI. On reaching Souastre they were taken by lorry to Authie Rest Area. Casualties to 7 April were one officer wounded, one other rank killed, and twenty-nine men wounded. By 15 April the 42nd Division had returned to the front line a few miles west of the positions they had held during the first days of the German Offensive, relieving the 37th Division in the Gommecourt-Hébuterne Sector. With this they inherited the responsibility for a complex defensive system. The sector was made up of three parts:

First: A front system of defences – an outpost line, including its own supports.

Second: A support system known as the 'Purple System,' on the ridge from Monchy-au-Bois to Fonquevillers to Gommecourt to Collincamps. It was this line that was to be held at all costs, along with the Sailly-au-Bois to Château de la Haie Switch, between the Purple and Red Systems.

Third: A reserve defence system known as the 'Red Line', on which divisions in Corps Reserve would assemble in case of attack.

After their rest at Authie the 1/7 moved to Coigneux between 12-15 April, from where they worked on the Château de la Haie switch line. The following day they were relieved by 2/5 Battalion Loyal North Lancashire Regiment (57 Division Pioneers). Only a day later the battalion moved to the area round Fonquevillers where they relieved the 9 North Staffs (Pioneers), and for the rest of the month worked on the division's Purple Defence Zone.

Each of the 1/7 Companies was allotted to one of the division's Royal Engineers field companies: 'A' Company was with the 427 Field Company RE for work in Gommecourt Trench; 'B' Company was with the 428 Field Company, RE for work on the Hêbuterne Switch; 'C' Company was with the 429 Field

Lieutenant Guy Clifton Davis
1/7 Northumberland Fusiliers

Guy was the youngest son of Robert and Helen Davis of Orpington in Kent and was educated at Harrow School where he was a member of the school OTC between 1909 and 1912. He joined the Inns of Court OTC in 1914, and was granted a commission with the Northumberland Fusiliers in July 1915. He went to the Western Front on 17 January 1917 but was invalided home in June 1917. He went back ito France in October 1917. Unfortunately, he died from his wounds on 11 May 1918. Guy is buried in Wavans British Cemetery.

Company RE for work on Rum Trench. The War Diary records that ... *as a result of this detail Lieutenant Guy Clifton Davis was wounded and four other ranks were killed and a further 35 wounded.*[12]

The War Diary[13] for April also reports that several officers and men of the 1/7 were awarded medals for their gallantry:

Bar to Military Cross to Major Vernon Merivale MC

Military Cross to Captain S. P. Brooke Booth and Lieutenant J. Dodds

Distinguished Conduct Medal to 290123 Company Sergeant Major Robert Richardson. The citation for this DCM reads:

> *For conspicuous gallantry and devotion to duty when his company were advancing in artillery formation, under heavy fire, he greatly assisted the platoon leaders and later he dug two men out who had been buried, although heavy shelling was taking place at the time.*

Military Medals to 290792 Sergeant John William Nesbit, 61190 Acting Corporal Lawrence Healy, 40351 Sergeant Joseph Bradshaw and 291088 Private Joseph Bell.

During the first six days of May the 1/7 continued to labour on improving the defences in the Hébuterne area, primarily within the 'Purple' System, and on improving Beer and Rum Trenches, much of the time beneath a storm of enemy artillery: during 5 May Captain D. R. Heriot and two men of 'B' Company were wounded. On 6 May orders were received that the 42nd Division was to be relieved by the 57th Division; the 1/7 swapped places with the 2/5 Battalion Loyal North Lancashire Regiment. The relief was completed by 0330hrs (7 May), with the men retiring to Risignol Camp near Coigneux, where they lived under canvas. After three days of rest and training, the battalion – less one platoon per company – went back to work on the Château de la Haie switch, between Souastre-Fonquevillers Road to its northern boundary. The daily toil involved the joining up of Front Line posts, wiring the switch, and all manner of reconstruction, including the merging of the switch into the Red Line. Each company provided a mining platoon for the construction of deep dugouts, work which was personally supervised by Major V. Merivale. Any platoons not deployed in work detail were under training, with special attention being given to gas training and to the use of a rifle whilst wearing a respirator.

We are very busy nowadays building all sorts of erections, from deep dugouts to mess-rooms; digging trenches by the thousand yards and putting out barbed wire by the mile. It takes me all the morning to ride round the various jobs we have on hand. And then I have various kinds of workshops to look after, which I have erected in the rear. The next thing I am starting is a drawing office.[14]

Bivouac Camp, Rossignol, near Coigneux, June 1918
Author's Collection

In early June the 1/7 were still based under canvas at Coigneux and continuing their work on the Château de la Haie switch line. However, on 7 June, the day that Major B.R. Smail returned to the battalion from home leave in England, the 42nd Division was relieved by the New Zealand Brigade; the battalion was relieved by the Maori Pioneer Battalion. The 1/7 moved near to Bus-lès-Artois which was four miles east of Sailly-au-Bois and eleven miles north-west of Albert. Throughout the month a number of officers and men, suffering from illnesses, were sent to hospitals behind the front and in some cases were evacuated to England, including Major Vernon Merivale and Captain C. F. Armstrong. During the month, the battalion received a draft of four men.

The onset of July found the 1/7 labouring at Bus-lès-Artois. All three companies were involved. 'A' Company was occupied in the wiring of Country Trench situated between Collincamps to the west and Courcelles-au-Bois to the east and a redoubt known as Fort Hod. Digging of deep dugouts was also the order of the day. 'B' Company were involved in the deepening, widening and the laying of trench boards along the entire length of Sixth Avenue (east of Bertrancourt) to the front line and the construction of a strongpoint at Apple-Trees. They also laboured on a communication trench called Cheeroh Avenue. 'C' Company worked with the 42nd Divisional Royal Engineers on the building of a number of deep dugouts.

On 8 August, the *Battle of Amiens* marked the start of the British advance that culminated in the signing of the Armistice on 11 November 1918. Canadian troops were secretly moved to the Somme and took over the southern part of the Australian Front Line. The Canadians and Australians manned the line for the advance south of the River Somme. A French force was positioned at the southern end of the attack. To the north of the River Somme, British divisions formed up for the advance. The extent of the front was from Albert in the north and, for the Canadians, Villers Bretonneux in the south.

At 0420hrs, just before first light and in dense fog, nearly 100,000 British, Australian and Canadian soldiers opened the offensive using a brutal bombardment, 400 tanks, and wave after wave of infantrymen. The noise of the tanks trundling to the front had been masked by aircraft droning unseen in the sky above. This momentous attack completely overwhelmed the enemy's defences: 13,000 prisoners were taken and between 300 and 400 guns captured. By nightfall, the Allies had made an advance of between six and seven miles.

Charles Bean, the official Australian Historian, recorded:

> *A little later the mist suddenly cleared, and for a moment all eyes on the battlefield took in the astonishing scene: infantry in lines of hundreds of little section-columns all moving forward – with tanks, guns, battery after battery, the teams tossing their manes.*[15]

General Erich Ludendorff, the German Commander, wrote that:

> *… it was the Black Day of the German Army in this war. The 8 August put the decline of that* [German] *fighting power beyond all doubt. The war must be ended.*[16]

The infantry battalions of the 42nd Division were at first geared up to probing the enemy's defences and their determination to fight, but by 21 August they were involved in the main thrust against the enemy. During the first three weeks of August, 'A' and 'B' Companies of the 1/7 were attached to the various brigades of the 42nd Division that were holding the front, and on 17 August three Fusiliers were killed by artillery fire. One of these was 290102 Corporal Oswald Monaghan, aged 29, who had been part of the original force that arrived in France in April 1915. His grave can be found in Bertrancourt Military Cemetery.

On 25 August, following the advance made by the 42nd Division, the Northumberlands moved forward to Miraumont. 'A' Company's position was east of Puisieux-au-Mont whilst 'B' and 'C' Companies were billeted near Miraumont. All three companies were employed in repairing roads near Serre, Puisieux, Miraumont, Irles and Warlencourt. Even engaged in this work behind the front the Fusiliers were not totally safe: on 30 August, enemy shell fire inflicted further casualties, killing one and wounding a further six.

During August, the battalion received a draft of one officer and nineteen men. As August ended and September came in, all of the battalion's companies were working on clearing and repairing roads, literally following the German retreat. From their billets near Warlencourt they worked in the area Le Barque, Ligny-Thilloy and Beaulencourt. On 4 September the Battalion Headquarters of the Northumberlands moved east of Villers-au-Flos, five miles south-east of Bapaume.

We have moved forward about eight miles to-day. It is really most interesting and amusing. Our orders are to follow the advance and keep the roads clear. So every day or so we start off and go straight ahead till we hear that the Boches are in the next village. Then we just pick out the first convenient bank-side and push up some bivouacs for the night. The place I am sitting on now was the scene of a fight this morning. We have tidied it up, buried a few dead Germans and we are waiting for dinner. Today we found a store of German soda-water, and have got enough to keep us going for a week or two.[17]

Men of the 1/7 Battalion about to clear roads, near Serre, August 1918
Author's Collection

Day after day the 1/7 worked on restoring the infrastructure within the rear of the advance so that men and munitions could reach the fighting in as efficient manner as possible, although they were constantly being harried by enemy artillery.

The weather still keeps fine, which is the most important matter. The chief trouble we have is the shortage of water, as the Boches blow up most of the wells as they retire, or fill them up with filth. So, we have to send a long way back for it. Work continues on mending the roads in the area east of Bapaume around Villers-au-Flos, Barastre, Bus and Ytres.[18]

By 15 September the 1/7 had progressively moved eastwards to Frémicourt and were living in a camp which 'A' and 'C' Companies were helping to rebuild. This camp had been built by the British in 1917 and occupied by the Germans in March 1918. 'B' Company were continually labouring on mending roads within this area – which the Germans then took great delight in blowing up, leaving craters the size of houses.

Last night the usual Gotha came over and started dropping things on us. I went outside to see the fun. The German plane was pretty well over our camp and there were about six searchlights right on him. The anti-aircraft guns were going fast and furious. Suddenly they all stopped, and for a few seconds he flew on unmolested. Then suddenly one of our planes appeared from nowhere and pumped a stream of incendiary bullets into him at very close range. There was a big flash as his petrol tank burst; then a shower of red and green lights as his stock of fire-works went off; and finally, a terrific explosion as he hit the ground … that was the fourth German plane to be crashed in two nights.[19]

On 27 September a general advance was made by the 1 and 3 Armies (the 42nd Division was part of the 3 Army under General Julian Byng) which is now known as the *Battle of Canal du Nord*. The Northumberlands followed close on the advance and opened the Trescault-Ribencourt and Trescault to Beaucamps roads to traffic. By 30 September 'A' Company was working on the Beaucamps-Villers Plouich Road. The War Diary[20] for September records the deaths of three men, with twelve wounded, and the arrival of a draft of seventeen men.

On October 1 the Battalion's Headquarters moved to Vélu, while its companies were spread far and near, labouring on the roads leading to the front. On 3 October the HQ moved to Villers Plouich, where Captain J. Welsh re-joined the battalion. Following the attack by VI Corps (now known as the *Battle of Cambrai, 8-9 October*) the 1/7 travelled eastwards to Lesdain, six miles south of Cambrai, where 'B' Company worked on bridges over the Escault Canal near Crèvecoeur-sur-l'Escault and 'A' and 'C' Companies toiled on the roads between Lesdain and Esnes. The 1/7 were constantly on the move eastwards and by 12 October they had moved five and a half miles further east to billets in Beauvois-en-Cambrésis; 'B' Company was doing the heavy work of filling in craters left by the retreating Germans in the Cambrai to Le Cateau-Cambrésis road. As for 'A' Company, their priority lay in eradicating craters along the Caudry to Quiévy road and with 'C' Company they laboured on the roads around Quiévy, Viesley and Barastre and the approaches to bridges over the River Selle. The front line ran just east of the River Selle.

German troops retreating eastwards through Northern France
as the Allied push intensified, October 1918
Author's Collection

I have just been around the billets of the companies. They are without exception the best the men have ever had since we came to France. But we shall probably move again before long and leave our nice billets. We shall not have much difficulty in getting others as the Boches are going back so rapidly that they have no time to blow all the houses up.[21]

South of the front held by IV Corps, the *Battle of the Selle* opened on 17 October on the western side of Le Cateau. Here XIII Corps faced three German Divisions, two of which were the 204th and 243rd Wurttemberg Divisions – regarded as first rate units. In the early hours of 20 October, the 42nd Division (IV Corps) were involved in a surprise night attack and secured the high ground east of the Selle. In response, the 1/7 HQ moved further east to Viesley. All three companies were toiling in extremely challenging conditions on the approaches to both sides of the bridges over the River Selle, from Barastre and Belle Vue towards Solesmes. The next day, with the Royal Engineers doing the blasting work, they were on the western side of the River Selle clearing the debris from two railway bridges which had been demolished, blocking the main road into Solesmes, as the Germans retreated. This Herculean task involved working around the clock. Surprisingly, only one Fusilier was reported as being wounded whilst working in these demanding conditions.

It has been an interesting day. I went into a village, or rather a small town, which had been captured a few hours before. It was a queer sight to see all the civilians standing about in the streets among the dead Germans that our people had shot or bayoneted. In one street about one hundred yards long I counted twenty dead Boches. They had bolted out of the houses they were billeted in when our men arrived on the scene. Young French girls and children were walking about and taking not the least notice. I suppose they are so happy at being rescued that they have no time to think about what people at home would call a horrible sight. The streets had all been barricaded with household furniture, and the owners were trying to sort out their belongings, most of which were badly damaged.[22]

Four days later the Battalion – less 'C' Company who remained at Viesley – moved into billets in Solesmes. 'A' and 'B' Companies were detailed for road duties between Solesmes to Marou and Solesmes to Belle Vue. 'C' Company's responsibilities were for the approaches to the bridges and for maintenance and repair of craters in the strategic roads west of the River Selle.

> *The refugees are still coming in. They transport all their belongings in the most weird vehicles pushed by hand. The Tommies are very good to them, and you often see them shoving the carts along the road. The male citizens always take their hats off and stand bare-headed when I ride past. At first I thought it was an embarrassing form of extreme politeness. On asking one of them why he did it, he told me the Boche officers made them do it under severe penalties. Since learning that, I hate to see it. But they have been so down trodden, and ill-used that all the spirit has been knocked out of them. The first morning we were in this house the two women came into the mess before we were up and scrubbed the floor etc. We soon stopped that; but honestly, they could hardly understand our making our own servants do it and much less making our men clean-up for them as well. They said they had to do it for the Boches and had better reason to do it for us. People at home have not the slightest idea what they have escaped.*[23]

No deaths at the front were recorded for the Northumbrians during the month, and they were reinforced by a draft of three officers: Captain J. Welsh, Lieutenant R.W. MacMullen and Second Lieutenant J. Dodds MC, along with thirty-two other ranks.

A file of German prisoners marching to the British rear after their capture
Author's Collection

For the first four days of November the battalion remained at Solesmes, although 'C' Company was still at Viesley labouring on the road east of the Selle.

Our band won the Divisional competition today for the best original composition for a march. It is to be adopted officially. Yesterday we won the final of the Divisional Association Football Competition. Prisoners are streaming through today, being pelted with much mud by the civilians.[24]

The 1/7 Battalion Band
Author's Collection.

Later, Liddell wrote:

Great times here just now. A big battle is under way, and as far as one can learn the Boches are fairly on the run. Mayos and I rode forward about eight miles this morning close up to the line, looking for future billets. We had quite an interesting time. This billeting job is quite exciting nowadays. Our troops are so thick on the ground that there are never enough houses to go around. Consequently, as soon as one finds out that a village has been captured, you dash off with half a dozen men and a lump of chalk. The chalk is used for writing up, 'Reserved for 7ᵗʰ NF' on the doors (if there are any doors) of the best houses you can find. The men, with two days' rations, are left to dispute the matter with the next billeting party, who are sure to turn up and try to kick them out. As there are scores of people playing this game there is some ill-feeling and bad language displayed. This morning we were rather late, and consequently found the village we made for already commandeered. We dashed on to the remains of a large farm, which proved to be empty except for a dozen Boches. They, I suppose, were prisoners, but no one was looking after them. In fact, they looked quite lost and miserable. However, we were not bothering with them; and I 'sat on' the farm whilst Mayos rode back and collected some men. He duly arrived back with the billet guard, and off we went home. The roads about here are packed for miles with our troops going forward and Boche prisoners streaming back. They do not worry much these days about finding escorts for the prisoners. They just wander back on their own and in their own time.[25]

On 5 November, the battalion took up billets in Le Quesnoy, (seven and a half miles northeast of Solesmes) whilst 'C' Company were housed near Beaudignies. On the following day, the battalion moved further east to Le Carnoy and worked on filling in craters in the roads through the Mormal Forest. The 42nd Divisional Front ran from Bavay through Petit Bavay to Pont-sur-Sambre.

It has been pouring solidly for two days, and we have been following the Boches all the time. But we are quite happy and enjoying the war.[26]

The advance drove further and further eastwards, and by the afternoon of 7 November the 1/7 had moved to Petit Bavay; for the next two days they worked on the roads through Mormal Forest and on a bridge in Boussières-sur-Sambre (about 4 miles south-west of Maubeuge). Specifically, 'A' Company worked at Vieux-Mesnil, 'B' Company was at Boussières-sur-Sambre and 'C' Company at Neuf Mesnil working on the roads to Hautmont.

We had rather a stiff day of it yesterday. At 2pm I received orders to move the battalion through a forest (the Mormal Forest) to a place about 10 miles away. All the companies were out in different directions, and had to be collected. As it is dark at 4pm, there was not much time to get forward and look for billets. In addition, it was raining, and had been raining for two days. No one knew whether the roads were passable, if the bridges had been blown up or not, etc. I rode on ahead with my groom, sent the Adjutant (Captain S. P. Brook Booth, MC) to look for some men who were on an outlying job, and arranged a place in the middle of the forest where I should meet him later. I found that owing to the road having been blown up it was impossible to get the battalion the way I wanted; so I left my groom to stop them and went on myself. I reached my destination just as it was getting dark, and found there was a small village of twenty-five houses and several other people besides myself looking for billets for troops. I set off back to my groom, but could find no sign of him. It was so dark you could not see your hand; the roads were so narrow and packed with guns, transport, etc. It was no fun scrambling through all the traffic on a horse, every now and then riding bang into an over-turned wagon, or floundering into the ditch at the side with two feet of mud in it. To cut a long story short, I rode about the forest for nearly seven hours, and eventually found most of my people, including Captain Booth and Captain Lidderdale, whom I rode into by accident in the dark. It was by their language that I knew them. We got everyone under cover (packed like sardines) by 2am and then had some food. We hope to move on to-morrow to a town (Hautmont) which has just fallen into our hands.[27]

On 9 November, as the front shifted east, the whole battalion (less 'B' Company and the Transport Section, who remained at Boussières-sur-Sambre) moved to Hautmont. All sections of the battalion were toiling to repair bridges that had been destroyed by the retreating Germans – a Sisyphean task.

Captain Lidderdale is leaving us, I am sorry to say. He is going home to be demobilized. Great fun to-day. We marched into quite a big town this morning, and the usual scene occurred. We tried to get in last night, but the Boches received us with a dose of machine-gun bullets. There was some misunderstanding as to whether the place was really ours or not. The troops who were detailed to 'mop up' the town could not get on with the work owing to the civilians rushing out to welcome them. We do not expect to stay here long as the Boches have gone back about twelve miles since last night. We had a very big job on to-day, bridging a river (the Sambre) and not enough men to do it. So, they sent us a lot of Boche prisoners to help. It was most amusing to see our Geordies hustling them around and making them work, talking to them in a mixture of Tyneside and French.[28]

That night the battalion stood down and moved into billets for a much-needed rest, in the eastern part of Hautmont. They were to stay there, undergoing training, until the end of the month.

It is certainly a funny war. At present no one seems to know either where the Boches have got to, or if we are supposed to be fighting them. We get no news at all, just rumours, and then a paper several days old. You can ride about in the open, well forward of our most advanced infantry, without any interference. It is said that some of our cavalry is ahead of us. I am sure I shall be ill with drinking so much coffee. The great notion of the civilians is to get you inside the house, give you coffee, and tell you all about their sufferings. I would love to see a few German towns going up in smoke.[29]

On 11 November, Germany signed an Armistice and at 1100hrs all hostilities ceased. It was a momentous day, but, sadly, although the war had ended, men were still dying. The Battalion War Diary records that, between 16 November and the end of the month, five Fusiliers died in hospital of 'natural' causes. These deaths would almost certainly be from pneumonia or influenza, both of which were rampant. In the middle of November word was received that Lieutenant Francis Merivale had died of pneumonia, see Chapter Thirteen, *Aftermath*.

In December, 'B' Company and the Transport Section remained at Boussières-sur-Sambre. These two groups of men were providing working parties to the Royal Engineers. On 6 December, 'C' Company moved to Boussois east of Maubeuge near the Belgian border. Here they worked on the roads, again filling in large craters. Also on this day, Second Lieutenant J. Dodds MC departed with a platoon of Fusiliers, to begin the preparations for the 42nd Division's movement to Charleroi. Beginning on 14 December the rest of the battalion marched in stages towards this Belgian city. On that first night they rested at Élesmes, on the night of 15 December at Crois-les-Rouvercy, and then the nights of 16 and 17 December at Épinois.

On 18 December 1918, Liddell wrote from Épinois:

I fear I am going to lose the greater part of the battalion very soon, as I am having to supply full particulars about the number of pitman I have. I asked one of the men to-day if he would like to go to the Rhine; and he replied that if it were all the same to me he would prefer the Tyne. Coming in to this village yesterday, the first thing which struck the eye was a large notice, saying, 'Welcome to the brave English soldiers.' It seems to cause the men a vast deal of amusement. Although they had marched about 12 miles they were strutting along the street and slapping their chests and shouting out, 'That's us, that is.' [30]

The battalion eventually arrived in Charleroi on 18 December.

The originals of 1915, at Charleroi 1918
Author's Collection

On 20 December 1918, Liddell wrote:

I am losing one hundred and ten of my best men, who are being sent home for demobilisation. I am afraid the band, the football team and the transport will be pretty well ruined. Well, the sooner we get home the better. It is rather sad though to see the battalion melt away. [31]

Until the end of the year the whole of the battalion remained in Charleroi supplying working parties to the Royal Engineers. During this month 204 men were demobilized, five under their long service agreement and 199 Coal Miners (under Group 3). Even so, the battalion received a draft of fifty-three soldiers. They celebrated Christmas and New Year at Charleroi, their last before leaving for home.

During January 1919 the 1/7 continued to provide working parties to the Royal Engineers. The battalion received a further draft of ten men, but steadily its strength was reduced through demobilisation, in this month by six officers and, under Group 3 (coal miners), by a further 169 men. February saw further diminution in the battalion's strength with three officers and 239 Fusiliers demobilised. During March the battalion was reduced to cadre strength, through demobilisation and the transfer of officers and men to other units.

By 10 March the 1/7 could muster only six officers and forty-eight men, one of whom was 290135 John A. Snaith who was by now serving as Acting Regimental Quartermaster Sergeant. He had enlisted in the middle of 1909 and arrived in France in April 1915. With others, he first saw the utter cruelty of war at first hand at *St Julien*, on 26 April 1915. Another of the originals was 7/1230 Pte Matthew Copeland from Byker (right).

At 1900hrs on 11 April, the 1/7 Battalion cadre embarked for Antwerp, sailing on to the UK on 14 April. It had been very nearly four tough years since these now battle-hardened Territorials had first arrived in France, on 21 April 1915.

Embarkation of the cadre at Antwerp, April 1919
Author's Collection

CHAPTER THIRTEEN

AFTERMATH

Everyone suddenly burst out singing;
And I was filled with such delight
As prisoned birds must find in freedom,
Winging wildly across the white
Orchards and dark-green fields; on – on – and out of sight.

Everyone's voice was suddenly lifted;
And beauty came like the setting sun:
My heart was shaken with tears; and horror
Drifted away ... O, but Everyone
Was a bird; and the song was wordless;
The singing will never be done.

'Everyone Sang' by Siegfried Sassoon

During the Great War, nearly 4000 men from the four, front-line Territorial Battalions of the Northumberland Fusiliers were killed. There were, in addition, at least two junctures at which men who had enlisted in the Territorials were reassigned to other battalions. The first of these came in the late summer of 1916; a raft of men were sent to bolster the depleted battalions of the Tyneside Scottish and Irish following their calamitous advance during the infamous 'First Day of the Somme'. The second was following the catastrophic losses suffered by the 149 Brigade in May 1918 after which its battalions were reduced to cadre strength; a large number of men were dispersed to other battalions of the Northumberland Fusiliers, particularly, the 1, 2 and 8 Battalions. These would continue the fight to the end. There were, of course, further casualties in the 2/7 Battalion, deployed for garrison duties in Egypt.

And after the Armistice … after final handshakes with 'brothers' who had shared their particular inferno … men returned to a changed world. Many, no doubt, were able to pick up where they left off, more or less; these were the fortunate ones, who stepped off the train intact in mind and well as in body. Others, broken by the trials of war, died at home. Some of these would not be officially recognised. One such, or at least until recently, was 4/2761 Private Walter Rutherford, aged 20, who died on 28 April 1917. In March 1916 he was admitted to North Staffs Infirmary suffering from tuberculosis, contracted in the trenches. He was discharged from the army in July 1916 and died at home in the following April. Until recently his death was not recognised by official bodies, but in 2015, after representations, an official headstone was erected by the CWGC in St Michael's churchyard, Wark, Northumberland.[1]

But not everyone could transcend the bleak rigour of living with death, or with the fear of it. Other men lived on, but not as the men they might have been. Many were disabled in body or mind, indeed often in both, and were thus unemployable. Tragically, the war made many returning soldiers into poor husbands and fathers, haunted by horrors too awful to share. With appalling irony, they survived, but as an embarrassing burden on the back of the very society they'd fought for.

Up to the middle of 1916 and the onset of conscription, the enlistment for the four battalions was generally from within the county of Northumberland. After this, conscripted men from all over the country were drafted, including Norman Gladden.[2] By the end of the war in 1918, there remained but a small body of men and officers who had disembarked in France in 1915. Northumberland is therefore graced with abundant war memorials; nearly every village has its own shrine, often with names inscribed that relate directly to those who gather round in silence on Remembrance Day. Many commemorate at least one of the lionhearted miners, ship builders and farmers who fought with 149 Brigade on the Western Front. Take, for instance, the memorials found in the small villages of the North Tyne Valley, a predominately rural district dotted with the vestiges of mining operations, with the small town of Bellingham in the north.[3] These bear the names of over 59 Territorials, mainly from the 1/4 Battalion. In Hexham, a large market town, there are 68 men honoured, again from the 1/4 Battalion.[4] In comparison, Ashington – once the biggest coalmining village in the world – has a memorial that commemorates 128 Territorials who served mainly with the 1/7 Battalion.[5] Memorials in the industrial lands in the south east of the county have a similar number of names.

All four battalions of 149 Brigade have memorials to the redoubtable soldiers and their contribution to Britain's victory:

Opening of the Memorial Arch to the 1/4 Battalion Northumberland Fusiliers
Hexham, 22 October 1919
Author's Collection

On 27 October 1919, in Hexham (the Headquarters of the 1/4) Lord Allendale, Chairman of the Northumberland Territorial Forces Association, unveiled a commemorative arch on Beaumont Street in honour of the 1/4 Battalion Northumberland Fusiliers. The memorial was conceived by Mr J. T. Robb as a personal thanksgiving for the safe return of all three of his sons from the war. The arch dates from the late 17th or early 18th Century, and once stood at the entrance to the White Horse Inn on Fore Street. It was moved in 1919 at the expense of Mr Robb, who owned a large family-run department store in the town, to its present site at the entrance to the Abbey Gardens. On either side of the arch there are bronze plaques, dedicated to the 4 (1/4) Battalion Northumberland Fusiliers; in 1998 these were restored and re-gilded, work funded by the Royal Northumberland Fusiliers Association.

Plaques to 1/4 Battalion Northumberland Fusiliers
found on either side of the Memorial Arch, Hexham.
Author's Collection

In Walker Park, which is in the Walker district of Newcastle upon Tyne, stands a simple obelisk dedicated to the 1/5 Battalion Northumberland Fusiliers, whose Headquarters were based at the Drill Hall in Walker. It was unveiled on 24 May 1921 by Colonel E.P.A. Riddell CMG DSO and was dedicated by the vicar of Longhurst, the Reverend A.S. Wardroper. The obelisk was designed by Messrs Graham and Hill of Newcastle and built by Mr George Carr on a plot donated by Newcastle Corporation. The memorial originally included bronze plaques which were later stolen, and which have been replaced in stone. Following this restoration, the memorial was unveiled again on 30 July 2016 by Lieutenant General R.V. Brims CB CBE DSO.

The original plaque stated:

Fifth Battalion
Northumberland Fusiliers
In memory of the Officers and Men
of the Battalion who gave their lives
for their country
in the Great War
1914 – 18
Erected by members and friends of
the Battalion.
Quo Fata Vocant

1/5 Battalion Northumberland Fusiliers Memorial
Walker Park, Scrogg Road
Newcastle-upon-Tyne
Author's Collection

On 30 November 1924, General Sir Percival S. Wilkinson unveiled a memorial to the 1/6 Battalion Northumberland Fusiliers in the old graveyard of St Thomas' Church, St Mary's Place, Newcastle, near to the battalion's Drill Hall in Northumberland Road opposite the City Hall and Northumberland Baths. The memorial takes the form of a statue of St George and the Dragon and is 'dedicated to the memory of the officers, non-commissioned officers and men of the VIth Territorial Battalion Northumberland Fusiliers who gave their lives in World War I'. Later plaques were added for the 43 and 49 Battalions of the Royal Tank Regiment.

1/6 Battalion Northumberland Fusiliers Memorial
St Thomas' Church, Barras Bridge, Newcastle upon Tyne
Author's Collection

In the ancient St Michael's Church on Bailiffgate in Alnwick, the 1/7 Battalion is commemorated on a bronze plaque. It was unveiled on St George's Day 1932 by Major General Geoffrey Fielding and was dedicated by Canon Margin.

The plaque states:

Erected by the Officers

Non-Commissioned Officers and Men of the

1/7th Battalion Northumberland Fusiliers

In memory of their comrades

35 officers

719 other ranks

who fell in France in the Great War

1914 – 1918

In Belgium two memorials associated with 149 Brigade were raised. One, a fifty-five feet tall obelisk erected near Oxford Road Military Cemetery in the hamlet of Wieltje, was unveiled on 1 September 1929 by Field Marshal Lord H. Plumer. The inscription reads:

Pro Patria

To the enduring memory of all ranks of the

50th (Northumbrian) Division

who fell in the Great War

1914 -1918

Later, an inscription was added to mark those in the 50 Division who gave their lives in the Second World War. On the two sides are listed the units which made up the 50 Division in the Great War, including 149 (Northumberland) Brigade. The second is to be found in St George's Church, Ypres, where there is a brass plaque which reads:

To the glory of God and

In memory of all ranks of the

5th Northumberland Fusiliers

who gave their lives in the

Great War 1914 -1918

There is no memorial to the Territorial Force Battalions of the Northumberland Fusiliers in France.

As bells rang with news of the Armistice, in many families in Northumberland 'everyone suddenly burst out singing' as Sassoon's poem suggests, celebrating the end of the Great War. And after that came the homecoming of sons, of husbands, friends, fiancés … men returning – however much changed – from the battle front. But of course there were many for whom the day that peace was announced was just another day of mourning – it must have been hard indeed to rejoice at such a time.

It must undoubtedly have been a sorrowful day for Edward and Annie Hunter of Gosforth, Newcastle, who tragically lost two sons on the same day, 26 April 1915, while they were serving with the 1/6 Battalion.

Captain George Edward Hunter
1/6 Northumberland Fusiliers

George was born in Newcastle upon Tyne in 1887, the eldest son of Edward and Anne Cunningham Hunter. He was educated at Aysgarth school and Charterhouse before attending the Royal Grammar School in 1895. Later he studied architecture as a profession and whilst at Crackett and Burns Dick he was made an Associate of the Royal Institute of British Architects. Later he joined his father's firm, Hunter and Henderson, stockbrokers, Newcastle upon Tyne. In 1904 he joined the 3rd Volunteer Battalion Northumberland Fusiliers as a second lieutenant. In 1908, when the Territorial Force was formed, he joined the 1/6 Battalion and was gazetted captain. He embarked for France with his regiment on 20 April 1915 and was killed by a fragment of a shell near St Julien on 26 April, aged 28, whilst leading 'C' Company. He is commemorated on the Menin Gate Memorial to the Missing.

A brother officer wrote: *He led his men with great courage and total disregard for himself, and was right in front of the enemy's position when he was killed by a shell fired at short range.*[6]

Captain Howard Tomlin Hunter
1/6 Northumberland Fusiliers

Howard was born in Newcastle upon Tyne in 1888, the youngest son of Edward and Anne Cunningham Hunter. He was educated at Aysgarth school and Charterhouse before joining the Royal Grammar School in 1895. From here he went to Durham University, continuing his studies in surgery at the Royal Victoria Infirmary, Newcastle, St Bartholomew's Hospital, London, and in Vienna. He joined the Third Volunteer Battalion as a second lieutenant in 1906 and when the Territorial Force was formed in 1908 joined the 1/6 Battalion. In 1912 he was gazetted captain. He embarked for France with his regiment on 20 April 1915, and was killed near St Julien on 26 April, aged 26, whilst leading 'D' Company. He is commemorated on the Menin Gate Memorial to the Missing.

A writer in the *Durham College Medical Gazette* stated:

We have all heard with pride and aching heart of his entry into action. The first torrent of bullet and shell only seemed to increase his absolute indifference to danger, and his example and courage infected the whole company. He led his men through a crossfire of machine guns and shrapnel trying to reach the German trenches by a series of rushes. When close to his objective he was struck on the leg but stuck to his job, gamely cheering on his men. We can imagine his bitter disappointment when he had to fall out so near to the end of his task. While being helped to the rear he was struck again in the chest and almost immediately dropped dead.[7]

Could it be any worse for the family? Well, yes. Their daughter Una lost her fiancé:

Lieutenant Arthur Richmond Garton

1/6 Northumberland Fusiliers

Arthur was born in Dublin, Ireland, the only son of Captain William George and Francis Helen Garton of Wimbledon. He was employed by the Bank of England in Newcastle upon Tyne and was engaged to Una Hunter sister of George and Howard Hunter. He embarked in France on 20 April 1915 and was killed in action, aged 26, on 26 April. In spite of heavy machine gun fire and shelling, Arthur cut a gap in the wire and, turning around smiling, said, 'Come on boys! We will get at them now', but he was killed before going much further. Arthur is commemorated on the Menin Gate Memorial to the Missing.

The late Thomas Hudson Bainbridge, formerly head of the firm Bainbridge & Co Ltd, a major business in Newcastle (now part of the John Lewis Partnership) and Kate Bainbridge, lost two sons during the war:

Signaller H. Patton, Royal Engineers, wrote of Lieutenant Thomas Bainbridge:

The Germans use gas shells, which blind you and poison you in no time, and don't give you a fighting chance. As for snipers, they do terrible lot of harm. There were many of these fellows popping at us going through. They are dressed in khaki. After we got through, we stopped at a place where Lieutenant Bainbridge had broken into a house and caught two spies. After getting through, and along the road, we were then put in the centre of a horseshoe trench with Germans all around. Shells were coming in from all sides. All one could do was to throw one's self flat on the ground and trust to luck.[8]

Lieutenant Thomas Lindsay Bainbridge

1/5 Northumberland Fusiliers

Attached Divisional Signal Company,

Royal Engineers

Thomas was born in 1882 in Newcastle upon Tyne, the third son of Thomas Hudson and Kate Bainbridge of Eshott Hall, Felton. He was educated privately in Colwyn Bay, North Wales, later qualifying as an electrical engineer, working in the shipyard of Swan Hunter and Wigham Richardson of Wallsend. In 1902 he joined the Royal Engineers (Volunteers) as a Second Lieutenant but resigned his commission in 1904. In 1908, following the inauguration of the Territorial Force, he joined Durham University OTC and earned a commission with the 1/5 Northumberland Fusiliers, becoming a Lieutenant in October 1913. His technical expertise made him an ideal candidate as a signalling officer. Thus he embarked for France on 20 April 1915 as commander of No. 2 Section of the Northumberland Divisional Signal Company. He was killed on 27 April 1915, aged 33, while gallantly carrying a message over ground which was being heavily shelled. He is buried in Birr Cross Roads Cemetery.

At the Newcastle Wesleyan Synod at Durham a letter was read out describing the burial of Lieutenant Bainbridge:

It was a beautiful moon-lit night, as we carried the bodies down the lines wrapped in blankets and lying on stretchers. As we passed each entrenched battalion the men stood to attention. At about a quarter of a mile from the trenches, on a piece of ground where about six other officers lie buried, we laid them to rest. The guns were roaring on every side, and the huge fireballs the Germans threw into the air illuminated the sky. Lieutenant Bainbridge was a plucky and good fellow.[9]

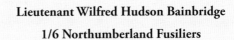

Lieutenant Wilfred Hudson Bainbridge

1/6 Northumberland Fusiliers

Wilfred was born in 1884 in Newcastle upon Tyne, the son of Thomas Hudson and Kate Bainbridge of Eshott Hall, Felton. He was educated at the Leys School, Cambridge. Before the war he was a director of his grandfather's department store. He disembarked in France on 2 May 1915, days after his brother had been killed. On 3 March 1916, Wilfred, the battalion's adjutant, was on a tour of inspection of the frontline trenches when he was wounded in the head by a sniper's bullet. At a local casualty clearing station he was operated upon for a fractured skull, appearing on course for recovery and was transferred to the Duchess of Westminster's Hospital near Étaples. Sadly, he developed meningitis caused by a subdural abscess and died in his sleep at 2230hrs on Wednesday 15 March 1916, aged 33. Another brother, Emmerson, was at his bedside. Thomas is buried in Étaples Military Cemetery.

In a tribute in the *Newcastle Journal*, his brother said of Wilfred:

And he was a Christian, too. His work was always well but quietly done. He was always modest, he was always kind. His life was that of an ideal sportsman, clean and straight. He never failed in anything he undertook to do, and he numbered as his personal friends all those with whom he ever came in contact, at work or at play. His humour, his voice, and his indescribable charm were all used for noble ends.

For soldiers in peace time, for the very poor in the slums of Newcastle, for the sick and suffering, he had for years given not only money, which is sometimes easy, but his leisure, which is always hard, and he lived with a great purpose before him, and he died having achieved it.

Proud may be the mother who bore him, the school which nurtured him, the country whose flag enfolded him, and the Church whose padre buried him.[10]

When the 1/7 disembarked in France on 21 April 1915 the roll held the names of three Merivale brothers: Vernon, John William and Francis, the sons of Professor John Herman and Blanche Merivale of Togston Hall, Acklington.

Captain John William Merivale
1/7 Northumberland Fusiliers

John was born in 1887 in Newcastle upon Tyne, the son of John Herman and Blanche Merivale of Togston Hall, Northumberland. He was educated at Sedbergh School, St Edward's Oxford and Queen's College Oxford, where he received a degree in law in 1909. Following this he enrolled as a solicitor with Wilkinson and Marshall of Newcastle. Also after leaving Oxford he joined the 1/7 Northumberland Fusiliers but in 1912 he resigned his commission. In 1913 he married Blanche Liddell and in 1914, Margaret was born. At the onset of war John volunteered for service with the 1/7 and disembarked in France on 21 April 1915. He was killed on 15 September 1916 whilst leading 'A' Company in their attack. He is buried in Bazentin le Petit Communal Cemetery.

Within weeks of receiving news of the death of his son, Prosfessor John Herman Merivale went down with influenza; he appeared to be on the road to recovery until pleurisy and pneumonia set in.

His obituary stated:

> *It is probable that the loss of his son, Captain J. W. Merivale, who died of wounds and the fact that Lieutenant Vernon Merivale (another son) had been wounded had affected his health.*[11] [Vernon survived the war - A.G.]

Francis Merivale (opposite) was to die of influenza in November 1918 in Rouen. In the summer of 1919 Blanche Merivale, mother of John and Francis and widow of Professor Merivale, died at Middleton Hall, near Leeds, after a short illness at the age of 63. Her funeral took place at Amble West Cemetery. So much sorrow, in just one family.[12]

Lieutenant Francis Merivale
1/7 Northumberland Fusiliers

Francis was born in 1895, in Amble, Northumberland, the youngest son of Mr John Herman and Blanche Merivale of Togston Hall, Northumberland. Between 1909 and 1913 he was educated at Haileybury College, Hertfordshire. He disembarked in France on 21 April 1915 as a second lieutenant, rising to lieutenant. As the war dragged to an end, Lieutenant Francis Merivale was rushed to hospital suffering from pneumonia and influenza; he died at one of the hospitals surrounding Rouen, aged 23, on 17 November 1918. This was a tragic end to a promising young man who had been on the Western Front with the Northumberland Fusiliers since April 1915. He is buried in St Sever Cemetery Extension, Rouen.

The Merivale Family in Happier Times
Courtesy of J. A. A. Bruce

Pte Edward Riddle Hedley
1/4 Battalion
Northumberland Fusiliers
Killed: 14 February 1916
Author's Collection

Pte James Hedley
1/4 Battalion
Northumberland Fusiliers
Killed: 8 April 1916
Author's Collection

Within a few weeks of each other, 4/866 Private Edward Riddle Hedley, (left) and 4/677 Private James Hedley (right), serving with the 1/4, were killed in action in Belgium. They were two of the four sons of George and Jane Hedley of West Woodburn, a small village nestling among the rolling sandstone hills in the heart of rural Northumberland. George was a stone-mason. Edward, aged 22, had served in the Territorials since 1911, and was killed on 14 February 1916 while the battalion was manning trenches near Sanctuary Wood.[13]

The War Diary of 1/4 Battalion records:[14]

On the afternoon the enemy shelled Hooge Ridge and followed this by an unsuccessful attack against the sector held by the Rifle Brigade. Shells fell into the trenches held by the fusiliers, killing four soldiers and injuring another dozen.

Edward is buried in Railway Dugouts Burial Ground, where a large number of Fusiliers lie together.

James, aged 24, was the eldest son and was killed on 8 April 1916. A pre-war member of the Territorial Forces, he worked as an apprentice joiner. At the time of his death the 1/4 were manning trenches in the Wytschaete Ridge sector:

Instead of the high narrow trenches of Hill 60, these were mostly mere breast works with little or no back protection. And the communication trenches were hardly deep enough to afford protection from sniping and indirect fire.[15]

James was sheltering in a dugout which received a direct hit. He and another soldier were killed outright; four others were wounded. He is buried in La Laiterie Military Cemetery, along with a number of others from the 1/4.

This was not the end of this family's sorrow. Another son, Joseph Collinson Hedley, was conscripted on 15 May 1916, on reaching eighteen. Following basic training he was posted, after his nineteenth birthday in 1917, to the 1 Battalion Northamptonshire Battalion with the service number 40682. During the summer of 1917 Joseph was invalided from France to the County of Middlesex War Hospital in St Albans with frostbite and trench foot to his hands and toes. His toes needed amputation and he later developed consumption. On 10 September 1918 he was discharged from hospital, with no hope of recovery, and died in the company of his friends on 11 October 1918. He was buried in St Cuthbert's Churchyard, Corsenside.[16]

On 25 April 1915 the 1/7 was ordered to advance in order to fortify positions being held by Canadian troops that had been fighting against tremendous odds and were exhausted:

> *At last between 10 and 11pm, under cover of the night, we were relieved by other troops, and retired to almost the same place from where we started in the morning. ... The battalion in these operations lost about 150 killed and wounded including the two young Wakes* (Wilf and Tom of Bamburgh, both killed by the same shell.)[17]

Pte Wilfred Hereward Wake
1/7 Battalion
Northumberland Fusiliers
Killed: 25 April 1915
Author's Collection
Pte Thomas Henry Wake
1/7 Battalion
Northumberland Fusiliers
Killed: 25 April 1915
Author's Collection

The 'two young Wakes' were 7/1598 Private Wilfred Hereward, aged 20, (left) and his elder brother 7/1989 Thomas Henry, aged 25, (right). They were the sons of Richard and Mary Wake who lived in the gatehouse of Bamburgh Castle. Wilfred was a pre-war Territorial, enlisting in early 1914, whilst his brother joined up soon after the declaration of war. Thomas worked as a house painter and Wilf as an apprenticed tailor. Both of their names can be found on the Menin Gate Memorial to the Missing in Ypres.

An unknown Northumberland Fusilier composed a poem in the trenches about the two brothers from Bamburgh, the day after he saw them fall:

The Canny Lads from Bamburgh

We soon got face to face with Huns,
Who had their big 'Jack Johnson' guns,
They tossed the shrapnel in by tons,
On the canny lads from Bamburgh.

And it just seemed to be our luck,
But on we went with British pluck,
When a piece of shrapnel came and struck,
Two canny lads from Bamburgh.

They faltered, then on their face they fell,
Beside them I knelt down as well,
And how they died just I can tell,
The two canny lads from Bamburgh.

Rather than be German slaves,
They lie buried amongst the braves,
I wrote on wood across their graves,
The two canny lads from Bamburgh.

They volunteered to cross the sea,
To fight for king and country,
And fell for England's liberty,
The two canny lads from Bamburgh.

All the boys join in and send
Their best respects to all their friends;
On Providence, it all depends,
On the canny lads from Bamburgh.

Even if the poetry is simple stuff, no one can doubt the sincerity and love behind the words.

On 15 September 1915 near High Wood during the *Battle of Flers-Courcelette* two brothers from Hexham, 4/3318 Ralph and 4/909 John Edward Newton, were killed. They were the sons of Ralph and Rachael Newton of Prior Terrace. John, aged 21, was a gardener and a pre-war Territorial who had enlisted at the end of 1911. His younger brother Ralph, aged 19, also a gardener, had enlisted in late 1915. Both are commemorated on the Thiepval Memorial to the Missing. Three other Newton brothers enlisted in the 1/4: Thomas (200690) James (267157) and William (4/1163), all of whom survived.[18]

Pte James Mead
1/4 Battalion
Northumberland Fusiliers
Killed: 15 September 1916
Author's Collection

Pte Henry Mead
1/4 Battalion
Northumberland Fusiliers
DoW: 22 September 1916
Author's collection

In the same action Henry and Jane Mead of Fern Hill, near Acomb, Hexham, would lose their two oldest sons: 4/2274 Frederick James Mead, aged 26, (left) and his brother 4/1869 Henry John Mead, aged 24, (right) who died on 22 September. Both were single men who worked on the estate of Captain James Cuthbert (killed in action with the Scots Guards at Loos). Both are commemorated on the Thiepval Memorial to the Missing. A third son, Charles, served with the Argyll and Sutherland Highlanders and survived the conflict. [19]

After all the horror came the Treaty of Versailles in 1919, forged in an icy climate of anger, desire for retribution, uncertainty and post-war depression. It comes as something of a surprise to find that – even then – people were easily distracted from political reality by reading society gossip and other superficial news. Robert Graves, a veteran and writer, who wrote his own masterly Great War story, recalled:

The Treaty of Versailles shocked me; it seemed destined to cause another war some day, yet nobody cared. While the most critical decisions were being taken in Paris, public interest concentrated entirely on three home-news items: Hawker's Atlantic flight and rescue; the marriage of England's reigning beauty, Lady Diana Manners; and a marvellous horse called The Panther – the Derby favourite, which came in nowhere.[20]

Today, long after even the 'another war' that Graves presciently mentioned, many thousands of people every year make the effort to visit the Great War battlefield memorials; they wander in silent, awestruck reverence along the seemingly endless rows of gravestones. They scan the monolithic towers and arches of Menin, Thiepval and Tyne Cot for names of grandfathers, great grandfathers … feeling a rush of pride and gratitude at the sacrifice that they and others made for the common good. This book has been written, in the same spirit of humility, for that 'sturdy race of men', to whom it is dedicated with my affection and undying respect.

When England sets her banner forth And bids her armovr shine, She'll not forget the famovs North, The lads of moor and Tyne; And when the loving cup's in hand And Honovr leads the cry, They know not old Northvmberland Who'll pass her memory by.

References

Introduction

1. Buckley F. *War History of Seventh Northumberland Fusiliers.* Grierson, Newcastle upon Tyne, 1919.

Chapter One: The Beginning – the route to the Western Front

1. IWM AC 9253 Reel 5, Dorgan, John William ('Jack')
2. *Berwickshire Advertiser,* 2 July 1909
3. 1/4 Battalion Notes: 20 June 1912, *St George's Gazette,* June 1912.
4. 1/6 Battalion Notes: 24 June 1912, *St George's Gazette,* June 1912.
5. IWM AC 9253 Reel 5, Dorgan
6. Appendix 1. Territorial and Reserve Forces Act. (7 Edward VII., Cap. 9)
7. Messenger C, *Call to Arms: The British Army 1914 to 1918,* Cassell Military Paperback, 2006, p.98
8. Appendix 1. Territorial and Reserve Forces Act. (7 Edward VII., Cap. 9)
9. *Manchester Guardian,* 5 August 1914
10. Harbottle G, *Civilian Soldier 1914 – 1919: A Period Relived,* Private Publication, Newcastle upon Tyne 1919, p.9
11. Ibid, p.9
12. Ibid, p10
13. IWM Archives, Document 440, *Private papers of E W Cotton*
14. Harbottle,1919, p.11
15. Ibid, p.11
16. Ibid, p.15
17. 1/4 Battalion Notes: Blyth, 22 December 1914, *St George's Gazette,* January 1915
18. 1/4 Battalion Notes: Blyth, 22 February 1915, *St George's Gazette,* February 1915
19. *Berwick Advertiser,* 23 October 1914
20. *Morpeth Herald,* 1 January 1915
21. *Newcastle Journal,* 4 May 1915
22. 1/7 Battalion Notes: Blyth, *St George's Gazette,* April 1915
23. Brown M, *Tommy Goes to War,* J M Dent & Sons Ltd 1978, p.39

24. Ibid, p.39

Chapter Two: Second Ypres. The Battle of St Julien

1. Harbottle, 1919, p.17

2. Buckley 1919, p.6

3. Hossack Anthony R, *The First Gas Attack,* www.firstworldwar.com, 22 August 2009

4. Bunbury, 1915, p.13

5. Ibid, p.13

6. IWM Archives, Document 440, *Private papers of E W Cotton*

7. Bunbury, 1915, p.14

8. IWM Archives, Document 440, *Private papers of E W Cotton*

9. Ibid

10. MacDonald L, *1915: The Death of Innocence,* Penguin, 1997, p.219

11. Armstrong William Watson, *My First Week in Flanders,* Smith Elder, 1916

12. Bunbury, 1915, p.19

13. Buckley, 1919, pp.11-12

14. Ibid, p.12

15. Ibid, p.12

16. *Berwick News and General Advertiser,* 25 May 1915

17. WO 95/2828, *War Diary 1/5 Battalion Northumberland Fusiliers*

18. Harbottle, 1919, p.21

19. IWM AC 9474 Reel 3, Harbottle G

20. Harbottle, 1919, p.23

21. WO 95/2829/1 *War Diary 1/6 Battalion Northumberland Fusiliers*

22. *Berwick Advertiser,* May 1915

23. Buckley, 1919, p.120

24. Harbottle, 1919, p.23

25. Bunbury, 1915, p.23

26. Buckley, 1919, p.13

27. IWM AC 9253 Reel 9, Dorgan

28. Buckley, 1919, pp.13-14

29. Ibid, p.14

30. *Berwick News and General Advertiser*, 8 June 1915

31. Armstrong William Watson, 1916, pp.24-25

32. MacDonald L, 1997, p.265

33. Buchan J. *A History of the Great War Volume 2,* Houghton Mifflin, 1923

Chapter Three: After St Julien, May-June 1915

1. Bunbury, 1915, p.35

2. Grint A I, *In Silent Fortitude. In Memory of the Men of the North Tyne Valley who Fell in the Great War,* Ergo Press, Hexham 2011, p.44

3. Grint A I, *The Faith and Fire Within. In Memory of the Men from Hexham who Fell in the Great War* Ergo Press, Hexham, 2006, p.40

4. Ibid, p.40

5. Bunbury, 1915, p.39

6. IWM Archives, Document 440, *Private papers of E W Cotton*

7. Bunbury, 1915, pp.41-42

8. Buckley, 1919, pp.119-120

9. Bunbury, 1915, p.44

10. IWM Archives, 9474, Reel 3, Harbottle G

11. WO 95/2828. *War Diary 1/5 Battalion Northumberland Fusiliers*

12. Ibid

13. IWM Archives, Document 440. *Private papers of E W Cotton*

14. Bunbury, 1915, p.58

15. *Hexham Courant,* 17 June 1915

16. *Hexham Courant,* 29 May 1915

17. WO 95/2828. *War Diary 1/5 Battalion Northumberland Fusiliers.*

18. WO 95/2829/1 *War Diary 1/6 Battalion Northumberland Fusiliers*

19. Wyrall E, *The Fiftieth Division 1914-1918,* 1939, Reprinted Naval and Military Press, 2002, p.81

20. Buckley, 1919, p.20

21. Ibid, p.21

22. Ibid, p.22

23. Ibid, p.22

24. Ibid, p.22

25. Ibid, p.22

26. WO 95/2829/1 *War Diary 1/6 Battalion Northumberland Fusiliers*

27. WO 95/2828. *War Diary 1/5 Battalion Northumberland Fusiliers*

28. WO95 2826/1. *War Diary, 149 Infantry Brigade*

Chapter Four: Armentières Sector

1. Harbottle, 1919, p.41

2. WO 95 2826/2, *War Diary 149 Brigade*

3. IWM Archives, Document 440, *Private papers of E W Cotton*

4. Wyrall E, 2002, p.91

5. Buckley, 1919, p.24

6. Grint A.I, 2006, p.87

7. Ibid, p.87

8. IWM Archives, Document 440, *Private papers of E W Cotton*

9. WO 25 2828/1 *War Diary 1/4 Battalion Northumberland Fusiliers*

10. IWM Archives, Document 440, *Private papers of E W Cotton*

11. Ibid

12. WO 25 2829/1, *War Diary 1/6 Battalion Northumberland Fusiliers*

13. Harbottle, 1919, p.44

14. Ibid, p.45

15. IWM Archives, Document 440, *Private papers of E W Cotton*

16. Buckley, 1919, p.27

17. WO 95/2828, *War Diary 1/5 Battalion Northumberland Fusiliers*

18. Buckley, 1919, p.27

19. WO 95/2828, *War Diary 1/5 Battalion Northumberland Fusiliers*

Chapter Five: Around the Salient

1. WO 95/2828, *War Diary 1/5 Battalion Northumberland Fusiliers*

2. Buckley, 1919, p.28

3. Ibid, p.29

4. Ibid, p.29

5. WO 95/2830, *War Diary 1/7 Battalion Northumberland Fusiliers*

6. WO 95/2828/1, *War Diary 1/4 Battalion Northumberland Fusiliers*

7. WO 95/2590, *War Diary 1/6 Battalion Northumberland Fusiliers.*

8. WO 95/2828, *War Diary 1/5 Battalion Northumberland Fusiliers*

9. Buckley F, *Q.6.A. and other places*, Spottiswoode and Ballantyne, London,1920, p.22

10. Ibid, p.24

11. Ibid, p.25

12. Ibid, p.25

13. Ibid, p.31

14. Buckley, 1919, p.32

15. Grint AI, 2011, p.83

16. Buckley, 1919, p.32

17. Ibid, p.33

18. Buckley, 1920, p.39

19. Ibid, p.39

20. Ibid, p.42

21. Ibid, p.43

22. Harbottle, 1919, p.56

23. Grint A I, 2006, p.101

24. WO 95/2830, *War Diary 1/7 Battalion Northumberland Fusiliers*

25. Grint A I, 2006, p.103

26. WO 95/2590. *War Diary 1/6 Battalion Northumberland Fusiliers*

27. Buckley, 1919, p.41

28. Buckley, 1920, p.65

Chapter Six: The Somme

1. WO 95/2828/1, *War Diary 1/4 Battalion Northumberland Fusiliers*

2. WO 95/2830, *War Diary 1/7 Battalion Northumberland Fusiliers*

3. WO 95 2826/4, *War Diary, 149 Infantry Brigade*

4. WO 95 2809/2, *War Diary, 50 Division*

5. Buckley F, 1919, p.42

6. Ibid.

7. Ibid, p.44

8. Ibid, p.45

9. Grint AI, 2006, p.136

10. Grint AI, 2011, p.124

11. Wyrall, 2002, p.159

12. Ibid, p.161

13. Gladden N, *The Somme 1916, A personal account,* William Kimber, London, 1974, p.110

14. Wyrall E, 2002, p.165

15. WO 95/2828, *War Diary 1/5 Battalion Northumberland Fusiliers*

16. Buckley, 1919, p.121

17. Buckley, 1920, p.148

18. Buckley, 1919, p.48

19. Buckley, 1920, p.93

20. WO 95/2828, *War Diary 1/5 Battalion Northumberland Fusiliers*

21. Buckley, 1920, p.94

22. Boraston JH, *General Haig's Dispatches, December 1916 – April 1917,* Dent and Sons 1919, p.75

23. Buckley, 1919, p.53

24. Ibid, p.53

25. Buckley, 1920, p.104

26. Wyrall, 2002, p.197

27. Ibid, p.197

28. Ibid, p.199

Chapter Seven: The Arras Sector

1. Buckley, 1919, p.57

2. Ibid, p.57

3. *St George's Gazette,* 30 June 1919

4. Buckley, 1920, p.148

5. WO 95/2830 *War Diary 1/7 Battalion Northumberland Fusiliers*

6. WO 95 2827/1, *War Diary 149 Brigade*

7. WO 95/2830 *War Diary 1/7 Battalion Northumberland Fusiliers*

Chapter Eight: The Affair at Houthulst Forest and the Winter of 1917/1918

1. Buckley, 1919, p.65
2. Ibid, p.65
3. Ibid, p.65
4. Ibid, p.65
5. Ibid, p.66
6. IWM AC Pickard J 8946 Reel 14
7. WO 95/2828/1 *War Diary 1/4 Battalion Northumberland Fusiliers*
8. IWM AC Pickard J 8946 Reel 14
9. Buckley, 1919, p.68
10. Ibid, p.68
11. Ibid, p.68
12. Ibid, p.69
13. Ibid, p.69
14. Ibid, p.70
15. Ibid, p.70
16. Ibid, p.70
17. Ibid, p.71
18. Ibid, p. 146
19. WO 95/2590. *War Diary 1/6 Battalion Northumberland Fusiliers*
20. Wyrall, 2002, p.250
21. Ibid, p.250
22. Ibid, p.250
23. Ibid, p.251-252
24. WO 95 2828/2, *War Diary 1/5 Battalion, Northumberland Fusiliers*
25. Buckley, 1919, p.72
26. WO 95 2828/1, *War Diary 1/4 Battalion, Northumberland Fusiliers*

Chapter Nine: The German Advance across the Somme, March 1918

1. WO 95 2828/1, *War Diary, 1/4 Battalion Northumberland Fusiliers*

2. Callin R W, *When the Lantern of Hope Burned Low.* J Catherall, Hexham 1919, p.8

3. WO 95 2829/1, *War Diary, 1/6 Battalion Northumberland Fusiliers*

4. IWM, Joe Pickard. AC8946 Reel 11

5. WO 95 2829/1, *War Diary, 1/6 Battalion Northumberland Fusiliers*

6. Callin, 1919, p.17

7. WO95 2827/3, *War Diary, 149 Infantry Brigade*

8. Callin, 1919, p.18

9. Ibid p.18 and p.27

10. Wyrall, 2002, pp.289-90

11. WO 95 2829/1, *War Diary, 1/6 Battalion Northumberland Fusiliers*

12. Ibid.

13. Ibid

14. Wyrall, 2002, pp.299-300

15. WO 95 2828 *War Diary, 1/5 Battalion Northumberland Fusiliers*

16. Wyrall, 2002, p.302

17. WO 95 2829/1, *War Diary, 1/6 Battalion Northumberland Fusiliers*

18. Callin, 1919. P.28

19. WO 95 2829/1, *War Diary, 1/6 Battalion Northumberland Fusiliers*

20. Callin,1919, p.28

21. WO 95 2829/1,*War Diary, 1/6 Battalion Northumberland Fusiliers*

22. IWM, Joe Pickard, AC8946 Reel 16-17

23. IWM, Joe Pickard, AC8946 Reel 17

24. Callin, 1919, p.30

25. Edmonds J E. *History of the Great War: Operations France and Belgium 1918, Appendices 20, p 131*

Chapter Ten: The German Offensive on the Lys

1. WO 95 2811/2, *War Diary 50 Division*

2. IWM Document, 12344, Bagley A E. transcript account, pp 2-3

3. Ibid. p 3.

4. Ibid. pp 3-4.

5. Callin, 1919, p.40

6. Ibid, p.42

7. WO 95 2829, *War Diary 1/6 Battalion Northumberland Fusiliers*

8. IWM Document, 12344, Bagley A E. transcript account, pp. 5-6.

9. Ibid, p. 6

10. Wyrall, 2002, p.326

11. IWM Document, 6709, Thompson A

12. IWM Document, 12344, Bagley A E. transcript account, p. 10

13. Ibid, pp. 12-13.

14. Ibid, p 13.

15. Wyrall, 2002, p.332

16. IWM Document, 6709, Thompson A

17. Ibid

18. IWM Document, 12344, Bagley A E. transcript account, p. 27

19. Ibid, p. 27

20. Ibid, p. 30

21. Callin, 1919, p.53

22. WO 95 2827/3, *War Diary 149 Brigade*

Chapter Eleven: Annihilation under French Command, May 1918

1. Kinaid-Smith M, *The 25 Division in France and Flanders,* Published 1920, reprinted 2001 by Naval and Military Press, p.250

2. Riddell EPA, W0 95 2811-3, *War Diary of 50 Division*

3. Ibid

4. Ibid

5. Ibid

6. WO 95 2828, *War Diary, 1/4 Battalion Northumberland Fusiliers*

7. Ibid

8. Callin, 1919, p.579.

9. Riddell EPA, WO 95 2811-3, *War Diary, 50 Division*

10. WO 95 2828, *War Diary 1/4 Battalion, Northumberland Fusiliers*

11. Callin, 1919, p.58

12. Jackson H W. WO 95 2824/4 *War Diary, 149 Brigade*

13. Blanchard D, *Battle of the Aisne 1918: The Phantom Sector,* Pen & Sword, 2015, p.82

14. Ibid, p.82

15. Ibid, p.83

16. WO95 2828, *War Diary, 1/5 Battalion Northumberland Fusiliers*

17. Van Emden R, *Prisoners of the Kaiser. The last PoWs of the Great War,* Pen & Sword, 2009, p.23

18. WO 95 2828 *War Diary, 1/5 Battalion Northumberland Fusiliers*

19. Ibid

20. Ibid

21. Riddell EPA, WO 95 2811-3, *War Diary, 50 Division*

22. Callin, 1919,

23. Riddell EPA *WO95 2811-3, War Diary, 50 Division*

24. Weber T, *Hitler's First War: Adolf Hitler; The men of the List Regiment and First World War,* OUP, 2010, p.287

25. Callin, 1919, p.62

26. Jackson HC, WO 95 2811-4, *War Diary, 50 Division*

27. Conan Doyle A. *The British Campaign in France and Flanders January to July 1918.* Hodder and Stoughton, 1919, p.183

28. WO 161 100/412 *Private Joseph Hodgson, 1/4 Northumberland Fusiliers, returning Prisoner of War Interview.*

29. Van Emden, 2009, p.24

30. Ibid, p.155

Chapter Twelve: Pioneer Battalion

1. Buckley, 1920, p.177

2. Ibid, pp.177-178
3. Buckley, 1919, p.73
4. Buckley, 1920, p.193
5. Morpeth Herald, 20 November 1922
6. Buckley, 1920, p.195
7. Ibid, p.198
8. WO 95 2650/4, *War Diary 1/7 Battalion Northumberland Fusiliers*
9. Buckley, 1919, p.77
10. Ibid, pp.77-78
11. Ibid, p.78
12. WO 95 2650/4, *War Diary 1/7 Battalion Northumberland Fusiliers*
13. Ibid
14. Buckley, 1919, p.79
15. Bean C.E.W. *Official History of Australia in the War of 1914-1918. Vol 6,* p.528
16 Luddendorff, E, *Luddendorf's Own Story Vol 2,* Harper and Brothers, New York, p.326
17. Buckley, 1919, p.80
18. Ibid, p.80
19. Ibid, p.81
20. WO 95 2650/4, *War Diary 1/7 Battalion Northumberland Fusiliers.*
21. Buckley, 1919, p.81
22. Ibid, p.81
23. Ibid, p.82
24. Ibid, p.82
25. Ibid, p.82
26. Ibid, p.83
27. Ibid, p.83
28. Ibid, p.84
29. Ibid, pp. 84-85
30. Ibid, p.87
31. Ibid, p.87

Chapter Thirteen: Aftermath

1. Grint A. I, 2011, p.373
2. Gladden, 1974, pp. 45, 93, 95
3. Grint A. I, 2006
4. Grint A. I, 2006
5. www.ashingtonmemorial.com
6. *Newcastle Journal,* 8 May 1915.
7. Tilbrook S, www.longlongtrail.co.uk/brothers-died-in-the-great-war
8. *Newcastle Journal,* 15 May 1915.
9. *Shields Daily News,* 14 May 1915
10. *Newcastle Journal,* 26 March 1916
11. *Newcastle Journal,* 20 November 1916.
12. *Morpeth Herald,* 18 July 1919.
13. Grint A I, 2011, p.88
14. WO95 2828. *War Diary, 1/4 Battalion Northumberland Fusiliers.*
15. Buckley, 1920, p.42
16. Grint A.I, 2011, p.378
17. Armstrong William Watson, p.20
18. Grint AI, 2006, pp.137-138
19. Grint AI, 2011, pp.121-121
20. Graves R, *'Goodbye to All That',* Penguin Essentials Edition, 2011, p300

Appendix A

Killed in action 24 – 27 April 1915

1/4 Battalion

Other Ranks:
Sergeants & Lance Sergeants:

94 William Glendining
785 Victor Elton Scott
    Corporals:
1873 William Hartley
539 John Robson
1685 Robert Venables
    Lance Corporals:
919 Norman Davidson
1701 Fred Lee
798 Frederick William
    McGann
968 Thomas Orr
757 Robert Thomas Potter
1592 Ernest Woodman
    Private:
1756 John Edward Adams
2097 Edward Archer
836 Obediah Armstrong
1319 Thomas Bailey
1765 Alfred Blacklock
806 Alfred Septimus Palmer
    Brown

1335 Gordon Brown
1961 Thomas Brown
1567 John Edward Cade
1327 Joseph Cunningham
1526 William Kendall
    Dickinson
824 Thomas Donaldson
2248 William Donnelly
4/2517 John Elliott
4/1348 James Fenwick
4/2449 Thomas Forester
4/2275 William Fox
4/2431 John Leadbitter
    Gibson
1872 John Grierson
1721 Andrew Rutherford
    Hall
1855 Arthur John Herdman
616 Matthew Hudson
1811 Arthur Jowsey
2100 William Keenan
1699 Fred Kirby

2071 Thomas O'Neill
2123 Matthew Patterson
1719 William Paxton
2279 George Pearson
1197 William Gillis Pearson
1958 Joseph Pigdon
1883 Robert Scott
964 Benjamin Slack
4/1185 James Smith
1404 William Soulsby
2021 William Spence
1851 Cecil Croft
    Thompson
1981 John Thompson
2201 George William
    Campbell Usher
2468 John Wade
1760 Isaac Hopper
    Whitaker

1/5 Battalion

Officers:
Major Foutain O'Key Colbourne Nash

Other Ranks:
Lance Corporal:

1423 GeorgeThompson
    Privates:
2712 John William Abbott

1522 James Arnold
2356 James Close
2589 William Coates

1728 Robert Ferguson
2565 William Heron
2458 David Keith Tullock

1/6 Battalion

Officers:
Captain George Edward Hunter
Captain Howard Tomlin Hunter
Lieutenant Arthur Richmond Garton
Lieutenant Edmund Mortimer
Lieutenant William Black Noble
Second Lieutenant Edward Noel Mather

Other Ranks:
Sergeants & Lance Sergeants:
2103 John Beck
869 Neville Brook
2230 Donald Ellis
6556 Robert Edward Lamb
1326 William Lumley
2170 Arthur Nunnerley
580 Anthony Potts
1469 Thomas Craighull Wilson
1973 Thomas Wynne
Corporals:
3196 David Amers
2019 James Binning
1503 Harry Hetherington
1974 Peter Weddell
Lance Corporals
2452 James Henry Hogg
1434 Adam McWinnie
2748 Frederick John Strasenburg
Private:
2602 John Cecil Allen
3356 John Farquhar Armstrong

3203 George Arthur Atkinson
2877 Benjamin Bashton
2378 Robert Beattie
3386 Francis Edward Bell
3387 Rueben Bezer
2382 John Boag
2391 Arthur Irwin Bridge
3213 Alexander Burgess
1068 Allan Henry Byrne
1754 Roger Crawley
1764 James William Croney
2325 William Cummings
2543 Amos Curry
3470 John Thomas Ellis
1546 Albert Epstein
1577 Bartley Evans
2628 William Fawcett
2150 Lewis Edward Franks
3247 Henry Gibson
1845 Stanley Gray
3391 George Greaves
1509 Gilbert Gregson
2587 Samuel Humble

2618 John Jackson
2748 Alfred Frederick Percy Jennings
2901 Peter Lamb
1803 Francis Watson Moore
2384 William Morrison
2393 Alfred Naitby
1712 Charles Newall
2000 Alexander Nixon
3508 Edward Henry Perry
3381 Richard Ralphs
2853 Thomas Job Raynor
2860 William Albert Ridley
1945 William Robertson
2339 Raymond Robson
2554 Edgar Blanchland Sanderson
2330 Arthur Sutton
2593 George Urwin
1138 Herbert Waller
1000 Thomas Wardle
2820 Alexander Caverhill Welsh

1/7 Battalion

Officers:
Second Lieutenant Alan Williamson Kent

Other Ranks:
Sergeants & Lance Sergeant:

1770 Thomas Harrison
25 Robert Hedley
98 James Huntley
7885 Robert Stephen
    Mossman
1871 James Wilson
    Corporal:
1447 James Dalby
2148 Thomas Hope Fell
    Lance Corporal:
1949 James Goodfellow
1443 William McLeod
2108 Alexander Noble
    Private:
2233 George Young Allon
1541 William Anderson
1948 Albert Coulthard
2236 George Curtis
2427 Laurence Fealey
2362 George William
    Geggie

1305 John Edward Harrison
2408 Thomas Hartley
2120 John Harvey
1700 Hugh Hudspith
1665 Fred Irving
2052 James Jeffrey
1384 Leon Jones
2295 Frederick Lyons
2435 Alexander Mackay
1575 Harold Marston
2340 William McCloud
1269 John Middleton
2438 Hugh Miles
2786 William Nairn
2786 Albert Ernest Nichol
1816 Robert Nicholson
2254 John Oliver
1359 Edwin Hindmarsh
    Patterson
1419 William Potts
2603 John Purvis

2265 James Robson
1394 Thomas Robson
2079 John Scott
2190 John Shepherd
2031 William Watson
    Smailes
2233 Thomas Stonehouse
1457 James Tait
3008 Matthew Taylor
1313 Harry Goodwin
    Thompson
1989 Thomas Wake
1598 Wilfred Hereward
    Wake
2238 Ben Broomfield
    Weightman
2141 John Wood

Appendix B

Killed in Action: 15 September 1916

1/4 Battalion

Officers:
Headquarters Company
Lieutenant John Angus Bagnall
'A' Company:
Captain John Thomas Henderson
Second Lieutenant Kieth Patrick*
'B' Company:
Captain Lionel Davey Plummer
Second Lieutenant Henry Archibald Long
'C' Company:
Second Lieutenant Joseph Thomson Melville*
'D' Company:
Captain Henry Hogarth Bell
Second Lieutenant Joseph Fleming*
Second Lieutenant George James Balfour*
* Attached from Higland Light Infantry
Lieutenant Vernon Taylor
Attached Machine Gun Company

Other Ranks:

Company Sergeant Major:
855 Christopher Rowell
Colour Sergeant:
236 Alfred Hetherington
Sergeant:
1860 James William Cocker
2141 Benjamin Cuffe
497 Edward Dunn
1018 Frederick Armstrong Forster
936 Surtees Forster
2805 James Hamilton
593 Frederick Harvey
2296 Alfred Holbrook
1764 George Percy Miller
1038 William Peebles
1839 Thomas Scott
Lance Sergeant:
20 Richard Brooks
1712 Norman Charlton
Corporal:
2148 Robert Armstrong
1136 John Chambers
2104 Joseph Daniel Cleugh
201110 Edward Spence Richardson
2268 Joseph Robinson
342 Walter Herbert Spark
1407 Thomas Welsh
1223 John Wheatley
Lance Corporal:
2505 Ernest William Bell
1793 John Bushby
2999 Tom Cowler
3059 Tom Bell Dodd
2784 Michael Hastings
1219 Hamilton Hoggarth
2936 James Adam Jamieson
1677 Alfred Lindsay
alias Alfred Lindsay Armstrong
940 Fred Maddison
200447 Matthew Martinson
1022 Samuel McGuire
1814 Charles Reed
2190 William Rowell

200385 James Sheppard
200425 John Shields
2911 Henry Simpson
2900 Thomas Sowerby
1400 Thomas Wilkinson
Private:
3278 Tom Abbot
201179 Frederick Charles Alderman
2783 Robert Ancrum
2776 William Anderson
1808 Edwin Armstrong
1828 Ernest Armstrong
4073 Arthur Atkin
1411 Robert Atkin
1802 Atkinson Joseph
9013 Charles Bailey
3024 Thomas Banton
3499 Robert Bates
9010 Beales Jack William
200856 Frederick Beattie
3585 George Carhill Beaulah
3274 James Bell
2078 Richard Bell
201038 Edward Thomas Bennett
201356 John Wilfred Bentley
3506 William Henry Beswick
2597 Robert Blackburn
3447 James Braddock
4173 Thomas Brogan
3491 Arthur Brookhouse
204012 Alfred John Brown
3662 Arthur Brownett
3551 Harold Bulson
2326 Robert Burn
9014 Arthur Butler
1576 Thomas Butters MM
1530 Charles Cade
4116 Thomas Carter
9018 Ben Chamberlin
3322 Edward Charlton
2247 Frederick Charlton
899 George Chilton

3226 James William Clynes
2065 George Cockbaine
1993 Thomas Codling
3980 Ernest Cook
204016 Fred Cook
3445 Albert Leverton Cooper
4140 Edward Cooper
2651 William Cooper
3616 John James Coulson
3570 John William Cousins
3596 George Cross
1767 Ralph Crozier
3323 George Davidson
2692 Joseph Davison
4193 James Dixon
3454 John William Dixon
2273 Alfred Armstrong Dodd
1485 William Dodd
3352 John Dodds
3430 George Dunning
201393 William Henry Emberton
1012 Arthur William Errington
38985 Bertie Evans
204022 Maurice Ethanuel Everitt
3428 Harold Fleetham
201226 Charles Flint
2801 William Gatens
1127 Robert Alexander Gibb
4019 Joseph Gibson
1785 James Gould
4187 Thomas Foster Graham
3436 Percy Graves
201364 Samuel John Gregory
4004 William Henry Grocott
4179 John Lisman Hart
200718 Arthur Harvey
200890 Albert Henderson

3089 Thomas Holliday Henzell
2921 Joseph Heron
4027 Henry Hibbert
4024 Thomas William Hill
4123 Thomas Hodgkinson
201369 John Houseman
1373 Henry George Hubbock
3417 Robert Hunsley
1282 Charles Hunter
1797 George Hunter
1353 John Pearson Hutchinson
1041 William Irwin
958 Solomon Jemison
3669 John Keetley
4021 Ernest Kirkham
9039 Frederick Walter Lambert
1048 James Lane
3427 Walter Large
1357 William Leathard
200640 John Lee
2611 Moses Lindsay
2822 Thomas Lindsay
3311 James Lisle
3591 Edward Lonsdale
1754 Isaac Marshall
2005 James Marshall
3852 Frederick Matthews
2026 William McCombes
3563 John McLean

3118 John Donald McLean
2274 Frederick Mead
2953 John William Meldrum
1009 Edward Milburn
3137 William Mills
1086 Thomas Mounsey
2773 William Murray
4112 Arthur Frederick Nash
3715 William Naylor
1016 Thomas William Nelson
1788 Thomas William Nevin
3711 George Henry Newton
909 John Edward Newton
3318 Ralph Newton
3210 Jonathan Nicholson
204033 Charles Percy Niker
9046 Harry Norman
1877 John Oliver
2813 Francis John O'Malley
9054 Jack Parnell
3434 George Moses Pepper
9006 William Robert Platfoot
1335 Thomas Potts
3367 John Gardener Purvis
2007 George Roberts
2117 John Roberts

1305 James Edward Robinson
436 John Thomas Robson
2433 Joseph Henry Robson
2452 Tom Robson
1724 Archibald Rutherford
2211 Joseph Herbert Rutherford
201229 William Edwin Scurr
201337 Herbert Benjamin Sherwin
3565 Charles Skelton
4063 Albert Smith
3013 Edward Stanley Smith
3262 Henry Smith
1868 Robert Armstrong Smith
2315 Richard Thomas Strong
2619 John Suddes
3263 Joseph Vickers Temple
2235 John Thompson
3568 John Robert Trowell
1385 Norman Venus
3313 Thomas Wallbank
1231 John William Whann
1752 Alexander White
3023 William Wightman
200154 Thomas Wright
2528 John William Young
1972 Robert Young

1/5 Battalion

Other Ranks:
Private:
4229 Charles Beadell
242402 Arthur Bentlety
4514 Joseph Carter
2346 William Andrew Chapman
4922 Lawson Craythorne
2124 John William English
8058 Frederick Featherstone

4421 Alfred Seymour Gibson
1933 Joseph Henry Golightly
267502 Guy Grainger
2607 Augustus Herron
240707 Samuel Aldridge Hood
242386 John Lisle

7109 John Robert Needham
1793 George Philipson
8117 Lawrence Reed
241090 Stanley Rogers
240974 John Williams

1/6 Battalion

Officers
Captain Trevor Carlyon Tweedy

Other Ranks:
Company Sergeant Major:
3234 Stephen Laws
Sergeant & Lance Sergeant:
2297 James Norman
Allison
2481 Jonas Smith
Corporal:
2835 John Foster Goodban
4753 Hyman Kurtzman
Lance Corporal:
4413 Frederick Atkinson
3662 Robert Henry Bradley
2070 Christopher Charlton
2747 Roy Ferguson
3314 Owen O'Dowd
8110 David Phillips
Private:
2401 Matthew Baptist
2357 James Batey
5121 Robert Batty
8022 George Herbert
Billett
8017 John William Boam
3883 Thomas Boe
4338 Ralph Briggs
8003 Robert Thomas
Gibson Brown
4055 Henry Burke
4723 William Chapman
3444 Thomas Cross

267888 William Dabell
2335 William Dawson
4212 Leonard Dodds
3730 John Farrow
4316 Robert Huggins
Fletcher
8063 Joseph Gibson
8059 George Goodwin
265771 Robert Graham
8064 Charles William
Grainger
3426 Lawrence Grieve
3380 John Thomas Laurie
Hall
267514 Ernest Harrison
265244 George William
Harrison
5443 Frederick Hibbert
8077 Charles Oswald
Hopcroft
265543 Charles Hornsby
4418 Hugh Hoy
4057 George Hughes
4347 John Keir
4806 Patrick Lamb
4170 Albert Lawson
8101 Albert Bolton Mace
2131 Thomas William
Maughan

1716 Joseph McGowan
4272 John Melville
1807 James Monaghan
265902 Nicholas Murphy
4549 John James Nelson
4116 Rueben Nelson
8112 William Blackett
Pearson
5131 Thomas Power
4140 John Harry Purdy
5170 Charles Ralph
8121 Ernest Harold Roach
5632 Joseph Henry
Robinson
4793 Samuel Robinson
265687 William James
Robinson
4286 Maddison Robson
4763 George Sanderson
8126 John Shale
265911 John Slight
3400 John Taylor
1923 James Tweddle
1661 Robert Walker
4570 Edward Whittaker
4339 Charles Whittle
265453 William Wilkinson
5063 Robert Wilson

1/7 Battalion

Officers:
Captain John William Melville
Second Lieutenant John Ivor Grey
Second Lieutenant Arnold Stroud (1/4 NF attached 1/7NF)
Second Lieutenant Baron Brooke Booth

Other Ranks:

Company Sergeant Major:

1272 Bertie Foster

Sergeant & Lance Sergeant:

1903 Robert Baxter
953 William Joseph
    Clancey
2170 Arthur Gray
290196 James Hood
265 Ernest Logan
1244 Alexander McNab
1494 Gilbert Swann

Corporal:

1207 Thomas Oswald
    Austin
2556 Ralph Craze
290824 Robert Dodds
2051 Frank Lough Pringle
1673 Edmund Webb

Lance Corporal:

2208 James Butler
290805 Edward Chesterton
290697 Peter Coxon
291118 William Lawson
2220 William Lyall
3427 James Purdy
2394 Tom Pybus
290537 Harold Shotton
291005 William Taylor

Private:

3391 James Backhouse
4526 Herbert Blow
2080 Alexander Borthwick
1487 John Brewis
2646 William Buddle
3755 Alfred Chisam
2799 Henry Colquhoun
291267 Ernest Constable
4394 Robert Cook

3339 John William Crook
290767 George Dinsdale
2425 John Brydon Douglas
1505 William Dumble
2562 George Humble
    Edwards
3808 John Evans
4500 Harry Arnold Everson
29814 Ernest Fewster
290515 Andrew Forrest
4491 John William
    Handley
6039 Stanley Harrison
6041 Christopher Bailey
    Heckels
3815 Adam Davidson Hill
290996 john Hinson
291003 Robert Hunter
6145 John William George
    Johnson
3775 Robert Stanley
    Johnson
290964 John Laidlow
291021 Henry Lee
290840 Robert Long
3731 Thomas William
    Lorimour
291203 Edwin W Lovely
290692 George Robert
    Mason
290654 Brian Mawson
3521 John McDonald
6068 Frank McKenna
1005 Frederick Charles
    Middleton
290808 William Morgan
3617 Edward Moss

292180 Daniel Mullen
291065 John Charles
    Nottingham
4130 Arthur Nutty
201242 James Oxendale
290421 Robert William
    Patterson
6094 Harry Robinson
292197 James Robson
2635 David Rollo
290434 John Rutherford
290974 Thomas Rutherford
290075 Arthur Sample
3730 Albert Schofield
3289 Peter Stacey
291135 Thomas Strother
2081 Richard Swan
3602 John James Tait
1702 Matthew Tait
291005 George Taylor
2872 John Thomas Templey
291010 Thomas Thompson
2939 George Todd
2348 Robert Turner
290713 Thomas Vosper
291058 James Wealliams
202218 David Wells
3108 Thomas Williams
292222 Arthur Hart
    Wilson
2290498 James John
    Wilson
291113 Thomas Wilson
2072 William Wilson
292223 Alexander Wood
292234 Sydney John Wood
292224 Richard Wragby

Appendix C

Killed in action 1/4 Battalion

13-19 November 1916

Officers:

Captain John Wilfred Robinson

Other Ranks:
Sergeant & Lance Sergeant:
200006 William Anthony
   Charlton
1783 John William Pearson
   Private:
9007 Bertie William Adcock
5206 Herbert Alfred Boast
1618 George William
   Boustead
202141 Frank Bradbury
5083 James Brown
5123 Cecil Burton
2257 Ernest Cartman
202166 Ben Cartwright
5093 William Francis Church
3299 John Clarke
200267 William John Crisp

5304 Joseph Davies
5133 Ernest Leopold Douglas
5397 Richard Dover
200679 Thomas Elliott
4094 William Oxley Elshaw
202668 John Glass
3685 Wilfred Hardwick
5397 Harold Hiscock
9331 Frederick Francis Holton
6988 Bernard Jones
2786 Harvey MacKey
3441 William Marples
2841 John Mulholland
9048 William Francis
   Newman
1341 George Oliver

5107 Arthur Ernest Pyatt
5106 Henry Pyatt
5024 Stanley Rouse
202017 Reginald George
   Thorneycroft
5141 Daniel Walden
5155 Harry Ward
5153 Herbert Howard
   Wilford
5156 Alfred George
   Woodward

1/5 Battalion

Officers:
Lieutenant Norman Wilfred Lawson
Second-Lieutenant Thomas Nelson Melrose
Second- Lieutenant Arthur Edward Moorhouse

Other Ranks:
Sergeant & Lance Sergeant:
1642 Thomas Barras MM
241367 James Ernest
   Bilham
2496 Archibald Buchanan
240093 Philip Deagle
1845 Thomas Henry Dixon
   Corporal:
7001 Edwin Adamson
240552 Robert Robson
6620 Joseph Scott
7027 Robert Sneddon
240640 Robert Owen
   Webb
   Lance Corporal:
240179 Cornelius Buckley
2623 George Fairless
240353 William Mitchell
6558 Frederick William
   Riseborough

240455 William Scott
   Private:
241770 Felix Edward
   Alexander
2668 Joseph Archbold
7225 John James
   Armstrong
7070 Edward Atkinson
240731 George Atkinson
2596 Thomas Atkinson
   MM
241781 Ernest Baker
6628 Thomas Barker
241131 Claude Harold
   Ivan Barrs
7076 Arthur Bayes
6506 George Bennett
241340 George Samuel
   Bills

240880 Robert Blackett
241020 William Boyle
4687 Arthur Butler
242283 Joseph Stanley
   Campion
241372 James Albert Carter
242341 Thomas Chapman
24025 Anthony Charlton
242226 Charles Chatfield
241043 Samuel Jobling
   Craig
6629 Joseph Crawford
240448 William James
   Crawley
241785 William Crisp
241786 John Cross
241788 Alfred Stark Davey
241976 Charles Docherty
1462 George Douglass

242287 Edward Smith Evans
240986 Joseph Fee
241393 Aaron Finkle
5776 Herbert Foulsham
241113 Samuel Garrett
242348 Charles Garrod
240102 George Gilbert
2323 John Graham
241797 Sydney Guyett
6680 Denton Haigh
241919 Harry Haigh
241974 Walter Halford
242011 James Hanson
240963 George Hardy
7158 Frank Henry Harris
241982 Thomas Heron
7212 Herbert Hindley
6665 Charles Henry Hodgson
241984 Edward Jackson
241924 Frederick Jackson
240884 Henry George Johnson
6740 William Lambert
241878 Thomas Lindsay
1754 William Longworth
240708 John Lowery
241889 Robert MacComb
240393 Alfred Makepeace MM
7102 Vincent Matthews
6546 George William Mayne
241987 George McCarthy
241990 William McClay

2466 Norman George McKenzie
241093 Henry Gilbert Measham
240171 Henry Merrilies
3068 Ventors Miller
242302 Frank Morris
241988 William Morrison
240561 William Mullen
243306 Henry Newton
2271 George Nichols
6783 John George Noble
6550 George Henry Nunn
241936 Arthur Ogden
241937 Brook Whitley Parkin
241940 Harry Parkinson
241816 Armine Pike
241893 John William Purvis
242367 Coupland Rackham
241948 William Ramsey
241947 Ernest Ramsden
241034 Robert Ramshaw
4134 John Raniggan
242311 Albert Fred Richardson
2168 Mark Richardson
242371 Abraham Riley
241859 Earnest Cairns Riley
241858 John Robinson
240891 William Robinson
240852 Reginald Robson
242368 William Rogerson
240853 Thomas John Rush

241945 Arthur Edward Rushworth
7020 Norman Samuel
240079 James Sheardown
6769 James Smith
242312 Charles Stocks
242373 Thomas Stonehouse
242313 James Swinden
240711 Robert Tait
241892 John Telford
4149 James Temple
6737 William Holdsworth Terry
240406 Edward Thompson
7057 Percy Tindall
241827 Cyril Bertram Tucker
241980 John Tulip
7064 Walter Henry Wordsworth
240217 John Watson
242406 Tom Watson
242244 John Thomas Webster
241846 Leslie Wells
241828 Eric Spencer Wilkinson
241894 Joseph Wilson
241187 Hugh Wimms
241964 John Wood
241011 Robert Wright
242384 Francis Young

1/6 Battalion

Officers:
Captain Andrew Smith

Other Ranks:
Sergeant & Lance Sergeant:
4571 Thomas Smith Scott
    Lance Corporal:
3491 Victor Cecil Hope
3385 Joseph Maskey
8129 David Vincent
    Shillito
        Private:
3327 Elliott Ashton
7590 Henry Beake
7518 Frederick James
    Cooper
7743 Frank Haldenby

7543 Albert Hallam
4987 George Holmes
1591 Thomas Leach
7061 George Martin
1540 John Matterson
    Midgley
7553 Charles Percy
    Oakham
5062 Robert Perdue
7605 Ernest Pym
7606 William Seal
3223 William Taylor

7611 William Charles
    Wheeler
7531 George Wild
2754 Ernest Wilson

1/7 Battalion

Officers:
Second Lieutenant Alan James Derrick
Second Lieutenant Frederick James Larken
Second Lieutenant Edward Grey Lawson
Second Lieutenant Dominic Roe Dathy O'Daley
Second Lieutenant Fletcher Hugh Lionel Woods

Other Ranks:
Sergeant & Lance Sergeant:
1057 Stanley Chambers
290049 George Dunn
290418 James Piercy MM
1430 James Richardson
2030 George Robinson
291712 William Wood
        Corporal:
290234 Arthur Bowman
291728 Wiliam Thomas
    Peake
    Lance-Corporal:
291008 John Aitchinson
291006 John Alexander
1593 John William Athey
4545 Charles William Dale
290284 Thomas Davidson
291101 John Grey
290524 Archibald William
    Lockhart
290104 Henry Miller
2232 George Wilson Purvis
3077 Joshua Ray

290444 George Gilbert
    Shiell
5645 Charles Wilson
        Private:
3504 William Anderson
292114 Thomas Arnell
290599 George Avery
293321 John Arthur Ernest
    Bailey
2502 Albert Baker
292603 Harry Banks
7005 Leonard Horace
    Barber
291122 Thomas Edgely
    Barclay
290837 Thomas Baron
292257 John Henry Batey
5512 James Blakey
292260 Harry Artur Bolam
292607 Victor Francis
    Brodie

7182 Reginald Charles
    Bryan
292616 Harry Carter
290577 John Clark
292692 Ernest Arthur
    Clayden
292264 William Collins
292310 William Henry
    Cooper
291719 John Curry
292618 Edward William
    Darrell
290050 Alexander James
    Davidson
290925 Robert Davison
292272 John Willie
    Douglas
7134 James Downs
292621 James Edward
    Drake
291075 Adam Sherlaw
    Elliott

290887 John Thomas Embleton
291260 Herbert Everatt
292278 Arthur Foster
291684 Robert Gibson
7045 William Gifford
290306 Herbert Goward
292633 Harry Grant
2940 Andrew Gray
291646 Lancelot Gregory
292284 Robert Gutherson
292640 Harry Hare
3524 George Hartley
292711 Frederick William Hilton
291726 Robert Albert Holmes
292709 Richard John Hopkin
7054 Thomas George Hubbard
292262 Samuel Robert Hutton
292280 George Jenkins
291032 John Johnston
7196 Frederick Jordan
290651 John Robert King

7210 Stanley Harrison Latham
291732 Godfrey Marriott
6181 Henry Salt Marsay
290935 Thomas Marshall
290403 Nicholas Maughan
292172 Henry McGuin
6147 George Young Metcalfe
6075 David Thomas Moreton
291116 James Murray
291733 Ernest Newton
291699 Frank Nixon
291071 Roger Patten
290657 George Patterson
291722 Fred Pearce
292700 Edward George Pearse
3771 Robert Henry Pringle
292303 Matthew Lee Prudhoe
1605 George Reavley
292266 James Reynolds
291742 Alfred Ripton
1979 William Lawson Ritchie

291659 Thomas Robertson
290441 Thomas Robson
290633 Edmund Ross
292259 Edward Carr Rowland
292277 Joseph Scott
291747 Nathaniel Smith
291749 James Smith
290820 James Tate
291756 John Tittley
5636 Robert Turner
291754 Robert Turner
291639 John Joseph Wadie
291702 Robert White
291764 Shadrach White
291720 George Thomas Whitehead
291705 Wilfred George Wickes
292704 Thomas Rutherford Wills
55808 James Wise

Appendix D

Killed in action 26 October 1917

1/4 Battalion

Officers:
Lieutenant Robert Arthur Abbas Simpson
Second Lieutenant Ryde Guild Rayner
Second Lieutenant William Ruddy
Second Lieutenant David Arthur Smith
Second Lieutenant David Lindsay Young

Other Ranks:
Sergeant & Lance Sergeant:
200081, William Dickinson
200525, John Robson
235253, John Watson
Corporal:
202199, Walter Brown

242300, William Haydon Linwood
204624, Robert Mitchell Newell
200520, John Edward Taylor

Lance Corporal:
203088, Christopher Burns
204570, Thomas George Colman
200798, Albert Logan
16083, Anthony Millington
242310, Reginald Revell

200547, Robert Henry Ridley
200751, William Teasdale
46884, Hugh Miller Templeton

Private:

241773, George Walter Anthony
202894, Lionel Victor Armes
200766, Frank Armstrong
235071, Harry Attrill
203288, Christopher Ayling
35604, Sam Bowyer
204070, Harry Braybrook
203289, James Brisley
235107, James Brunt
202157, George Busfield
203290, William Button
202520 James Candish
202222 John Robert Carneby
202914, Lious Carrick
205164 Thomas Pattison Chisholme
202034, Joseph Alfred Colling
204474, Terence Colton
43093, Robert Raymond Cooper
203299, Albert Edward Crisp
204630, Tom Dale
202278, Bainbridge Davidson
202174, Edward Carr Dawson
204064, Frederick Charles Dean

235080, George Dodds
290923, Walter Douglas
203351, Richard Dunman
203305, Charles John Edward Dunn
203244, Edward James Dwyer
200863, Robert Ellwood
202837, Edward Eyton
203272, Bertram Frederick Bruce Falconer
365394, James Fawcus
202244, Robert Ferrell
202208, Richard Fielden
200644, Matthew Frazer
203219, Ralph Gair
203247, John Glover
202213, Walter Gradon
202926, John Seymour Grant
201986, Frederick Harley
202272, Alexander Henderby
266045, Benjamin Hill
292671, David Samuel William Jones
202111, Sydney John Jordan
204618, William Kelly
203318, Alfred Edmond Kingshott
202358, John Thomas Kirtley
203369, Thomas Leach
204615, Thomas Logan
203323, Herbert Tom Manning
35555, Edward Matson
203682, Alexander McCaffery

242510, Ernest William Monkman
201094, William Todd Moore
201907, George Edward Newman
204483, Michael Nicholson
204401, Ernest Joseph Palmer
201914, George Parker
235232, William Parkin
201858, Herbert Thompson Petfield
201491, Thomas Cochrane Reid
201800, William Robson
203640, Richard Rogers
202125, Charles Ryder
201939, John Sanderson
315354, Samuel Sanderson
203129, Walter Slassor
235067, John Surtess
44624, Frank Thorington
41233, John Towey
242212, Ernest Percy Trotter
9466, Richard Turner
290724, Robert Wade
243197, Wilfred Ward
22/969, Archibald Watson
242005, George William Williams
47970, Alfred Albert Wilmshurst
202832, John Wilson
291953, Samuel Woodcock
202035, William John Worth
242265, Harry Wright
5058, James Wright

1/5 Battalion

Officers:
Second Lieutenant William Gibson Verrill
Second Lieutenant William White Wilkin

Other Ranks:

Sergeant & Lance Sergeant:

240771, Peter Anderson
240284, Joseph Andrew Hawthorn
240140, Arthur Farm Taylor
240050, Alfred Willis

Corporal:

242329, Robert Atkinson
241833, George Crisp
240979, John William Hadaway
243178, William Kears
242491, John Nunn
263078. Alexander Wallace
240295, Arthur Wilson
241831, George Robert Woods

Lance Corporal:

240164, Robert Brown
242433, William Conway
240324, William Cowie
241335, Ernest Bertram Gooda
241310, William Gumsley
44835, Benjamin Kitchener
45095, George Low
44844, Charles William Luxton
242524, William Noble
242363, Fred Parkinson
240682, Albert Smith
263088, Walter Smurthwaite
243188, William Stephen Storey

Private:

242529, Matthew Addy
241897, George Angus
242493, David Edward Archbold
240327, John Arkle
242520, James Armstrong
242017, Sydney Armstrong
242014, Albert Ash
35478, John Astley, John
242556, Thomas William Baggaley

19/417, Arthur Ernest Baglish
3/9024, James Barbour
33532, Norman Barker
45065, Frederick Thomas Barton
242336, Frederick Blacknell
44922, William Arthur Innocens Blandford
263073, Edward Norman Bolam
44867, Walter Bonsall
44936, James Orlands Bridge
44914, William Henry Brittain
242448, Albert Brookes
242082, John Brown
18/1390, Henry Brunton
44941, Frederick Oliver Cain
240402, Samuel Carline
263096, George William Carr
45069, William Thomas Catling
242090, Edward Charlton
242045, Arthur Henry Clack
241783, Albert Arthur Clayton
242532, Lewis Costello
241004, George Craig
263079, Robert Craig
242281, Henry Cuthbertson
242178, William Joseph Dagleash
44946, William Davies
240115, Richard Dinsdale
240375, Joseph Dodds
242286, Thomas Dolan
16271, Albert William Dunn
242453, Harold Brown Cotterill Elliott

44954, Donald Evans
44959, Edward Fairthorpe
44864, Benjamin John Morton Field
45082, Bertie Fifield
44958, George Ernest Finlayson
35689, Bertie Flannagan
27/249, Archibald Fullard
242421, William Gates
24584, Robert Gibbon
240688, Samuel Joseph Gorman
24214, Walter Graham
243152, George Green
27/290, John Green
241346, Thomas Groves
44865, Walter Gundry
242180, Woodhead Haigh
44876, Henry George Hall
240738, Robert Hall
45086, William Harry Hall
44978, Charles Hallewell
44968, Colin Halliday
45058, Herbert Hardy
242537, George Grievson Harwood
241283, Arthur James Hawley
242535, Thomas Albert Hewitson
44963, Valentine Hibbert
263052, Joseph Homes
241872, Robert Hudson
3203, James Hutchinson
38647, James king
44991, Andrew Leech
242356, Robert Lendrem
243174, William Thwaites Longstaff
242413, John Edward Lowdon
240349, Samuel Lowdon
242511, William Mackle
46757, Edwin Mallalieu
241107 Arthur Marshall
241989, Edward Maughan

241060, Lacey Mayes
263023, Philip Mckenna
242116, Bernard Mckevitt
240760, Daniel McNally
241365, Joseph Mead
241417, Alfred John
Mellars
45000, George Edward
Mellor
240014, Charles Norman
Merritt
57582, Thomas Miller
242418, William Miller
263085, Ralph Moore
44995, Horace William
Morley
45061, Henry Mulhearn
44895, William Nicholas
Musgrove
44916 Douglas Napier
45002, Frank Newton
44886, David Arthur Page
240019, Richard Park
242199, Neil Patrick
240149, John Harrison
Patterson
242031, Charles Ambrose
Payne
44917, Albert Pedlar

241995, Joseph Purdy
242481, William Ramsay
40595, Harry Rayner
242120, John William
Reed
202123, Albert Edward
Reynolds
242445, Frederick Charles
Rhodes
263065, Fred Yates Roberts
45017, Robert Roberts
241380, Henry Percy
Robinson
241979, William Robinson
240239, Jacob Robson
45059, Francis Archer Roe
44906, Max Leopold
Rosher
44921, William Ross
242124, John Taylor Rutter
241569, Ernest Sanderson
241863, Matthew Scott
242129, Albert Shepherd
240874, Ernest Simpson
201929, Arthur William
Slack
241861, William Smith
241953, William Smith
45030, William Stafford

25/1295, Robert
Stephenson
243189, William
Stephenson
263044, John Stockdale
242460, William Straughan
45029, Arthur Sunderland
45040, Harry Taylor
240795, John Young Taylor
241383, William Taylor
45037, William Stuart Tegg
241960, John Thompson
242525, William Tonothy
242145, Joseph Dixon
Turnbull
242463, John Turner
242382, Samuel Ward
263025, Thomas Ward
44918, Herbert Noble
Warren
241845, Edgar Harold
Waters
291664, Alfred Watson
240365, Thomas Dodds
Wood
44858, George Walter
Wright

1/6 Battalion

Officers:
Lieutenant Ronald Lidderdale Guy
Lieutenant Philip Shaw
Lieutenant Harold Kenyon Temperley
Lieutenant Stanley Dawson Simm Tucker
Second Lieutenant John Herbert Shaw

Other Ranks:
Lance Corporal:
265211 George Henderson
Private:
2678347 Ralph Herbert
Blenkinsopp
44280 Thomas William
Charles Boynette
267400 Edgar Cole

267200 Charles Glew
45147 Wilbert Greenwood
267131 Claude Henry
Hubert
265899 John Jones
34137 Samuel Lawrence
36558 Ernest Ebenezer
Leonard

36500 Frank Martin Pallant
267320 George Philip Read
266110 Albert Robinson
201721 John William
Thompson
267100 Robert Thompson

1/7 Battalion

Officers:
Lieutenant Frederick Anderson Brown
Lieutenant James Angus Scott
Lieutenant Arthur Penton Strong
Second Lieutenant Gerald Danby Doucet
Second Lieutenant Robert Thompson

Other Ranks:
Sergeant & Lance Sergeant:
235170, George Leighton Adamson
290396, George McLeod
242488, William Russell
290695, Thomas Simpson
291703, George Thomas Thompson
Corporal:
16/330, Thomas Davidson
290291, John Egdell
290345, Alexander Murray Henderson
290154, William Meurs
290801, Robert Riddle Robson
Lance Corporal:
291818, Ernest Allen
292110, William Appleby
290618, Adam Dennison
291681, Allfred Ridgway
290608, William Tait
290749, Robert Walker
Private:
291819, Richard Atkinson
291781, William Beaumont
292121, Horace Robert Betts
267683, Frederick Thomas Brown
266764, Albert Edward Browning
25/803, Thomas Ernest Burn
205165, Thomas Burt Burrow

30/66, John Cassidy
291995, Thomas Clifton
18750, Thomas Crow
292068, Richard Docherty
204747. Miles Farrell
291060, Thomas Fotheringham
28/219, George William Gallirhir
291886, William Joseph Garrard
291889, Samuel John Stather Goatley
291798, Edward Grant
203358, Edward George Grant
292039, Peter Haley
205122. Ernest William Hebdon
290325, John Hepple
291725, John William Hodgson
35406, William James Hodgson
36488, Arthur George Humphries
205174, Thomas Hutchinson
291975, Thomas Ireland
205171, Robert George Janson
292042, Charles Edward Colman Jee
205130, Edwin Jevers
291928, Thomas Walter Keeble

290781, John Keeney
291788, Harry Kelsall
293116, Charles Edwin Kirby
291677, William Rainey Knott
290092, Frederick Lazenby
25/1060, John Edward Leonard
292169, John William Lowdon
290746, James MacKenzie
36476, John Mandsley
18841 John Thomas Matthews
10202 Thomas Soulsby McDougall
291780, James McWalters
291213, Henry Mickleborough
202848, James Milne
30/189, William Moreland
291877, Jacob Morton
291980, Herbert Nash
292227, Robert Nield
291836, Wilfred Noble
292183, John O' Malley
21/762, George Parker
291921, Frederick Alfred Peacey
19/489, Fred Priest
292657, Mark Racklin
2050005, Thomas Renwick
266783, Alfred Rich

291633, William Alexander Robertson
205044, Charles Robinson
11716, Joshua Hedley Rutter
291807, Charles James Rye
24231, William Hicklin Savigar
292230, Frank Sims
310034, George Albert Smith
35404, Robert Morrison Smith

291986, Albert Stephenson
24/1289, Joseph Stewart
203907, Sam Swift
291920, John Timlin
291989, William Henry Tomkins
291107, James William Turnbull
291969, James Joseph Turner
23137, William Wall
291814, Harold Hastings Walling

2911881, John Wallis
36486, John Watson
205170 William Ernest Watson
290499, Robert Weightman
290501, Thomas Henry Weightman
293114, Archibald Welch
204703, Jon Wheatley

Appendix E

Killed in action 21 March – 2 April 1918

1/4 Battalion

Officers:
Captain Thomas William Gregory
Lieutenant Tom Clough Lund
Second Lieutenant Thomas Hall
Second lieutenant John Hamilton

Other Ranks:
Sergeant & Lance Sergeant:
18185, William Baker
26/1193, John Gibson Robson
200423, William Baty Tiffin, MM
Corporal:
204598, John James Reynolds
36151, George Frederick Sheward
200442, Thomas Davison Varty
Lance-Corporal:
34811, George Allan
19/1778, Hugh Barlow
202156, Joseph Batty
202033, Arthur Cowley
17420, Percy Cowley
200874, Edward Isaac Hilton

46434, William Alfred Jolly
200938, George Liddell
200404, Richard Middleton
204592, John Slater
Private:
15771, William Ackroyd
20215, John Fitton Armitage
202907, Hayden Baldwin
35665, Ignatius Baron
201344, Charles Bishop
204009, James Bott
32229, James Brannan
48557, Frank Broad
202154, Joe Brook
235192, Benjamin Brown
38907, Percy Brownridge
28/2, Daniel Bullmore
59955, Roy Gideon Clifford
34/795, John Cowans
202084, Donald Daniel

59957, Arthur James Douglas
365233, Peter Doyle
235249, Willie Eastwood
16/1092, Robert William Embleton MM
59962, Albert Edward Exley
204398, Frederick Gibbs
235250, William Hobson
203727, Charles John Howe
202108, Fred Ireson
203202, James Laidler
235101, Morris Leschinsky
201899, Charles McDonald
201906, Lancelot Mortlock
21903, Clifford Mugg
32/469, William Parkinson
20116, John Pencott
203208, George Rawson
201020 Joseph Roberts

29598 James Smith
44627, William Henry Townson
16/1030, James Walker
201968, Thomas Ward

21166, William Ward
34309, John, Widdowson
201198, Frederick James Harold Willis
203204, Thomas Wilson

202135, Herbert Wing

1/5 Battalion

Officers:
Captain James Cunliffe Leask
Second Lieutenant Arthur Coulson
Second Lieutenant Thomas Nettleship
Second Lieutenant Joh McIntosh
Second Lieutenant Walter Henry Markham

Other Ranks:
CQMS:
Andrew Jervelund
Sergeant:
204501, John Thomas Boyd
263040, Robert Dryden
Corporal:
201673, Herbert Smith
Lance Corporal:
16/296, Robert Peirson
243185, David Richardson
Private:
263029, Sydney Allen
24/1595, James Atley
59928, Alfred Benjamin Benstead
59936, Frank Brazeas
59931, Thomas Briggs
240367, Robert Brown
235346, William James Cady
30/369, Harry Collins
48048, John Dickinson

235360, Peter Flitton
40959, Norman Greenwood
11451, William Grey
242462, Joshua Hainsworth
47372, Hall, William Hall
205072, Ernest Ives
341327, Carl Hugh Victor Johnson
48340, Arthur Lane
25/360 George Leigh
41377 Bernard Lowe
40565, Charles Henry Lunn
211452, James Edward Mann
242028, Alfred Measures
240765, James Murray
18129, John William Palmer
235410, Harold Pendrick
25/1225, John Potter
242474, Frank Scholfield

61335 George McDonald Simms
242128, Joseph Simpson
16/1416, Daniel Smith
242001, Matthew William Smith
5/5197, Thomas Stevenson
25095, Reginald Thompson
34862, George Edward Turner
46146, Albert Edward Vanstone
242394, Charles Wheeldon
240264, Joseph Henderson Williams
240556, James Young

1/6 Battalion

Officers:
Captain Keaisley Mathwin Drummond MC

Other Ranks:

Company Sergeant Major:

235168, Robert Douglas Harbron

Sergeant & Lance Sergeant:

267062, Herbert Spencer Bullimore

265466, Michael Foggin Lamb

265234, Thomas Lewis

265772, Joseph Wright Williams

Corporal:

267314, Harold Boyd

267482, Robert William Dent

267505, Lewis Henderson

265871, William Wright

Lance Corporal:

265877, James Currie

267385, Robert Henry Little

266212, Thomas Vangard

Private:

45196, Thomas Herbert Allchurch

267407, John Sidney Bell

267250, Frank Bennett

54593, Christopher Boynton

36492, James Silvester Clarke

366699, Arthur James Cockcroft

45264, Frederick Crann

265108, James Richard Dempsey

60088, Walter Douglas

265601, Thomas Dunlavy MM

16/647, William Dickie Eaton

267197, Fergus Edgar MM

36499, Robert Arthur France

45136, Owen Giles

41270, William Henry Groome

265324, William Gaston Duval Hall

267203, Thomas Hamilton

28/64, Charles Thomas Hawes

29881, William Heaton

52767, Richard Hill

266949, James William Holmes

265959, Michael Hoy

36556, Benjamin Hutchinson

28/117, John William Kelly

366836, Norman Kennedy

34260, Harold Sydney Langdon

52827, James Lawson

16720, William Duke Leatham

40559, Thomas Lodge

16/1270, Richard William Longstaff

267091, Arthur Love

266294, Thomas Makepeace

235135, Michael McCardle

202789, William McQuirk

366861, George Frederick Monteith

267521, Joseph Moore

36526, John Newton

43138, Robert Young Patterson

36506, Edward Charles Paul

44285, Henry William Powell

265659, Frederick Purchase

265874, Sidney Rea

267416, Robert Reed

267319, John Shannahan

235394, Edgar Thomas Sharpe

265229, William Simpson

30/107, William Skipper

267309, James Slack

265194, Frederick Stephenson

297041, William Sutherden

267121, Harry Thompson

267398, George Throne

267577, Archibald Stanley Tickell

267171, Arthur Tomlinson

45115, Ronald Walter Viles

201874, Fred Wagland

45201, Frank Wainwright

267002, Walter Robert Wakley,

43148, Robert Walker

267122, Ernest Whittaker

267352, Robert Wilson

45262, Arthur William Woolnough

Appendix F

Killd in action 9 – 15 April 1918

1/4 Battalion

Officers:

Captain Geraint Davies MC

Lieutenant Edgar Watson Stiles

Second Lieutenant Charles Montague Davison

Second Lieutenant A H Lawson

Other Ranks:
Sergeant & Lance Sergeant:
200424, Samuel Gleaves
30/162, John Wright
Corporal:
37413, Joseph O'Neill
Lance Corporal:
200483, Albert Clarricoates
235226, Herbert Pearson
204588, Charles Smith
58344, John Embleton
Turnbull
46193, Sidney William
Wheble
Private:
203342, Willian Agombar
34296, James Edward Allen
66471, George Richard
Bale
66467, Clifford Sidney
Barradell
6648, Horace Lewis Bond
316117, Abraham David
Burt
204576, Stanley Carter
37393, Arthur James
Cherry
205684, Frederick
Dennison
29/239, Edwin Dyson
58171, John William Guest
58219, Thomas Arthur Hall
66521, Samuel Halliday
58250, Samuel Harley

291934, George Harris
204026, George Henry
Horn
64597, Robert Hubbard
58358, John Henry
Humphreys
8157, John Pearson Ince
29/1060, Freeman Jackson
58379, Frederick Monston
Jenson
203364, George Jessup
66532, Arthur Johnson
56266, Thomas Jones
16/1733, James Major
68987, James Mason
201042, Thomas Theodore
McAdam
66539, Harry Meade
204612, Charles Henry
James Meek
204301, Bertie Mileham
201905, James Millborrow
68991, Joseph Alexander
Miller
36387, Frank Edward
Morley
66543, James Arthur
Muffin
66541, John Thomas
Murphy
6123, Walter Naylor
40411, Fred Neal

22/1242, James Ogden
37414, Patrick O'Neill
66552, Norman Clarence
Padgett
66560, George Potter
66562, Walter Powell
69023, William John Ritchie
48520, William Robertson
69027, Thomas Salmon
51065, Christopher
Simpson
47123, William Henry
Stocks
365882, Henry Swannack
60946, Edward Octavius
Thompson
32643, William Thwaites
39591, Harold Towse
69055, George Robert Vyse
69058, Harry Walker
31883, George Herbert
Watson
47973, Henry Alfred
Weaver
41609, Thomas Wilkinson
36314, Arthur Williamson
37119, John Williamson

1/5 Battalion

Officers:
Lieutenant Alfred John Field MC

Other Ranks:
Sergeant & Lance Sergeant:
240441, Albert Bushell
40354, Ralph James
Corporal:
240989, James Clennett
Cleminson

242230, William
Hinchcliffe
45090, William John
Holness
40358, Thomas Jones

65736, Samuel Myatt
Lance Corporal:
23/391, Thomas Bengal
61174, Edward
Addenbrookes Fletcher

18212, Robert Gibbs
31/78, Louie Herbert
242231, Albert Edward Hornby
240004, William Logan

Private:
65600, Thomas Henry Armes
240334, Edward Atkinson
65604, William Aungles
65605, Frederick Arthur Avery
65607, John Henry Bainbridge
42771, William Barker
69084, Walter Edward Barnett
69084, Albert Victor Bickerton
242162, Andrew Bell
69086, Arthur Edward Bellerby
69089, Harold Braddon
65621, Harold Briddon
34312, Frederick Leonard Broadhurst
235341, Edgar Ernest Brown
42846, Thomas Byrne
242417, Thomas Cassidy
56003, Raymond Tom Castle
240902, John Chapman
69104, Alfred Francis Clarke
37851, Robert Coleman
65638, Lewis Cowling
65644, Leonard Crowther
20872, William George Davis
65646, Edwin James Archer Dawson
65647, John Dean
240676, John Duffy
42892, John Edwards
69120, Thomas Edmond Fawell
65654, James Fielding
241170, William Goadby

65673, Jesse Frederick Goodband
69130, George Halfpenny
65679, William Henry Hall
69136, Lawrence Hill
65688, Charles Frederick Holden
65694 John Hunter
60086, George Jones
69146, William Jupp
69150, Edward Key
27/404, Joseph William Knapper
18975, William Henry Knight
18419, John William Lackenby
46848, Alex Lafferty
44905, George Henry Landers
69156, Thomas Turner Lee
67712, William Lee
240119 Hutchinson Lindsay
65718, Stanley Littlewood
61301, Robert Duncan Livingstone
240885, George Logan
240876, Percy Longstaff
240348, Thomas Lough
69162, Martin MacDermot
243137, James Main
341120, Alfred Makepeace
44999, Harold Marsden
65722, David McCaughey
69164, Frank Meakin
69165, George Mercer
54619, William Morgan
65742, Thomas Orr
240371, William Dobson Pattison MM
51449, George Alfred Pickering
34/446, Harry Pollard
242012, John William Quinn
34971, Oliver Randerson
45016, Will Thomson Redfearn

235388, Albert John Reeves
65755, Oakey Rhodes
66726, Joseph Roberts
240282, Richard Robinson
203287, Charles Rowe
66725, Thomas Rowley
44782, William Rusling
65759, George Rutherford
65766, Harold Thomas Shaw
66733, Percy Shorey
41547, Benjamin Siswick
66742, Edward smith
75771, Oswald Seymour Smith
66729, Robert Smith
21/1396, William Stoddart
241840, Sidney Robert Swatman
66753, William Tait
66751, Ernest Taylor
65781, Joseph Arthur Tupping
200833, Joseph Turnbull
292213, Albert Percy Turner
66756, Frederick Charles Usher
16/433, George Wallace
31972, James Walton
66764, William Wheatley
47983, Edwin George White
65791, Maurice Leonard Wiltshire
44893, Robert Wright
65793, William Henry Wright

1/6 Battalion

Officers:
Lieutenant Arthur William Leech MC
Second Lieutenant Garibaldi Matthewson Waggott

Other Ranks:
Sergeant & Lance Sergeant:
265571, Samuel Brookes
265235, James France MM
66294, Ernest Hoyle
Corporal:
265658, Robert Henry
Archer
Lance Corporal:
267276, James Harris
267367, Charles Lancaster
265667, John Thomas Scott
Private:
2656149, Benjamin John
Adams
66308, George William
Appleby
43088, Thomas Archbold
59916, Lewis Armstrong
265124, Alfred James
Bacon
66317, George Black
66313, George Joselyn
Bloomfield
267327, Thomas Breeze
66316, William Brown
20501, Patrick Burke
43231 George Armstrong
Carr
66319, George Charles
Clapham
235423, Edward Charles
Coates
267257, Frederick Cole
45251, William Alfred
Cooke
66641, Ernest Henry Corps
267259, Henry Barton
Coulson

66324, John Lambert
Cowan
66326, James Cowie
265625, George Denton
MM
66647, Robert Dixon
66534, Thomas Kitchener
Fletcher
267493, Johnathan Forster
52815, Fred Foulkes
316331, Ernest Alfred Fox
36552, Frank Fretwell
66658, George Garratt
36554, John Gerard
66341, Wilfred Arthur
Grattidge
366766, Thomas Windsor
Guite
36555, George Henry
Haigh
265369, William Hall
66354, Alfred Hodgson
66358, John Huddart
266034, James Hughes
54204, Charlie Hunt
267030, John William Iles
66669, Arthur Ingle
39065, Samuel Dowes
Ingram
66361, Herbert Johnson
203984, Thomas Andrew
Bryson Kemp
66675, Lownsbough King
16547, Robert William
Kirkman
66367, Arthur Lacey
66375, Wilfred Lee

52805, Henry William
Lewis
66677, William Lindsey
66678, Bolam Loud
45268, Edward Henry
Marks
66697, George Shipley
McIntyre
31425, Leonard Metcalfe
66696, John George
Middlemass
66695, Samuel James
Mitchell
66382, Joseph Stanley
Morris
66694, William Morton
66384, Cyril Mottley
36533, Peter Murphy
66386, Henry Musgrave
66701, Charles Keith
Naden
66391, Frederick Newman
69173, John William
Newsome
66394, William Newton
79174, George William
Nicholson
16/1252, Francis O'Connor
66706, William George
Pansey
66401, Frederick Parr
66712, Albert James Pears
66708, William Pearson
66710, Cecil Charles
Philips
66406, Edgar Philips
69180, Arnold Pitts
69182, Henry James Pootle

69185, William Henry Quinn
69187, Stanley George Randall
66410, Sydney Ridley
266079, William Ridley
66411, Lionel Arthur Rippin
66412, James Allen Robinson
66570, Robert Robinson
266071, John Robson
266252, William Robson
69191, Howard Rooker
69193, Leslie Arthur Scruton
69194, Thomas Edward Selby
265504, Edward Shortt
66585, Samuel Shuker
45231 Edward Harold Shuttleworth

69199, William Leonard Siddalls
66595, James William Siddle
69200, Frederick Bertram Simpson
66427, William Skeggs
66584, Ernest Smith
265733, John Smith
66951, Tom Smith
69209, John Robert Speck
69214, Fred Stead
69217, Leonard Stobbs
66433, Leonard Stone
202254, Arthur Storey
66577, William Stubbs
66574, Albert Maurice Stubley
69219, Thomas Summerbell
36531, Gordon Sunderland
52931, Israel Surfas
66588, Percy Sutcliffe
66505, Ernest Theakstone

52733, William Thomson
66598, Reginald Thornton
66439, Charles Thorp
201032, Fred Tiffin
66440, William Till
69227, Arthur Tomlinson
66599, Wilfred Tunney
36517, George Turner
69234, Henry Turner
66446, Percy John Viner
69239, Benjamin Warsap
66628, John Watson
66615, Thomas Vincent Joseph Watson
66609, Jake Whitley
66279, William John Wilkins
66617, Alfred Williams
69189, Reginald Williams
266086, George Wombwell

Appendix G
Killed in action 27 – 30 May 1918
1/4 Battalion

Officers:
Lieutenant Colonel Bertram Dees Gibson
Captain John Martin Benson
Captain David Thompson Turner
Lieutenant William Saville Jones
Lieutenant Robert Henry Smallwood
Second Lieutenant Albert Elelyn Morris
Second Lieutenant John Edmund Farwell
Second Lieutenant Henry Robson Tully
Warrant Officer George Fewster

Other Ranks:
Sergeant & Lance Sergeant:
200467, William Alders
200572, Nehimiah Allport
237017, Elva Robert Jasper
Corporal:
200065, William Cuthbert

78980, Harold William Pickett
Lance Corporal:
40355, Thomas Collinwood MM
44579, George Walter Cooper
202262, William Dean

78985, William Wesley Stares
Private:
66475, Frederick Barber
203153, James Bates
200067, Charles Bowman MM

200009, Edward John Brown
200545, John Buckham
78850, Charles Percy Campbell
59945, Robert William Clerkwell
75862, Ernest Chell
66492, William Cecil Coleman
75868, Leonard Arthur Cooke
75853, John Foster Cox
75864, Isidore Cecil Cross
242419, John Davey
78995, Harry Francis Douch
78986, George Albert Graves
291932, Thomas Harper
75877, Harry Frank Hartley
291255, Thomas Heffron
75878, George Heslop
267202, William Hillaby
21/1275, William Hunter

200755, George Hutchinson
27/1037, Thomas Irwin
79009, Alfred William Keeley
45864, Lewis Kenyen
79013, Charles George King
68972, Robert Edward Lawson
75890, Joseph James Lay
75889, Hubert Loughlin
204077, George Mears
75920, Christopher Mellor
75622, Frederick George Mercer
75624, Granville Milles
10268, James Milner
66545, William Mitchell
66536, Aubrey Lemuel Moore
58383, John Henry Mould
75627, Arthur Edward Munday
75636, Isaac Pattison
54105, Edgar Prosser
58102, John Edward Reed

203160, William Richardson
43423, James Robert Kemp Rutherford
75668, Charles Smith
267550, Horace George Smith
201071, John Somerville
75912, Theodore Staff
75673, Harold Sudgen
75439, Albert Edward Symonds
75769, Bertie Harold Thomas
204488, John Thompson
66627, George Alfred Wallis
201951, Cycil Lawton Whiteley
75715, Frederick Richard Willis
75918, George Edward Wilson
75917, James Arthur Wilson
75705, Albert Wood
61902, Edward Wright

1/5 Battalion

Officers:
Captain Neville Marriott North MC
Lieutenant Henry McDonnell Anderson
Lieutenant Ernest Vernon Sargeant
Second Lieutenant James MacMeeken
Second Lieutenant John Hamilton McMurdo
Second Lieutenant Edward Philipps
Second Lieutenant John Ernest Porritt
Second Lieutenant William Eustace Priestnall
Second Lieutenant John Barnett Slack

Other Ranks:
Sergeant & Lance Sergeant:
30292, Thomas Birney
340296, Anthony Scott
237082, Alfred James Woodley
Corporal:
65743, William Poulson Paish

242517, Thomas William White
75758, John George Wilson
Private:
75780, William Ashworth
23/683, Harry Allan
61834, William Henry Allan

75826, James Rushby Allison
75834, Horace Joseph Boot
59935, Percy Bowker
241772, Robert James Brinded
61987, Thomas Burns

75840, William Butler
241391, William Edward
 Byers
243169, Edward Carr
36837, George William
 Chafer
4948, Charles Thomas
 Davison
340361, David Douglass
65652, Richard Elves
41946, Alfred Ewbank
340793, George Fawcett
61802, Walter Firth
61873, Arthur William
 French
241082, Thomas Gardham
242184, Bernard Lewis
 Grainger

61848, James Walker Hazell
340829, Gordon Hoggart
 Hill
61777, William Hughes
16/424. Randolph Jackson
204183, James Jones
260043, George Ernest
 Lawton
242358, Tim Lowe
36383, Herbert Rawson Lumb
40412, Patrick Joseph
 Moran
69170, John Holmes Moss
241812, William Davis
 Murchie
24878, Lawrence Murray
242202, Francis Railson
48354, Thomas Rendall

65757, Lawrence Ricketts
75798, Alfred Raymond
 Robinson
61770, Archie Leonard
 Sawford
75800, Herbert Shields
200249, Louis Spark
61814, Charles William
 Starkie
242969, George Stokoe
242372, David Sword
242063, Richard Teale
235408, Albert Henry
 Turner MM
260051, Walter Tyne
241913, George Vincent
25/1330, Matthew Wright

1/6 Battalion

Officers:
Lieutenant Allan Ryder Hall
Second Lieutenant William Jenkin David

Other Ranks:
CQMS:
265366, Arthur Nelson MM
Sergeant & Lance Sergeant:
202505, Edwin Banks
45153, Charles Walter Day
24308, William Edward
 Gallon
Corporal:
40284, Herbert James Ashton
265993, John Edward
 Edwards MM
58355, Matthew Andrew
 McFeat
16/607, Henry Alfred
 Padgham
Lance Corporal:
267236, Frederick Carnill
Private:
75326, Horace Adams
45130, Sydney Arundel
59919, Charles Barlow

75531, William Thomas
 Battams
75309, Herbert Bell
366898, Charles Edward
 Bleasby
75935, Henry Robson
 Cairns
265906, Elsden Corkin
75290, Harold Coulton
35370, Herbert Stanley
 Cowell
66300, Charles Richard
 Moses Dale
267484, Charles Edward
 Dazley
266175, Henry English
75573, Plimsoll Dean Farr
75579, Walter Fowler
75582 George Gardner
267509, Francis Henry
 Hearnshaw

66666, George Robert Hobson
75607, George Albert James
75613, Charles Jones
66364, Richard Kay
267389, Fred Langhorne
75503, James Page
75378, William Thomas
 Pattenden
75219. Thomas Pickering
75236, Arthur Radford
75252, George Hubert Scott
69188, George Shields
75251, Joseph Swarbrick
66614, Herbert Ward
16/783, William Wallace
 Winter
75272, John Wolfenden
66624, Percy Woods
36516, Robert McCondach
Young

BIBLIOGRAPHY

Armstrong William Watson, *My First Week in Flanders,* Smith Elder, 1916.

Baker C, *The Battle for Flanders,* Pen & Sword, 2011.

Barton P and Banning J, *Arras,* Constable, 2010.

Bean C.E.W, *Official History of Australia in the War of 1914-1918, Vol 5.*

Blanchard D, *Battle of the Aisne 1918: The Phantom Sector,* Pen & Sword, 2015.

Boraston J H, *General Haig's Dispatches: December 1915 – April 1916,* Dent and Sons, 1919.

Brown M, *Tommy Goes to War,* J M Dent & Sons Ltd, 1978.

Buchan J, *A History of the Great War Volume 2,* Houghton Mifflin, 1923.

Buckley F, *Q.6.A. and other places,* Spottiswoode and Ballantyne, London,1920.

Buckley F, *War History of Seventh Northumberland Fusiliers,* Grierson, T.M. Newcastle, 1919.

Bunbury W J, *A Diary of an Officer: with the 4th Northumberland Fusiliers in France and Flanders from April 20 to May 24 1915,* J Catherall. Hexham, 1915.

Callin R W, *When the Lantern of Hope Burned Low,* J Catherall, Hexham, 1919.

Campbell P J, *The Ebb and Flow of Battle,* OUP, 1979.

Conan Doyle, A, *The British Campaign in France and Flanders January to July 1918,* Hodder and Stoughton, 1919.

Corrigan G, *Mud, Blood and Poppycock,* Cassell, 2004.

Dixon J, *Magnificent But Not War,* Pen & Sword, 2003.

Edmonds J E, *History of the Great War: Operations France and Belgium 1918,* Appendix 20

Gladden N, *The Somme 1916: A personal account,* William Kimber, London, 1974.

Graves R, *'Goodbye to All That',* Penguin Essentials Edition, 2011.

Grint A I, *In Silent Fortitude: In memory of the men of the North Tyne Valley who fell in the Great War,* Ergo Press, 2011.

Grint A I, *The Faith and Fire Within: In memory of the men of Hexham who fell in the Great War,* Ergo Press, Hexham, 2006.

Harbottle G. *Civilian Soldier 1914 – 1919: A Period Relived,* Private Publication, Newcastle upon Tyne, 1919.

Hart P, *1918: A Very British Victory*, Weidenfeld and Nicolson, 2008.

Hart P, *The Somme* Weidenfeld and Nicolson, 2005.

Hart P, *Voices from the Front,* Profile Books, 2015.

Hewitson T L, *Weekend Warrior: From Tyne to Tweed,* History Press, 2006.

Keegan J, *The First World War*, Hutchinson, 1998.

Kinaid-Smith M, *The 25 Division in France and Flanders,* 1920, reprinted 2001 by Naval and Military Press.

Lewis-Stempel J, *Six Weeks*, Orion, 2011.

Lloyd N, *Passchendaele: A New History*, Penguin, 2017.

Luddendorff E, *Luddendorf's Own Story Vol 2,* Harper and Brothers, New York.

MacDonald L, *1915 The Death of Innocence,* Penguin, 1997.

Messenger C, *Call to Arms: The British Army 1914 to 1918,* Cassell Military Paperback Edition, 2006.

Moses H, *The Gateshead Gurkhas*, County Durham Books, 2002.

Neillands R, *The Death of Glory*, John Murray, 2007.

Nicholls J, *Cheerful Sacrifice*, Pen & Sword, 2005.

Norman T, *The Hell they Called Hugh Wood*, Pen & Sword, 2003.

Prior R and Wilson T, *Passchendaele: The Untold Story*, Yale, 2002.

Rawson A, *Somme Offensive March 1918,* Pen & Sword, 2018.

Steel N and Hart P, *Passchendaele: The Sacrificial Ground*, Cassell, 2000.

Stevenson D, *With our Backs to the Wall*, Allen Lane, 2011.

Van Emden R, *Prisoners of the Kaiser: The Last PoWs of the Great War,* Pen & Sword, 2009.

Van Emden R, *Boy Soldiers of the Great War*, Headline, 2005.

Weber T, *Hitler's First War: Adolf Hitler; The Men of the List Regiment and First World War,* OUP, 2010.

Wyrall E, *The Fiftieth Division 1914-1918*, 1939, Reprinted Naval and Military Press, 2002.

Newspapers and Journals

Berwickshire Advertiser, 2 July 1909.

Berwick News and General Advertiser. 25 May 1915.

Berwick News and General Advertiser, 8 June 1915.

Hexham Courant, 17 June 1915.

Hexham Courant, 29 May 1915.

Morpeth Herald, 20 November 1922.

Newcastle Journal, 15 May 1915.

Shields Daily News, 14 May 1915

Newcastle Journal, 26 March 1916

Newcastle Journal, 20 November 1916.

Morpeth Herald, 18 July 1919.

Berwick Advertiser, 23 October 1914.

Morpeth Herald, 1 January 1915.

Newcastle Journal, 4 May 1915.

St George's Gazette (Northumberland Fusiliers) Vols XX-XXXVIII, 1902-1920

War Office Documents

Appendix 1. Territorial and Reserve Forces Act. (7 Edward VII, Cap. 9)

National Archives

WO 95 2828 *War Diary 1/4 Battalion, Northumberland Fusiliers*

WO 95 2811 *War Diary, 50 Division*

WO 95 2826 *War Diary 149 Brigade*

WO 95 2828 *War Diary 1/5 Battalion Northumberland Fusiliers*

WO 95 2590 *War Diary 1/6 Battalion Northumberland Fusiliers*

WO 95 2650/4, *War Diary 1/7 Battalion Northumberland Fusiliers*

WO 161 100/412 *Private Joseph Hodgson, 1/4 Northumberland Fusiliers, returning Prisoner of War Interview.*

Internet Sites:

www.ashingtonmemorial.com *(Grint A I)*

www.firstworldwar.com

www.longlongtrail.co.uk

www.greatwarforum.org

www.tynemouthworldwarone.org/project.html

www.rytonwarmemorials.org.uk

www.findmypast.com

www.ancestry.com

Imperial War Museum Resources (Transcriptions of Oral Accounts)

IWM Document, 12344, *Bagley A E, transcript account*

IWM Archives, Document 440. *Private papers of E W Cotton.*

IWM AC 9253, Dorgan John William, 'Jack'

IWM AC 9474, Harbottle George

IWM, AC 8946, Pickard Joe

IWM Document 6709, Thompson Alexander

INDEX

Portuguese Army Formations

Divisions:

Brigades:

INDEX OF INDIVIDUALS